Intelligent Multimedia Systems

A Handbook for Creating Applications

Intelligent Multimedia Systems

A Handbook for Creating Applications

Randy M. Kaplan

Wiley Computer Publishing

John Wiley & Sons, Inc.
New York • Chichester • Weinheim • Brisbane • Singapore • Toronto

Executive Publisher: Katherine Schowalter

Editor: Marjorie Spencer

Managing Editor: Micheline Frederick

Electronic Products, Associate Editor: Michael Green

Text Design & Composition: SunCliff Graphic Productions

Designations used by companies to distinguish their products are often claimed as trademarks. In all instances where John Wiley & Sons, Inc. is aware of a claim, the product names appear in Initial Capital or ALL CAPITAL LETTERS. Readers, however, should contact the appropriate companies for more complete information regarding trademarks and registration.

This text is printed on acid-free paper.

Copyright © 1997 by John Wiley & Sons, Inc.

All rights reserved. Published simultaneously in Canada.

This publication is designed to provide accurate and authoritative information in regard to the subject matter covered. It is sold with the understanding that the publisher is not engaged in rendering legal, accounting, or other professional service. If legal advice or other expert assistance is required, the services of a competent professional person should be sought.

Reproduction or translation of any part of this work beyond that permitted by section 107 or 108 of the 1976 United States Copyright Act without the permission of the copyright owner is unlawful. Requests for permission or further information should be addressed to the Permission Department, John Wiley & Sons, Inc.

Microsoft® Video for Windows™, © 1995 Microsoft Corporation. All rights reserved.

Library of Congress Cataloging-in-Publication Data

Kaplan, Randy M., 1955-
    Intelligent multimedia systems : a handbook for creating applications / Randy M. Kaplan.
       p.   cm.
    Includes bibilographical references.
    ISBN: 0-471-12040-5 (alk. paper)
    1. Multimedia systems.   2. Artificial intelligence. I. Title.
QA76.575.K37   1997
006.7'8--dc21   96-39308
                                                                              CIP

Printed in the United States of America
10 9 8 7 6 5 4 3 2 1

Dedication

There are two people I want to mention in this dedication who have been influential in similar ways, but separated by many years. One of these is a mentor from the past; the second is a friend from the present.

Whenever one sets out to accomplish a goal, a couple of ingredients are key to reaching that goal. One of these is belief in oneself—to be able to say, "I can do this." A second ingredient is to have people around you who will say, "You can do that."

About twenty years ago, when I was an undergraduate in college, I had a computer science professor who was, at that time my favorite teacher. His name was James B. Maginnis. I learned recently that Professor Maginnis passed away. His passing saddens me because it is like a bright star going out. His style was vibrant and challenging, and yet at the same time he was realistic. He also told wonderful stories, as he knew such people as Grace Hopper. These characteristics made me enroll for each and every course he taught and his advice still lives on in me. When I have occasion to teach I try to follow his example. In his classes I always felt, "I can do this." For this original spark, I want to dedicate this book in part to Professor Maginnis.

Back when I decided to try to write a book, I wrote quite a few proposals. I sent them to many publishers, and received as many rejections. I decided to make one last attempt—a long shot, and wouldn't you know it, this was the one that was accepted. I only marginally believed I could write (I have been told so many times about the failings of my abilities in this regard), but I really wanted to prove this wrong. Without an editor who believed, this would have never been possible for me.

The second person to whom this book is dedicated is Diane Cerra, my first editor at John Wiley, who said by her actions, "You can do this."

Randy Kaplan
1997

Contents

Preface	xiii

Chapter 1 Introduction — 1

Merging Technologies	1
Multimedia and Artificial Intelligence	4
Important Definitions	5
The Basics	11
Multimedia Applications	12
Text	12
Sound	13
Images	13
Video	14
Glue	15
Tools	16
Artificial Intelligence	16
Rule-Based or Expert Systems	18
Knowledge Representation	19
Tools	22
Other Books	24
Intelligent Multimedia Systems Revisited	25
The Rest of the Book	27

Chapter 2 Multimedia Authoring Tools — 33

Introduction	33
Developing Your Own Multimedia Tool Versus Using a Commercially Available Tool	34

Language-Based Versus Graphic Interface–Based Tools   35
   The Interaction Language   35
   The IL Language in Greater Detail   43
   IL's Doorway   58
   Authorware Professional for Windows   62
   Recap   96
The Importance of Paradigms   99
   Developing Multimedia Using Time Lines   99
Visual Basic as a Multimedia Authoring Tool   110
   Introduction to Visual Basic   111
   The ATM Simulation in Visual Basic   111
   Some Comments about Visual Basic and the ATM Simulation   129
Chapter Summary   130

Chapter 3 The Multimedia Database   133

Introduction   133
   Databases   133
   Knowledge as Media   137
Architecture   140
   Records in the Multimedia Database   141
   An Example   143
   Viewers, Loaders, and Operations   145
   Retrieving Media by Content   148
   Retrieving Media by Characteristic   150
   Creating a Multimedia Database   151
Chapter Summary   151
Suggested Reading   152

Chapter 4 Tools for Intelligent Applications   153

Introduction   153
Making a Thinking Machine   154
The LISP Programming Language   155
   A Brief LISP Tutorial   157
Logic as a Programming Language   170
   A Brief Prolog Tutorial   177
   Deriving Rules for the Operation of the Toaster   190
Expert Systems and Expert System Languages   190
   What Is an Expert System?   191

A Small-X Tutorial	194
Rules to Make a Toaster Work	196
Chapter Summary	203
Suggested Reading	205

Chapter 5 Knowledge Representation   207

Introduction	207
Many Approaches for Many Reasons	208
Symbolic Representations	208
Semantic Networks	209
Introduction to Semantic Networks	209
Using Semantic Networks	213
Creating Your Own Semantic Networks	217
Representing a Semantic Network	218
A Tool for Creating Semantic Networks	219
Logic Representations	236
Introduction to Logic Representations	236
Using Logic Representations	244
Representation Structure	248
Using Frames	254
A Tool for Creating Frames	260
Chapter Summary	284
Suggested Reading	285

Chapter 6 Models   287

Introduction	287
Introducing Models	288
Why Models?	289
Qualitative and Quantitative Models	291
A Mini-How-To Guide	292
Step 1: What are the Components in the Mechanism?	293
Step 2: Identify Which Componets Represent Sub-components of the Mechanism and Which Represent Connections between Mechanisms	294
Step 3: Identify the Relationships between Components in the Model	294
Step 4: Identify Implicit Relationships in the Mechanism	295
Step 5: Specify the Rules of Operation of the Model	296
Step 6: Test the Model	298

Model Examples	302
PROUST	302
A Process-Oriented Model	307
Knowledge, Metaknowledge, Meta-metaknowledge	310
A More Complete Toaster	311
Step 1: What are the Components of the Mechanism?	311
Step 2: Identify Which Components Represent Subcomponents of the Mechanism and Which Represent Connections between Mechanisms	313
Steps 3 and 4: Identify Relationships between Components in the Model	314
Step 5: Specify the Rules of Operation of the Model	316
Step 6: Test the Model	330
Chapter Summary	339
Suggested Reading	340

Chapter 7 A Toaster Tutor 343

Introduction	343
Just What Is an Intelligent Tutor?	344
The Tutoring Domain	345
Now That We Know What It Is, What Do We Want It to Do?	346
Tutor Design	346
Story Board	346
How It Works	359
Tutor Models	364
Student Model	366
Instructional Model	381
Simulating the Simulation	391
Chapter Summary	400
Suggested Reading	401

Chapter 8 Natural Language Processing and 403
Intelligent Multimedia

Introduction	403
Multimedia and Natural Language Processing	405
Natural Language Processing—The Details	405
Propositions Are the Key	430
Application Example 1—An Automatic Illustrator	431
Elements of the Automatic Illustrator	432

Application Example 2—A Foreign Language Tutor Named Habla	439
Pedagogy	440
A Proposed Description of Habla	447
Chapter Summary	448
Suggested Reading	451

Chapter 9 The Future of Intelligent Multimedia — 453

What Does the Future Hold for Intelligent Multimedia?	453
Advances in Artificial Intelligence	454
Neural Nets	454
Genetic Programming	465
Advances in Multimedia	470
Virtual Reality and Environments	470
The Internet	473
Suggested Reading	477

Appendix A CD-ROM Information — 479

System Requirements	480
The WINVIDEO Subdirectory	481
Implementation Platform	481
User Assistance and Information	481

Index — 483

Preface

Intelligent multimedia. Just what does this mean? To answer the question, we must consider what has happened to the personal computer in the last few years. The personal computer can no longer be considered just that, a personal computer. Over the past few years, it has become much more—a sort of general information appliance. It can deliver data to its users as text (the original presentation media), as sound, and as still and moving pictures. The personal computer and television are beginning to converge. Televisions are being discussed with capabilities like those of personal computers and likewise personal computers are being discussed that are a lot like televisions. What does this convergence mean to multimedia software developers?

Multimedia software will have to process data that are significantly richer in content than is typical of textual data. Multimedia programs manipulate sound data, graphics data, and moving picture data like video and animation. The proliferation of CD-ROMs filled with these kinds of data for viewing and interaction provides proof of the need for programs that can interact intelligently with these data and its users. Multimedia developers should consider the opportunities offered by this rich data as consisting of both possibilities for manipulation and interaction.

Most CD-ROMs currently available are of the point-and-click variety. The software programs manipulating multimedia data are strictly scripted programs constraining how a user views the multimedia data contained on the CD-ROM. No matter how complex a multimedia program is, it usually cannot make accommodations to the user. This constrained use of multimedia is primitive and represents only the first stages of what will eventually be possible. The purpose of this book is to introduce intelligent systems technology (artificial intelligence) and discuss how it can be used (embedded) in a multimedia system.

Intelligent multimedia is the marriage of two disciplines: multimedia software development and intelligent software development. You may not recognize the moniker "intelligent software development," but these are the software components typically called artificial intelligence programs.

Multimedia offers tremendous potential to embed artificial intelligence. In particular, adding intelligence to a multimedia program may unconstrain a previously constrained program. Instead of letting the program guide the user through multimedia data, an intelligent multimedia program can act as a true guide, varying itself according to the needs and desires of the user. This is the view of intelligent multimedia of the future—no multimedia systems incorporate intelligence to this extent today—but we can see the promise of intelligence in the context of multimedia software development by considering what tools are available and how they can be used. This book provides an overview of the available tools (both multimedia and intelligent), proposes some potential applications, and presents an example of intelligent multimedia.

Three elements were critical to the content of this book. The first was to provide an overview of tools for creating multimedia applications. The reader coming from a background of intelligent system development would find this a useful introduction to some of the tools and approaches for creating multimedia systems. The second area of focus is to provide an overview of intelligent systems technology. Multimedia application developers would most likely find this material useful in understanding the various technology and techniques that can be used to develop intelligent systems. The third key area of focus is the marriage between multimedia and intelligent systems.

How do we marry systems that present multimedia to systems that will reason about them? The answer to this question is the third focus area in this book. How can a multimedia application be created that contains the information necessary for reasoning about the application? To provide a significant example of this mechanism, the book describes a significant application called the Toaster Tutor. The Toaster Tutor is an example of the marriage of artificial intelligence and multimedia into a system that presents information about a toaster and allows a user to repair a broken toaster. The system combines several different types of media and reasoning systems to exemplify how multimedia and artificial intelligence can be combined into an functional intelligent multimedia system.

Programs used to create the intelligent multimedia system described in later chapters are included on the CD-ROM that comes with this book. Throughout most chapters are examples of tools that can be used by the reader to develop various aspects of intelligent multimedia systems. For example, one of the tools provided allows a user to create a frame database. Frames are just one way to store complex information used by reasoning systems. The Toaster Tutor uses a database of frames to store information about the toaster, and this frame database is then used to display information about the toaster and to reason about how the toaster operates. Other tools the reader may find useful are also included. For example, the Toaster Tutor uses a small expert system shell to simulate the toaster's operation. The shell, documentation for the shell, and source code have also been included.

One of the interesting things that often happens when writing a book of this kind (and I suspect any book) is that the very task of writing generates new ideas and opportunities. For instance, when I was writing about the tool for frames, many new ideas and features would come to mind. One idea was to provide a searching mechanism to locate frames in the frame database. Unfortunately, part of the task of writing a book is to finish, so I could not explore each and every nuance, idea, and program feature that came to mind. As you are reading this book and considering its content, you may wonder why I did not include certain things. My explanation is one of time (wanting to finish writing this book) and space (not creating a multivolume work). The wonderful thing about this is that you can explore these ideas using the contents of this book and the examples on the CD-ROM as a starting point.

If you decide to work with any of the Windows-based examples you will need to have Microsoft's Visual Basic, Version 3.0. The required extensions to Visual Basic used by each of the application will be installed with it. Although I have not recompiled the code in Microsoft Visual Basic Version 4.0, there is no reason why the code should be incompatible.

Even when there were no graphics displays, no sound cards, and no full screen video; when we used punched cards to communicate with the computer I felt it was a kind of canvas on which anything could be built. Multimedia makes this idea more of a reality. I hope the information provided in this book enriches the kinds of multimedia or intelligent systems you might build.

Randy Kaplan
April 1997

A Note About the Applications Included with This Book

The applications included with this book are examples to supplement the descriptions contained in the book. As such, certain features of the included applications may not be implemented and are left to the reader as an exercise. Though the applications have been tested no software is fool proof. If you should encounter any problems with the software, please let John Wiley & Sons know. They will in turn contact me, and I will do my best to resolve the problem if possible.

Intelligent Multimedia Systems

A Handbook for Creating Applications

CHAPTER 1

Introduction

Merging Technologies

For the longest time our perception of the computer was as a machine to perform complex and/or highly repetitious calculations. In the 1950s a fundamental shift in our view of computers occurred. Computer scientists realized that computers were not only fantastic calculating engines but also fantastic tools for manipulating symbolic information. This meant that computers could do "other kinds" of calculations, not just arithmetic calculations. The ability to do other kinds of calculations depended on something called representation.

Mathematicians are consummate representers. Their profession could be called the premier representation profession. When a mathematician can successfully devise a representation for a problem and the manipulations for that representation, the key to solving a problem is at hand. Mathematicians understand the power of representation.

Interestingly enough, the idea that a computer could manipulate a representation other than for arithmetic came from the scientists working in the field that is the subject of at least half of this book—artificial intelligence. Computer scientists studying artificial intelligence used the computer for manipulating symbols to represent ideas, concepts, and other objects involved with human thought and intelligence.

In a way the work done by computer scientists set the stage for what would come years later. If it is possible to represent human thought objects symbolically and carry out computations on these objects, what else could be represented and computed? In the answer to this question several technologies merge and manifest themselves in present-day computing systems.

It has always been possible to use a computer to store text. Characters can be encoded into a digital representation, and the representation can be readily processed and stored in a computer system.

Characters and multiple characters (text) represent the first deviation from data traditionally associated with the computer. Assigning a numeric value to each and every printable character makes it possible to manipulate characters and text as if they were numeric data. Printers can interpret these special numbers (special because of their interpretation) and print them as the characters the numeric values represent. In order that all computers use the same code, a standard encoding has been created. The code used for text is called American Standard Code for Information Interchange or ASCII.

Text is a means to convey information. As such, it is also a medium (the means) through which information is expressed. Several other kinds of media are used by humans to convey information: sound, pictures, animation, video, and movies. For the media to be available for manipulation by computer, a code has to be invented for sound, photos, and video. The code must be a digital one so that a computer can easily process it. The problem is that sound, pictures, and video are not inherently digital. A black and white photograph, for instance, has many shades of white through black, that is, a continuum of shades. You can identify these shades, but they are not discrete. In other words, you cannot easily identify one gray from another in a black and white photo. **Digitizing** an image involves just this process of discretizing the individual shades of gray in a black and white photo and then encoding this discretization into an economical file format. Although this description of digitizing a photograph is a simplification of the process, encoding a picture in this way makes it possible for a personal computer to use pictures in the same way as text.

So far I have described various types of media and why computers can process these types of media in the same way that computers process text. From individual media to multimedia is a short step. Multimedia is the combination of two or more media types for conveying information. For example, television is one of the oldest multimedia devices.

A relatively recent entry in the field of multimedia is the personal computer. The "recentness" of this entry is due to the commercial availability of the hardware and software needed to record and view various kinds of media. Because this hardware and software makes it possible to view various kinds of media, we say that the hardware and software enables a capability for multimedia. The hardware and software are called enabling technology.

The enabling technologies for multimedia that can be identified include hardware for recording and playing sound, hardware and software for viewing and creating graphics, and hardware and software for recording and playing video and animation. These enabling technologies to view and record the various kinds of media present only a part of the enabling picture. Several other technological developments also enable computer-based multimedia capability.

To play or record sound, video, or graphics a significant amount of computational power is necessary. The evolution of personal computer technology has placed a significant amount of processing and computational power on our desktops. The development of computational power has certainly further enabled the computer's ability to manipulate multimedia.

Multimedia is also a memory-intensive application. It would not be possible to run any present-day multimedia programs in 64 KB of memory. Multimedia requires large amounts of memory to store the data that represent sound, video, or graphics. Hard disk storage has evolved so that multigigabyte hard disk drives are available for under $500, and CD-ROMs provide an inexpensive means to store and distribute multimedia programs and data.

The physical ability to process and store multimedia information has led to a class of computer programs to access this information. Because a typical CD-ROM can have hundreds or even thousands of individual media, text, graphics, images, video, animation, and sound represent different types of media that can be manipulated like any other data a computer can process. The programs accessing the media must facilitate and assist a user with access to the media. The task of these programs is more like that of a navigator whose responsibility it is to keep track of where you are and where you may go in the multimedia. I like to think of these programs as multimedia navigation programs in that they assist a multimedia program user with locating and viewing media.

A recent example of this kind of program is Netscape's Navigator World Wide Web browser. This program is capable of viewing and navigating through many different kinds of media. In the case of the Navigator, the media are spread out over many different computers over a very large area. An amazing and significant characteristic of the Navigator is that it represents a standard approach to managing multimedia.

Computers can display and process multimedia data as they can any other data, but this processing only consists of what is specified by the programmer. A computer's ability to manipulate these different kinds of data (sound, graphics, and video) is largely dumb. The computer does not understand the sound, graphics, or video. Imagine the tremendous potential if it were possible for a computer to understand something about the sound, graphics, or video. The capability of using multimedia data intelligently will distinguish the next generation of multimedia applications. To accomplish this it will be necessary to merge multimedia technology with the technology of artificial intelligence.

Multimedia and Artificial Intelligence

It may seem that the idea of merging multimedia technology with artificial intelligence is far-fetched. After all, what does one have to do with the other? The answer to this question lies in the potential for adding intelligence to a system.

For example, the most popular computer interfaces to many computer programs are the visual or graphic user interfaces. To interact with a computer, one moves a pointing device like a mouse to buttons, menus, or hot spots and presses a button on the pointing device. Instead of using an interface like this, imagine an interface where you could converse with a computer system in a spoken language.

In a system where the interface was spoken language, we would not have to learn new skills for interacting with the computer. Furthermore, a system that could understand natural language could also understand another very important kind of media—text. Natural language processing is only one aspect of artificial intelligence that may have tremendous potential when combined with multimedia.

Another area for application of artificial intelligence in multimedia is in media understanding. In this mode, artificial intelligence programs act as experts and choose media for presentation of specific kinds of information. Envision a kind of multimedia assistant that can collect and assemble media in a presentation format; in carrying out this task, the assistant can reference various media from multiple databases and assemble a presentation fulfilling a specific request. This task would require expert programs to understand and select media and also programs expert in media presentation.

These expert programs are examples of a specialty in artificial intelligence called expert systems. An expert system is a computer program that behaves like an expert. In doing so, the computer is using expert knowledge to perform expert tasks. Because expert knowledge is typically limited in its availability, a computer-based expert capability can make expertise more readily available.

Important Definitions

To set the context for the discussion to follow, here are definitions for multimedia, artificial intelligence, and artificially intelligent multimedia systems.

Multimedia is the conveyance of text, sound, still photos, and full motion video in a seamless and uniform environment. The environment supports each media type and the continuity between them. Computer-based multimedia uses the computer as the seamless environment for presentation of different types of media.

Artificial intelligence is the creation of computer programs that enable the computer to do tasks that would normally and naturally be carried out by humans. The term "artificial intelligence" was coined by John McCarthy in the 1950s. McCarthy is one of the intellectual fathers of artificial intelligence and is also the creator of the programming language called LISP. LISP is used to create computer programs for artificially intelligent applications. Over the years, the term "artificial intelligence" has fallen out of favor. Even McCarthy has expressed disappointment that this term has remained the name of this field of study for such a long time. In a recent collaboration, Marvin Minsky, another intellectual father of artificial intelligence, has used the term "machine intelligence," which is a more descriptive term of what artificial intelligence is all about.

The tasks (and subdomains) that are explored by artificial intelligence researchers include vision (how the brain sees), game playing, natural language understanding, planning and problem solving, robotics, speech understanding, and expert systems (systems that behave like a human expert).

An **artificially intelligent multimedia system** is one that combines multimedia technology with the technology of artificial intelligence. More specifically, an artificially intelligent multimedia system is one whose multimedia elements (text, sound, still photos, and video) can be controlled by program elements that are instances of artificial intelligence programs.

If artificial intelligence programs are to operate on a multimedia database, then that database must be structured to accommodate its use in an artificially intelligent system. It is not enough, as in the typical multimedia application, to allow a program to control the display of multimedia data. In this case the program can distinguish between text, sound, graphics, and video. It does not know how the text, sound, graphics, and video are related or anything about the meaning of the media.

In a typical multimedia navigator, links between media are set by the developer or programmer. The navigator can follow the links between the media. In an artificially intelligent multimedia program, the program can look at the links as a kind of information. The links tell the program how information is related. Of course, the links can be used to navigate through information, but the links can now also be used for other purposes.

For example, suppose we have a multimedia database containing information about toasters. Among other things, the database shows how a toaster works. This is accomplished through text, still photos, graphics, sound, and animation. The information in this database is organized so that a user can learn how a toaster works. The links between information in the multimedia database describe how components of the toaster are related. Now, suppose we want to show how to make repairs to the toaster. How can we accomplish this with the same multimedia database? Using the same links that connect elements of the multimedia database, problems can be created by the system and presented to the user of the system. The user can try to "fix" the toaster. Using the same multimedia database we are able to (1) describe how a toaster works and (2) show how to repair toasters. Artificial intelligence technology can be used to accomplish this.

Figure 1.1 is an example of a multimedia database. It doesn't look like a typical database—after all how many databases do you know of that look like this? Where are the records in this database? What are the elements to be stored? Even so, Figure 1.1 does represent a database of information.

Relationships and elements are clearly defined. More important, the multimedia database specifies two important semantic relationships—*attached-to* and *controls*. *Attached-to* gives information about how to assemble a toaster. We should be able to write a computer program that (1) can create a toaster from its components using the *attached-to* relationship and (2) make the toaster work using the *controls* relationship.

8 CHAPTER 1

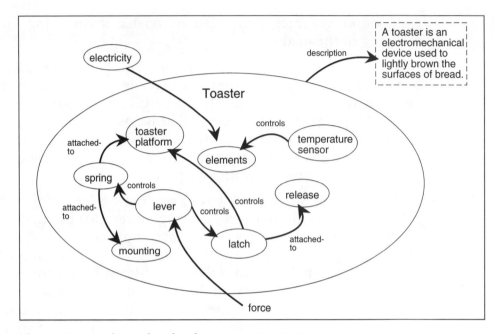

Figure 1.1 Multimedia database, version 1.0.

The semantics of the controls relationship defines how the components interact with one another. You would expect descriptions of the control interactions attached to the *controls* relationship. For example, the release controls the latch. This can be seen when we look at how the release and latch are attached to one another. This is shown in Figure 1.2. As you can see in Figure 1.3, if the release is

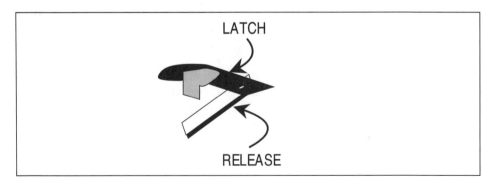

Figure 1.2 Latch and release engaged.

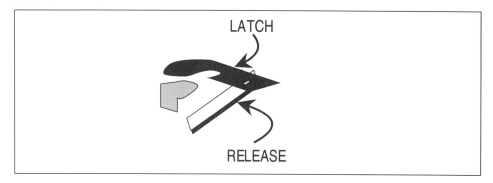

Figure 1.3 Latch and release disengaged.

pulled, then the latch disengages. This could be expressed formally by the following relationship.

pull(release(left)) → pull(latch(left))

You will notice that Figures 1.2 and 1.3 use diagrams to represent the various components of the toaster. Actually, the database can be augmented to include this information. The revised database is shown in Figure 1.4. This database now includes component pictures. Of course we could use the pictures to create some of the subassemblies of the toaster. An example of such an assembly is shown in Figure 1.5. This figure shows how the release, latch, handle, and toast platform all relate to one another. With some additional information placed in the database, subassemblies such as the one shown in Figure 1.4 could be derived directly from the database.

A multimedia system that mixes text with images, produces diagrams, and demonstrates the operation of a device demands a rich representation of the information describing that device. Figures 1.1 and 1.4 show some of this information. Of course, there must be information about the way objects are assembled. Once assembled, how do the various components operate and how are the operations of individual components related to the operation of the components as a whole or in groups? This information is encoded into the database as a series of rules that represent component behavior.

Information stored in the multimedia database is called **content** and is developed independently of the multimedia system. Content is transformed into something compatible with multimedia sys-

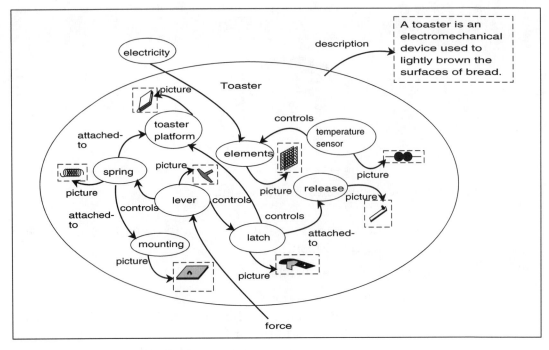

Figure 1.4 Multimedia database, version 2.0.

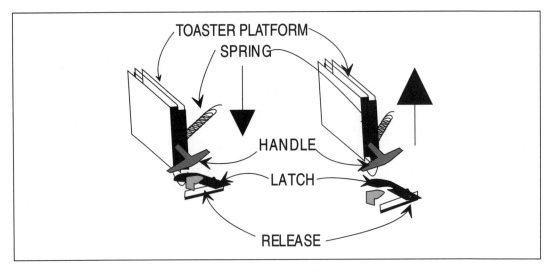

Figure 1.5 Operation of the latch, release, handle, spring, and toaster platform.

tems. The database includes the means to display information contained in it. This idea of a database that contains many different kinds of information is not typical of our idea of a standard database.

The use of the database metaphor (multimedia as database) is important because it is a framework in which we can think about creating multimedia systems. The database is not simply a viewer that allows one to present different kinds of multimedia. Rather, the database is also a processor for multimedia data that can use descriptions of the multimedia contained in the database to assemble different kinds of presentations.

This handbook is about assembling multimedia systems that use artificial intelligence. It is about how to use the idea of a database as the foundation of this kind of system. This handbook is also about using artificial intelligence to enhance the processing capabilities of multimedia systems. If rules are encoded into the multimedia database describing component operation, artificial intelligence algorithms and programs can enable the components to operate as their counterparts would operate in the real world.

This thumbnail sketch has been a brief introduction to multimedia and artificial intelligence. The next sections review in more detail the elements comprising a multimedia system and the nature of the components of artificial intelligence that would create more powerful multimedia systems.

The Basics

Throughout, this discussion has mentioned many (if not most) of the elements and components of multimedia. Now, a more orderly presentation of the ingredients of multimedia is in order. This section is an overview of the rest of the book and is divided into two parts. The first part describes the ingredients of multimedia, the second part, the elements of artificial intelligence.

At various times the preceding discussion referred to the kind of software that is developed when developing a multimedia system or application. Besides a system or application, multimedia software constitutes a kind of presentation of information. The interface of a multimedia system deals precisely with the presentation of many different kinds and forms of information. Whenever any software is created it should be preceded by a plan for its implementation. This is typically called the software design. A presentation has a similar entity associated with it. The plan associated with a multimedia presentation is called a **script** or **story board**. Both script and design are needed for a multimedia application.

Multimedia Applications

Text, graphic image, animation, video, font, authoring tool, digital audio, image, bitmap, color, and event-driven. What do all of these terms have in common? Each one is an important aspect of the creation of multimedia applications. The assembly of these various elements into a cohesive production can make use of any or all of these. Understanding what each of these is and how they relate to one another is important for the creation of successful multimedia applications.

Text

It would be relatively easy to skip over text as an element of multimedia. After all, whenever any nonpicture or nonsound information is presented, it is typically taken for granted that text will be used to present the information. Consider this book. Its fundamental presentation media is text. Books like this one are created so that the font(s) used are relatively uniform. With multimedia, this need not be the case. Consistency plays a very important role, but consider the available palette of fonts. Hundreds of different fonts are available in many different sizes and can be underlined, italicized, bolded, or any combination of these—and these are only the visual features of individual characters of the text. Characters are aggregated into words, words into sentences, sentences into paragraphs, and paragraphs into columns or pages. If we think of a character as a one-dimensional object, then these can be aggregated into larger units like paragraphs. A paragraph has a height (number of sentences) and a width (number of words in a sentence) and is therefore two-dimensional. If we continue the analogy to geometrical objects, lines can be combined into various two-dimensional objects such as rectangles and circles. Visually, two-dimensional units of text can be "shaped" in just this way. This is another visual feature of text. But it doesn't end here.

Besides the visual features of text, there is also the choice of what to describe, how it will be described, when it will be described, and so on. Text, as a part of multimedia, should not be, I repeat, should *not* be, taken for granted. After all, the printed word revolutionized communication. Should such an important element be taken for granted? I don't think so...

Sound

It may seem that if we can use the written word to express some information, sound might be unnecessary. This is true only if we think of sound as the spoken word. Sound is much more than this and, like text, is something we often take for granted—but not always. For example, the only thing produced by a radio is sound, so it is very difficult to take sound for granted when listening to the radio. What would it be like to listen to a movie without its sound track?

A multimedia presentation can include sound, and this should be considered an important part of the script. The different kinds of sound that can be included are spoken word, recorded live sounds (sound effects), recorded music, and computer-controlled music. As for text, quite a palette is available, and careful consideration should be given to what will be used in any multimedia presentation.

Images

If text and sound are often taken for granted, images are just the opposite. After all, a picture is worth a thousand words. When I showed the example of the toaster database, I represented it pictorially. Tremendous amounts of information can be presented with images. A picture is an extremely compact but rich representation of information. It is no wonder that visual information is key to any conveyance of information.

We can distinguish several different kinds of images. The earlier figures in this chapter are diagrammatic. Diagrammatic images are distinguished from others by the elements of the representation. In a diagrammatic representation, the elements of the diagram are strictly defined. We could say there is an alphabet used in the diagram. The toaster database uses a small set of elements consisting of circles, text labels, and one-ended arrows. The second of the toaster diagrams contains smaller graphic elements in addition to diagrammatic elements.

A graphic element is not constrained by any set of symbols. A graphic is typically drawn and referred to as a drawing. In addition to drawn graphic elements, graphic elements can be collected by scanning them. Scanning is the process of converting hardcopy (paper) images into computer-based (electronically encoded) images.

A sequence of images may be displayed with a small delay between them. When the images represent a sequence, such as the movement of a graphic element, the result is an animation. Each image represents a "cel" of the animation, and hence the name *cel animation*. So, in addition to still graphics, graphics that simulate motion can be created.

Video

The ability to use a personal computer to display in real time, full motion video just as you would watch on television, is a very recent development. The technology required to do this is very complex and is very computationally costly. In this mode, the personal computer is acting as a video player. The ability to make a personal computer display full motion video makes the computer a complete self-contained media machine. Until recently, a videotape player or videodisk player would have to be connected to a special graphics adapter that incorporated the capability to display both video and graphics. The external video tape player or video disk player would be controlled by the computer. The drawback to this is that it requires an additional device. More important, all of the media needed must be present on the media player. If all of the media could not fit on one disk or tape, the system user would have to change tapes or more than one player would be needed. This made the process very cumbersome and prone to problems—as is true with the addition of any new hardware.

With the computer as the "total" media device, many different media sources can be stored. These can be programmatically assembled on demand, making the presentation process significantly easier and more versatile.

Glue

Since the advent of word processors, drawing programs, and graphic user interfaces (GUIs) in general, the term "cutting and pasting" has taken on a new meaning. Before these programs, cutting and pasting was just that—cutting using scissors and pasting using real glue. Paste was particularly important because it held things together. If the paste wasn't the right kind, then the things pasted would fall away from what they were pasted to.

Many of the computer-based tools appearing today serve as a kind of paste for multimedia. For example, many of the newer word processors will allow the display of text, sound, graphics, and so on. The glue is the word processing document in this case. There are also specialized tools that provide glue. Examples of tools are programs like Macromedia's Director and Netscape's Navigator.

When we think about the metaphor of glue, we want to think about two things. First, what sort of glue is provided? How does it allow different media to be pasted together? Second, what information does the glue allow to be stored with the media? Does the glue allow descriptions of the media that can be used by other programmatic elements? Or is the glue passive, only allowing media to be pasted together? The more information that can be used as part of the glue, the more powerful the system.

Tools

The discussion of glue mentioned tools that act like glue. The tools that make the glue represent only one class of glue. We can identify several classes of tools that come into play when considering multimedia. A summary of these tools is shown in Table 1.1.*

Quite a bit could be written about the tools listed in Table 1.1. In fact, each deserves a book of its own. I will be coming back to particular examples and issues with these tools in later discussions in this book. For now, you should understand my goal is not to explain how to use these tools in detail, but rather how to use them to assemble an intelligent multimedia system. No one tool listed in Table 1.1 has the capability to support what I have been calling artificially intelligent multimedia. Together, with some additional machinery, they can build intelligent multimedia systems.

Artificial Intelligence

The machinery to create intelligent multimedia is derived from tools, algorithms, and methods of artificial intelligence. In fact, quite a few techniques of artificial intelligence could be applicable. Some of these are more appropriate than others, and in general two aspects of artificial intelligence are particularly relevant. The first of these is knowledge representation. This is a particularly important aspect of artificial intelligence, as most artificial intelligence programs use knowledge as data—a concept different from the typical computer program.

A second class of artificial intelligence methodologies particularly relevant to creating intelligent multimedia are expert systems. These can provide the capability to make decisions in the presentation and operation of a multimedia system. Both of these classes of artificial intelligence tools are discussed briefly in the next two sections.

---

*Some of the tools listed in Table 1.1 have been replaced during the course of the writing of this book. Table 1.1 is meant to provide the reader with a sampling of the kinds of tools available for creating multimedia applications.

Table 1.1 Summary of Multimedia Tools

Tool Class	Description	Examples	Class Function
Word processing programs	These programs handle primarily text, although most current programs (like Microsoft's Word for Windows Version 6.0) allow pasting of different kinds of media.	Microsoft Word for Windows 6.0 WordPerfect for Windows	Multimedia source material authoring
Drawing programs	The production of graphic images is accomplished with these programs. Most current programs have the ability to create 3-D images.	Paint for Windows PC Paintbrush Micrografix DRAW for Windows Micrografix Designer Adobe Illustrator	Multimedia source material authoring
Animation creation programs	An animation creation tool is a means by which a multimedia author can create graphic-based animations (cartoons).	Disney Animation Studio Autodesk Animator Pro Macromind Director Macromind Authorware MotionWorks MediaShop	Multimedia source material authoring
Multimedia authoring programs	This class of tools makes up the primary class of tools for creating multimedia.	Microsoft Multimedia Viewer Macromind Authorware Asymmetrix Toolbook Macromind Director Hypercard	Multimedia assembly (although it may be typical that some of these tools have means to create multimedia source materials)
Multimedia manipulation programs	These programs allow a user to manipulate the different kinds of multimedia. For example, a wave editor gives a user the means to modify sound .WAV files (a kind of sound file). Similarly a video editing program would allow a user to edit video for a presentation.	Gold Disk VideoDirector WaveEdit for Windows Adobe Photoshop Micrografix Photomagic	Multimedia manipulation

Rule-Based or Expert Systems

Rule-based systems, or expert systems as they are sometimes called, make up one class of artificial intelligence applications. Rule-based systems have certain characteristics that make them particularly useful and appropriate for this purpose. Chief among these characteristics is how knowledge is represented in a rule-based system. In a system of this kind, knowledge is expressed in the form of rules. A rule has the basic form

>if something-is-true then do-something

The **something-is-true** part of the rule is a specification of a conditional expression, such as

>$a = 5$

or

>jeffrey is male

The **do-something** part of the rule is some action to be done if the condition of the rule is true. This part of a rule may cause one or more variable values to change, or display some information to the user of the system.

A rule-based program consists of a series of rules like the one shown. The program will focus on a particular decision-making process. For example, an expert system might be used to identify fish when given a certain set of characteristics. In order to accomplish this, each rule-based system rule can access a common area of computer memory called **short-term memory**. Short-term memory can be used to store variables, their values, and other kinds of symbolic objects. The conditional part of a rule tests variables and symbols in short-term memory when a rule-based program is running.

An expert system interpreter runs a rule-based program by scanning the rules that make up the program. The scanning process looks for rules whose conditions are satisfied. More than one rule may have a condition that is satisfied. If more than one rule has a satisfied condition, one rule is selected, and the actions (**do-something**) of that rule are processed.

It may seem that rules are best suited to represent decision-making processes. In reality, the rule representation can be used for tasks other than decision making. The meaning of a rule is the primary concern of knowledge representation.

Knowledge Representation

Data manipulated in computer programs usually is interpreted by people to have some specific meaning. For example, a record of data in a payroll program may consist of several numbers. These individual numbers are called **fields**. By themselves the numbers are meaningless. We need to know precisely how to interpret each of the numbers. An interpretation of the data in the record makes the data meaningful. This record (in the case of payroll data) could contain three fields: employee number, hours worked, and salary. The data in the record is said to *represent* this information.

We can take this idea one step further and create data records that represent more complex entities. The more complex entities I am referring to, called knowledge representation structures (a big name for records), can be used to represent human knowledge, that is, the knowledge you and I have in our heads. One example of a knowledge representation structure is a rule.

An important characteristic of a knowledge representation is the type of data contained in it. Much of human knowledge is symbolic—we invent symbols to represent different types and kinds of knowledge. You are looking at one very common symbol system—words written on a page. Representational symbols typically consist of one or more names and a related or imposed structure. The names and structure together form the knowledge representation. A rule has a precise structure. Although it was originally represented as,

    if something-is-true then do-something

it can also be presented as a pair of structures.

    ((condition(s)) (actions(s)))

where both the condition and action have well-defined structures consisting of operations and symbols. The toaster can be used to clarify the idea of rules for knowledge representation.

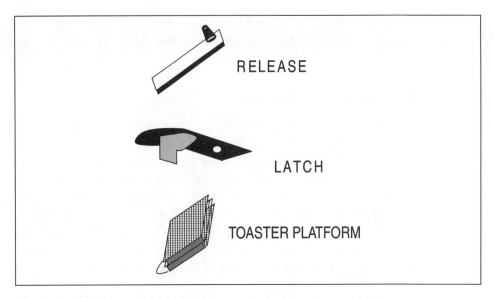

Figure 1.6 Release, latch, and toaster platform components.

Suppose we want to describe the operation of the release, latch, and toaster platform. In order to do this I need to define some symbols to represent these components. I can use the names of the components for this purpose. Pictures of the components are shown in Figure 1.6.

I want to describe the operation of these components, so one of the things I will do is to specify some of the actions that can be performed by each of the components. These actions can be represented symbolically. Words represent the actions. The actions for each component are summarized in Table 1.2. With this table of symbolically represented actions and components, I can describe

Table 1.2 Summary of Components and Associated Actions

Component	Action	
Release	atRest	pulled
Latch	engaged	disengaged
ToasterPlatform	up	down

Table 1.3 Summary of Components and Their Associated States

Component	Possible States	
Release	release(atRest)	release(pulled)
Latch	latch(engaged)	latch(disengaged)
ToasterPlatform	toasterPlatform(up)	toasterPlatform(down)

the various states of each component. I can use a functional notation for this as shown in Table 1.3.

I can begin writing rules that describe the operation of these components with these possible states. The conditions of the rule contain one or more states of the toaster components. The actions, conclusions, or consequents of the rule specify updated states for the components of the toaster. For example, I can describe the relationship between the latch, release, and toasterPlatform in terms of the following rules.

if release(pulled) then latch(disengaged)

if latch(disengaged) then toasterPlatform(up)

The toaster would require many rules like these to describe its complete operation. As you might imagine, it is possible with these rules to describe both operating and defective states of the toaster. Although I have represented a mechanical device with these rules, it is also possible to represent other kinds of things. For example, with rules that are similar to these but somewhat more complicated, it is possible to represent a person's behavior. Certain very complex computer games contain sets of rules that describe how the characters of the game behave. This same idea can be used for other kinds of multimedia applications.

It is possible to represent complex applications with rule-based systems and other kinds of knowledge representation schemes. This brings us back to the very important idea of knowledge as data.

One key to creating an intelligent system is the ability to encode knowledge describing a particular domain into a data structure representation. The data structure representation is only that, a repre-

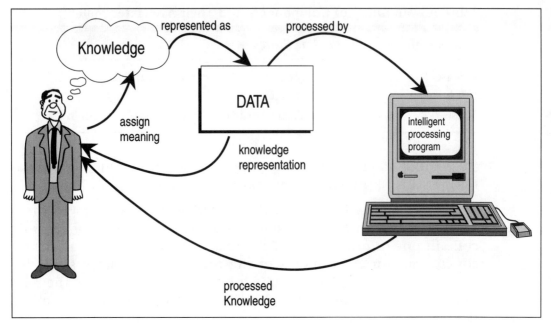

Figure 1.7 Summary of relationship between person, knowledge, data, and computing system.

sentation. The meaning assigned to the representation is determined by whoever will use it. By structuring and formalizing a representation for knowledge, especially in a form or structure that can be processed by a computer, the representation attains the distinction of being a kind of data. Just as programs can be written to process data, programs can be written to process knowledge. The programs that process knowledge-type data will perform functions implementing some aspects of intelligence. This relationship between knowledge, data, and intelligent programs is a foundation of intelligent systems. The relationship is summarized in Figure 1.7.

Tools

Just as there are tools for creating multimedia programs and applications, there are also tools for producing artificial intelligence applications. One reason the tools for artificial intelligence are described separately from the multimedia tools is that no commercial or public domain tool yet explicitly combines the features of a multimedia tool and an artificial intelligence tool. That is the reason for this book—to describe how these individual tools can be combined.

Tools for artificial intelligence can be divided into two classes: programming languages for developing artificial intelligence applications and programs designed for creating artificial intelligence applications. The latter differ from the former in that they typically are designed to create specific types of applications, such as expert systems.

There are three typical artificial intelligence programming languages: LISP, Prolog, and Smalltalk. Each of these languages represents a different approach to creating programs for artificial intelligence. Each also allows easy manipulation of symbolic data.

LISP is probably the best-known and oldest of these languages. It is a procedural language like C or BASIC, but here the similarity to these common languages ends. LISP is based on a uniform data representation. This representation is called a list and can be used to represent very complex structures. The same structures that represent data in LISP are also used to represent program functions. This uniform representation allows for substantial power in a language.

Prolog differs from LISP in its underlying paradigm. Prolog implements a logical paradigm. Like LISP, the representation of data and program is uniform. Although Prolog is also able to manipulate lists, its representation is in the form of logical clauses.

The remaining language, Smalltalk, is an object-oriented language. Like LISP and Prolog, it was designed for creating applications that manipulate symbolic information. In Smalltalk, the representation consists of objects that communicate by sending messages. One important aspect of Smalltalk is the concept of inheritance. In complex systems, inheritance can facilitate economy in representing complex systems and promote code reusability.

The other class of tools for artificial intelligence are those specifically designed for creating intelligent systems. Most original tools for creating artificial intelligence applications were originally constructed as layers on top of LISP, but now these tools are independent of LISP for various reasons. The most common artificial intelligence tools are those for creating expert systems. These are called expert system shells.

Expert system shells are called this because they contain the mechanism to create expert systems. They are expert systems without the knowledge that makes them an expert system. The knowledge is "filled-in" to create the expert system. These shells are of particular interest because they are best suited for the representations and mechanisms for intelligence in multimedia systems.

Another kind of tool is one providing a specific representational mechanism. One representation scheme in artificial intelligence systems is based on a data structure called a *frame*. A frame is a generalized data structure that can be used to represent symbolic information. As part of its definition, it supports inheritance. Tools exist for creating and maintaining frame-based knowledge representations. A summary of these tools for creating intelligent systems is shown in Table 1.4.

Other Books

In the last couple of years many books have been published about multimedia and the tools that can be used to produce multimedia applications. On my bookshelf alone, I have a dozen or more books about the subject. Needless to say, there are books presently in production that will appear before and after this book does. Some of these new books will give detailed descriptions of the tools I will be describing. The point of this book is not to repeat these detailed descriptions.

This book is about how to assemble tools for creating multimedia and tools for creating intelligent systems. Multimedia tools can be very powerful by themselves, but by themselves, they seldom make use of the multimedia for any purpose other than presentation. Reasoning about the contents of the multimedia or the presentation must be delegated to specialized components in the system.

Table 1.4 Summary of Tools for Intelligent Systems Implementation

Tool Class	Description	Examples	Class Function
Languages	Certain languages are specifically designed for the purpose of creating intelligent systems. Among other important characteristics, these languages facilitate symbolic manipulation.	LISP Prolog Smalltalk	To implement intelligent systems.
Expert systems and expert system shells	A specialized tool for creating intelligent systems. The characteristics of specialization include the type of knowledge representation (rules) and the paradigm implemented by the expert system.	M.4 (an embeddable expert system shell) EXSYS (a standalone expert system shell)	To implement rule-based expert systems.
Knowledge representation tools	These are tools used to represent symbolic data—specifically data used to represent knowledge. Knowledge representation systems typically are part of systems that reason with knowledge.	Prolog (logic-based knowledge representation) KL-ONE (and its successors)—a noncommercial inheritance network	Representing various kinds of knowledge contained in and used by an intelligent system.

Intelligent Multimedia Systems Revisited

I have defined an intelligent multimedia system to be one that combines the elements of multimedia and the elements of artificial intelligence. So far I have treated these elements separately. This is because multimedia and artificial intelligence represent two separate fields or disciplines. The chapters in this book are arranged so that the reader unfamiliar with multimedia tools and techniques can gain some familiarity with these and likewise so that those unfamiliar with artificial intelligence can learn about the relevant tools and techniques. Eventually these two kinds of tools come together later in this book in an example of an intelligent multimedia system—an intelligent tutor.

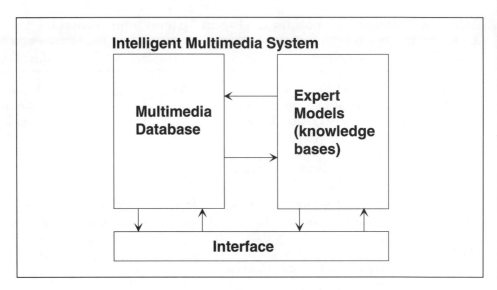

Figure 1.8 Typical plan for an intelligent multimedia system.

An intelligent tutor is a kind of intelligent multimedia system that uses multimedia to convey information. If we think about intelligent multimedia systems as being constructed according to a typical plan, then Figure 1.8 depicts a general structure for intelligent multimedia systems.

In Figure 1.8 an intelligent multimedia system is depicted as consisting of three elements: a multimedia database, one or more expert models making up the intelligence for the intelligent multimedia system, and the interface providing for interaction with the system.

The interface is the means by which the intelligent multimedia system can receive input from a user. The interface passes on user input to the knowledge bases or to the multimedia database. The knowledge bases and multimedia database represent more than just data, they also represent programs. For example, the multimedia database includes programs that are able to display animation or play sound.

The multimedia database is the container for all media used by the intelligent multimedia system. The multimedia database may actually contain the media if the database is the physical container for the media files. It may also be a logical container if the media files are stored in individual files. In either the physical or logical case, the multimedia database facilitates access to the media contained in the media files. The simplest kind of database may be a list of the available media. A more complex type of access to the database would be an index providing for rapid retrieval of the different media from the database.

The knowledge bases contain one or more expert models able to react to user input through the interface component. An expert model may select media to be displayed or analyze user input to determine the next action of the multimedia system. Another kind of expert model could assemble presentations, and yet another may know how to understand spoken English to respond to spoken user input. The various kinds of knowledge contained in the knowledge base can make decisions about the media contained in the system and make use of these media. Rather than write an explicit program to perform specific tasks, the knowledge can specify how the intelligent multimedia system will respond to various situations. In the case of an intelligent tutoring program, the intelligence makes decisions about what to tell the users as they are working on problems formulated by the intelligent tutor. The characteristic that makes an intelligent multimedia system stand out from a typical multimedia or artificial intelligence system is a merging and interaction between media and intelligence.

The Rest of the Book

Systems that combine multimedia and intelligence can be used for, among other things, education, training, and recreation. I mention these applications to establish a context in which to consider these systems. Their true power is in the system's ability to oversee access to the many types of information contained in the system.

Chapter 2 reviews some tools available for multimedia development. I discuss several classes of tools in this chapter and describe the advantages and disadvantages of using them. It would be easy in this chapter to become lost in the details of a particular tool. Rather than do this I will review different types of tools, and outline how they are used to create multimedia applications. From this discussion you should be able to select one or more tools appropriate for your particular application. In this chapter, a sample multimedia application is also presented and implemented in two different tools. The reader can gain some insight into the tradeoffs of selecting one tool over another.

Chapter 3 introduces the concept of a multimedia database. Unlike its text and data counterpart, a multimedia database can be used to store text, graphics, images, videos, animation sequences, and digital sound. Key to this database is a relational structure that can be used to access the information contained in the database.

Chapter 4 describes some of the tools presently available for developing intelligent systems. This chapter is the counterpart to Chapter 2 for intelligent systems and describes the two major programming languages for creating intelligent applications: LISP and Prolog. Most of the tools for developing intelligent applications were derived from these languages, so this will provide the reader with a good foundation of the principles on which these languages are based. A third tool described in this chapter is one for developing expert systems. As you will see, some of the intelligent multimedia systems presented in subsequent chapters make use of expert systems to implement the intelligence embedded in them.

Chapter 5 discusses knowledge representations. A knowledge representation is a computer-based memory structure used to store and manipulate knowledge. This is a particularly important subject, as the very nature of intelligent systems depends on the representations they will use. Chapter 5 describes rules, frames, and facts among other kinds of knowledge representations.

Chapter 6 discusses models. A model is a representation of a mechanism or process in the real world. Models are very important when developing any multimedia application, as they form the basis for the operation of the application. A general description of a model is given and then followed by a discussion of three important kinds of models: domain, student, and instructional.

A domain model contains information about what an intelligent multimedia system will present. For example, if the intelligent multimedia system is a tutor for repairing televisions, then the domain model will contain knowledge about television repair.

In an intelligent tutoring system the student and instructional models together represent the teacher in the system. These models are invisible to the user and are only apparent because they control the behavior of the instructional system. Of course, the sophistication of these models can vary from very simple rule-based models to complex models based on rules and statistics.

Now that we know what we want to represent, it is time to tie this to the kinds of media that we will want to use. The knowledge representation described in Chapter 5 lends itself nicely to the task of representing both knowledge of the system and also those things that will be used to augment the knowledge. For example, when we are describing the latching mechanism of the toaster, it might be useful to show how this mechanism functions with an animation. The knowledge representation will "point to" the related animation so that it can be called upon when needed.

Chapter 7 describes a complete intelligent multimedia application. I will present the design and implementation of a kind of intelligent multimedia system called an intelligent tutor. An intelligent tutor is a computer program that acts like a teacher. The tutor, called Toaster Tutor, teaches a student information about how to repair a toaster and also how to solve problems. An interesting feature of the tutor is that it represents the toaster device, so you can use the system to simulate the process of using the toaster. You can watch what happens when you use the toaster and what effect your repairs will have. You will be able to see how to represent devices in this chapter and how to fashion a course around these device representations.

The knowledge representation used in Chapter 7 is primarily frame and rule based. Artificially intelligent programs called expert systems are used throughout the tutor to implement its intelligence. In Chapter 8, a different type of artificial intelligence application is described. Chapter 8 focuses on the use of natural language processing in intelligent multimedia. Natural language processing is the capability of the computer to process written or spoken language and understand the language it processes.

The last chapter, Chapter 9, considers several frontiers of computer science and how they relate to intelligent multimedia systems. Often the literature about these avoids them or considers them as a separate discussion subject and is (rightly) criticized for this. For this reason, I will discuss neural networks and virtual environments and how they relate to intelligent multimedia systems. A neural network is a computing device that is patterned after the organization of the brain. It consists of many small interconnected analog processors. Unlike a traditional computing device, a neural network is "programmed" by teaching it how to recognize things. A neural network has a memory by virtue of the learning process.

Neural nets can be used for constructing pattern recognizers. They may have great potential for guiding an intelligent multimedia system. For example, one area where a neural network may have an impact is in assessing performance and recognizing student problems. A neural network could be trained to recognize good performance and poor performance and guide feedback to the student in both situations. In a traditional intelligent multimedia system this would be accomplished by a rule-based program that would have to be explicitly specified. In a neural network, the network would learn.

A second important technology that may have a significant impact on the development of multimedia and intelligent multimedia systems is genetic programming. Genetic programming uses an approach similar to that used by cells to reproduce. I will introduce genetic programming and describe how it might impact intelligent multimedia.

It is unarguable that the Internet and the World Wide Web have changed our ideas of computing, information, and communication. Likewise, I would be remiss if I did not attend to the Internet's affect on intelligent multimedia. The section in Chapter 9 about the Internet presents some ideas of how intelligent multimedia and the Internet might be joined to create new kinds of intelligent multimedia systems.

Another important cutting edge technology goes by the name **virtual environment**. A virtual environment is a computer-generated environment. Imagine a computer that can take you into a laboratory and allow you to carry out experiments. Virtual environments are roughly classified into three categories. The simplest are computer-based simulations in which you sit at a computer and interact with an environment created by the computer. Games like SimEarth and SimCity are examples of this type of virtual environment.

A second type of virtual environment is the virtual reality environment. In this environment, the user wears special headgear and body gear to interact with the computing system. The headgear produces three-dimensional images. The user's view is restricted to what the computer generates, so it appears as if the user is part of whatever environment the computer generates. In its most typical form, the user wears a glove that is monitored by the computing system. The system can respond to hand gestures.

The third class of virtual environments are ones in which the environment is responsive to the user. Unlike virtual reality, no special "clothing" is worn. The environment can be manipulated directly by the user.

CHAPTER 2

Multimedia Authoring Tools

Introduction

Let's begin with a very simple definition of a multimedia authoring tool:

> A multimedia authoring tool is a computer program that allows an author to create a program that will present graphics, images, sound, video, and animation.

Several requirements are implicit in this definition. First, the multimedia tool should simplify the process of creating a multimedia program. That is to say, it should be the Phillips screwdriver that fits the Phillips-head screw. It is important for a multimedia authoring tool to facilitate the process of multimedia authoring.

Second, the multimedia authoring tool must provide for multimedia. In other words, the tool should be able to display various kinds of multimedia including graphics, sound, text, animation, and video. This should be part of the tool, or easily incorporated into the tool. Some tools can be augmented with components that have additional capabilities, and this would adequately meet our needs.

Third, a multimedia tool should not be a closed box. It should allow doors and windows between the inside and outside. Sometimes in the creation of a multimedia application you will encounter a development wall. If the multimedia authoring tool does not have a doorway to the outside, you may not be able to get over this wall. On the other hand, if the multimedia tool does have a door to the outside world, then such development walls might be overcome by using a tool outside of the multimedia authoring tool environment and then passing the results back into the environment. Most of the more recent multimedia authoring tools do provide doors between the inside and outside.

Finally, multimedia applications are typically highly interactive. This means there must be provision in the multimedia tool for interactivity. All of the GUI devices we have all come to know should be part of the multimedia tool. For example, if you are going to author multimedia hypermedia applications, then the multimedia authoring tool should provide some GUI tool that represents a button. If not, then this may not be the tool for your purpose.

Developing Your Own Multimedia Tool Versus Using a Commercially Available Tool

The selection of any tool for creating a complex application should be done with great care. Usually, commercial tools will not meet all of the requirements of a project and tradeoffs have to be made. Creating your own tool appears to be a viable option in this case. There are several important questions to ask when you are considering the option to create your own tool as an option. Do you *really* have a good reason to do this? Do you *really* have the time to do this? Do you *really* want to do this? Creating your own multimedia tool is a very costly approach and should be considered in this light. Later in this chapter I will describe a DOS-based multimedia authoring tool developed for a large-scale intelligent tutoring program. Over 4 million lines of code have been written in the language defined for this tool. Although the project was successful and met the project requirements I would consider my options carefully before choosing this approach again. Too many tools meet the requirements now, and most of these tools have substantial capabilities beyond my own effort. Consider the question of home growing *very carefully* before choosing this approach to tool selection and creation. If you cannot find a tool that fits the bill, first consider what it will take to extend one that exists. If you still find yourself without the needed capabilities, see if you can find a tool that allows you to add the capability through a door. Only as a last resort should you choose to grow your own tool.

Language-Based Versus Graphic Interface–Based Tools

This section discusses two tools for creating multimedia applications. One of these is a tool named the Interaction Language or **IL**. IL is a language I grew to develop an intelligent multimedia application. Although this language has no intelligence per se, it was designed with the "hooks" for intelligence, so you could connect it to the outside world and it would be able to use intelligence from somewhere else. The reason I want to discuss IL is that (1) it is a fairly simple language that will illustrate some of the elements of a multimedia authoring tool, (2) it is a DOS-based language, (3) it implements the basic paradigm of a tool to create interactive applications, and (4) I have included it on the CD-ROM included with this book.

The second tool I will describe is the multimedia courseware tool named *Authorware Professional for Windows*. This tool has been around a long time for the Macintosh. A couple of years ago it was ported to the Windows environment, and this is the version I will discuss. The point of this discussion is to compare two very different types of tools that allow you to do the same thing—to create multimedia applications. The goal is to give you a basis for some of the differences between tools so that when you go to choose a tool, you will be armed with some useful information.

The Interaction Language

IL is a little language designed to facilitate the development of multimedia applications on IBM PC–compatible computers. The fundamental motivation for creating a language to author multimedia applications was that at the time there were no similar authoring programs that met all of our requirements. We decided that whatever we used had to be simple enough to be used by nonprogrammers, and that we should be able to readily extend the language as we needed. Our client chose the development and delivery platform (the PC), and because of this we could not make use of the many tools available for the Macintosh at the time. All of these reasons converged to give birth to the IL language.

When IL was first conceived, it was as a little language—a specialized programming language with few statements. In fact, when IL was first conceived, it had no more than 10 different kinds of statements, but as with most software, demands were made upon it that could not be met (one of the reasons to grow your own), so we extended it. It now consists of over 50 distinct statement types that support multimedia application development. These are shown in Table 2.1.

When you look at Table 2.1, you can guess what some of the statements do simply by their name. For example, the DISPLAY statement is used to display graphic images. The statement allows a graphic image contained in a graphic image file in the .PCX format to be displayed at a specified position on the display screen.

What makes IL a language specifically designed for implementing interactive multimedia applications? There are two characteristics of IL that make it appropriate for this purpose. First, IL implements an **event-driven** paradigm. An event-driven paradigm is one in which the computer watches for events to occur. When a specific event occurs, the computer examines a table of responses to events that might occur and finds one that matches the particular event that did occur. If a response is found, the computer executes the response and waits for another event to occur. If no response is defined for the particular event, then the computer goes back to waiting for other events.

The event-driven paradigm is especially appropriate for creating multimedia applications because these are programs that typically incorporate significant amounts of interaction. One of the most common types of events is a button press or click. Another is pressing one or more keys on the keyboard.

Table 2.1 IL Statements

ACTIVATE	ENDTEST	RESTOREIMAGE
BEEP	FADEIN	RESTORESTATE
BUTTON	FADEOUT	RETURN
BUTTONCURSOR	FORWARDVIDEO	REVERSEVIDEO
CALL	FREE	RUN
CALLMACRO	GO TO	SAVEIMAGE
CCALL	HALT	SAVEPALETTE
CHAIN	HIDEVIDEO	SAVESTATE
CHAINRETURN	INC	SEARCHVIDEO
CLEARDISPLAY	KEEPSCREEN	SET
CLOSEFILE	KEY	SETBUTTON
CLOSELIBRARY	LOADPALETTE	SETCHROMA
CLOSEVIDEO	MACRO	SETCURSOR
CONCAT	MOUSEDOWN	SETCURSORCOLOR
CURSORMAP	MOUSEUP	SETEFFECT
DEACTIVATE	MOVEVIDEO	SHOWVIDEO
DEC	NOINITSCREEN	SINGLESTEP
DEFINE	OPENFILE	SIZEVIDEO
DELAY	OPENLIBRARY	STILLVIDEO
DELETE	OPENVIDEO	STOPVIDEO
DISABLE	PALETTE	TEST
DISPLAY	PLAYVIDEO	TEXT
DISPLAY LIST	READFILE	TIMEOUT
DRAGGABLE	READFRAME	VARIABLE
ENABLE	RESET	VIDEOINDEXOFF
ENABLECURSORMAP	RESETCURSORMAP	VIDEOINDEXON
END	RESETMOUSE	WRITEFILE

The second characteristic of the IL language that makes it appropriate for the development of multimedia applications is that it facilitates and simplifies the activities necessary to create these applications. For example, defining buttons and recognizing button events are elements of the IL language. As I mentioned earlier, displaying graphics is also a function of the IL language. A good tool

Programs in IL

A program in IL is called a **script**. Each script consists of one or more **parts**. Each part has at least one and no more than two **sections**. If a part has only one section, then it will consist of a series of **actions**. If a part has two sections, then it will first consist of a sequence of actions and then be followed by a sequence of event definitions. A part can be labeled. Parts in an IL script are like functions or subprograms in more classic programming languages.

When a part is executed by the IL interpreter, the first thing that happens is that the actions of the script part are executed. The table of IL statements is also a table of the actions that can be used in the first section of a script part. A sequence of actions can display a graphic that can serve as a menu. A sequence of actions could also display a video sequence or some text.

The other section of a part contains event definitions. There is one event definition for each event to be recognized. If, for example, you want to respond to three different mouse click events, you would define three different events, one for each distinct mouse click event. The IL statement used to define events is called the ON statement. An ON statement looks something like

    ON <event> {GO TO label|CALL label|RETURN}

Think of the ON statement as a way of saying "On this thing happening, do some other thing." The "this thing" could be a mouse click or a keyboard entry. The "some other thing" might be to display a graphic image at a particular location. By the way, the "this thing" is the event.

What Kinds of Events?

Four types of events can be recognized in the IL language.

- A mouse event
- A keyboard event

- A variable event
- A timer event

A mouse event is one naturally involving the mouse. Since many different things can be done with the mouse, mouse events can actually represent a significant number of different kinds of events. For example, pressing the left or right mouse buttons represents an event. Pressing the left or right mouse button at a certain location on the display screen represents a similar but slightly different kind of event. IL can respond to a significant number of mouse-based events.

A keyboard event is one that involves pressing a key on the keyboard. IL can recognize two kinds of keyboard events. One of these kinds of events is when any key on the keyboard is pressed. The other is when a specific key on the keyboard is pressed. Of course, there can be many other kinds of keyboard events, but these are the two kinds IL can respond to.

A variable event is one that occurs when an IL script variable attains a specific value. In other words, events can be associated with variable values. So, if you want to change the behavior of the program after a user does the same thing several times, you could do so by triggering an event based on the value of a counter variable.

The remaining type of event is a timer event. A timer event is one where a certain amount of time passes before an event occurs. This type of event is useful when you want to give a user a limited amount of time for a particular interaction.

GOTO*ing versus* CALL*ing*

The latter part of an ON statement specifies what will happen when the event occurs. This specification is made by branching to a new script part. The branch can be made in one of two ways—by going to the new script part or by calling a new script part.

As I mentioned earlier, script parts are very much like functions or subprograms in a traditional computer program. By going to a new script part you are simply branching to that part. The IL interpreter will not remember anything about where you came from to get to that part. Each time you branch to a new script part, the events that can be recognized are set to those in the script part. This is to say they replace any events from a previous script part. Using a GOTO branch in an ON statement allows each script part to locally control its branching.

In the case of the CALL branch in an ON statement, the IL interpreter will remember where the branch to the new script part was made from, just as would happen if a program function were called. The new script part will be processed, and if a RETURN action is encountered, the current script part being processed will be replaced by the one that called it. In this way, scripts can set up very specific contexts for reacting to the actions of a user.

There are a couple of important points to remember about this branching. First, when a RETURN action is made to a previous script part, the display will not be updated unless that script part (the one returned to) does the updating. This is the responsibility of the IL script writer. Second, a RETURN action always causes a return to the beginning of the script part. Unlike typical program functions, which return to the point of the call, IL takes a slightly different approach and returns to the beginning of the calling script part. Let's look at a couple of examples. In the IL script that follows, two graphics will be displayed, each depicting a button. The purpose of the script is to identify which button was pressed and to display some text identifying the button.

Program Listing 2.1 Sample IL script

```
display button1 at 150 100
display button2 at 350 100
on mousedown at button1 call b1id
on mousedown at button2 call b2id
on key go to exit
end

b1id: text font hlv37.gft at exact 125 250 foreground 15
      background 0 set
button 1 was pressed
return
end
```

```
b2id: text font hlv37.gft at exact 125 250 foreground 15
         background 0 set
      button 2 was pressed
      return
      end

exit: halt
end
```

This script has a total of four script parts. The first of these is unlabeled, and the remaining three script parts are named **b1id**, **b2id**, and **exit**. When the script is processed by the IL interpreter, the display will appear as shown as Figure 2.1. Pressing the left mouse button with the mouse arrow positioned over the button labeled 1 results in the display shown in Figure 2.2. Likewise, pressing the left mouse button with the mouse arrow positioned over the button labeled 2 results in the display shown in Figure 2.3. While the script is running, you can press on these buttons any number of times and the display will change accordingly. Let's look at the script a little closer.

The very first script part at the beginning of the script contains two sections. In the first section, the two graphics representing the buttons are displayed by the IL statements,

```
display button1 at 150 100
display button2 at 350 100
```

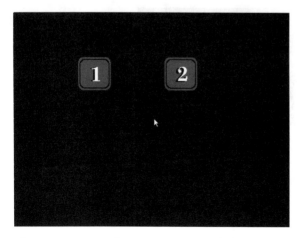

Figure 2.1 Simple IL script initial display.

Figure 2.2 Pressing button 1 and the resulting display.

Following the display of the two button graphics, the next script section defines three events that will be recognized by this script part. These are a mouse press at the button 1 graphic, a mouse press at the button 2 graphic, and pressing any key on the keyboard.

The section named **b1id** contains an action that displays text. The text indicates that button 1 was pressed. The TEXT action is quite versatile. With it you can display text anywhere on the dis-

Figure 2.3 Pressing button 2 and resulting display.

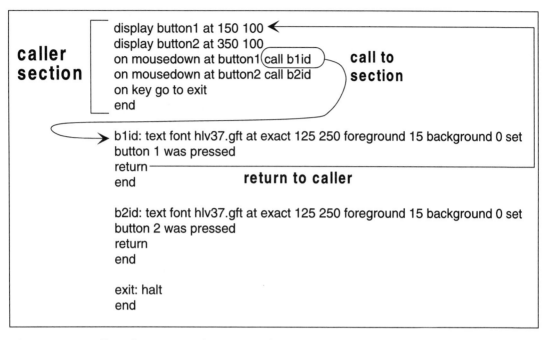

Figure 2.4 Call and return paths in simple IL script.

play, in a specific background/foreground color combination. You can also specify a font used for the text display.

Following the TEXT action is a RETURN action. When this action is processed by the IL interpreter, a branch is made back to the script section caller. In this case, the branch is made to the first script part. The activity of call and return is depicted in Figure 2.4.

A GOTO branch is used in the third event in the first script section. This type of branch is used in the event because this event is used to terminate the script. A CALL branch is not needed here, as there is no need to remember the call because the script will terminate.

The IL Language in Greater Detail

The basic elements of the IL language have been defined: the ability to display graphics and the ability to specify events that will be recognized by the IL interpreter. As you saw from the previous examples, event definitions and actions can be combined into a script to create a highly interactive application. The ON statement and DISPLAY statement are quite versatile by themselves. Of course, I have not described much of the versatility of these two statements and many of the others that are part of the IL language. This section describes the ON statement and DISPLAY statement in greater detail and some of the other statements that comprise the IL language.

The ON Statement in Detail

The syntax of the ON statement is shown in Table 2.2.

ON statements define events in an IL script. The various events that can be recognized include mouse events, keyboard events, button events, variable test events, and menu events.

The two kinds of mouse events that can be recognized are named MOUSEUP and MOUSEDOWN. At present, the only button recognized as an event is the left mouse button. As the names imply, it is possible to recognize an event when the left mouse button is pressed or when it is released. These two kinds of mouse events can be processed when they occur anywhere on the display in ON statements like,

```
ON mouseup CALL ...
ON mousedown CALL ...
```

Likewise, the event can be restricted in several ways. The location of the event can be specified as a discrete rectangle on the display, a particular point, or the name of a graphic displayed in the current script section. The sample script uses this latter technique to constrain the mouse event to the position of button 1 or button 2:

```
display button1 at 150 100
    .
    .
    .
on mousedown at button1 call b1id
```

Besides constraining a mouse event by naming a graphic displayed in the script section, you can also do this by specifying a rec-

Table 2.2 Syntax of the ON Statement

Form	ON *event* ((((CALL | GO TO) *label*)	RETURN)

event:
MOUSEUP, MOUSEUP AT *location*
MOUSEDOWN, MOUSEDOWN AT *location*
KEY, KEY *char*
BUTTON *name* (ON |OFF)
TEST *condition*
MENU *name item*

location:
RECTANGLE *ulx uly lrx lry* (BOX)
x y
fileName

char:
any keyboard character including ^n denoting the new line character.

condition:
variableName
variableName comparisonOp Constant
DRAGGABLE name AT IMAGE imageName

name:
any sequence of characters beginning with an alphabetic character

variableName:
the name of a declared variable

comparisonOp: (one of) gt, lt, le, ge, eq, ne

constant:
(string | integer)

string:
a sequence of characters enclosed in quotation marks

integer:
a sequence of digits

imageName:
the name of an image displayed in the current program section

item:
an integer denoting a menu item (# of the item)

tangle or a point on the display. A rectangle is defined by specifying the upper left and lower right points of the rectangle. A point is defined by specifying the coordinate of the point. Examples of these events are:

```
on mousedown at rectangle 100 100 300 400 call ...
on mouseup at 100 200 call ...
```

Simple keyboard events can also be defined. Just as there is an unconstrained and constrained version of the mouse event, there are also unconstrained and constrained versions of keyboard events. For a keyboard event, not specifying any key for the event allows any key to trigger the keyboard event. Specifying a particular key in an event makes the event triggerable only on pressing the specified key. Example keyboard events are:

```
on key call ...
on key x call ...
```

The next class of events are based on IL buttons. So far, the scripts presented use events based on simple mouse events. The events recognized are individual and for any script section must be redefined as they are needed. If certain interactions will be repeated across screens, it may be more convenient to define buttons for these interactions.

A button, like the events defined earlier, consists of an area of the display identified by a graphic that can be clicked on by placing the mouse cursor over the graphic and pressing the mouse button. In IL, a button is a graphic object that can be reused for user interactions. A button is defined in a button definition.

A button definition consists of the following items:

- Coordinates of the button
- A graphic for the button in the up or "nonclicked" state
- A graphic for the button in the down or "clicked" state
- Code to be executed when the button is up
- Code to be executed when the button is down
- Button type
- What to do when the button is disabled

An example of a button definition is

```
button:     quit
at:         320 240 370 290
whenup:     quitbttn
whendown:   quitrev
upcode:     set quitv 1
            set endv "terminate"
            end
downcode:   set quitv 0
            display textbox at 125 412
            end
mode:       nostay
erase:      no
end
```

A button can be one of two types: **STAY** or **NOSTAY**. When a STAY-type button is clicked, it will stay in the position it is clicked into.

A NOSTAY button is one that only goes into the down or ON state momentarily when it is clicked. As long as the mouse button is pressed, the button will stay down. When the mouse button is released, the button will return to the up position. The different behaviors of STAY and NOSTAY are useful for different purposes in applications, which is why this aspect of button behavior can be defined.

The related event, the ON button event, can be defined for the activity of an enabled button. Buttons can be enabled and disabled as they are needed in an IL script. A button event can respond to a button in the ON state or the OFF state. Each button has a name used in the event definition. Examples of a button event definition are

```
ON button x ON call ...
ON button x OFF go to ...
```

The next kind of events are those involving tests. A test event can be one of two types. The first type of test event is one involving testing the value of IL variables. An IL variable can be defined and used throughout an IL program. The test event can be triggered when a variable becomes nonzero or when a variable achieves a specific value.

The second type of test event is one triggered by a special IL entity called a draggable. A draggable event occurs when a draggable is moved to a specific display position. A draggable is a graphic object that can be moved to any position on the screen by clicking on the object and dragging the graphic object to its new position.

Like buttons, draggables are defined with a special definition statement. To define a draggable it is necessary to specify a name for the draggable, the graphic image, and a starting position on the display for the draggable. An example of a draggable definition is:

```
draggable dragit file object at 0 0
```

Event definitions for the three types of test events are:

```
ON test x call ...
ON test y eq "alpha" go to ...
ON test draggable foo at image object call ...
```

The second event definition contains a simple conditional expression, **y eq "alpha"**. Six comparison operations are available, **gt** (greater than), **lt** (less than), **le** (less than or equal), **ge** (greater than or equal), **eq** (equal), and **ne** (not equal).

The test draggable event requires the specification of a previously defined draggable and a previously displayed graphic image (the target graphic for the object). The event is triggered when the draggable touches the target graphic.

The remaining event definition is a MENU event, which is triggered when a menu item is selected by clicking on it with the mouse. Menus are defined with a MENU definition statement. Part of this definition is a series of items. Each item is one entry in the menu and is referred to by its specification. The event definition for a menu item consists of a specification of a menu name and an item name, for example,

```
ON MENU fileMenu option Open call ...
```

One remaining event type I need to define is a time-based event. For this event, a certain amount of time passes and an event

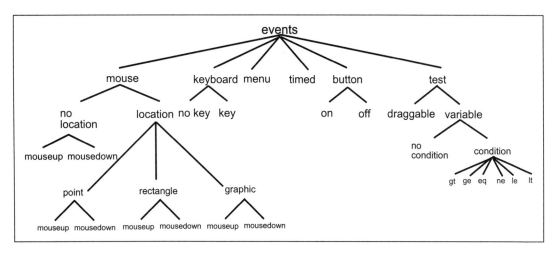

Figure 2.5 Summary of event types.

is triggered. Unlike the previous event definitions, the timed event is defined by a different IL statement, the TIMEOUT statement. In this event definition a time is specified and a called branch-to, for example

```
TIMEOUT 10 call ...
```

A summary of event types is shown in Figure 2.5.

IL Actions

IL actions allow an IL program to carry out relevant multimedia tasks such as displaying graphics and text. Some of IL's more significant actions will be described in this section.

The DISPLAY Action

The DISPLAY action is used to display graphic images at a specified position on the display. The graphics file format supported by IL is the .PCX format. This format is widely used and supported by many graphics programs. If the graphics program does not directly support the .PCX file format, chances are the program can import and export graphic files in this format.

In its most basic form, the DISPLAY action requires you to specify the name of the graphics file and the *x* and *y* coordinates where the graphic will be displayed. An example of the basic DISPLAY action is

```
DISPLAY graphic at 32 412
```

This example displays the filenames graphic at location *x* = 32 and *y* = 412.

The next version of the DISPLAY action allows a variable to be used to name the graphics file and variables used for the *x* and *y* coordinates of the graphic image. Any combination of variables and constants can be used in a display statement. The following code excerpt shows an example of a DISPLAY action using variables.

```
VARIABLE fileName xpos ypos
SET fileName "button"
SET xpos 124
SET ypos 244
DISPLAY fileName at xpos ypos
```

As has been described so far, one display statement must be used for each graphic to be displayed. Sometimes this can make each graphic seem to appear individually, which may be an undesirable effect. To avoid this, a variant of the DISPLAY action allows multiple graphic images to be displayed at once. This variant is named the DISPLAY LIST action. In the DISPLAY LIST action, you name a series of graphic files to be displayed. All graphics files in the list will be assembled into a display in memory, and the composite image in memory will be displayed. The form of the DISPLAY LIST action is:

```
DISPLAY LIST
    display clause 1
    display clause 2
         .
         .
         .
    display clause n
ENDLIST
```

A **display clause** consists of the name of the graphics file and the position at which it will be displayed. Any number of **display** clauses can be included in a DISPLAY LIST action. An example of a DISPLAY LIST action follows.

```
DISPLAY LIST
    systmenu at 0 0
    f15bttn at 32 22
    quitbttn at 32 412
ENDLIST
```

The third variant of the DISPLAY action allows a programmer to display a graphic with a predefined effect. The specific effect, delay, step size, and direction of the effect can all be defined. The specific effect and related parameters are all defined by a related action named SETEFFECT. The DISPLAY action to display a graphic with an effect is:

```
DISPLAY WITH EFFECT graphic at 0 0
```

The TEXT Action

Although a graphic may include text, it is useful to have a way to display text independent of any displayed graphic. This is the purpose of the TEXT action. The TEXT action requires the specification of several parameters in addition to the text to be displayed. To display text, it is first necessary to specify a font. Fonts are contained in files and specified by naming the required font file.

After the font name, the position of the text is specified. There are two ways to specify the position of text to be displayed. Coordinates for the display of text can be specified in exact screen coordinates (x, y) or as row and column according to the size of the font.

The foreground and background colors of the text are specified following the coordinates of the text. The colors are specified according to palette indices. For a 16-color palette, the foreground and background colors are specified as numbers from 0 through 15.

The remaining parameter defines how the text will be displayed. This is called the display operation. There are three available display operations. They are named SET, AND, and OR. SET means the bits of the display will be set exactly to the bits of the text. The AND operation means the bits of the text are ANDed with the display bits and the OR operation ORs the bits of the text with the bits of the display. An example of a TEXT action is:

```
TEXT FONT hlv37 at 1 1 FOREGROUND 15 BACKGROUND 0 SET
first line of text
second line of text
%%%
```

The text follows the specification of parameters and can span multiple lines. The sequence of text must end with a triple percent (%%%). Sometimes it might be useful to set the text while a script is running and dependent on user actions. It is possible to store text in a variable and use the variable as the source for the text display. The syntax for the TEXT action changes slightly when using a variable for this purpose. An example of this variation of the TEXT action is:

```
VARIABLE sometext
SET sometext "first line of text|second line of text"
TEXT FONT trm15 AT EXACT 160 410 FOREGROUND 15 BACKGROUND 1
    SET FROM sometext
```

In the example the text variable was set to the value

```
"first line of text|second line of text"
```

The or-bar (|) is used to denote a new line. When the text is displayed, it will be displayed on two separate lines.

When the amount of text to be displayed is sufficiently large, it may be inconvenient to store a large amount of text in a variable or to enter the text as part of a script. For these circumstances, text can be read from a file and displayed according to TEXT-action parameters. This version of the TEXT action also involves a slight variation in the syntax of the action:

```
TEXT FONT hlv37 AT 1 1 FOREGROUND 15 BACKGROUND 1 SET FILE
    myfile.txt
%%%
```

When the amount of text to be displayed is sufficiently large and the area for the display of the text is constrained, it is sometimes appropriate to display the text in a region that can be scrolled. In such a region, buttons are used to reposition the text being viewed. For example, 20 or 30 lines of text can be displayed in

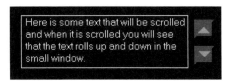

Figure 2.6 Scrollable text region.

an area that is 5 lines high. An example of a scrollable text region is shown in Figure 2.6.

To define a scrollable region, it is necessary to define two buttons. One will be used to scroll the text in the up direction, the other to scroll the text in the down direction. A scrollable region is defined by attaching the buttons to the text region and also defining the height of the region. An example of this version of the TEXT action is:

```
TEXT FONT hlv37 AT 1 1 FOREGROUND 15 BACKGROUND 1 SET
FILE sometext.txt
SCROLL up upbutton down downbutton height 5
%%%
```

Cursor Antics

The cursor can be a very useful tool, and being able to change the cursor for an application may be a useful device. For example, changing the cursor is a way to give visual feedback about the function or purpose of a display element. Active areas of the display can be denoted using the cursor.

The mouse cursor can be redefined as needed. IL has two different ways to accomplish this. There are 12 standard cursors available: hand, pencil, mouse, magnifying glass, clock, arrow, question mark, up arrow, left arrow, crosshairs, magnifying glass with a plus sign, and magnifying glass with a minus sign. The standard cursors are shown in Figure 2.7.

At any time the cursor can be reset to one of the 12 predefined cursors. This is accomplished with the SETCURSOR action:

```
SETCURSOR 0 5 hand
```

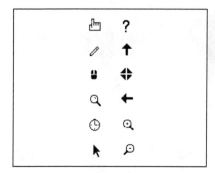

Figure 2.7 Standard IL cursors.

If you need to change the cursor periodically, the SETCURSOR action is a good way to do it. Sometimes, though, it is more convenient to define where on the display the cursor is to change. For this reason, you can define a cursor map. This map defines the cursor for specified rectangular regions. Wherever no cursor is defined in the map, the default cursor (arrow) is used. As the cursor is moved through the defined regions, it will automatically change. More than one cursor map can be defined in an IL script.

A cursor map is defined as a series of rectangular regions. Each region has a cursor associated with it. An example of a cursor map definition is:

```
CURSORMAP cmap
cursor at 0 0 250 356 is hand
cursor at 251 0 529 178 is pencil
cursor at 251 179 529 356 is magnifier
ENDMAP
```

In this definition, there are three cursor regions. The regions defined by the cursor map **cmap** are shown in Figure 2.8.

Cursor maps do not go into effect until they are enabled. A cursor map is enabled with the ENABLECURSORMAP action and the name of the cursor map. The cursor map **cmap** is enabled by

```
ENABLECURSORMAP cmap
```

Finally, when a cursor map is no longer needed, the map can be eliminated by resetting the cursor map to its default state. This is accomplished with the RESETCURSORMAP action.

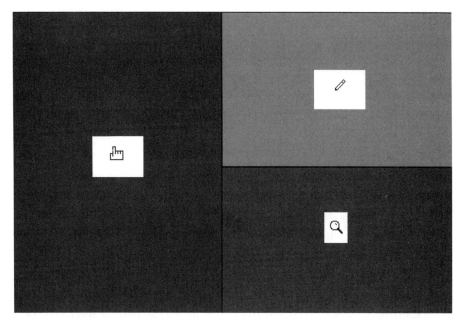

Figure 2.8 Cursor map regions.

Menus

No system for creating interactive applications would be complete without the capability to display and process menus. I have already described the event related to menus (the ON MENU event). A menu is the means by which a list of items can displayed, and a user can select one or more items from the list. An IL menu definition allows the characteristics of the menu and the menu items to be defined.

Menus are specified in a menu definition. Like a button definition, a menu definition consists of several lines beginning with a DEFINE MENU statement and ending with an END MENU statement. Each menu has a name, and an IL script can have as many names as are needed by the application.

Characteristics such as the location, colors, border, and title are also defined in a menu definition. In addition to these characteristics, a menu can have one or more items associated with it. An item will be displayed in a vertical list. An example of a menu definition is:

```
DEFINE MENU fileMenu
ITEM "OPEN"
ITEM "NEW"
ITEM "CLOSE"
ITEM "EXIT"
ROW 1
COLUMN 5
BORDER SINGLE
BORDERCOLOR 3
TITLE "File"
TITLECOLOR 2
END MENU
```

To be part of a display, a menu needs to be activated. When activated, the menu just defined will appear as shown in Figure 2.9.

One of the more interesting characteristics of IL menus is that their characteristics may be changed while a script is running. For example, if a menu would grow as a result of a user interaction, this can be accomplished by the SET MENU action. The SET MENU action allows the row, column, border type, background display, title, title color, border color, foreground color, background color, and item to be redefined while the script is running. The basic syntax of the SET MENU action is:

```
SET MENU menu-name PARAMETER-NAME PARAMETER-VALUE
```

The SET MENU action to modify items in the menu has a slightly different syntax. In this SET MENU statement it is necessary to specify the index of the menu item and the string for this item. An example of this action is:

```
SET MENU fileMenu ITEM 4 "SAVE"
```

Figure 2.9 Menu displayed from menu definition **fileMenu**.

Variables

The remaining topic of this IL sampler is variables. All variables in an IL script are global to the script. Variables are a useful means to keep track of state information in a script, function as counters, and maintain text information. In an IL script variables need to be declared but are not typed. Variables obtain types when they are assigned values. Reassigning a variable value may change the type of the variable.

Sometimes a script might become too large to be loaded into memory at one time. Scripts may be split into parts under these circumstances, and one script may load and run another script. This is called chaining, and the operation is the same as the CHAIN statement of the BASIC programming language. Between chains (when one script chains to another) an IL script writer can preserve all variable values. When the variable table is preserved, information is passed from one script to another in this way.

A variable is declared in a VARIABLE action. The VARIABLE action is like the BUTTON and MENU definition statements because the action causes a variable to be defined. The variable can then be used throughout an IL script. The syntax of the VARIABLE definition action is:

```
VARIABLE variable1 variable2 ... variablen
```

An IL script can have any number of VARIABLE actions, and a VARIABLE action can have any number of variables declared in it.

Variables are manipulated with several actions. A variable is assigned a value using a SET action. The syntax of the SET action is:

```
SET variable name
```

IL currently supports three types of values that can be used in a SET action: integers, real values, and strings. A string is a sequence of characters enclosed in quotation marks.

To facilitate the use of a variable value as a counter, two actions are provided. These are decrement (DEC) and increment (INC). As the names imply, the DEC action reduces the value of an integer valued variable by 1 and the INC action increases the value of an integer variable by 1.

Earlier in this chapter, I described an event based on testing variable values. In addition to these events, there is also a conditional action called the TEST action. The TEST action consists of a TEST followed by a sequence of actions, followed by an ENDTEST statement. The statements enclosed in the TEST...ENDTEST are executed only if the result of the test is true. An example of a TEST action is:

```
TEST alpha ge 32
    DISPLAY image1 at 0 0
    DISPLAY image2 at 12 52
ENDTEST
```

IL's Doorway

So far, all you have seen are aspects of IL that allow an IL programmer to create an interactive multimedia presentation. This discussion has mainly focused on graphics and text as the primary media, but IL also can use other kinds of media. One very important aspect of this discussion is how IL can interact with external applications—specifically those supporting the development of intelligent applications. To be possible, IL must have some way to communicate to the environment outside of IL and also receive communications from this environment. There are two aspects of this ability to transfer information between environments. The first is how IL can be mixed with another environment; the second is how IL can communicate with that environment.

When I speak about communication with another environment, I am really referring to how IL will transfer data into the other environment and vice versa. One way in which this can be accomplished is to make the environments the same. For example, the IL language interpreter is implemented in the C language. If the IL interpreter (a C program) can become part of a larger C program, then that C program could pass data to the IL script and vice versa. Of course, it is not as easy as it sounds.

There are two steps to processing an IL script. The first step involves translating a script into a form that can be run. IL statements are processed to extract the type of the statement and the associated parameters for the statement. Once this is accomplished the appropriate code in the interpreter can be called to actually execute the IL statement. The part of this process where an IL script is translated into a form that can be executed is something that happens once. A structure is built for a script that can be executed, and this structure remains in memory until the script is terminated. This means the translation part of the IL script execution process is not needed after an IL program is translated. All that is needed is the part of the IL interpreter that runs the structure in memory for the IL script. This separation between the translation process and the execution process gives us a way to embed an IL script in a C program. The element of the IL interpreter responsible for running an IL script can be separated from the translator part and made a C function that can be called from within a C program. The result of all this is that a C program can run an IL script. Of course we left out one important part—how does the IL script get translated into the necessary memory structure?

Translation of the IL script is accomplished by making the translation element of the IL interpreter able to produce a file containing the memory structure representation of an IL script. The interpreted or translated file can be loaded by the C-callable version of the IL interpreter and then executed. The ability to translate an IL script, save the translation in a file, and then execute the translated file gives us all that we need to embed an IL script into a C program. Once this is accomplished, any application that can interact with a C program can also interact with an IL script. The relationship between the IL interpreter and the embeddable version of IL is shown in Figure 2.10.

Figure 2.10 shows an IL script being processed by the IL language translator. The translator produces an executable representation of the program. This representation is processed by the Interpreted language processor, which results in the IL script being run. So far this is the way we have been thinking about IL scripts.

When an IL script is embedded into a C program as shown in Figure 2.10, the IL language translator produces a file. The file, called the translated IL script, is the script in translated form. The IL language interpreter can produce a file like this for any script. Embedded into the C program is the interpreted language processor.

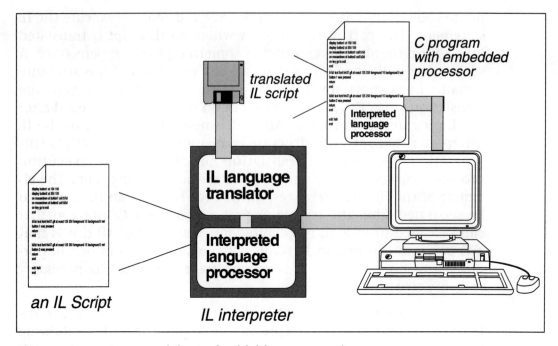

Figure 2.10 Structure of the embeddable version of IL.

This C function can load a translated IL script and execute the script from within the C program. A script is run by calling the C function that contains the interpreted language processor and passing to it two pieces of information. The first is the name of the translated script; the second is a special data structure in which variables can be passed to the IL script and later can be used to pass information back to the C program.

Passing Information to the Script

Information can be passed between the C program and the IL script via the parameter structure. The definition of a parameter structure is:

```
struct parameterStruct
{
    char *name;
    int type;
```

```
    int vtype;

    union valueUnion
    {
       int ival;
       double rval;
       char *sval;
    } value;

    struct parameterStruct *next;

};
```

This structure is composed as a linked list allowing as many variables as necessary to be passed to the interpreted language processor. The **name** field of the structure contains a string that names a variable. This string represents one of the variables declared in the IL script. The **type** field contains an integer representing the kind of parameter. The three kinds of parameters are **p_in**, **p_out**, and **p_in-out**. As the names imply, the first specifies a parameter used for input to the running script only, the second stands for a variable that is copied back to the C program, and the third represents a variable that is copied into the IL script and back to the C program.

The **vtype** field is a specification of the value type of the variable. This field can be set to **t_int, t_real,** or **t_string**. Closely associated with the variable type is the variable value. A union is used to hold the value. It consists of three fields: **ival** for integers, **rval** for real values, and **sval** for strings. The field **next** will be set to NULL, if this is the last parameter passed to the IL script, or it will be set to point to the next parameter.

Prior to calling the embedded IL interpreted language processor from within a C program, a linked list of parameter structures is created. When the interpreted language translator is called, a pointer to the linked list is passed. In the compiled IL script that will be processed by the interpreted language translator, each of the variables named in the parameter linked list structure will be declared in the script. If the parameter list names the variables **alpha**, **beta**, **gamma**, and **delta**, then there will be a variable statement in the compiled IL script. When the language processor is called, it copies all of the values in the parameter list that are defined as input or input/output values into the corresponding variables of the IL script. The values in these variables from the C program can then be used by the IL script.

On exit from the IL script (when the script halts), the last thing the interpreted language processor will do is to transfer values from variables in the IL script to the parameter structure. Only variables that are defined as output or input/output will be copied back to the C program.

A C program is the basis for incorporating intelligence into an IL-based program. Because many other programs communicate with C programs, this IL doorway allows much flexibility in choosing tools to create the intelligent portions of multimedia systems.

Authorware Professional for Windows

The IL approach is just one approach to take to implement an interactive application. Creating a visual application using a programming language like IL is a disadvantage because it is not possible to immediately view the visual result of the program. Some of the guesswork in creating the application is in the placing of the visual components. It would be much easier if it was possible to place the actual visual components (such as buttons and menus) on the display as opposed to specifying their position. In fact, such a visual development tool is not part of the IL tool set. Authorware Professional is an entirely visual environment for creating applications. All of the components that can be part of an application can be placed on a display during the program development process. Look at the example of an Authorware Professional Screen in Figure 2.11.

The example shown in Figure 2.11 consists of the usual window elements—a title bar across the top of the window and a fairly typical Windows-type menu bar—but then in the main window area are two more elements. On the left is a toolbar. This tool bar contains the programming elements of Authorware Professional. The second element of the main window is another window. This window con-

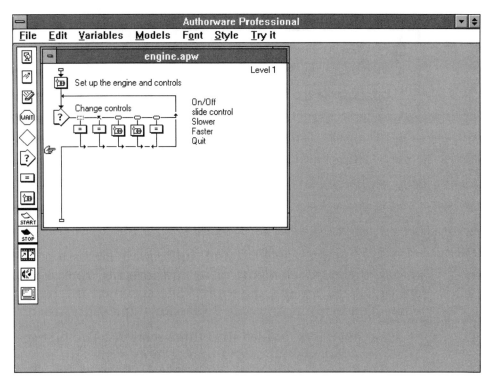

Figure 2.11 Sample Authorware "authoring" display.

tains an Authorware Professional program. As you can see in Figure 2.12, an Authorware Professional program resembles a flow chart. Programming-like symbols are connected to one another. In a short time I will describe the function of the various icons. For now, it is important to understand these are the "statements" of the Authorware Professional language.

The tool bar, shown in more detail in Figure 2.13, contains a series of icons. Each of these icons represents a visual function, or a programming specific function. The underlying paradigm of Authorware Professional is very similar to IL. Authorware Professional is an event-driven language that responds to various types of events including button presses and keyboard entries. Authorware Professional makes use of another paradigm in addition to the event-driven paradigm.

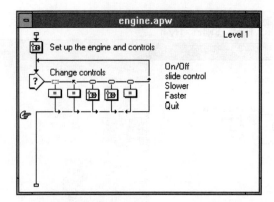

Figure 2.12 An Authorware "program."

The intended application of Authorware Professional was educational; therefore, elements of an Authorware Professional program are organized around questions. The specified interactions are all embedded in an Authorware Professional question structure.

The tool bar is divided into three sections. The first section contains the fundamental programming tools of the Authorware Profes-

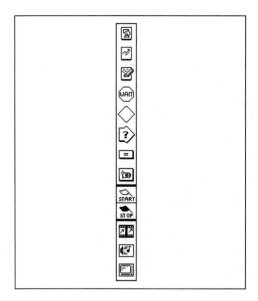

Figure 2.13 Authorware tool palette.

sional language, the second section contains tools used for debugging, and the remaining section contains tools for embedding various types of media into an Authorware Professional application.

The first icon, ▩, is a tool that allows a programmer to insert text and/or graphics into an Authorware Professional application. Complex graphics can be created with this tool.

The next tool, ✎, creates animation. This tool creates a kind of animation called a path animation. Path animations involve specifying an object and the path along which that object will move. While running this particular element, Authorware Professional will move the object along the specified path.

Graphic elements on a screen can be erased when they are no longer needed. In IL, this was accomplished by redrawing a screen or drawing over a graphic element. In Authorware Professional this is accomplished with the ✎ icon. This icon is very flexible because many kinds of erasures can be specified (e.g., wipes and slides).

Sometimes it is necessary to insert various type of delays into an application. One type of delay is the kind that causes a display to remain for several seconds, another stops the application. The ⏱ icon is used to insert delays into Authorware Professional applications.

No programming language would be complete without a way to act on a decision. The ◇ icon is used for this purpose. If you remember your flowcharting symbols, you will recognize this as the standard decision symbol.

As I mentioned earlier, another important part of the Authorware Professional paradigm is the question. A question is inserted into an Authorware Professional application with the ⌕ icon. This icon allows for the various interactions Authorware Professional supports. When you insert this icon into an application and add an element to the question, you get a small window as shown in Figure 2.14. You can see by Figure 2.14 that Authorware Professional supports a very rich set of interactions.

Associated with interactions are tests. In order to make an Authorware Professional application respond in different ways to a user, the ▭ is used to test the result of the interaction. In some

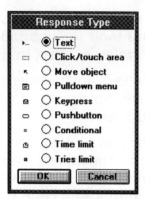

Figure 2.14 Types of interactions supported in a question.

ways, this programming element works like the decision element, and it is important to know when to use one as opposed to the other.

Authorware Professional has the ability to encapsulate code. An Authorware Professional program page could become cluttered very quickly. The 🔲 icon allows a section of Authorware Professional code to be encapsulated into the icon. Double clicking on the icon in an Authorware Professional program display causes the "code" in that icon to be displayed.

The 🏁 and 🏁 icons are used for debugging. These icons can be inserted anywhere in an Authorware Professional application. It is then possible to run the application from the start flag to the stop flag and watch for the desired behavior.

Three icons can be used to insert media into an application: 🎞, 🔊, and 📹. The first is used for inserting animations into an applications of the cel variety. This type of animation consists of a series of images that are displayed one after another. The second icon, as you might have figured out, is used to insert sound into an application, and the remaining icon is used to insert video into an application.

The Semantics of a Visual Language

One of the most interesting things about learning a visual programming language is how you figure out the meaning of the elements of the language. Invariably, in visual programming languages like Authorware Professional, the meaning of a particular symbol may not completely be contained in a description of the symbol in the documentation for it. For example, the use of the ▨ (display) icon may seem straightforward, but when you begin to understand how this icon controls what and when is displayed, and more important, *why* it is displayed, you begin to see that things are not as black and white as they appear to be. The meaning of this icon includes much more than just the ability to display certain kinds of information in an Authorware Professional program.

This aspect of a visual programming language makes it difficult to describe on a statement by statement (or in this case icon by icon) basis. It is very easy to miss aspects of the semantics of the language. Rather than take the approach of describing each icon in detail, as we described each statement for the IL language, I will show how a typical, albeit somewhat complex, application is constructed in the Authorware Professional language.

A Sample Application—A Simulation of an Automatic Teller Machine

Suppose you wanted to create a simulation of an automatic teller machine so employees of a bank can demonstrate the operation of the teller machine without needing to have one in every office. One way to accomplish this is to create a computer-based simulation. The graphics would depict a replica of the front panel of teller machine as shown in Figure 2.15.

The simulation is meant to operate exactly like a real teller machine. A card will be inserted into the machine, and through a series of interactions, one can make deposits, withdrawals, and inquiries. What would a program for this look like in Authorware Professional? Figure 2.16 shows part of the simulation program.

Figure 2.16 is the top-level view of the program. Detail is embedded into this flow diagram in the ▨ icon. Each of these icons in Figure 2.16 contains Authorware Professional program code, flow diagrams that carry out various elements of the functionality of the automatic teller machine simulation. The excerpt shown in Figure 2.16 consists of seven icons. The first icon contains the program

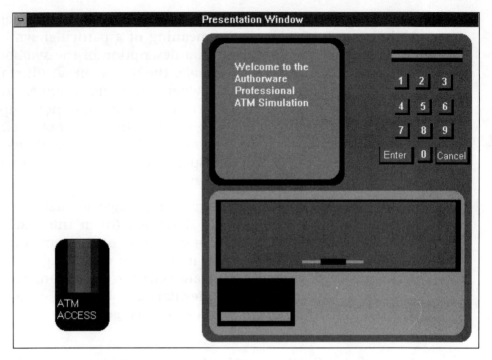

Figure 2.15 Simulated automatic teller machine display.

code for the "opening" of the simulation program. The opening consists of displaying an opening screen (depicted in Figure 2.17) and a button that allows a user of the simulation to start the automatic teller machine simulation.

The visual code associated with this opening screen is shown in Figure 2.18. The code consists of three icons. Most of the interactions associated with an Authorware Professional program are created with the ⟨?⟩ icon. This is the icon that allows the specification of the kind of interactions that occurs when the program is run. The particular interactions that occur are controlled by the icons attached to the ⟨?⟩ icon. In this case there is only one of these, and it is a "subprogram" icon (▣). In this case the icon contains no program code; it simply holds a place to allow an interaction, which in this case is a button click. Notice that in the flow diagram the ▣ icon has a small square attached to it. This is shown in Figure 2.19. It represents the kind of interaction that will occur as part of the question.

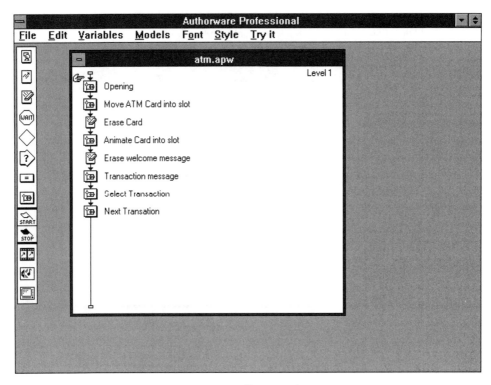

Figure 2.16 Part of the automatic teller machine program.

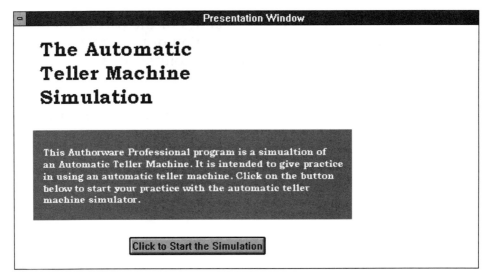

Figure 2.17 Automatic teller machine opening screen.

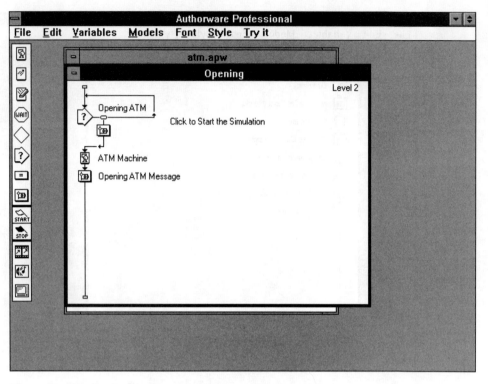

Figure 2.18 Code for the opening screen.

One of the interesting features of the part of the flow diagram that represents flow is the direction of the arrows. The direction of any arrow in the flow diagram is controlled by the nature of the interaction. As you can see in Figure 2.19, one arrow points back into the question icon and a second arrow points to the next icon in the flow below the question icon. As you might imagine, the direction

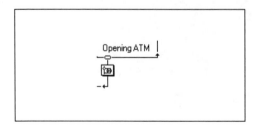

Figure 2.19 Icon for the interaction.

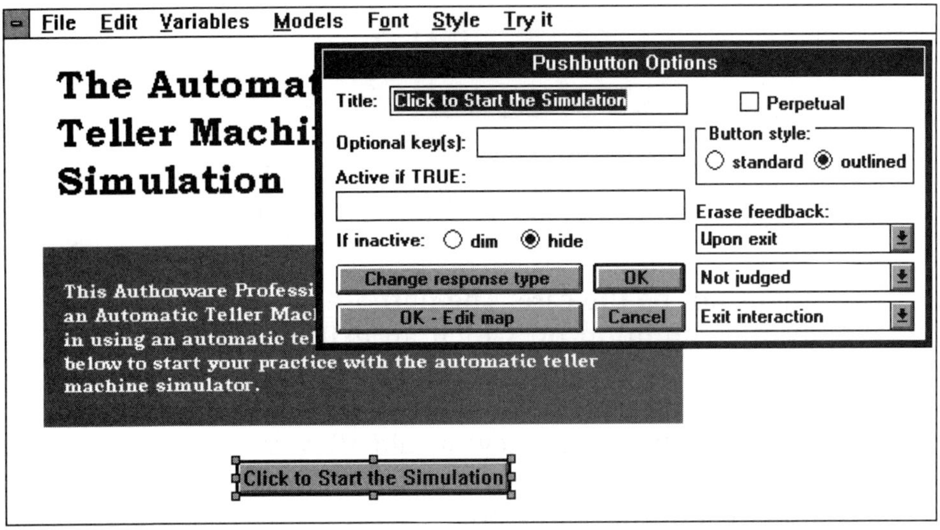

![Figure 2.20 dialog box screenshot]

Figure 2.20 Dialog box for the pushbutton interaction.

of the arrows depends on the nature of the interaction. This is controlled by a dialog box that can be called up when the small button icon is clicked on. The dialog box that is displayed is shown in Figure 2.20.

In this diagram you can see the choices for setting what happens as a result of the interaction. Each kind of interaction may have different features in this dialog box, but generally, there are several common to all dialog boxes. One common feature is whether the interaction is judged. You can see this setting in the pull-down menu on Figure 2.21, which shows **Not judged**.

The pull-down list shown in Figure 2.21 may seem a little odd. What is it we are specifying here? For the pushbutton, these choices really don't make much sense. For other interaction options, this

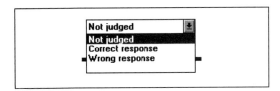

Figure 2.21 Response processing menu.

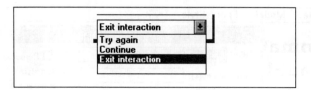

Figure 2.22 "Interaction exit" pull-down list.

might not be the case. The purpose of the pull-down list is to specify the condition on which an exit is made from the interaction. Let's suppose the interaction is a key press. Selecting the **Correct response** choice of this pull-down list would mean that only a correct response (the correct key) would allow you to exit from the interaction. Whether you exit the interaction or not is the function of another list of the dialog box, one shown in Figure 2.22.

With the list shown in Figure 2.22, you control what happens when. In the course of the interaction, the user enters the correct answer, an incorrect answer, or an answer that is not judged. You can have an interaction **Try again**, continue along in the interaction, or exit the interaction. Understanding these two pull-down lists is very important, because you can create a kind of loop in the program. Authorware Professional does not have an explicit looping construct, so it is important to know the different ways to create loops in an Authorware Professional program.

The opening screen shown in Figure 2.16 provides the user with a description of the simulation and the ability to start the simulation when desired by clicking the button on the screen. When that occurs, the simulated teller machine will be displayed. This display is shown in Figure 2.23.

Before getting into the code of the simulated teller machine, let's discuss how the graphic for the simulated teller machine was created. When you select the ▧ icon, you are presented with a tool palette. This palette contains several drawing creation tools and is shown in Figure 2.24.

Although it is small, the drawing palette provides the basic functions needed to create basic and not so basic graphics. The auto-

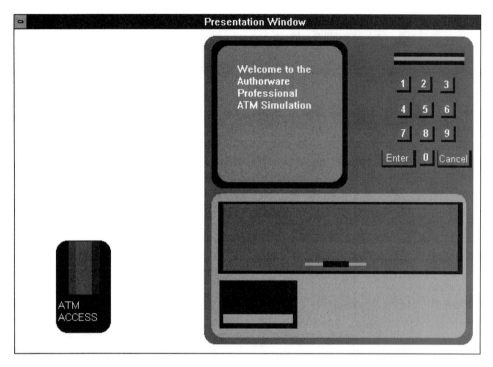

Figure 2.23 Simulated teller machine.

matic teller machine simulation (shown in Figure 2.25) was created with this tool palette. The way graphics are organized in an Authorware Professional program is particularly important. The small palette of tools allows Authorware Professional to have precise control over each graphic object that is drawn. This is much different from graphics in IL. In IL, graphics are created outside of IL and used in an IL script via the DISPLAY action. Authorware Professional treats graphics as distinct objects because they are rendered inside the program.

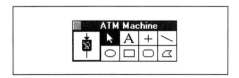

Figure 2.24 Drawing tool palette.

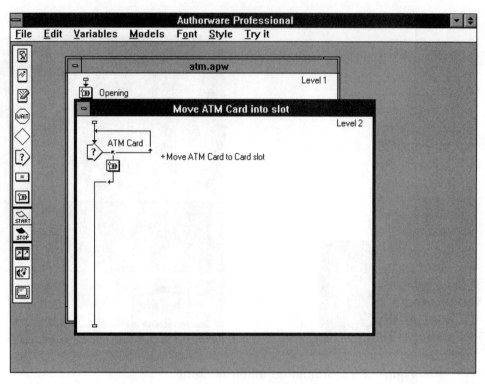

Figure 2.25 Move ATM ACCESS card to ATM slot.

The icon denotes the selection tool. With this icon you can select a component of a graphic (any object drawn with the toolkit) and manipulate it. Manipulations include setting the color of the graphic object, the size of the graphic object, and its position.

To create a textual graphic object, you use the A icon. With this icon you can insert text into a graphic in a specific font of a certain size and with certain characteristics (such as color, boldface, underlining, etc.). The text can be fixed (you enter it when you create the text object) or variable (you specify a variable name in the text field). The latter allows you to have dynamically changing text depending on the state of the program.

The , , , , and icons are all used for creating figures of various shapes and sizes. The tool is used to create lines, is used for squares and rectangles, for circles and ellipses,

◻ for rounded corner rectangles, and ⬠ for polygonal shapes. A graphic figure may be drawn filled or unfilled, transparent, solid, or textured. The color of an object may also be specified. Finally, the + icon is used to create straight lines at 0 degrees, 45 degrees, and 90 degrees.

Each and every object drawn is a *separate* object. The separateness of an object is maintained or lost depending on whether it is drawn in one container or many containers. A container is a display object represented by the ▨ icon or the interaction (⟨?⟩) icon. Why is this important to understand?

There are many times when you want to place a graphic on a display (like the ATM ACCESS card), want to manipulate it (move it to its slot), animate it into the slot, and make the last bit of the access card disappear. To accomplish this, the ATM machine and the ATM ACCESS card *must* be in different containers so that the ATM ACCESS card can be manipulated by itself.

Now, let's continue with the discussion of the ATM program in Authorware Professional. Looking at Figure 2.26, you can see the following group of icons. There is an interaction icon ⟨?⟩ attached to a single interaction labeled ⟲. This icon denotes a drag interaction. In this interaction, a graphic object is dragged to a target location. The target is programmatically specified. The ATM ACCESS card is a graphic contained in the interaction container (⟨?⟩). If the card is dragged to its target, in this case the ATM machine slot, the next part of the program will run. If the card is dragged anywhere else on the display, it will remain in that position and nothing will happen.

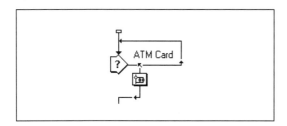

Figure 2.26 Icons to move ACCESS card.

The exit to the next part of the program is controlled by the branch line out of the subprogram box ( ),

and the return to the interaction is controlled by the loop from the interaction back to the interaction ( ).

The subprogram icon ( ) is a "dummy" box used solely as a placeholder for the drag interaction.

When the ATM ACCESS card is dragged to the location of the slot, the ATM machine will accept the card. This is accomplished by a simple frame animation consisting of five frames in the icon labeled **Animate Card into Slot**. This icon, in turn, contains a sequence of six icons labeled 100%, 80%, 60%, 40%, 20%, and 10%. The first of these icons displays 100% of the ATM ACCESS card at the ATM card slot, pauses, and then erases the display. This is repeated for a graphic containing 80% of the card, 60% of the card, and so on. The code screen for this is shown in Figure 2.27.

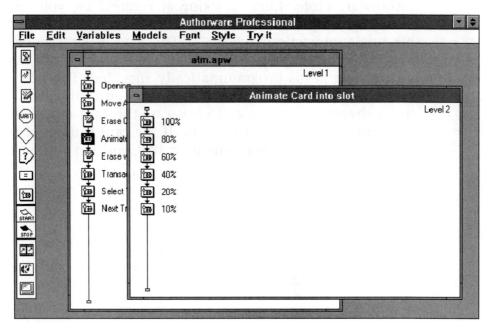

Figure 2.27 Code for animating ATM ACCESS card.

MULTIMEDIA AUTHORING TOOLS

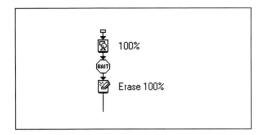

Figure 2.28 Code for displaying one frame of the ATM ACCESS card animation.

Each subprogram icon used to display a part of the card contains the icons shown in Figure 2.28. An example of one frame of the animation is shown in Figure 2.29. After the ATM ACCESS card is accepted by the ATM machine, the simulation will ask for the kind of transaction wanted by the customer. The display for this is shown in Figure 2.30.

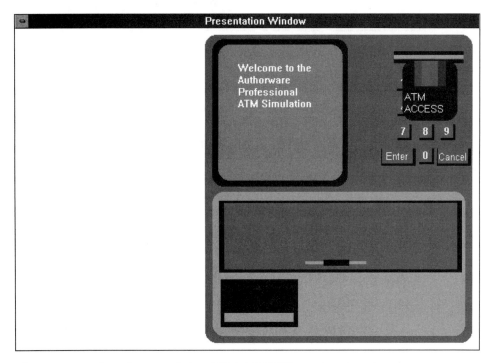

Figure 2.29 One frame of the ATM ACCESS card animation.

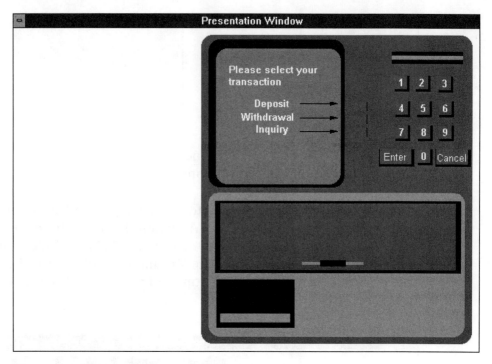

Figure 2.30 Transaction type selection screen.

It is instructive to see how variable text can be output to an Authorware program screen. There is no "output" statement per se in the traditional sense, but there are text fields that can be placed on a screen by way of the tool palette.

Remember, the [A] icon is for placing text fields. When a text field is placed, you can type the text in that field directly or paste a variable in the field. This allows you to have text that can change dynamically during an Authorware program run. To set text in a pasted variable, we use the assignment icon and insert a statement that assigns a value to the pasted variable into this icon. An example of this is shown in Figure 2.31.

The text pasted in Figure 2.31, "Please select your transaction" is exactly the same as the text that appears on the presentation screen of Figure 2.30.

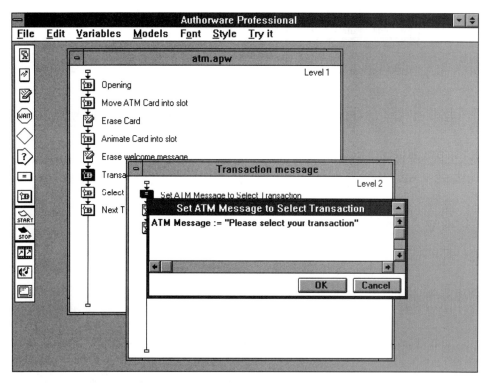

Figure 2.31 Setting a value of a pasted variable.

The code for processing the transaction consists of an interaction icon (?) and three interactions attached to the icon, one interaction for each of the three possible transactions, as is shown in Figure 2.32. Clicking on the appropriate button will activate the code in the related interaction. Let's consider what happens when processing the Deposit transaction.

The **Deposit** interaction consists of a series of activities that prepares the display for the interaction and then invokes the interaction. This is represented by the last icon of the program screen shown in Figure 2.33.

The actions for preparing the ATM machine before the Deposit interaction consist of erasing the message shown on the ATM screen for selecting a transaction and also erasing the buttons displayed on the screen for this purpose.

80 CHAPTER 2

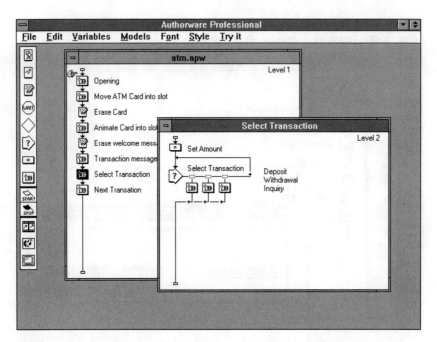

Figure 2.32 Topmost level of transaction handling code.

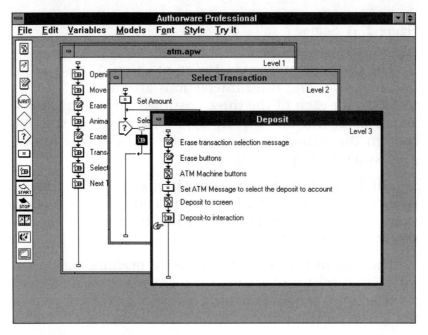

Figure 2.33 Deposit interaction code.

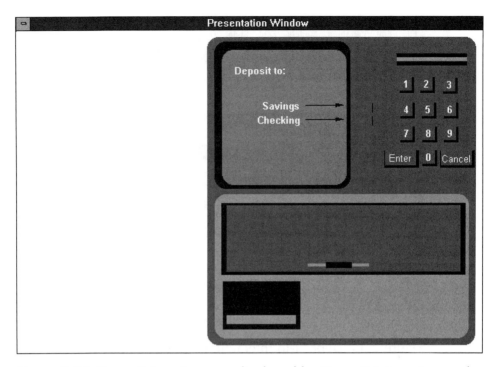

Figure 2.34 Deposit target screen displayed by Deposit interaction code.

Next, a set of buttons is displayed to allow the ATM user to select an account (savings or checking). The resulting screen is shown in Figure 2.34. The transaction selection code is similar to the deposit-to selection code. It consists of an interaction icon that has two icons attached to it—one for each account that could be selected (see Figure 2.35).

Selecting the deposit-to account leads to the next two parts of the transaction. In the first part of the transaction the ATM user will enter the amount to be deposited, and in the second part of the transaction the envelope is inserted into the ATM machine. The transaction code is shown in Figure 2.36.

Getting the deposit amount involves erasing the deposit-to message and erasing the account selection buttons. A new message is displayed that asks the ATM user to enter the amount of the deposit. The ATM amount entry screen is shown in Figure 2.37.

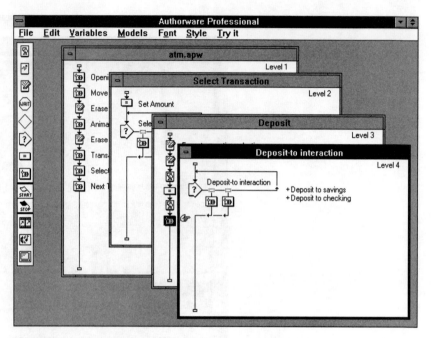

Figure 2.35 Deposit-to interaction code (when an account is selected).

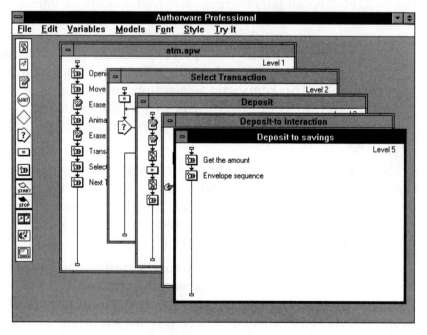

Figure 2.36 Code to handle the rest of the Deposit-to interaction.

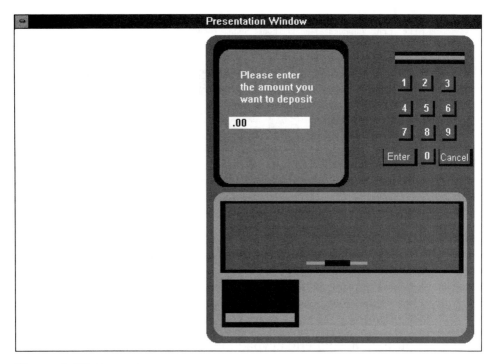

Figure 2.37 Deposit amount entry screen.

Notice in Figure 2.37 that the keypad consists of 12 buttons. Each of these buttons in the keypad is a separate entity in the amount code. A separate piece of code is written for each digit button. The interaction code is shown in Figure 2.38.

The amount is accumulated in a variable. The variable is named AMOUNT. Initially the variable AMOUNT is set to zero. Every button on the keypad that is depressed is added to the variable AMOUNT. Before the value of the digit is added, the AMOUNT will be multiplied by 10. This shifts the amount in AMOUNT to the left. Every time a new digit is pressed, the amount moves to the left as it does in a real ATM. Figure 2.39 shows the AMOUNT accumulation code for the keypad digit 1.

The screen shown in Figure 2.40 was created by pressing the 2 button, the 5 button, and the 0 button in that order. Notice that the total AMOUNT displayed is $250.00, just as we would expect. Once an amount in entered, an ATM user will press the **Enter** key. Since

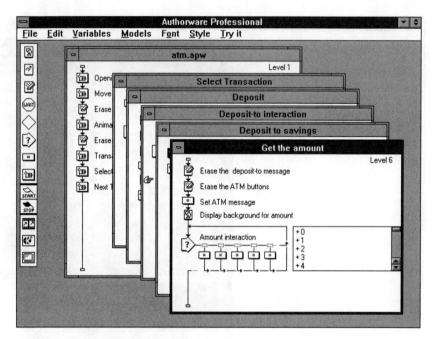

Figure 2.38 Numeric keypad interaction code.

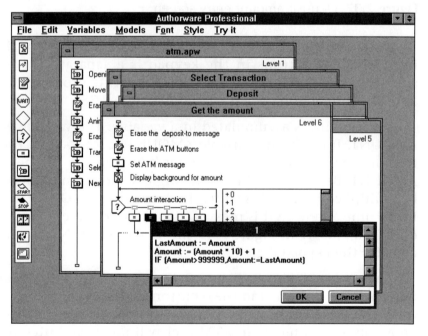

Figure 2.39 Code for adding 1 to AMOUNT.

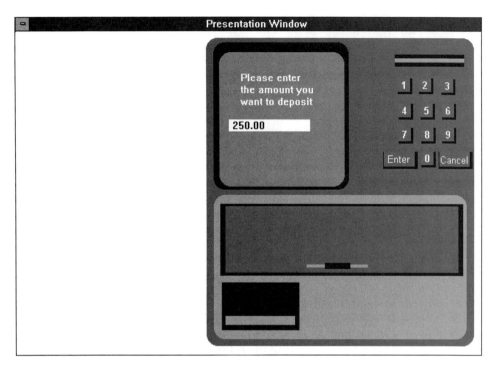

Figure 2.40 ATM screen after the buttons 2, 5, and 0 are pressed.

this is a deposit, the Enter key causes the simulation to be the "envelope" sequence. The topmost level of this sequence is shown in Figure 2.41.

The envelope sequence begins with the erasure of elements not needed for the sequence. The ATM amount and last ATM message are erased. Then a new ATM message is displayed. This message instructs the ATM user to insert the deposit envelope in the deposit slot. This screen is shown in Figure 2.42.

The first part of the envelope sequence is a simple animation for the envelope slot. In this animation, the slot appears in the slot apparatus on the bottom left of the ATM. At the end of the slot animation, a deposit envelope appears to the left of the ATM. The code for the slot animation is shown in Figure 2.43. At the end of the slot animation, the screen appears as depicted in Figure 2.44.

Because it is not possible to physically place the envelope into the ATM slot, we need to simulate this in some way. To accomplish

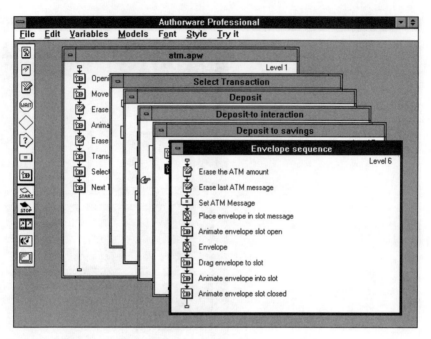

Figure 2.41 Topmost level of code for the envelope sequence.

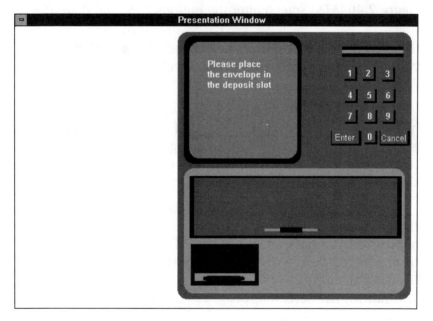

Figure 2.42 Display for the beginning of the envelope sequence.

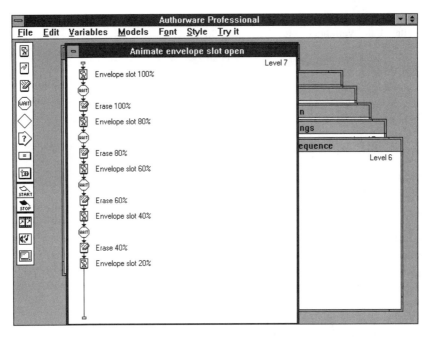

Figure 2.43 Code to animate the envelope slot open.

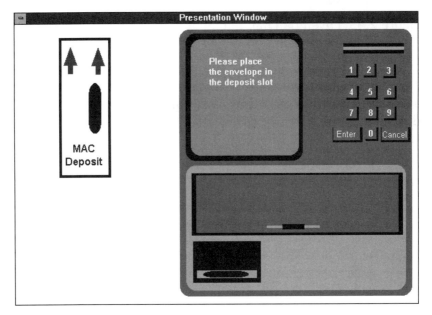

Figure 2.44 Screen at the end of the slot animation sequence.

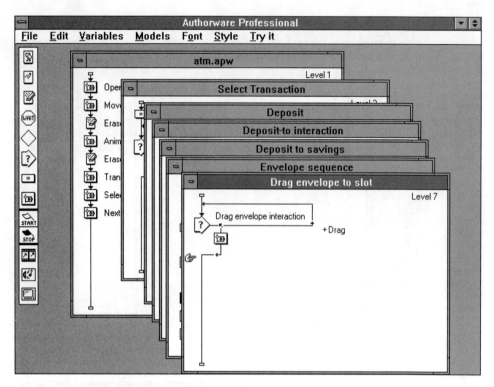

Figure 2.45 Envelope Drag interaction.

this, the ATM user will use the mouse to drag the envelope to the slot. This is accomplished with an interaction icon, where the interaction is specified as a drag to a target. As long as the envelope is dragged to the vicinity of the slot, the next part of the simulation will take place. The Envelope Drag code is depicted in Figure 2.45.

Let's take a closer look at the Drag interaction. The interaction code is displayed in Figure 2.46. When you double click on the inter-

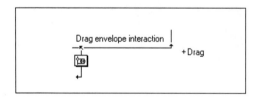

Figure 2.46 Drag interaction code.

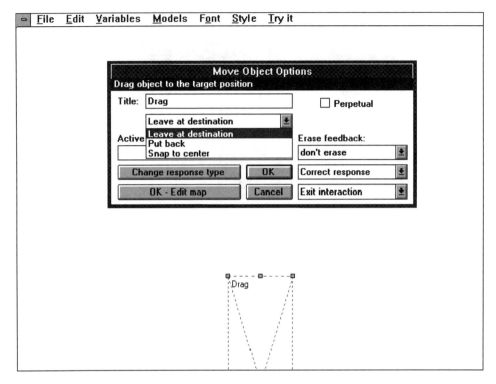

Figure 2.47 Details of the Drag interaction.

action icon, a dialog box appears. This is shown in Figure 2.47. Notice that in Figure 2.47 the details of the drag interaction are specified. One of these details is specified in the drop down menu shown in Figure 2.47. In this menu, the characteristic at the end of the drag is specified. The three choices are **Leave at destination**, **Put back**, and **Snap to center** (of the target). At the bottom of Figure 2.47 is a partially cut off rectangle with an X through the center. This is the target of the drag interaction. The envelope is dragged to this position, which coincides with the position of the slot. To show how the target area coincides with the envelope slot, Figure 2.48 shows the target overlaid on the part of the graphic containing the slot.

It makes sense that all of these elements must be specified for an interaction involving dragging an object to a specified location. In Authorware, the specification is accomplished visually as shown in Figure 2.48.

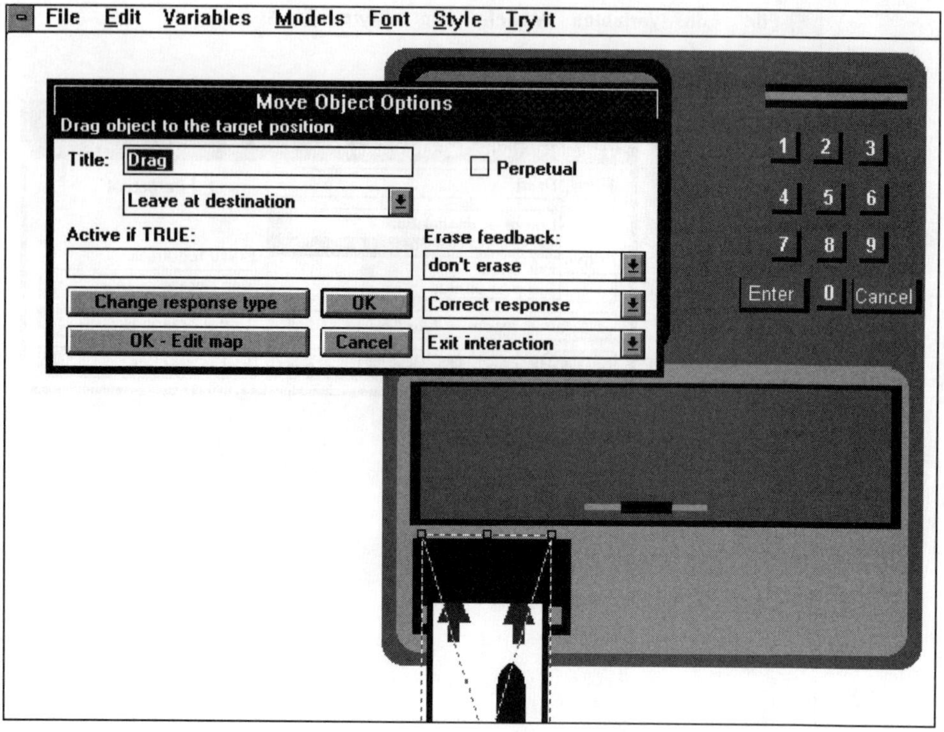

Figure 2.48 Drag target overlaid on slot graphic.

When the envelope is dragged to the target location (at the envelope slot), the envelope is "taken in" as it would be at a real teller machine. Part of this sequence is shown in Figures 2.49 and 2.50. There are actually five steps to this animation, and it is accomplished by the series of code icons shown in Figure 2.51.

Each of the code icons in Figure 2.51 consists of three steps. The first erases the previously displayed envelope (displayed by the previous code icon). The second step displays the new portion of the envelope, and the third step creates a short pause before the next code icon is executed. The code for this sequence of steps is shown in Figure 2.52.

At the end of the envelope animation sequence, another animation sequence begins. This is the envelope slot closing sequence. Like the other animation sequences discussed so far, the slot closing

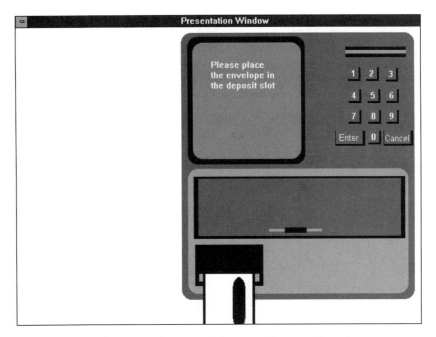

Figure 2.49 The 40% frame of the envelope animation sequence.

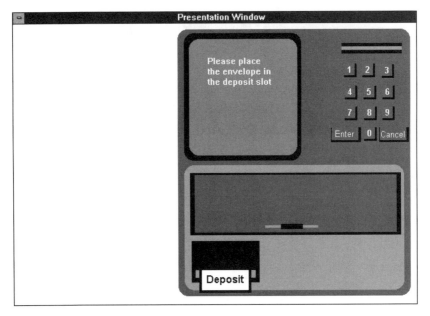

Figure 2.50 The 20% frame of the envelope animation sequence.

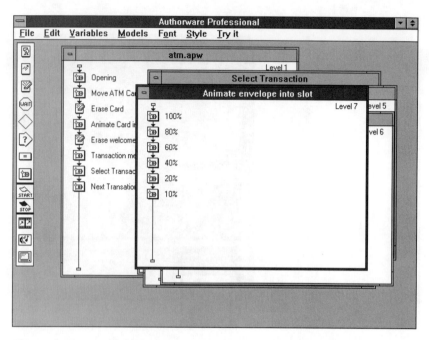

Figure 2.51 Code for the envelope animation sequence.

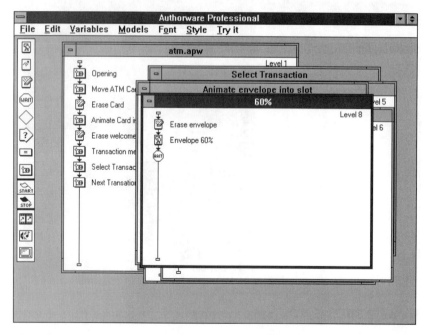

Figure 2.52 Code for one step of the envelope animation sequence.

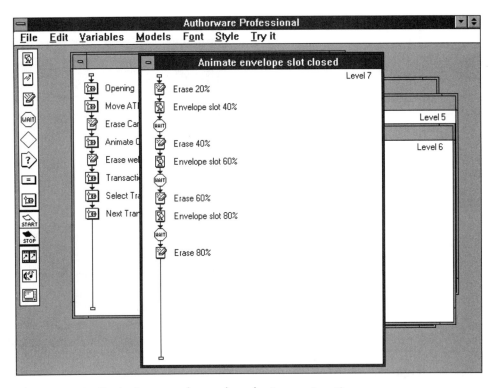

Figure 2.53 Code for envelope slot closing animation sequence.

sequence consists of a series of erasures, displays, and delays. Each subsequent display shows the slot less open. The envelope slot closing animation sequence is shown in Figure 2.53.

The transaction is completed, and now we want to ask the ATM user if he or she wants another transaction. The display for this is shown in Figure 2.54. If the ATM simulation user does not wish to continue, he or she may click on the **No** button and the ATM simulation will display the message shown in Figure 2.55 to the ATM user.

The Authorware code to handle this is like a lot of the interaction code I have shown and described earlier. In the case when the user selects **No** (no other transaction), the ATM is erased along with anything else that needs to be erased to clear the display. Then a closing message is displayed. After the closing message icon, a (WAIT) icon pauses the interaction and waits for a mouse click. The code for this is shown in Figure 2.56.

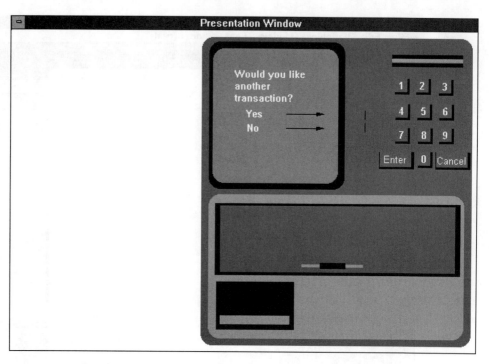

Figure 2.54 ATM another transaction display.

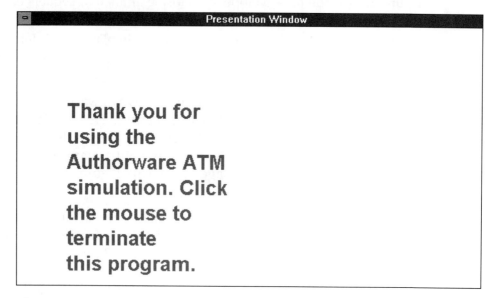

Figure 2.55 ATM simulation final screen.

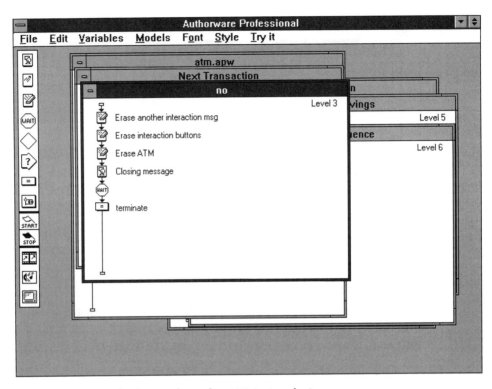

Figure 2.56 Code for ending the ATM simulation.

The WAIT icon has a series of options you can set. They include waiting for a mouse click, a key entry, displaying a button, and pausing for a predetermined amount of time. The WAIT icon dialog box options are shown in Figure 2.57.

Figure 2.57 Dialog box for the WAIT icon.

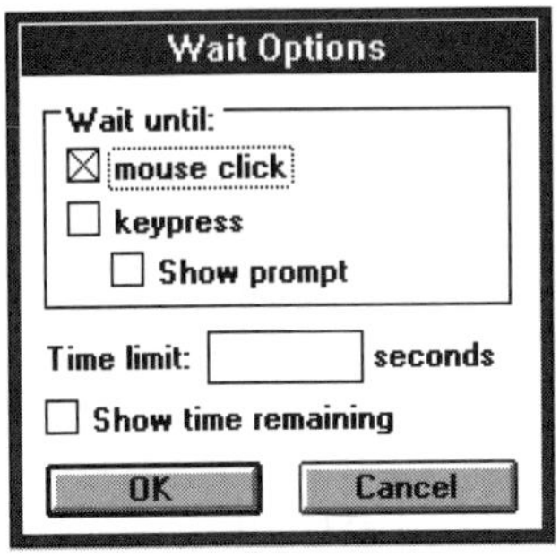

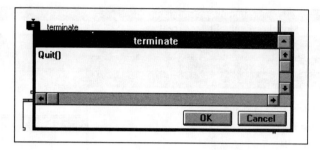

Figure 2.58 Function call to terminate Authorware.

The ▭ icon of Figure 2.56 causes the simulation to terminate. It contains a function call that ends the Authorware program and returns to Windows. The function call to accomplish this is shown in Figure 2.58.

If on the other hand a user wants to continue with the simulator, he or she would click the **Yes** button in Figure 2.54. The ATM message would be erased and the simulation would return to the beginning. This is accomplished by the code shown in Figure 2.59.

The code shown in Figure 2.59 contains two icons (in the window labeled **yes** in Figure 2.59). The second of these, the ▭ icon, causes the simulation to start again. This too is accomplished by a function call that branches to the beginning of the simulation. In Authorware, each icon is labeled as you write the code, and you can unconditionally (or conditionally) branch to any icon. The code contained in the ▭ icon that causes this branch is shown in Figure 2.60.

Recap

This section has given a thorough description of how an interactive program is crafted in Authorware and how visual-based programming differs from a language-based type of programming.

What you might have figured out from this discussion is that Authorware, like IL, is big on creating complex interactions but not so big on creating programs requiring sophisticated calculations of any sort. This book is about the marriage of multimedia and intelli-

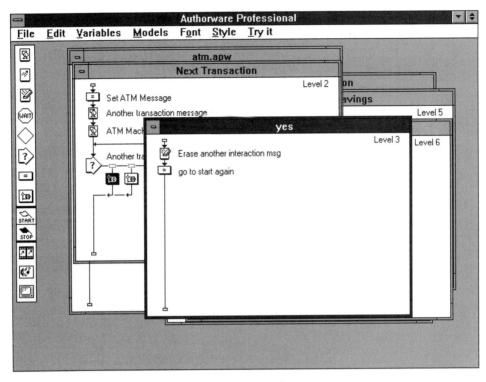

Figure 2.59 Code to restart the ATM simulation.

gent processing, so how is this accomplished with something like Authorware?

To give an Authorware simulation the ability to reason intelligently about program interactions, it is necessary to set up a link be-

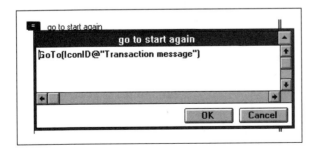

Figure 2.60 Unconditional branching code.

tween the multimedia Authorware program and the intelligent reasoning component. The link is the means by which the multimedia component passes information to the intelligence component. One kind of link for this purpose is a file. As long as Authorware can start other programs and read and write files, and as long as the intelligent application can read and write files, we have the means for multimedia and intelligent components to interact.

Another approach involves using Windows dynamic link libraries (DLLs) as the means for communications. A DLL is a library of program functions that can be called by a running program. By calling a DLL function, a Windows program is extended by the functionality of the DLL function. It is as if the DLL function is already part of the program that called the DLL. This means the intelligent components of an intelligent multimedia application can be encapsulated in a DLL called from the multimedia program, in this case an Authorware application. Authorware supports DLLs. The relationship between an Authorware program and a DLL function is shown in Figure 2.61.

In Figure 2.61, the Authorware program calls a DLL function in a DLL. Information is passed to and from the DLL function via the

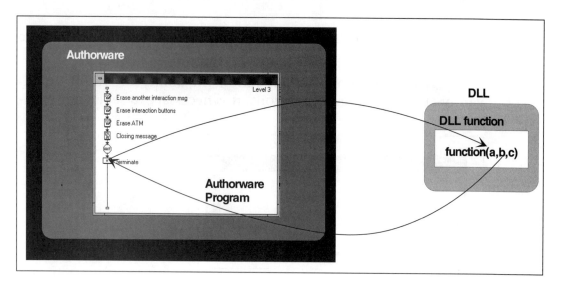

Figure 2.61 Relationship between Authorware, an Authorware program, and a DLL.

functions arguments. The DLL function performs some process that is not already supported in Authorware.

The Importance of Paradigms

One of the main motivations for creating a programming language or software development tool is to save work. High-level languages were created to reduce the number of statements a programmer would have to write. One statement in a high-level programming language will translate into many statements in an assembler language and possibly many more in a machine language. Would you rather write one high-level statement or 100 assembly language instructions? And the labor saving does not end here.

When a programming language implements a special paradigm, the language will save the programmer even more labor. This was a fundamental motivation underlying the creation of IL. Remember, IL implements an event-driven paradigm. The labor-saving aspect is that the programmer does not have to create the code for this paradigm each time it is needed. The code to recognize events can be substantial. In fact, the code that recognizes events in IL spans more than 15 full pages of C language code.

In multimedia, several different paradigms have appeared, including event or interaction driven, time line based, script based, and object oriented. It is very important to understand the underlying paradigm so that the tool can be effectively used. The next two sections describe two tools based on two different paradigms. One of these tools is based on the idea that sequences of multimedia events can be specified on a time line. The other is a tool I will use throughout this book that is based on an interaction-based paradigm.

Developing Multimedia Using Time Lines

Consider for a moment you want to create a simulation of some machine. It does not matter what the machine does. For our purposes it can do anything. For this purpose we invent such a ma-

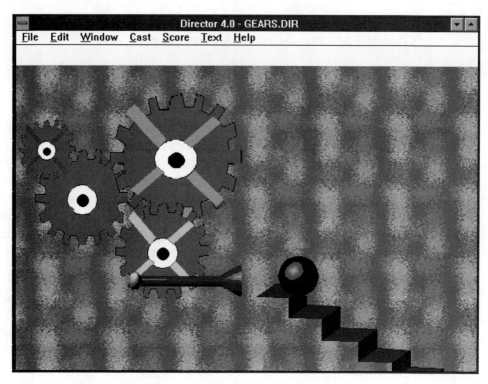

Figure 2.62 Screen depiction of our "any" machine.

chine, the purpose of which will be obvious and a depiction of which is contained in Figure 2.62. In case the purpose of this machine is not so obvious, it has been devised to push a bowling ball down a series of steps. The machine consists of several gears (four to be exact), a pusher arm, stairs, and a bowling ball. These elements are the "actors" of our any-machine simulation. Together the actors make the cast of the any-machine. The actual simulation consists of 15 frames in which the gears, pusher arm, and ball move at various times.

I have already described multimedia in terms of events that are recognized and acted upon. In the case of IL, the events were specified in a script and the time at which they occurred was specified by the sequence of statements in the script. Let's suppose another way to specify events is to do so by defining when the events occur. A convenient way to accomplish this is by using a time line. On this

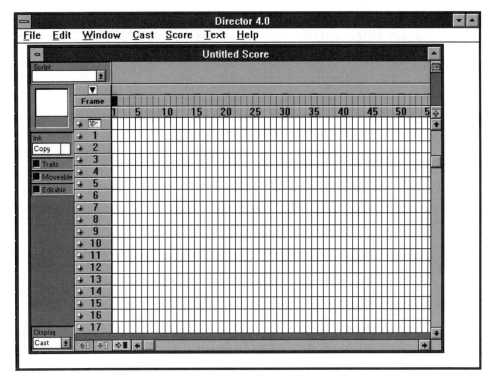

Figure 2.63 A "score" for specifying events.

time line we can place events, and an interpreter will make the events happen. Let's see what this might look like.

The grid shown in Figure 2.63 is the means in a program called Macromedia Director used to specify when events occur. The grid is called a score because in concept it resembles the score that a conductor of an orchestra would use to lead an orchestra. When first confronted, this score looks fairly daunting. The score becomes easier to use as you have practice using it.

In the score, the horizontal lines represent a sequence of events, usually related to a single actor. Of course, more than one actor may be placed in the score on a line if appropriate, but keep in mind that a line corresponds to a single sequence of events. If more than a single line is used, the events occurring at the same time will appear at the same time in the multimedia presentation. Certain lines have special labels (other than numbers). For example, there are two lines labeled with small speakers ( ). These are used to specify sound events.

The columns correspond to events. Each represents a distinct and discrete event in the score. Events are inserted into the score by selecting cast members (actors) and showing where and when they appear. In the case of our any-machine we have some 26 cast members. But this doesn't seem right. Looking at the any-machine in Figure 2.62, you only can count seven actors, right? Well, perhaps by looking at the cast, you can better understand why there are 26 cast members for the any-machine.

If you look closely at the cast window in Figure 2.64, you will notice that all of the cast members that appear in the simulation are present and then some. You will also notice each and every orientation of the cast members appears discretely as a member of the cast. Why is this so?

To show a gear turning, we need to show the gear in its various orientations as it rotates. In creating this simulation I chose to show four orientations of each gear. That is why for each of the four gears there are actually four cast members. To show a gear turning we show the first orientation of a gear, the second, and so on. In the

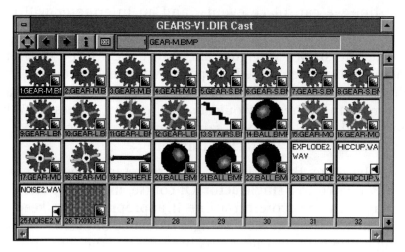

Figure 2.64 Cast members for the any-machine simulation.

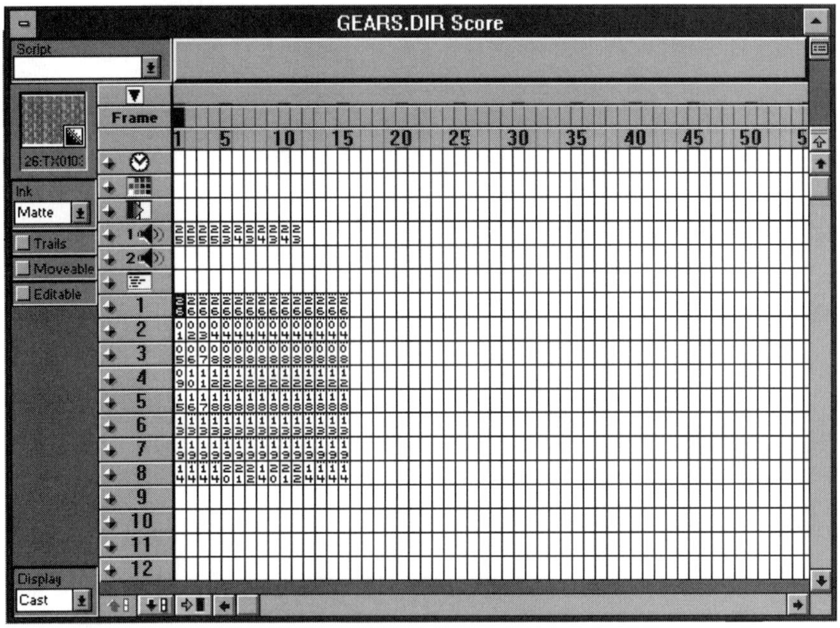

MULTIMEDIA AUTHORING TOOLS 103

Figure 2.65 Any-machine score.

score, each display of a cast member represents a discrete event. Let's see the score for the any-machine simulation.

In Figure 2.65 part of the score is now filled. The score consists of eight sequences of events of 15 frames in duration and a sound track consisting of 11 frames in duration. Looking a little closer at the score cells we can see they are filled in with numbers. Figure 2.66 shows the second line of the score more closely. In line 2 the following sequence of numbers appears:

01 02 03 04 04 04 04 04 04 04 04 04 04 04 04

Each of these numbers corresponds to a cast member: 01 refers to the first cast member, 02 to the second, 03 to the third, and so

Figure 2.66 Closeup of score line 2.

on. This line can be translated into the following sequence of instructions:

```
display actor 01
erase   actor 01
display actor 02
erase   actor 02
display actor 03
erase   actor 03
display actor 04
display actor 04
display actor 04
display actor 04
display actor 04
display actor 04
display actor 04
display actor 04
display actor 04
display actor 04
display actor 04
display actor 04
```

Notice that the activities in this list include displaying an actor and erasing it. The first three actors are displayed and erased. The fourth actor is simply displayed for the duration of the simulation. Why is this?

On a particular line of the score only one actor can be present. By placing different actors on the same line of the score we are telling Director to show a sequence of actors. To display a new actor, the one previously displayed needs to be erased. When the simulation gets to the event that displays actor 4, something different happens. Since this actor does not change for the duration of the simulation, there is no need to erase it. Director is smart enough to realize this and does not need to erase the display before each actor 4 display.

In Figure 2.65, the score contains nine filled-in score lines. Eight of these lines contain bitmap actors and one contains sounds. This means that during a single instant in the simulation nine distinct events will be going on at once, like nine musicians playing at the same time. You will see and hear nine different events each instant of the simulation. In total there are 15 instants in the simulation. You could figure out what happens in the score by looking at a line of the score and looking at the cast to see what is displayed or played (in the case of sounds). To show how the any-machine score represents different aspects of the simulation, I have annotated the score in Figure 2.67.

As you can see, the annotated score can be divided along several dimensions. The score is naturally divided into lines and columns

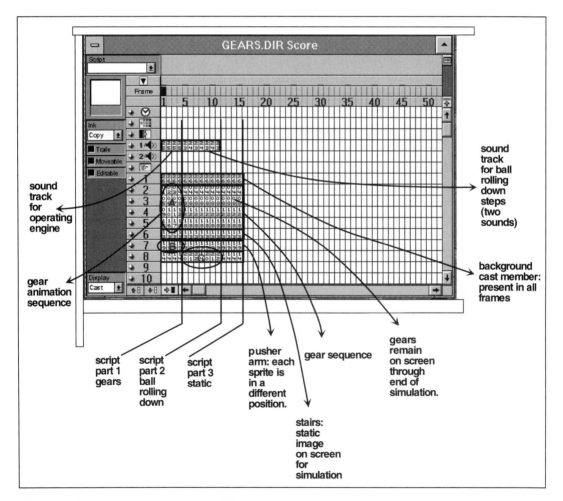

Figure 2.67 Annotated any-machine score.

that I have already described. By drawing lines on the score as I have, the score sections take on a meaning with respect to the simulation.

Vertically, the script consists of three parts. The first part of the score causes the gears to turn and the pusher rod to move to push the bowling ball. The second vertical section of the score is the part of the simulation where the bowling ball rolls down the steps. Finally, the third vertical section of the score is a static part where all components of the simulation remain on the screen when the bowling ball has reached the bottom of the stairs.

The sequences representing movement on the screen are labeled A, B, and C. Sequence A represents the four gears turning, sequence B is where the pusher arm moves, and sequence C is the bowling ball rolling down the steps. All other frames are static ones: They remain on the screen and do not change unless they participate in a moving sequence. This is an important part of the score-based paradigm. For a cast member to remain on the screen throughout a simulation, it must be present in the cells of the simulation on its line of the score. If the cast member is not present on the score it will disappear from the display of the simulation.

Interactive Score-Based Multimedia

You might ask how interactivity can be incorporated into the score. The score has a way to incorporate interactivity, but like Authorware, it is based on a language built into Director. The language is called Lingo.

To demonstrate an interactive version of any-machine, I want to add a cast member that functions as a switch. Actually I will add two cast members—one is a depiction of a switch in the ON position and the other is a switch in the OFF position. Initially, of course, the switch will be in the OFF position. The new version of any-machine is shown in Figure 2.68.

While the switch is on the OFF position, we don't want anything to happen. The machine is off. Clicking the mouse on the OFF switch causes a click to sound, the OFF switch to change to the

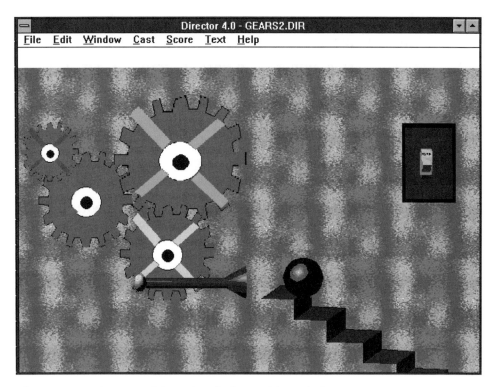

Figure 2.68 Any-machine simulation with switch.

ON switch, and the any-machine to start. So long as the switch is in the ON position, the any-machine runs—the simulation repeats itself until the ON switch is clicked again. Clicking the ON switch again causes a click to sound again, the OFF switch to be displayed, and the simulation to stop and return to the initial (OFF) state.

One of the interesting things about Director is where you can add scripts. Basically scripts can be added to anything in a score. But just what is anything? Scripts can be attached to frames, cast members, and sprites.

A frame is a cell in the score. Scripts are activated by way of events. An event associated with a frame is leaving or exiting the frame and going to the next frame. A script for a frame begins

```
ON exitframe ...
```

Following this statement are a series of actions supported in the Lingo language.

For cast members and sprites, scripts begin with a different event. A sprite is a copy of a cast member. A sprite occupies a cell of the score. A sprite can occupy any position of the stage and can be resized without affecting the cast member. The sprite is a copy of a cast member and has its own script associated with it. The event for a sprite is

```
ON mouseup
```

Cast members can also have scripts associated with them and, as for their sprite copies, the event associated with them is

```
ON mouseup
```

Having at least three different locations to place a script means we have to decide where to place the script. Do you place the script in the frame, cast, or sprite? Scripts that always run for a particular cast member should be placed in the cast member. If the script is placed in the sprite, then it will have to be copied to each and every sprite.

The functions of the switch in the revised any-machine are created by dividing the script into two parts. One part of the script corresponds to the OFF state of the switch and the other corresponds to the ON state of the switch. Conceptually the new score is organized as shown in Figure 2.69.

What happens in the score is as follows. In the OFF-state score a frame script is added with the following code.

```
ON exitframe
    go to frame 1
END
```

As this code specifies, it is an unconditional branch to frame 1, the frame that was just completed. This causes all of the cast member sprites to remain on the display.

The switch OFF cast member also has a script associated with it. The script is as follows:

```
ON mouseup
```

```
    go to frame 18
END
```

Clicking this cast member (a sprite in frame 1) causes a branch to frame 18, the start of the simulations core. The simulation runs through its last frame, and this frame has a script associated with it.

```
ON exitframe
    go to frame 20
END
```

Frame 20 is the beginning of the any-machine simulation. This unconditional branch causes the simulation to repeat itself. The simulation replaces the OFF-switch sprite by the ON-switch sprite. Along with the change in sprite, there is also a click accompanying the switch.

The ON switch has the following script associated with it.

```
ON mouseup
    go to frame 1
END
```

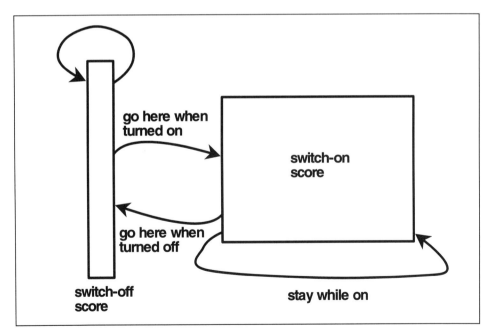

Figure 2.69 Conceptual organization of the revised any-machine script.

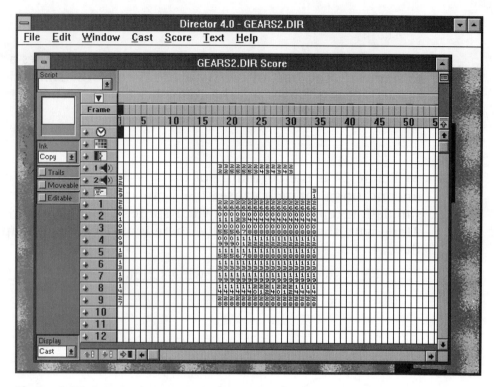

Figure 2.70 Interactive any-machine simulation score.

This completes the cycle. When the ON switch is clicked, the OFF-state score is shown, the switch changes to OFF, and the any-machine resets to its initial state. The complete score for the interactive any-machine simulation is shown in Figure 2.70.

Visual Basic as a Multimedia Authoring Tool

It would be impossible for me to cover each and every existing multimedia authoring presently on the market; therefore, in this chapter, I have selected a handful of those I feel are exemplary of the kinds of tools you might find and use for authoring multimedia applications. Closely tied to the number of available tools is the evangelism that sometimes comes along with the particular tool. I would be remiss if I left out Visual Basic because it represents a significant and important way to author multimedia applications in the Windows environment.

Just as there are many excellent books about multimedia tools, there are many books about Visual Basic. Consider the following a most brief introduction highlighting some of the basic features of Visual Basic and also those features making it a good multimedia authoring tool.

Introduction to Visual Basic

Visual Basic answers the question, "Is there a life after BASIC?" By creating Visual Basic, Microsoft has given new life to the original rationale for creating BASIC—namely, to simplify the process of developing applications in the Windows environment.

The paradigm underlying Visual Basic consists of three major components: events, forms, and reusable components. In Visual Basic, the stage on which interactions take place is the *form*. A form looks a lot like a window in Windows, as you can see in Figure 2.71.

The window labeled **Form1** in Figure 2.71 is a typical form in Visual Basic. This figure also depicts the Visual Basic design environment. On the left hand side of the screen is a set of tools, similar to Authorware. On the right hand side of the screen is another window containing properties for, in this case, the form.

A Visual Basic application can have any number of forms.* The **File** menu of the Visual Basic environment contains a selection to create new forms as they are required in the application.

The ATM Simulation in Visual Basic

In many ways, Visual Basic is somewhat like IL because you have to write code. With Authorware, there was a minimum of code to write. Visual Basic lies somewhere between Authorware and IL, be-

---

*There is a limit to the number of forms in an application, and you can learn about the exact limit in the Visual Basic documentation.

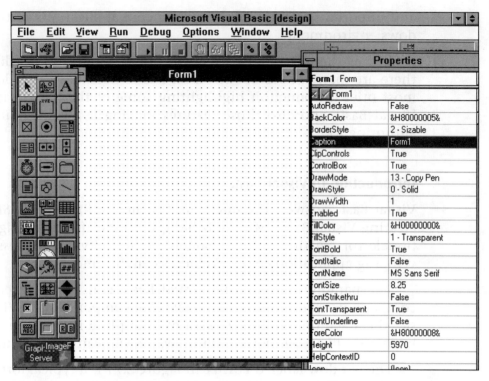

Figure 2.71 Sample Visual Basic form.

ing somewhat closer to IL in the amount of programming necessary to create an application. For example, in Authorware we did not have to code anything for dragging a picture across the screen. In Visual Basic all of the code to accomplish this must be implemented. This of course makes the task of implementing a draggable object more complex than it is in Authorware. So why use Visual Basic?

There are a couple of reasons. First, Visual Basic is cheaper than Authorware. Authorware can cost as much as $2000. Second, many products exist to extend Visual Basic. These are called components and can be plugged into Visual Basic. Third, and perhaps most important, Visual Basic is a *true* programming language and has things like data structures, which are important when incorporating intelligence into an application. By using the programming language features in Visual Basic, intelligence can be built directly into an ap-

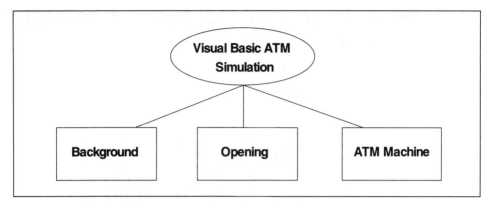

Figure 2.72 ATM application organization.

plication without using external components. This is much more difficult to accomplish in Authorware, as the language has only a limited provision for data structures and complex operations on these data structures.

Now let's have a look at what it is like to create the ATM simulation in Visual Basic. A Visual Basic application is divided into forms. Each form will have certain functionality associated with it. The Visual Basic ATM simulation will use the three forms shown in Figure 2.72.

The background form is simply that—a full screen form; in this case its color is white, which will lie behind any other forms that will be displayed. This form is displayed first when the ATM simulation starts up. The background keeps any objects on the screen under the background from being displayed, as sometimes happens in Visual Basic applications.

The opening form, shown in Figure 2.73, consists of the same display that first appears in the Authorware ATM simulation, complete with a button to start the simulation.

To create this form, I copied the Authorware opening screen into the Visual Basic form. This copied the picture of the Authorware button, which, when copied as a picture, has no functionality associated with it. A button needs to be placed on the screen, and the appropriate code also needs to be written for the button.

Figure 2.73 Visual Basic ATM simulation opening screen.

BackColor	&H80000005&
Cancel	False
Caption	Click to Start the
Default	False
DragIcon	(none)
DragMode	0 - Manual
Enabled	True
FontBold	True
FontItalic	False
FontName	Arial
FontSize	9.75
FontStrikethru	False
FontUnderline	False
Height	375
HelpContextID	0
Index	
Left	2400
MousePointer	0 - Default
Name	b_start
TabIndex	1
TabStop	True
Tag	
Top	4185
Visible	True
Width	2835

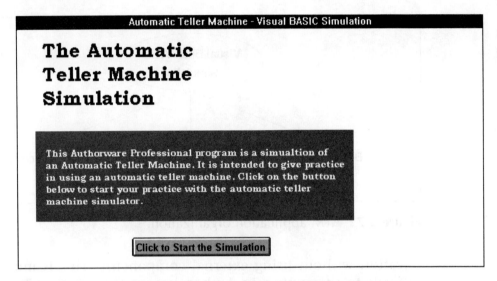

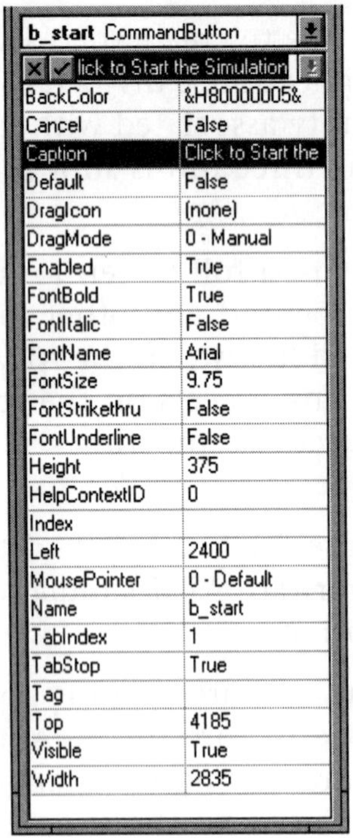

Figure 2.74 Button property list.

A button is added to an application by selecting the button tool and placing and sizing the new button on the form. The button, called a control, has properties and code associated with it. Each type of control has a set of properties associated with it. Different controls may share the same properties, such as width and height, but specific properties may apply to a single control. Figure 2.74 depicts the property list for a button.

Controls can have code associated with them. The code is organized around events, and each event associated with a control can have code associated with it. Like properties, events are associated with a particular control. Some events are common to many controls. Others are specific to only one control.

For a button, events such as CLICK, DOUBLE CLICK, MOUSEDOWN, and MOUSEUP are expected for this type of control. If you look at Figure 2.75, you will see in fact these events are part of the

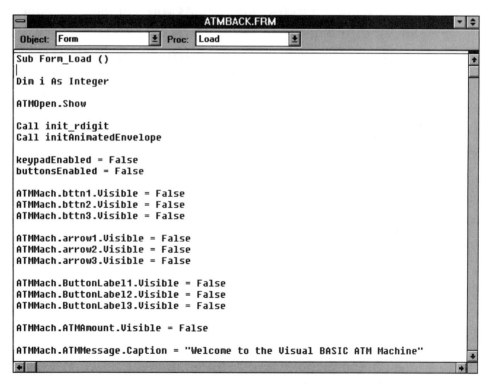

Figure 2.75 Partial listing of LOAD event code for the Background form.

available events for a button. An important event for forms is the LOAD event. When a form is first loaded, this event is triggered. If there is code in this event, then that code will be executed. This is a very useful event for doing things like initializations and any start up processing for a form that will be done initially. Figure 2.75 shows the LOAD event code for the ATM simulation.

Clicking on the **Start** button causes some initializations to occur (more about this later) and also causes the startup form to be hidden and the form containing the ATM to be displayed. Just as in the Authorware version, the ATM machine consists of the ATM card and ATM machine. Although seemingly trivial, just this bit of code represents an important difference between Authorware and Visual Basic. In Authorware, there is an implicit understanding about the sequence of events. In the Authorware icon sequence, one icon following another icon specifies the sequence of display events in the Authorware program. In a Visual Basic program, the sequence of actions is implicit in the program. As you will see, the sequence is embedded in the program code.

Figure 2.76 depicts an annotated version of the ATM simulation form. This is the main form in the Visual Basic ATM simulation in the sense that most of the action of the simulation occurs in this form.

You will notice in Figure 2.76 that there are "extra" elements, such as all of the ATM cards comprising the card animation sequence. This display is called the design time display because it shows all of the design elements used in the Visual Basic program.

On the left hand side of Figure 2.76 are four similar icons, each with a depiction of a small stopwatch. These controls, called timers, are used to control such things as animations and polling. Below the timers is the main image of the ATM card. This card is the basis for the form that is dragged to the card slot.

The display of the ATM consists of several controls, most of which cannot be seen in Figure 2.76. The top circle is where the ATM message will appear. This is the place where messages such as, "Select transaction" and "Please enter the deposit amount" will be displayed. Below the place for the ATM message are the labels for

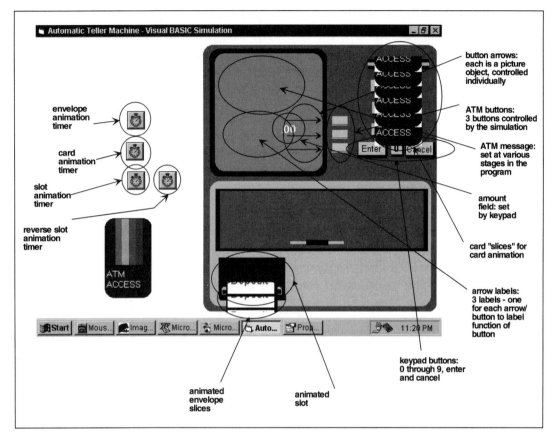

Figure 2.76 Annotated Visual Basic ATM simulation.

the ATM buttons (to the right of the display). Next to the labels are the arrows that are to make the connection between button and label clear. The .00 in the figure is the ATM amount. At the point in the transaction when an amount is entered, the amount will be displayed in this control.

The keypad is covered by the sections of the ATM card used in the card animation. A couple of the keys can still be seen (**Enter**, **Cancel**, **0**). Nine more digit keys are covered by the ATM cards. Each of the keys consists of two icons. One of these icons represents the button on the screen; the other represents the button when a key is pressed.

To the left of the keypad keys are three additional buttons. These are used to select options during the simulation process. To select the transaction, deposit, withdrawal, or inquiry, you would use these buttons. Like the keypad, these buttons consist of two icons, the button icon and the icon that appears when the button is pressed.

The animated envelope slices appear at the bottom of the simulated ATM. These are used in the envelope animation when the envelope is inserted into the insertion slot. Finally, below the envelope slices are the different frames used in the animation of the insertion slot opening and closing.

In Figure 2.77, you can see that the amount of detail that must be specified in the Visual Basic program is significantly more than is needed in the Authorware program. In fact, each and every element used in the simulation needs to be defined. Figure 2.77 depicts the various elements functioning together to create the ATM simulation.

Figure 2.77 shows all of the elements of the Visual Basic simulation. Each element is numbered and corresponds to the sequence of events in the running simulation. A description of the implementation follows the numbered annotations.

Step 1. The ATM card is dragged to the ATM card slot. The ATM card resides in its own form. When the simulation begins, and after the **Start** button is pressed on the initial screen, the ATM is displayed and the form containing the card is also displayed. At this point, the card is available for dragging.

Step 1a. Notice that the form containing the card also contains a timer control. This is a polling timer. A polling timer is used to test a condition periodically. In this case, the condition being tested is the arrival of the card form at the ATM slot. The Visual Basic code contained in the ATM card polling timer is shown in Figure 2.78.

You can see in the property list for the polling timer (Figure 2.79) that every 250 milliseconds (1/4 second) the timer "goes off." When the timer goes off, the code associated with the timer is executed. Setting timer to poll every 1/4 second will not overtax the processor—a shorter time means the processor must check the posi-

MULTIMEDIA AUTHORING TOOLS 119

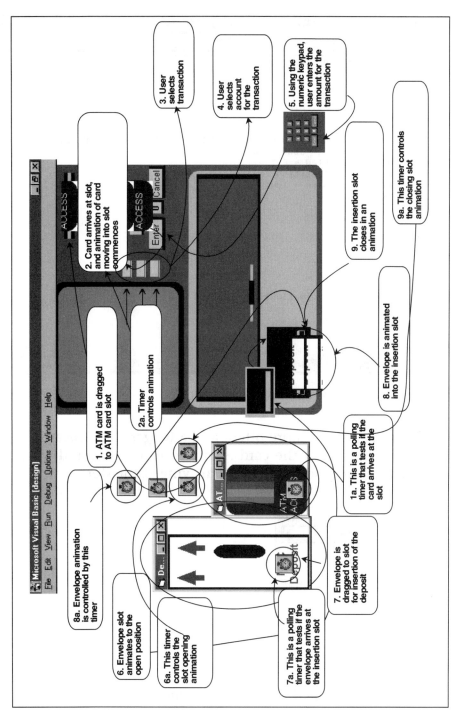

Figure 2.77 Visual Basic ATM simulation sequence.

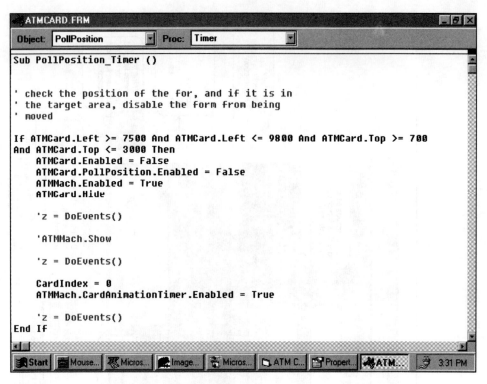

Figure 2.78 Card polling timer code.

tion of the card more often, and a longer timer means there might be a delay when the card is moved to the slot and when the program can respond to the card arriving at the slot.

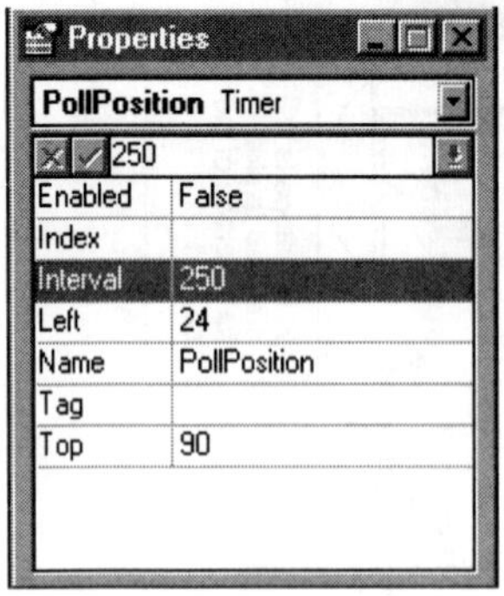

Figure 2.79 Property list for polling timer.

The code checks to see if the card is in a rectangle bounded by certain coordinates. These coordinates represent a rectangle around the area of the slot. The rectangle is large enough that if the card is placed more or less near the slot, it will be recognized as being at the slot.

If the card is placed near the slot, then it is removed from the display by "hiding" the form. After the card is erased, the animation sequence of moving the card into the slot is started by enabling the card animation sequence time. It is a good idea when using timers to remember to only have enabled one at one time. The polling timer is disabled in this code also.

Step 2. The card arrives at the slot and the animation of the card moving into the slot commences. There are several ways in which an animation of an object moving can be accomplished in Visual Basic. I use a primitive version of cel animation, but there are certainly more efficient ways to accomplish the same activity. To move the card into the slot, I create a series of pictures. Each picture shows a different slice of the ATM card as if the card were actually moving into the slot. Each picture is loaded into a Visual Basic picture control and made invisible until they are needed. A timer is used to control the animation, which consists of showing each of the card images, one after another, with a small delay in between. This is another application for a timer. The code contained in the card animation time is shown in Figure 2.80.

The code contained in the card animation timer does two things. First, it controls the animation, and second, it sets up the ATM for what follows in the simulation. In this case, after the card is inserted, the next part of the process is to select a transaction.*

When the event is triggered, the current card displayed is made invisible, and the variable **CardIndex** is incremented. This variable selects a card to display. The card control is a special one—it is a control array. Every control in a control array has the same set of properties, and the controls in the array can be referenced by an in-

---

*Yes, I know that the next step of the process would be to enter a PIN, but our ATM does not have this step.

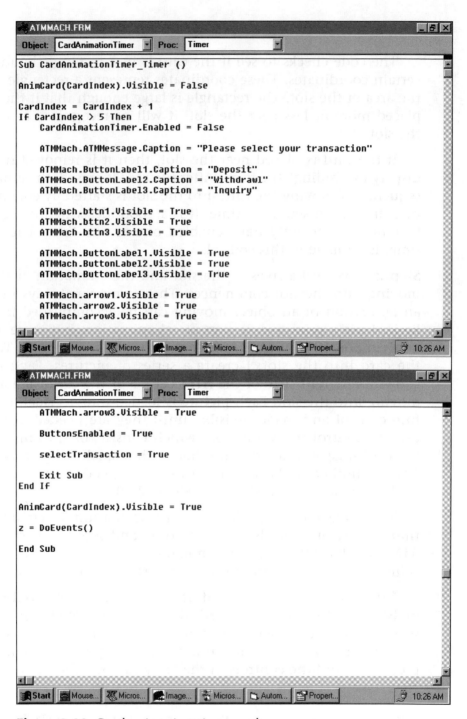

Figure 2.80 Card animation timer code.

dex. This type of control is especially good for doing the kind of animation we need to do.

After the variable **CardIndex** is incremented, its value is checked to see if the last card in the animation sequence was displayed. There are six cards in all and the index begins at zero, so if the variable is greater than five, all of the cards have been displayed. At this point the card animation timer is disabled. We don't want it going off after the animation sequence is completed. After this, the setup for the transaction selection phase of the simulation is performed.

Each control needed for the transaction selection phase is set as required. For example, the message to be displayed is set to "Please select your transaction," and the transaction buttons are labeled, **Deposit**, **Withdrawal**, and **Inquiry**. Because the controls are initially invisible, those needed must be made visible. Finally, the buttons must be enabled. Since these buttons are really simulated buttons, I set a flag that will be checked to see if the code should be executed for the button.

Step 3. The user selects the transaction. The user can select any of the three transactions. The only operational one in this simulation is the **Deposit** transaction. The display is in the state shown in Figure 2.81 when the user can select a transaction.

To create buttons like those in the Authorware simulation, I chose to implement them independently of the mechanism provided in Visual Basic. This is somewhat more complex, as you will see, but does allow some greater flexibility in how the buttons appear on the display.

To make a button flash or change when it is clicked, it is necessary to have two bitmaps. One of these is used when the button is in the up or OFF position; the other is used when the button is in the down or ON position. In this simulation, the buttons are rectangles, one colored blue (for the OFF position) and the other colored yellow. They are placed one on top of another and are made visible or invisible depending on whether the button is clicked. The code controlling this is shown in Figures 2.82, 2.83, and 2.84.

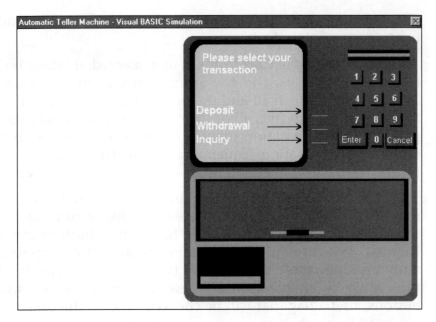

Figure 2.81 Simulated ATM ready for a transaction selection.

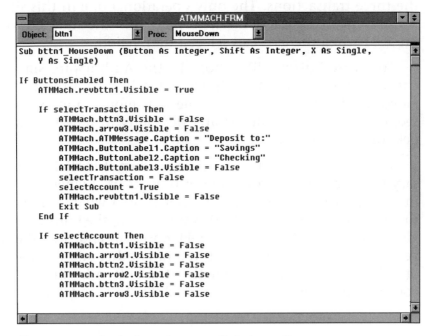

Figure 2.82 Code for a button click (part 1).

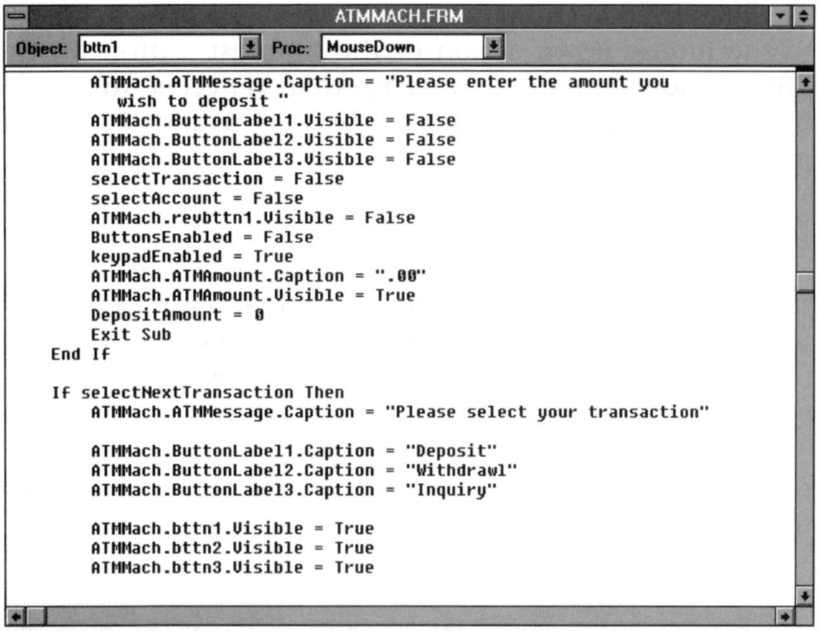

MULTIMEDIA AUTHORING TOOLS   125

```
            ATMMach.ATMMessage.Caption = "Please enter the amount you
                wish to deposit "
            ATMMach.ButtonLabel1.Visible = False
            ATMMach.ButtonLabel2.Visible = False
            ATMMach.ButtonLabel3.Visible = False
            selectTransaction = False
            selectAccount = False
            ATMMach.revbttn1.Visible = False
            ButtonsEnabled = False
            keypadEnabled = True
            ATMMach.ATMAmount.Caption = ".00"
            ATMMach.ATMAmount.Visible = True
            DepositAmount = 0
            Exit Sub
        End If

        If selectNextTransaction Then
            ATMMach.ATMMessage.Caption = "Please select your transaction"

            ATMMach.ButtonLabel1.Caption = "Deposit"
            ATMMach.ButtonLabel2.Caption = "Withdrawl"
            ATMMach.ButtonLabel3.Caption = "Inquiry"

            ATMMach.bttn1.Visible = True
            ATMMach.bttn2.Visible = True
            ATMMach.bttn3.Visible = True
```

Figure 2.83 Code for a button click (part 2).

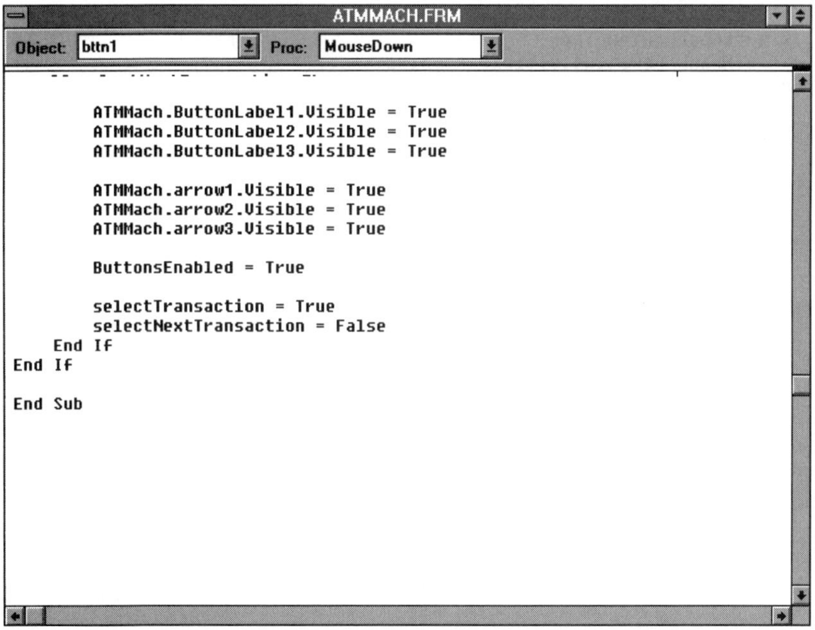

```
            ATMMach.ButtonLabel1.Visible = True
            ATMMach.ButtonLabel2.Visible = True
            ATMMach.ButtonLabel3.Visible = True

            ATMMach.arrow1.Visible = True
            ATMMach.arrow2.Visible = True
            ATMMach.arrow3.Visible = True

            ButtonsEnabled = True

            selectTransaction = True
            selectNextTransaction = False
        End If
    End If

End Sub
```

Figure 2.84 Code for a button click (part 3).

Figures 2.82, 2.83, and 2.84 show the code necessary to respond to the mouse down action of the topmost button on the display. This of course is much more code than is needed to flash a different bitmap to simulate a button. The code to do this is in the statement,

```
ATMMach.revbttn1.visible = true
```

This code makes the reverse or yellow bitmap visible. Likewise, there is a segment of code for when the mouse is released on a button. It is shown in Figure 2.85. The statement managing the blink (the only statement in this event handler) is

```
ATMMach.revbttn1.visible = false
```

This leaves us with the rest of the code for when the mouse button is pressed.

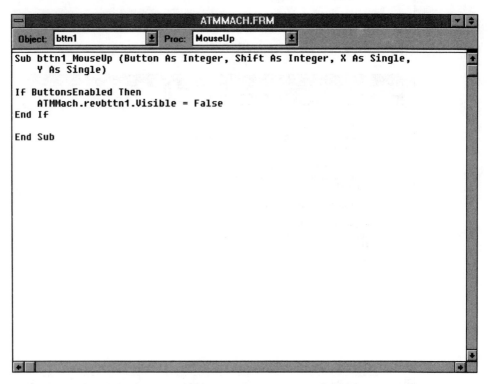

Figure 2.85 Code for a MOUSEUP event.

The topmost mouse button of the three that are displayed is a multifunction button. The purpose of this button changes as the program progresses. In a real ATM, you press the same button for different things, so our ATM behaves the same way.

The function the button performs is controlled by a flag that is set in the program. Three flags can be set:

```
selectTransaction
selectAccount
selectNextTransaction
```

When **selectTransaction** is true, the transaction has been selected and it is now time to set up for account selection. If you look at the code, you will see the labels for the buttons are changed to **Savings** and **Checking**, and the prompt is changed to "Deposit to:". Likewise, when **selectAccount** is true, the account has been selected and it is time to set up for entering the amount of the transaction. Notice that the code here makes the button labels and arrows invisible and enables the keypad for entry.

Step 4. The user selects the account for the transaction. I have already shown the code for this. The simulated ATM display contains a prompt asking the user to do this, and the buttons are appropriately labeled. When the user clicks the **Savings** button, the simulated ATM display is changed to request the amount of the transaction.

Step 5. Using the numeric keypad, the user enters the amount for the transaction. When the user selects the account, the screen prompt is changed to "Please enter the amount you wish to deposit." Along with this, a field will display the amount and the keypad keys are enabled for entry. You can see the code for this in Figure 2.86.

The keypad buttons are similar in how they operate and how they are implemented to the other buttons I have already described. One small difference is that instead of having separate controls, as is the case with the other buttons (**bttn1**, **bttn2**, and **bttn3**), the keypad buttons are implemented as two control arrays—one for the button in the up position and one for the button in the down position. It makes sense to do this because the code for each of the but-

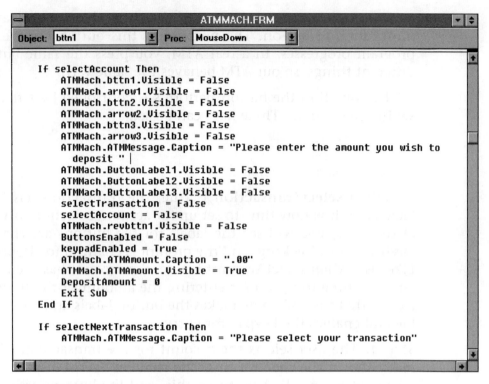

Figure 2.86 Code to enable amount input.

tons is the same. Instead of having to repeat the code 10 times, it only has to be written once. When the button is pressed, the reverse bitmap is displayed and the value of the digit is added to the accumulated amount total displayed in the amount field. When the button is released, the reverse bitmap is made invisible.

Step 6. Envelope slot animates to the open position.

Step 6a. This timer controls the slot opening animation.

Steps 6 and 6a represent another animation. Like the card animation, this animation is controlled by a timer, and also like the card animation, a sequence of pictures are displayed in succession to portray an opening slot in the ATM. The slot opens to accept the deposit envelope.

The slot animation uses a control array to contain each of the successive slot pictures. A nice side effect of using control array to store the slot pictures is that the sequence of pictures can be shown in the opening direction or in the closing direction depending on the direction of the index. Later on, this is how the slot is closed—by reversing the index direction from counting up to counting down.

Step 7. The envelope is dragged to the slot for insertion of the deposit.

Step 7a. This is a polling timer that tests if the envelope arrives at the insertion slot.

After the slot opens and the envelope is made visible, the ATM user will drag the envelope to the vicinity of the slot. The code to accomplish this is very similar to the code for dragging the ATM card to its slot. The code associated with the polling timer checks periodically on the position of the envelope. If the envelope is within the vicinity of the insertion slot (a predefined rectangle), then the animation sequence for the envelope is started.

Step 8. The envelope is animated into the insertion slot.

Step 8a. The envelope animation is controlled by this timer.

This is another bit of code we have seen before. A series of envelope slices are shown in a predefined sequence controlled by a timer showing each envelope picture. The sequence looks as if the envelope is traveling into the insertion slot.

Step 9. The insertion slot closes in an animation.

Step 9a. This timer controls the closing slot animation.

A second timer is used to "close" the insertion slot. As was mentioned previously, this is accomplished by running the slot opening sequence backwards. This in turn is accomplished by decrementing the slot picture index as opposed to incrementing it.

Some Comments about Visual Basic and the ATM Simulation

My purpose in showing the Visual Basic implementation of the ATM simulation is to give the reader a feel for the difference between implementing something like the simulation in Visual Basic and implementing the simulation in Authorware. Visual Basic requires more attention to the details of implementation, although all of the access to windows, buttons, and other windows-type controls is available in Visual Basic.

From appearances in the ATM simulation, it was easier to create a program for this simulation in Authorware than in Visual Basic. The problem arises when there is a desire to do anything involving programming or programming-like tasks. The facility for this exists in Visual Basic but not in Authorware.

For our purposes, Visual Basic represents a good starting point for creating intelligent multimedia applications. All of the features we would expect in a multimedia language are present, and we are also able to integrate Visual Basic applications with other external applications—namely, those providing the intelligence to our applications.

Chapter Summary

There are many different kinds of tools to create multimedia. It is possible to home grow a tool to create multimedia applications, although there are many tools that can be used off the shelf. This chapter described a home grown tool for developing multimedia applications called IL.

IL is a programming language for developing multimedia applications. It was developed as a little language that was easy to use and easy to learn. IL can display graphics and react to mouse and keyboard interactions. An IL program is called a script. Scripts consist of multiple parts, and each part contains two sections. One section contains a series of statements that display graphics and text; the other section defines the interactions that can take place in a script part.

Because there are no tools for creating both artificially intelligent and multimedia applications, it is important to consider how the artificially intelligent elements of the application can be incorporated into the multimedia elements. The approach used in IL is to enable IL to be embedded in other applications. In IL, this is accomplished by allowing IL to be called from other C programs.

IL is one paradigm for creating applications. It is a language-based paradigm. Using IL, a multimedia application is created by writing statements in the language. An alternative to the language-based paradigm is the visual paradigm.

Two off-the-shelf programs for creating multimedia applications are Authorware Professional and Macromedia Director. Authorware Professional is a multimedia authoring program that uses icons for program creation. Another authoring tool that uses a visual programming paradigm, Macromedia Director, uses a score-based approach to create multimedia applications.

The last authoring tool described is a programming language for the Microsoft Windows platform called Visual Basic. Visual Basic is a hybrid programming language, both visual and language based. The visual elements of the language allow the design and placement of Windows-based interface elements such as windows, menus, buttons, lists, and graphics. These visual elements can have code attached to them. The code is written to react to events that are defined for the visual elements. For example, code can be written to respond to a button click event.

In order to gain some insight into the differences when implementing applications in an authoring tool such as Authorware Professional and Visual Basic, the same sample application is presented in both of these tools. Authorware Professional facilitates the development of interactive applications, whereas Visual Basic provides the capabilities for a rich programming environment.

CHAPTER 3

The Multimedia Database

Introduction

Chapter 1, introduced the idea of a multimedia database. Any multimedia system requires a repository to store all of the media needed for the multimedia system. In this one repository picture, sound, sequence, description, and other multimedia information will be kept. A multimedia database presents a somewhat different set of problems than a typical database. In a typical database the bits and bytes usually represent numbers and text, which are easily interpretable by the database mechanism. Most database mechanisms, on the other hand, do not have a built-in means to display graphics, or video, or play sound. This chapter expands the concept of a database to encompass multimedia and describes some of the problems that are encountered when creating a multimedia database.

Databases

Database applications constitute a large percentage of the application domain for computers these days. Corporations guard their databases with zealous attention, as miners guard their claims. Typically such databases contain sensitive information about the operations of a company. A competitor obtaining database information may cause serious damage to the database owner. If they are so important, what is nature of these things we call databases?

Databases are not a new idea. In fact there were always databases. They were significantly less sophisticated than present databases. The decks of punched cards that were used as the recording medium for databases represented structured organizations of the data contained on them. The differences between these databases and those of the present are not only the structure represented in the organization of the data, but also the tools that are part of the database.

In the case of the punched cards, the programmer more often than not had to write the code that would manipulate the data contained on the cards. Sometimes this code could be reused. Anytime a new database was devised, code would have to be written to process it. Modern databases act more like containers, allowing a programmer to impose a structure on data and also provide the tools to manipulate that data. A key to this discussion is the idea of structure and tools. A multimedia database should contain the same sorts of things, tools and structure.

Although it is highly distributed, one example of a multimedia database is the database created by all of the content existing on the World Wide Web. The content of this database is not structured to the "field" level, but the World Wide Web database does have a structure imposed by HTML (Hypertext Markup Language). The WWW database has structure and also tools.

The database supported by the World Wide Web consists of a data type called a page. Pages are hierarchically organized. Each hierarchy has a root, sometimes called the home page. A page represents a container structure of the database, and the contents of a page can include text, graphic images, sound, animation, and video.

The WWW-database hierarchy is manifested by links. A link is a connection between two pages. In some ways a link represents an index in a relational database that gives access to another table record in the database. A link exists as a mouse clickable area on a page. Clickable areas are "hot."

Clicking on a hot area may produce one of several results. As I mentioned, one of these results is to cause the display of another page in the WWW database. Another is to cause other media to be displayed or played. Under these circumstances, a viewer or a player may be created to show or play the media. For example, if the media is a PostScript file, then a PostScript viewing program will be run for the user so they can view the PostScript file.

As I mentioned, structure is imposed in the WWW database by the links between pages. The system "understands" certain kinds of data and can invoke the appropriate mechanism to allow a viewer to see a particular kind of media. This kind of structuring mechanism allows for a particularly rich and powerful way to traverse large amounts of data with relative ease. Except for the programmatic control contained in a page, the database allows for little more than traversing pages and viewing media.*

The WWW database can be searched. Text search is supported by the WWW database, and several search engines that are part of the WWW database environment are available.

Although the WWW database supports text search, it does not support search of other kinds of media. For example, the only way I would know if a picture of the Peruvian mountains existed in the WWW database is if the image were titled in this way, or if the search engine used link information to find this picture. A true multimedia database should have retrieval capabilities for all of the media types that it supports. There might, for example, be a picture searcher, and a movie searcher, and a sound searcher. Technology for carrying out picture, sound, and movie searching should be developed.

For our purposes the WWW database offers a conceptual jumping off point for the functionality required in a multimedia data-

---

*The World Wide Web supports a richer document than I have described including behavior implemented by CGI (Common Gateway Interface) scripts or by Java. These capabilities add a new kind of medium—a programmatic medium to the WWW database.

Table 3.1 Functionality for a Multimedia Database

Requirement	Description
Data types to be stored	1. Numeric 2. Text 3. Formatted text (PostScript, TeX, etc.) 4. Graphic files (.GIF, .JPEG, .PCX, etc.) 5. Sound files 6. Movie file
Container types	Pages
Structuring mechanisms	Links between pages 1. Text 2. Graphics
Functions supported	Viewers for 1. Numeric data 2. Text data 3. Formatted text 4. Graphics files 5. Sound files 6. Move files 7. Pages Travel between pages Searchers for text

base. Table 3.1 is derived from my discussion of the WWW database.

These are the basic characteristics defining a multimedia database. It is possible to extend this table to include more functionality. For example, the WWW model does not include the ability to attach usable information to the links between pages. This information would be useful in determining the relationships between pages and understanding how one page relates to another in the database.

A database is a kind of container for data. When thinking about containers, think of the database as the largest container. In the case of the WWW database the container is the page. The page container is one that is largely unstructured and provides little organization to the data contained on it. Records in a traditional database consist of fields containing data. A record contains a group of related data, such as an employee record. In a multimedia database, a record could contain a set of related data. For example, a record might be created that contains a location, a text description of the location, pictures of the location, sounds from the location, and a movie of the location. A record could also be used to create other organizations. For example, records could hold sequences of multimedia information.

Most multimedia databases include a tool called a report generator. It is the means by which data is retrieved from the database and organized in various desirable forms. A report generator in a multimedia database would allow the display of sequences of multimedia information in various formats. The format could be a hypermedia format (traversing links between containers), a sequence of multimedia (as in a display consisting of a series of graphic images), or an overview of the contents of the database (as in a map of the multimedia contained in the database). The report could be interactive.

An interactive report is one that would configure itself according to events occurring as a result of viewing the report. Such events include mouse clicks or responses to queries during the presentation of a report. In this mode, the system could be used to present certain sequences of information as desired by the author. As you can see in Table 3.2, modifications to the multimedia database functionality table have been made to include some of the richer functionality I have just described. Table 3.3 defines the functionality of the report generator.

Knowledge as Media

In my description of multimedia I have listed media types familiar to us. Graphics, sound, text, video, and animation are all common

Table 3.2 Enriched Functionality for a Multimedia Database (added functionality displayed in italics)

Requirement	Description
Data types to be stored	1. Numeric 2. Text 3. Formatted text (PostScript, TeX, etc.) 4. Graphic files (.GIF, .JPEG, .PCX, etc.) 5. Sound files 6. Movie file
Container types	Pages *Structured pages* *Records* *Frames*
Structuring mechanisms	Links between pages 1. Text 2. Graphics 3. *Labeled links*
Functions supported	Viewers for: 1. Numeric data 2. Text data 3. Formatted text 4. Graphics files 5. Sound files 6. Move files 7. Pages Travel between pages Searchers for text 8. *Report generator for multimedia database elements*

types of media. Knowledge is a kind of medium that does not appear in the typical list of media.

Chapters 4 and 5 will describe tools for artificial intelligence and knowledge representation. Knowledge representations consist of special structures used by the computer to reason about both real

Table 3.3 Functionality for Report Generator

Report Generator Function	Description
1. Provide for multimedia display	Each media type has associated with it an appropriate viewer—a mechanism that handles the display or rendering of a medium on a particular output device. For example, graphic images may be output on a display, hardcopy, or a long-term storage device.
2. Use multimedia display functionality to create a multimultimedia report	A multimedia report is defined as a static representation of multimedia information contained in the media database. In a traditional report generator, a user of such a system will prepare a layout template. This template is a visual representation of what the report eventually produced by the system will look like. In the case of the multimedia database generator, the report generator will do the same thing—it will allow a user to create a template describing the output. The report generator for multimedia allows for complex presentation sequences that are appropriate for multimedia.
3. Support dynamic reporting capabilities	For the most part, once a report template is defined in a report generator, the reports produced are static. They present certain information and do not change. In a multimedia environment, there is a different situation. A multimedia report may allow for interaction. Under these circumstances, the report generator must provide for this.

world and abstract objects. In some cases these knowledge representations consist of sets of rules that specify how an object works or how a particular process is carried out. Knowledge representations are used to describe how languages such as English are written. Knowledge representations are also candidates for storage in the multimedia database.

Two issues are important to consider when thinking about knowledge as a media: how the knowledge will be retrieved and how the knowledge is related to other types of media in the multimedia database.

Knowledge retrieval is closely associated with knowledge use. When knowledge is retrieved from a database the retrieval could return the knowledge in its raw form. This could be a rule or a specification. As an alternative, knowledge could be retrieved and then put to use. These retrieval operations can be distinguished by calling the first a data-type query and the second a knowledge-type query. An example of a data-type query would be

> Retrieve rule 23

and an example of a knowledge-type query would be

> Retrieve a sequence of images that describe how to remove the cover from a toaster.

In the knowledge-type query, knowledge contained in the multimedia database is used to understand and then answer the query. This brings us to the second issue about knowledge in a multimedia database.

More often than not the knowledge in an intelligent system is used to manipulate other kinds of data stored in the system. In the knowledge-type query example here, the knowledge to process this query will make use of graphics, animation, or video in the database to satisfy the query. There is a relationship between knowledge media in the multimedia database and other types of media. The way that this is accomplished is important to consider when constructing the multimedia database. Chapter 5 describes a knowledge representation structure called frames that can support the relationship between knowledge and other media contained in the multimedia database.

Architecture

Because traditional databases do not have functionality for creating a multimedia database, modifications or adjustments need to be made to existing database to handle multimedia requirements. For example, media like sound and video do not have keys. How can a piece of multimedia be retrieved from a traditional database? This section gives an example of how this can be achieved and also discusses some of the issues relevant to multimedia databases.

Records in the Multimedia Database

A relational database is organized into tables. In turn the tables are organized into a set of rows. Rows serve the same purpose as records. A record is divided into fields. A field contains one element of the record's data. Remember, all fields in a record are related to one another. Two different approaches can be used to assign fields in a multimedia database. In the first approach, the media data can be incorporated into the database. In the second approach, the database points to the media data. For this approach, the media data reside in individual files external to the database. As in any other database, a field in the multimedia database will hold data. Each field holds one piece of data. A field will define the type of data it contains, the source of the data, and the actual data (or a pointer to it). A data field is diagramed in Figure 3.1.

In a database fields are juxtaposed into a linear sequence. This will not do in the case of a multimedia database. Linear sequences are only one possibility. Sequences in two or more media can run in

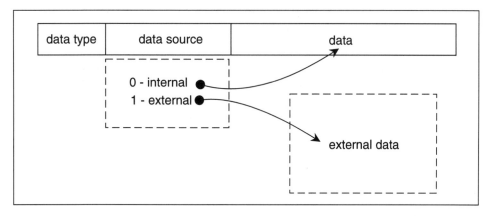

Figure 3.1 Logical configuration of a data field.

data type	data source	data	link to next field	time difference of link	type of link

Figure 3.2 Multimedia database record configuration.

parallel. For example, one sequence might be an animation and the second might be a sound sequence, such as a musical background. Another possibility is a network-like sequence of fields represented by hypermedia documents. Fields can also be related by subsumption. If one field subsumes another, then the subsumed field is contained in the subsuming field. A multimedia database record must be flexible enough to allow for these various types of relationships. A candidate record is shown in Figure 3.2. The three parts added to this record are the link to the next record, the time differentiation of the link, and the type of link.

The link to the next record is a pointer to the next record. The type of link specifies whether the record subsumes what it points to or is connected (in the case of linear juxtaposition). The time differentiation specifies whether the records occupy the same time, whether they are sequential, or whether the connected record occurs at a particular time.

Another useful piece of information in the case of media such as movies, animation, or sound is length. Length could be measured in frames of information or time. Since time would universally apply to all types of media, we will use time as the measure of length.

So far the multimedia record only describes physical characteristics of the media and how one record will relate to another. Equally important is the logical description allowing the record to be retrieved from the multimedia database. It is important to keep in mind how the multimedia is described, as it must be able to be used. The extended multimedia database record is shown in the Figure 3.3. To make the use of this record clearer, I will give an example shortly. First, though, some of the field data values need to be defined.

data type	data source	data	link to next field	time difference of fields	type of link	logical description of the data

Figure 3.3 Revised and extended physical multimedia database record.

THE MULTIMEDIA DATABASE 143

1. *Data Type or Media Type*

   The data type or media type describes the kind of multimedia data contained in the record. The different types include

Text	
Graphics	single images)
Animation	(multiple graphic images, "cels")
Movies	
Subsumption	(record combines others)
Script	(record contains program code)

2. *Data Source or Media Source*

   Data of media can be contained in a record, a file, or pointed to. The types are

   In a place
   In a file
   Pointer

An Aside

Fields, records, data types, and structures—sounds like computer science, *is* computer science. What does this have to do with multimedia? Multimedia authoring packages encapsulate much of this detail. There is an advantage to this, an author need not attend to the detail of it all, but there is also a price to be paid for this encapsulation of detail. The price is paid in the lack of flexibility. Understanding how information is stored, what needs to be stored, and why in the case of an authoring program will help you to understand how to expand your own capabilities. Of course, you can also design your own system (as is the point of this book).

An Example

To understand how the multimedia record can be used, I will show an example using our toaster. Suppose you want to show how the toaster latch release mechanism works. A small animation (se-

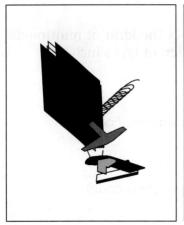  

Figure 3.4 (a) Mechanism latched. (b) Mechanism unlatched. (c) Mechanism up.

quence of graphic frames) and associated sound would be very useful for this demonstration. The media elements we have available to us are shown in Figures 3.4 and 3.5.

Three graphics in Figure 3.4 show the toaster platform and release mechanism in various positions. There is also a sound file associated with the latch releasing. To use the record representation, we will need file records—one for each media element and one to subsume the sequence. The resulting representation used is shown in Figure 3.6.

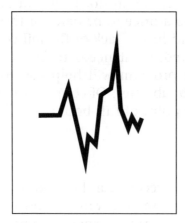

Figure 3.5 Toaster latch release sound.

THE MULTIMEDIA DATABASE 145

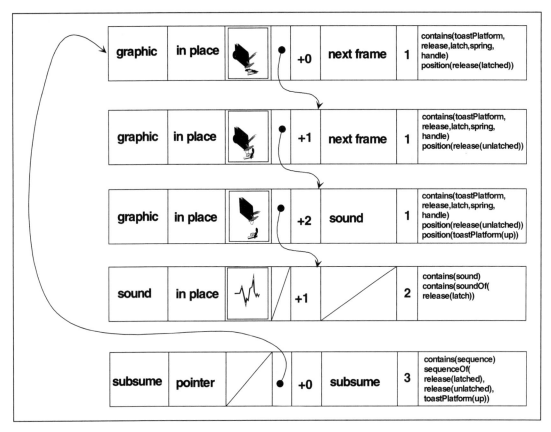

Figure 3.6 Multimedia database records for toaster platform sequence.

Viewers, Loaders, and Operations

To make use of the sequences of records in the multimedia database, I will define three kinds of mechanisms: viewers, loaders, and operations. A viewer is used to display a particular kind of media. It is important to understand what is meant by the term "display." This term makes sense when it is used for graphics, text, or movies. These media are meant for display, on a display. On the other hand, what does it mean to display sound? Sound is not displayed; it is played. Given the proper hardware, a sound file can be played by a computer. For this reason, I will use the term "display" in a generic sense. To display a sound means to play the sound. To display an animation means to show the animation with an appropriate animation player. The animation player uses the display of the computer to show a sequence of animation frames. For each media type, there is a *viewer* to display the media. In an object-oriented paradigm the media type (text, graphic, video, or sound) is an object and the object can receive a message whose name is view. In this sense the viewer belongs to the data type. Viewers like these are for individual media. There are viewers for graphics, sound, animation, video, and text. In the context of multimedia databases there is another important class of media viewers.

To retrieve specific kinds of media in a large multimedia database can be a complex task. This task can be facilitated by a viewer giving the user a view of the complete multimedia database. One way to accomplish this is with a viewer that summarizes the contents of the database according to classifications assigned to the media in the database. The view could be hierarchical, as shown in Figure 3.7, or in the form of a network, as shown in Figure 3.8.

A media type must be loaded before it is viewed. The purpose of a loader is to prepare a media type for viewing or manipulation. A specific loader is associated with each media type. Loaders move media files from their particular sources into the multimedia database or load a particular media on demand for display. The multimedia database will require a loader during the creation of a multimedia database.

A loader may not be physically separate from a viewer. In fact it may be part of a viewer. I distinguish between the loader and the viewer because the loader may require the ability to decompress the media when it is retrieved from the multimedia database so it can be viewed. Compression is an important consideration in a multimedia database as it is usually the case that media requires a large amount of storage. For example, a typical video sequence spanning no more than ten seconds of viewing time may require 60 MB of storage. Loaders will process the compressed media, expanding it into a viewable form.

Another function of loaders is to act as a means to store media in a multimedia database. The loading function is defined in two di-

THE MULTIMEDIA DATABASE   **147**

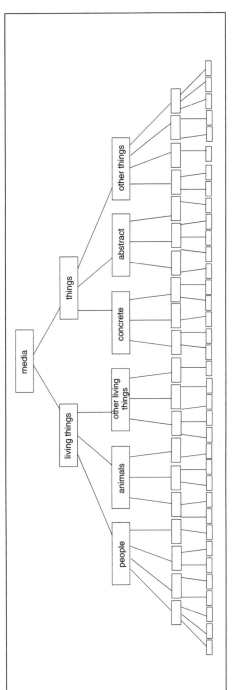

Figure 3.7 Hierarchical view of multimedia database.

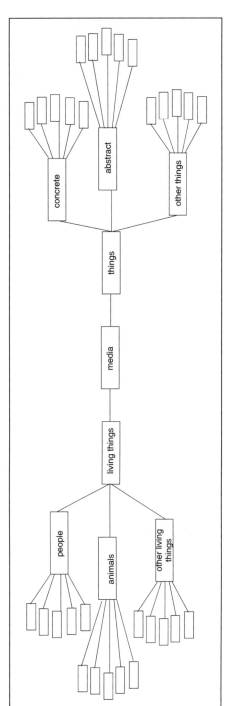

Figure 3.8 Network view of multimedia database.

rections. One is from the multimedia database to the viewer and the other is from the raw source of the media to the multimedia database.

A media type has a set of operations associated with it. The following operations are applicable to all media types.

- *PLAY.* Display (generic) the media on the appropriate output device at normal speed.
- *STEP.* Display (generic) the media on the appropriate output device on a frame by frame or unit by unit basis.
- *REWIND.* Rewind the media to a specified point.
- *FAST FORWARD.* Fast forward the media to a specified point.
- *STOP.* Cease any media operation in progress.
- *REVERSE.* Display (generic) the media on an appropriate display device in the reverse direction.
- *POSITION.* Position the media at a specified position (frame or unit).
- *SEARCH.* Locate a particular frame or unit in the media by content.

Retrieving Media by Content

The SEARCH operation deserves some additional discussion, as this is a particularly interesting and important topic when considering the different kinds of media to be searched.

In Figure 3.6 the last field in each contains some identification information for the media contained in the record. For example, the first record in the sequence contains the following identification information.

```
contains(toastPlatform,release,latch,spring,handle)
position(release(latched))
```

This information identifies the content of the media. In this case the media consists of one frame of the three-frame animation sequence. The content information can be used to retrieve the frame if needed by specifying a query like

```
contains(release) and position(release(latched))
```

or

```
contains(toastPlatform)
```

When creating a multimedia database, the burden of identifying content is on the database developers. If a media entry in the database has not been properly indexed, then a retrieval for that media might fail. Content indexing like this is a very difficult and time-consuming task. Other, more general approaches are being explored.

In the content indexing process it is possible to define several different levels of identification for entries in the database. At the lowest level is the physical image or the physical data that comprises the media. In the case of a graphic image, the physical data are the pixels that comprise the image.

At the next level are the object descriptions. In a graphic image an object description would consist of the primitive shapes that form the image. For example, a graphic image of a car would be described at the object description level as a set of shapes like rectangles, squares, and circles.

Image features consist of characteristics of the image. If the image contains rectangles, then the image feature level will describe the rectangle by specifying its dimensions and color.

The next level decribes the images by defining how objects in the image are related. If the image consists of several cars, then the association level will define the juxtaposition of the objects in the image.

The topmost level of description describes images according to their content. This is the level of description that was used in Figure 3.8, where the objects in the image are named and any relationships in the image are specified.

The examples just given are for graphic images and other types of visual media. It may not seem that the same levels of description could be used for a media like sound. At the physical image level are the bits that make up the digital sound representation. The object description consists of specifications of the slices of the digital sound waveform. The slices are grouped logically—for example, portions of the digital waveform whose frequency rises and portions of the digital waveform whose frequency falls. These portions comprise the object descriptions of the sound media.

Image features for sound consist of frequency and dynamics specifications, and the association level specifies how the sound changes over time. At the topmost level, the description describes the content.

One of the problems with retrieving media by content is that each image must be assigned some description of its content. If the multimedia database is large, this task can be time consuming. The retrieval of an image or sound requires that the content of the image or sound be recognized. This task is quite complex, as you might imagine. If an image can be classified by some other means, this might simplify the retrieval problem.

Retrieving Media by Characteristic

The lowest level of image classification is the physical image. This consists of the pixels that make up the image, the colors of the pixels, and so on. Suppose we want to retrieve images of a particular train. We have one image of the train available to us, but we want to find other images in the database. One way to accomplish this is to count how many times each particular color is used in an image. The result of this count is a kind of color profile of the image. The multimedia database is searched for an image with a similar color profile. If one is found, it is presented as a possible image of the train. A refinement of this approach is to count the number of color pairs in the image and use this profile to retrieve images from the multimedia database.

Pattern matching is another approach to retrieving a certain desired image from the multimedia database. Suppose we use the train again. We process the image of the train to transform it into a series of lines. The lines constitute a kind of pattern. Orientation, length, and connectedness can all be used as characteristics. The database is searched by retrieving an image, transforming it in the same way, and then comparing the candidate image's transformation to the sample image's transformation. If they match or come close to matching, then it is possible the candidate image is an image of a train.

Creating a Multimedia Database

A multimedia database is created from many sources. This makes it important to have the proper loaders for installing and retrieving media to and from the multimedia database.

In some cases multimedia may be authored by authoring or editing software. The authored multimedia is usually stored in a proprietary format and needs to be transferred directly in this form into the multimedia database. Paper documents can be stored in a multimedia database through the use of scanners. The scanner creates a picture of the document in an appropriate multimedia format. The loader can then load this picture into the multimedia database using a graphics image loader. Text documents can also be processed by an optical character recognition program so that the text contained in the document may exist in the multimedia database as text.

Sound and video can be recorded by the standard means and then digitized with the appropriate multimedia hardware. The digital version of the audio or video is loaded into the multimedia database by the appropriate multimedia loader.

The multimedia database creation process will include a step or steps to classify media as they are stored in the database. If the type of classification used is content classification, then the loader will be responsible for obtaining a classification that can be assigned to the media. The loading mechanism should also include a means to edit the classification after the file is stored in the multimedia database.

Chapter Summary

The multimedia database can serve as the repository for media used in multimedia applications. A multimedia database will differ from its traditional database counterpart in the kinds of data that have to be stored and the means of retrieval of the media.

The various kinds of media that can be stored in a multimedia database include graphics, animation, video, text, audio, and knowledge. Each of these has associated with it a viewer, which will display or play the media, a loader that is responsible for loading the media into a viewer or loading raw media into the multimedia database. The loader manages compression and decompression of the images when necessary. Each media also has a set of operations associated with it. These operations are supported in the viewer.

Knowledge as a media is an interesting departure from the other kinds of media stored in a multimedia database because of how it can be used. The knowledge contained in a multimedia database may be used to control how other media in the multimedia database are used or retrieved. For knowledge media we distinguish between two types of queries: a data-type query, which involves retrieving raw knowledge, and a knowledge-type query, which involves satisfying a request that requires some knowledge.

Multimedia stored in a multimedia database can be content classified. The classificiation is made so that media can be retrieved according to the classification. Content classification for a large multimedia database may be extremely time-consuming. Alternative means to carry out media retrievel automatically could be used. For example, characteristics at the physical level might be used to retrieve elements from the multimedia database. Pattern recognition is also an approach that may be used for media retrieval.

Suggested Reading

Chorafas, Dimitris N., *Intelligent Multimedia Databases*, Englewood Cliffs, NJ: Prentice Hall.

A good overview of multimedia databases from the standpoint of applications using them.

CHAPTER 4

Tools for Intelligent Applications

Introduction

Just what is it about tools for creating intelligent systems that make them different from the traditional tools for creating application programs? The same question could be asked about tools for creating multimedia applications. What makes these tools different from those for creating traditional applications? As we saw in Chapter 2, the functionality that is part of the language makes a tool appropriate or better for a particular domain of application. The same can be said for tools for creating intelligent applications—namely, the language supplies some critical function or functions key to the application domain.

Artificial intelligence and its intelligent applications have a history almost as long as computing itself. One can trace some of the reasoning leading up to the possibilities of machine intelligence back to John Von Neumann (see McCorduck, 1979). But if one could identify a time of beginning for artificial intelligence, that would be the Dartmouth Conference in the summer of 1956. This is where the "parents" of artificial intelligence "gave birth" to the field.

Needless to say this history lesson is not about multimedia or intelligent applications. I am primarily interested in recounting some of the history to you to reinforce the idea that some of the things I will describe in this chapter and the next have a long heritage, especially long if you measure this heritage in terms of the advances we have seen in computer technology. So, even if I do not give an adequate or sufficiently detailed explanation of why a particular tool has manifested itself in a particular way, there were cogent and (at the time) well thought out reasons for the formulation.

Making a Thinking Machine

What made those original thinkers think a computer could possibly simulate human thinking? Although there are many arguments pro and con, it is mathematics that provided a motivation for the idea that machines might be able to think.

As long ago as 100 B.C. humans were interested in thinking about thinking (see McCorduck, 1979, p. 6). The real thinking about thinking began with philosophers, mathematicians, and scientists. The approach was fundamentally the same—to codify the thought process in a mathematical representation. For quite a long time, logic was seen as the means by which human thinking processes could be represented. Of course, logic proved to be inadequate, which led to modified and more elaborate logics.

In their original incarnation computers manipulated numbers. They were gigantic calculators, nothing more. Or were they? Alan Turing established the connection between machine and thinking. One basis for this connection was an abstract machine* named the Turing Machine. The Turing Machine was and still is considered to be a universal computing device. Any computation performed on a modern-day computer can also be performed on a Turing machine,

---

*An abstract machine is a device that can be used to carry out computations. Unlike present-day computers, an abstract machine does not exist other than on paper. It is a mathematical device used to test and prove theories about computation.

though the process is somewhat more unwieldy than using a modern high level programming language. The Turing machine requires a program be entirely encoded into a coded alphabet. Turing believed any intellectual problem could be formulated as "find a number n such that ..." (McCorduck, 1979, p. 57), and thus the connection is established. Computers can manipulate numbers. All intellectual problems can be formulated as a problem of finding some number—a problem of computation. Logics provide the high-level representation. Logics are then encoded into numeric representations that can be computed. This is the basis for all ideas about symbolic computation.

In the following discussion of tools for artificial intelligence we must consider the first tools for creating intelligent applications because tools remain important and are still used for major development.* We begin with the lingua franca of artificial intelligence, LISP. LISP was the first language of artificial intelligence, and its conceptual underpinnings influence much about artificial intelligence applications and systems.

The LISP Programming Language

LISP, an acronym standing for List Processing Language, or more colloquially as Lots of Irritating Superfluous Parentheses, is a functional and symbolic language.

Until LISP, most high-level languages of the time were translated or compiled. This meant the basic programming process was

1. Write and code the program.
2. Compile the program.
3. See if the program runs. Examine results. Repeat from step 1 as many times as necessary.

---

*There is a trend of late to implement intelligent applications with C++. This is because of the nature of LISP and Prolog and the overheads they incur. Nevertheless, the philosophical basis for many applications comes from LISP and Prolog.

Anyone who has worked on the batch computing systems of the 1960s knows this process can be extremely time-consuming. To maximize the results of each and every run of the program, it was important to squeeze as much debugging information out of a run of the program as possible. One or more hours might intervene between each run, so it was necessary to make each and every run count.

John McCarthy introduced the idea of time sharing. Everyone got a slice of the processing time of the computer. Because the computer operated much faster than any human being, the computer would "be back" to give another slice before people felt they were waiting. With such a system it would not make sense to have a compiled language. A language processor giving immediate results would be much better in this environment. Language processors like this are called interpreters. Another significant aspect about McCarthy's formulation of LISP is that statements entered into a LISP interpreter offer immediate results, so, with a LISP interpreter, it is possible to enter a statement and watch the effect of that statement.

Unlike many other programming languages of the day or of today, the representation of the LISP programming language is uniform: In LISP the programming language and the data are one and the same. In LISP PROGRAM = DATA and DATA = PROGRAM. The implications of this were and are profound. A LISP program had access to LISP data, but LISP programs were LISP data, so LISP programs could be manipulated like any other LISP data. This means that LISP programs could be changed while a LISP program was running—a LISP program could be self-modifying.

LISP programs manipulate symbolic expressions. A symbolic expression is nothing more than a word with meaning in the context of the system. In languages like FORTRAN it would be necessary to create an array representing a string. The string could then be used to represent a symbol. In LISP, the representation of symbolic information and its manipulation are given as a part of the language. Symbols are concatenated into lists, which are the basic element of manipulation in a LISP program. A list can represent a list of symbols or a call to a LISP function. The interpretation of a LISP list is controlled by a LISP function named **eval**. The **eval** function defines how LISP programs are interpreted. Functions are constructed compositionally as lists of lists. All of these characteristics define some of the abstract basis and significant elements of the LISP language. Some of the basic statements of the language are presented in the next section.

A Brief LISP Tutorial

Basic Elements

The most basic element of LISP is the symbol. A symbol consists of a contiguous sequence of characters. Examples of valid symbols are

```
cat
dog
systemInitialization
np
```

Other primitive data types that can be part of a LISP program are integers, real numbers, and strings. These basic elements can be part of LISP lists.

Lists

A LISP list is a sequence of basic elements and/or lists enclosed in parentheses. For example, a simple LISP list would be

```
(domestic-animals dog cat hamster)
```

This is where parentheses begin to play an important role in the language. A list can also consist lists. The list just shown can be embedded in another list:

```
(animals (domestic-animals dog cat hamster)
         (zoo-animals monkey zebra giraffe))
```

As I said earlier, a program in LISP is a list. Following is an example of the definition of a simple LISP program.

```
(defun second (x) (car (car x)))
```

Basic Functions

An expression in LISP, called an s-expression, is in prefix notation. This means the name of the function (the operator) comes first in the expression followed by the operands of the function. Adding two numbers *x* and *y* would be represented as:

```
(+ x y)
```

The two most basic functions (and historically famous) are the **car** and **cdr** functions. These are famous because they come from the original implementation of the LISP language on a computer that had as part of its instruction set **car** and **cdr**.

The **car** function takes a single argument: a list. It returns as its result the first element of the list. The form of the function is

```
(car x)
```

where **x** must be a list. An example of the use of this function is

```
(car '((a b) c d e))
```

When applied to this list, the result of the function is

```
(a b)
```

The second of the two functions is **cdr** (pronounced cooder). When applied to a list, this function returns the rest of the list. The result of this function will always be a list, even if the list only has one element, its **car**. The form of the **cdr** function is

```
(cdr x)
```

where **x** is the list to which the **cdr** function will be applied. An example of the use of **cdr** would be:

```
(cdr '((a b) c d e))
```

The result of this application of the **cdr** function would be

```
(c d e)
```

Now suppose we wanted to construct a new function from the ones we know so far, **car** and **cdr**. It may not seem we can do too much with these functions, but humor me because this will get us to the next important concept. How could we construct a function that would return the second element of a list? What would be the second element of the list (**c d e**)? The element would be a **c**, but how would we get this functionally? In the list (**c d e**), **d** is part of the **cdr** of the first list. Actually, the second element is the **car** of the **cdr**. Functions can be combined in LISP, so the result of one function is the argument to another function. We could use the following expression to extract the second element of a list.

```
(car (cdr '(c d e))
```

It would be inconvenient if we had to write this expression each time we wanted to get the second element of a list. Another function in LISP is the function used to define new functions. When a new function is defined it becomes available as part of the LISP language. The name of this function is **defun**. The function definition for the second element of a list would be

```
(defun second (x) (car (cdr x)))
```

The **defun** function is a function of several arguments. The first of these is the name of the function, the second is the parameter list of the function, and the third argument is the body of the function—the statements executed for the function. For the definition of **second**, the body the function is (**car (cdr x)**). Like other functions, **defun** is evaluated like any other function in LISP—its value is computed and a result is returned (all functions return results). In the case of **defun**, the result of the function is the name of the function. We can even ask LISP to describe the function for us. Figure 4.1 shows the definition of the function and Figure 4.2 shows LISP's description of the function.

The specifics of Figure 4.2 are not important. You can see LISP has made the function named **my-second** part of the environment. Now I can simply use this new function directly as shown in Figure 4.3. Pause a moment and consider the implications of what we have just accomplished. We have extended the LISP language with a function of our own. This function is now part of the language. The interpreter "understands" **my-second** and knows what to do when it sees it in an expression. Because it can be extended, we can readily use LISP to define our own languages. In fact, many LISP systems have been implemented in just this way—by writing a language that sits on top of LISP.

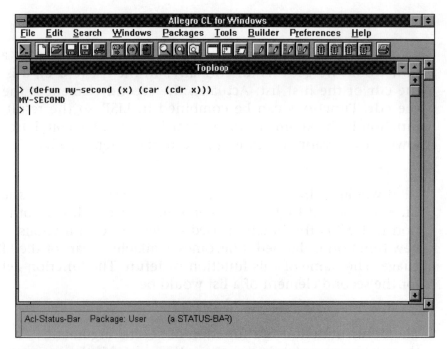

Figure 4.1 Defining the function **my-second**.

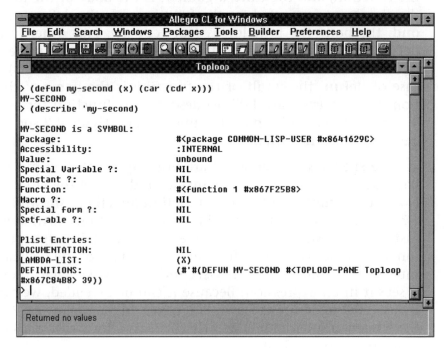

Figure 4.2 LISPs description of **my-second**.

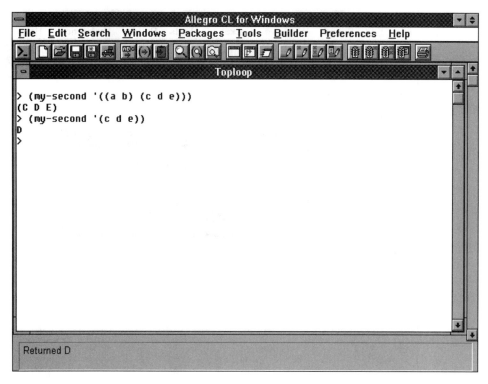

Figure 4.3 Using **my-second**.

Let's consider another function (the basis of this LISP interpreter), the **eval** function. Consider the expression

```
(eval '(my-second '(c d e)))
```

Notice in Figure 4.4 that in the first case, the result of the function is as before, namely a **d**. In the second case, an error was produced by the interpreter. What is the difference? Consider the difference between the two expressions.

```
(eval '(my-second '(c d e)))
(eval (my-second '(c d e)))
```

In the first expression the inner expression is quoted ('). The quote (') has a special meaning in LISP. In the second expression the inner expression is not quoted. I really have not answered the first question, and I have introduced a new question. What do quotes do?

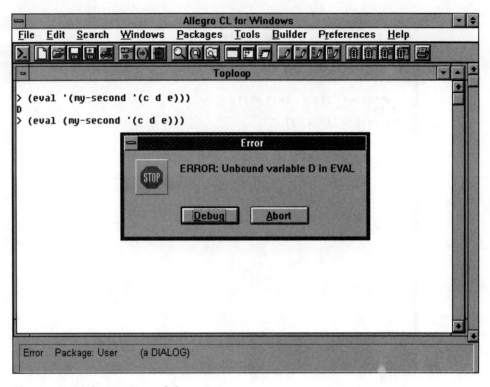

Figure 4.4 The LISP **eval** function.

The **eval** function is the fundamental function in LISP. (In fact, **eval** is so fundamental that the LISP interpreter is actually defined in LISP.) It evaluates each and every expression—this is most important to remember. The only time the **eval** function does not evaluate is when the expression is quoted ('). The quote tells the **eval** function not to evaluate the expression that follows. Actually, **quote** is a LISP function. The following expressions are equivalent:

```
'(a b c)
(quote (a b c))
```

The **quote** function when evaluated returns exactly its argument. Now let's reexamine why the first **eval** function worked and the second did not.

In the first case,

```
(eval '(my-second '(c d e)))
```

the result of **eval**ing the expression **'(my-second '(c d e))** is the **eval** of the expression **(my-second '(c d e))**, and the result of this **eval** is **d**. In the second case,

```
(eval (my-second '(c d e)))
```

eval evaluates the symbol **my-second**, determines it is a function, and applies the function to its argument. The result of this is **d**. Evaluating **d** delivers an error because **d** has not been assigned, thus the unbound variable error message.

As I mentioned, LISP can be defined in the LISP language. This is a true power of the LISP language. To gain a better understanding of the LISP language and to see some more LISP code, let's consider what a simplified version of the **eval** function might look like.

Program Listing 4.1 LISP eval function.

```
(defun lispEval (exp)
       (cond ((atom exp)
              (cond ((numberp exp) exp)
                    (t (getValueforAtom exp))))
             ((equal (car exp) 'quote) (cadr exp))
             ((equal (car exp) 'cond)
              (lispCond (cdr exp)))
             ((equal (car exp) 'setq)
              (lispAssignment
                   (cadr exp)
                   (lispEval (caddr exp))))
             (t (lispApply (car exp)
                   (mapcar #'(lambda (x) (lispEval x))
                       (cdr exp))))))
```

Much of this function you probably won't understand unless you have done some programming in LISP. This is okay though because I am going to explain how this function works. What is important about this function is that it represents most of the important concepts of the LISP language. These concepts include recursion, conditionals, and symbol processing.

LISP's conditional statement, that statement most like the IF statement of other programming languages, is called a **cond** statement. Like all other LISP constructs, the **cond** construct is a function; it returns a value. As you might imagine, the value returned is either a true or a false. In LISP, a true value is a special constant **true** or any non-**NIL** value. False is represented by the special constant **NIL**. Anything that is not **NIL** is true.

A **cond** statement is about as complex a LISP statement you can find, especially if you are a beginner. It consists of multiple clauses, and it is very important to get the clauses just right, or the **cond** statement might not work like you expected. Let's take a bird's-eye view of the **cond** statement. In its most basic form, it looks like this:

```
(cond
      (conditional clause 1)
      (conditional clause 2)
      (conditional clause 3)
      ...
      (conditional clause n))
```

This statement is like an If statement with multiple conditionals, sort of like

```
if a then b else
if c then d else
if e then f ...
```

Each conditional clause has two parts, a condition and a consequent (what is done when the condition is true), so a conditional clause has the form

```
((condition) (consequent))
```

The condition must evaluate to a LISP true or false value, and the consequent can be any series of LISP statements. The result of the **cond** statement is the result of the last LISP statement of the conditional clause whose condition evaluated to a true value.

The conditional expression of a conditional clause can make use of a LISP function that returns a true or false value, a function that returns a true or false value, or the special constant **t** that always returns a true value. The **eval** function contains several examples of LISP predicate functions.

The **equal** predicate compares two LISP expressions. The predicate will return a true value if the two expressions match exactly. If the expressions contain sublists then each sublist must match exactly, element for element, and the sublists must appear in the same order.

To test whether a LISP expression is an atom, a symbol, a number, a character, or a string, the **atom** predicate is used. If the argument of this function is one of these primitive elements, then the result of the function is true. Any other expression as an argument to **atom** will return a **NIL**.

The **(numberp exp)** expression tests its argument and returns true if the argument is a number and **NIL** otherwise. The last conditional clause of the **cond** statement of the **eval** function begins with the expression **(t (lispApply (car exp)**... The conditional expression of the conditional clause is a **t** which means the clause always evaluates to true. In the context of the conditional expression, this is the conditional clause that will always evaluate to true, and in the event no other conditional clause evaluates to true, the statements of this clause will always be evaluated. This is called the default conditional clause of the **cond** statement.

LISP is a language supporting recursion. You can see this directly in the **eval** function. The function is shown again with the recursion in italics.

Program Listing 4.2 LISP eval function showing recursion.

```
(defun lispEval (exp)
      (cond ((atom exp)
             (cond ((numberp exp) exp)
                   (t (getValueforAtom exp))))
            ((equal (car exp) 'quote) (cadr exp))
            ((equal (car exp) 'cond)
             (lispCond (cdr exp)))
            ((equal (car exp) 'setq)
             (lispAssignment
                   (cadr exp)
                   (lispEval (caddr exp))))
            (t (lispApply (car exp)
                   (mapcar #'(lambda (x)
                      (lispEval x)
                      (cdr exp)))))))
```

The use of recursion in LISP is typical. It is by far the easiest way to disassemble and process lists. Lists lend themselves to this kind of manipulation because they are hierarchical and nested structures. In the **eval** function, a complex LISP expression is evaluated by calling the **lispEval** function to evaluate its parts. The parts are then used as arguments to the first element of the expression (something that evaluates to a LISP function name).

Of course this leaves, "Is it possible to do iteration in a language that so easily supports recursion?" as an open question. In the original versions of LISP, iteration was accomplished with a form of the GOTO statement. In more modern versions of LISP, there are looping statements and a full set of true looping statements (which look like they have been borrowed from other, more traditional languages). In LISP, real programmers don't use loops; they use iterators.

The **eval** function contains a special function that begins **(mapcar #'(lambda (x)...** The **mapcar** function is one of a class of iterator functions having the form

```
(mapfff function list)
```

where **fff** specifies the particular iteration function. The interpretation of this expression is that the function **function** is applied to each element of list **list**. The function will return a list of results, each element of the list being the result of the individual application of the function to each element in the list. Map functions iterate through a list of elements. If you understand how these functions work, you seldom have to use true (loop-based) iteration in a LISP function, and using these iterator functions is more efficient than using true iteration. Let's consider an example before returning to the **eval** function. Suppose we wanted to create a function that would accept a list of lists and return the second element of each list. There are several ways this can be accomplished. It can be done recursively, with standard iteration, or with an iterator. By far, the iterator is the easiest. Here is how it is done.

We already have the function **second** that returns the second element of a list. All we have to do is place this function in an iterator, and we have it.

```
(defun all-seconds (alist)
    (mapcar #'second alist))
```

That's all there is to it. This function will do exactly what we want.

It is also useful and instructive to see how the same function could be implemented with a loop and with recursion. This will also introduce some new LISP functions to you. Let's first see how its done with a LISP loop.

Remember we said we will have a list of lists to which we want to apply **my-second**. To do this, we walk down the list of lists, extracting the second element of each sublist and adding it to the eventual resulting list. The code for this is:

```
(def all-seconds-2 (ll)
     (let (result (l ll))
          (loop
               (cond ((null l) (return result))
                     (t (setf result
                              (append result
                                      (list (my-second (car l)))))
                        (setf l (cdr l)))))))
```

In this version of the function, the LISP function **loop** produces the effect of an infinite loop. Any LISP expression inside of this function (you can have more than one) will be evaluated repeatedly until an explicit exit from the **loop** function is evaluated.

Notice I have used **cond** to perform the work of the function. In the first conditional clause of the **cond** function, I test to see if the list is empty with the **null** LISP function. If the list is empty, the loop will be terminated by the **return** function. The result of the loop will be the accumulated list of second elements of the sublists of the list.

Inside the function definition is another function I have not discussed. It is the **let** function. From the perspective of a historical view of LISP, **let** solves the serious problem of the address space being global, which was a characteristic of older LISP implementations. In early LISPs there was no variable scoping. The **let** function is one way common LISP has to create and initialize local variables. In **all-seconds-2** the variables **result** and **l** are locally declared, with **result** initialized to **NIL** and **l** initialized to the value of the original input list. These variables only exist inside the scope of the **let** function and are not available outside of this function.

Two other functions used in **all-seconds-2** are **setf** and **append**—**setf** is the assignment function of LISP and **append** is one of several functions that allow you to build lists. The form of the **setf** function is:

```
(setf place form)
```

where **place** is the location to store the result of evaluating **form**. A more traditional way to express this is

```
place := form
```

Remember form will be evaluated, and it is the result of the evaluation that will be stored in place. So, if you have something like

```
(setf x 1)
```

the **x** will evaluate to the number 1, whereas

```
(setf x (+ 1 3))
```

will result in **x** being evaluated to the number 4.

The functions **car** and **cdr** are what I like to call accessor or destructor functions. They are used to take apart LISP expressions. Without a corresponding set of functions to assemble lists, LISP would be pretty boring and not very useful.

Two of the most basic list construction functions are **cons** and **append**. The **cons** function is used to create lists by attaching the **car** of a list to the **cdr** of the list. It may seem strange to use these terms in this way, but **car** and **cdr** not only refer to functions, they also refer to the parts of a list. Each and every list has a **car** and a **cdr**. The **car** of a list is the first element of the list. This can be an atom or another list. The **cdr** of the list is the rest of the list without the first element. The **cons** function attaches a first element of a list to the rest of a list.

The **append** function does just what the name of the function implies. It is the concatenation function for lists. The **append** function is not the same as the **cons** function, and they should not be confused. The **append** function makes one list the next element of an existing list. The function is not destructive and a new list is the result of this function. An example of **cons** and **append** is

```
(cons 'a '(b c))           →      (a b c)
(cons '(a b) '(c d))       →      ((a b) c d)

(append 'a '(b c))         →      produces an error
(append '(a b) '(c d))     →      (a b c d)
```

Notice in each case of the **cons** function the result is a list. Notice that in the case of the first **cons** a list is produced, but the corresponding **append** produces an error. This is because the arguments to an **append** must always be lists, whereas the arguments to **cons** need not always be lists. Also notice that the results are different in the second example of **cons** and **append**. In the case of **cons** the result is a list consisting of a first element **(a b)** and elements **c** and **d**. The reason for this result is exactly how **cons** is defined. The first argument to **cons** becomes the first element in the resulting list. The second argument of the function becomes the rest of the list.

Returning to our discussion of the **all-seconds** function, I still need to show and describe a recursive version of this function. This version of the function is

```
(defun all-seconds-3 (l)
    (cond ((null l) nil)
          (t (append   (list (my-second (car l)))
                       (all-seconds-3 (cdr l))))))
```

This function works in the same way as the iterative function in the sense that the function walks down the original list, extracting the second element as the function progresses. The difference is that the function uses recursion to implement the processing of the original list and to accumulate the result of the processing.

The Common LISP language is quite a rich language, and space does not permit me to show all of the functions that are part of this language. Over the years it has evolved and now includes an object-oriented component among other important extensions. It may not be obvious at this point why a language like LISP might be more appropriate to create a reasoning program. LISP is well suited for this purpose because it allows for the manipulation of symbols, and symbols can be used to represent elements of reasoning, thinking, and real world objects.

Logic as a Programming Language

Around the time LISP was undergoing its fourth or fifth incarnation, when there were things like LISP machines and Xerox Dolphins (another computer whose operating system is based on LISP), there was a movement underfoot toward entirely different programming paradigms. Like most programming languages of its time, LISP was procedural. Both the step and time of the step were specified in the procedural paradigm. Languages like Smalltalk and Prolog then began to explore the possibility of eliminating the dimension of time from the programming task. These languages were some of the first examples of the declarative paradigm.

The language Prolog did not appear on the scene until the early 1970s. It was a European invention—Alain Colmerauer and Philippe Roussel are credited with the creation of this language. The motivation for Prolog was the desire to create a system to process natural language. Consider the following conversation between computer and user (from Colmerauer and Roussel, 1993).

User: *Cats kill mice.*
Tom is a cat who does not like mice who eat cheese.
Jerry is a mouse who eats cheese.
Max is not a mouse.
What does Tom do?
Computer: Tom does not like mice who eat cheese.
Tom kills mice.
User: *Who is a cat?*
Computer: Tom
User: *What does Jerry eat?*
Computer: Cheese
User: *Who does not like mice who eat cheese?*
Computer: Tom
User: *What does Tom eat?*
Computer: What cats who do not like who eat cheese eat.

What is the relationship between this example and a system that processes natural language and logic? What Colmerauer and Roussel understood is that the parsing process is similar to the process of logical proof. As it turned out, an automated proof procedure called resolution was available to Colmerauer and Roussel. To understand something about how Prolog works, let's consider how the proof procedure operates.

Let's suppose we have the sentence

The little boy played ball.

We can represent this sentence as a kind of linear graph with nodes labeled with sequential integers and edges labeled with the words in the sentence. This representation is shown in Figure 4.5.

Using a logical notation, another representation of the graph would be the series of facts

the(1,2)

little(2,3)

boy(3,4)

played(4,5)

ball(5,6)

Our next step is to write a list of rules in this notation (the logical notation) that when used, will describe how to construct a sentence. For example, one rule might define that a sentence is composed of a noun phrase and a verb phrase.

R1. s(x,y) → np(x,z), vp(z,y)

This rule is read: A sentence from node x through node y can be written as a noun phrase from node x to node z and a verb phrase from node z to node y.

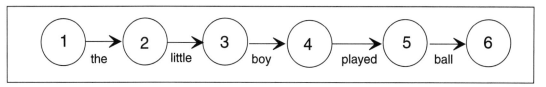

Figure 4.5 Linear graph representation of sentence.

Having defined the "sentence rule," I can define rules for other elements comprising a sentence. Two we know about from the sentence rule are *np* and *vp*. Here is another rule of the grammar:

R2. np(x,y) → det(x,a), adj(a,b), n(b,y)

This noun phrase rule can be read in a similar way as the sentence rule. A noun phrase from node *x* to node *y* is defined as a deteminer from node *x* to node *a*, followed by an adjective from node *a* to node *b*, followed by a noun from node *b* to node *y*. In a moment I will show how these rules are used. The rest of the rules of the grammar are

R3. vp(x,y) → v(x,a), n(b,y)

R4. det(x,y) → the(x,y)

R5. n(x,y) → boy(x,y)

R6. v(x,y) → played(x,y)

R7. adj(x,y) → little(x,y)

R8. n(x,y) → ball(x,y)

It is easiest to understand how these rules can be used by actually seeing them in use. To do that, I will make use of the original linear graph representation shown in Figure 4.6 Beginning with this graph, I will select rules to use to "build up" from the terminal nodes of the graph. In the first level of the graph, each edge/node pair is labeled. Above each of the nodes added to the graph, I have also shown the rules used to create that part of the level. For this

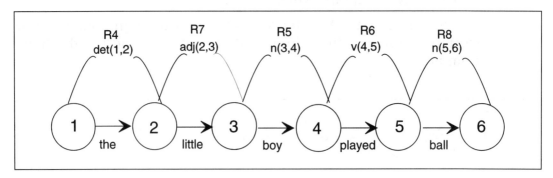

Figure 4.6 First level of derivation/parse tree.

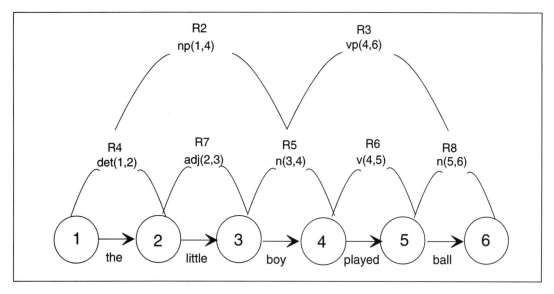

Figure 4.7 Adding the **np/vp** level to the tree.

level, we label nouns, verbs, and so on. At the next level (Figure 4.7), nodes are combined again to form more abstract structures—in this case, noun phrases and verb phrases. Finally, I can add a root node to this graph using rule R1. Notice that in Figure 4.8, all of the words of the original sentence are used up. Notice also that the numbers of the nodes involved in a particular rule element have replaced the variables in the elements. We know, for example, there is a determiner from nodes 1 to 2 from *det*(1,2).

I showed the process because it is important to understand how a sentence can be derived given a sequence of rules called a grammar. We can use the very same rules to prove the sentence is a valid one under the specified grammar.

As I mentioned earlier, there is a relationship between deriving a sentence in a language and proving the sentence is a part of the language. Before beginning there is one important concept we must understand.

Suppose we have a series of statements, X, Y, and Z, and suppose we want to prove a statement A; that is to say, under the conditions that X, Y, and Z are true, we also want to show that A is true. How

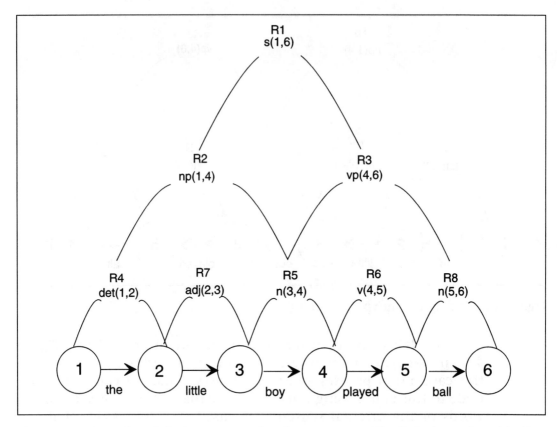

Figure 4.8 Completed derivation tree for the sentence "The little boy played ball."

can we do this? One way is to try to do the proof directly. We can try using the statements X, Y, and Z and any rules we know involving X, Y, and Z to prove the truth of A. For humans this is a good procedure. For computers it is not so good. Why? For simple systems like the one described here, the task would be a simple one for humans or computers, but as the system becomes more complex (more statements and more rules), the amount of work that must be done to prove a statement may not be able to be finished in an acceptable amount of time using a computer. Refutation is another way to accomplish the same thing.

If we want to prove A, then let's see if not A (the refutation of A) is consistent with the series of statements. If not A is inconsistent with a series of statements then A must be true. In other words, A and not A cannot be part of the same series of statements if the system of statements is consistent. The task of proving A becomes one of showing that not A is inconsistent with the system. I will now prove that the sentence "The little boy played ball" is a sentence in the grammar we specified using the proof procedure as I just described it.

We start by refuting there is a sentence encompassing nodes 1 to 6.

    1. not s(1,6)

From rule **R1** we know a sentence is actually composed of an *np* and a *vp*. Therefore our refutation of (1) becomes

    2. not np(1,z), vp(z,6)

Proceeding in this way, we know an *np* is defined as a *det*, an *adj*, and an *n*. Using this rule (R2), we can rewrite the refutation. The result of this is

    3. not det(1,a), adj(a,b), n(b,z), vp(z,6)

R4 is a rule for *det(x,y)*. Step 3 is rewritten:

    4. not the(1,2), adj(2,b), n(b,z), vp(z,6)

As this point in the procedure, we have our first inconsistency. This inconsistency is brought about by the fact *the*(1,2). Two things happen: The inconsistency reduces what has to be proven, we throw out the elements of the inconsistency, and in the process variables become bound to values. The result is

    5. not adj(2,b), n(b,z), vp(z,6)

I will now finish the proof that *s*(1,6) is true.

    6. not little(2,3), n(3,z), vp(z,6)

    7. not n(3,z), vp(z,6)

    8. not boy(3,4), vp(4,6)

    9. not vp(4,6)

    10. not v(4,z), n(z,6)

    11. not played(4,5), n(5,6)

12. not n(5,6)
13. not ball(5,6)
14. □

All of the terms have canceled. Thus, *not* s(1,6) is inconsistent with the series of statements.

What I have shown here is the proof procedure used in Prolog. I have also shown this same procedure lends itself very well to showing that a sentence is part of a grammar. Although many of the details have been left out of this description, one of the important aspects of this process is called unification. Unification is the logical process of matching that goes on during the proof procedure.

When we encountered a fact like

the(1,2)

in the proof procedure we needed to match that against a fact or statement in our system. The matching process is called unification. In other words, the element *the*(1,2) in step 4 of the proof procedure, unifies with the fact *the*(1,2) of the list of facts and statements of the grammar. In this case the unification is simple, it involves two elements that are exactly the same. The unification process can involve variables and very complex structures.

Another important aspect of the proof procedure as implemented in Prolog is called backtracking. In our simple example the rule or fact chosen at a particular step in the proof procedure was obvious: The selection process was simple. In the more typical case, the rule or fact to choose may not be so obvious because more than one can be chosen. The selection of one of the rules or facts at a particular time may be incorrect. We might proceed down a path where many elements have been shown to be inconsistent but arrive at a dead end, where not all elements are inconsistent. Under these circumstances, if there are other rules or facts to try, we must go back and try them to see if a successful proof can be produced. The combination of backtracking and unification makes Prolog an extremely powerful tool.

The power of Prolog, like the power of other rich-paradigm languages, is that something is made available to the programmer for free. Prolog supplies its own pattern-matching engine (actually a generalized pattern-matching engine), and because Prolog has a built-in searching process (backtracking), this does not have to be implemented by the programmer. The programmer can take advantage of these features in writing programs.

If a programmer needs to write something like a planning program or expert system, two types of intelligent applications requiring pattern matching and backtracking, it can be written more directly in Prolog because the language supplies the functionality.

A Brief Prolog Tutorial

Like LISP, Prolog has primitive elements called symbols. A symbol is a string beginning with a lowercase letter and representing some object or relationship. Examples of Prolog symbols are

```
male
female
joe
edward
likes
large
```

The next type of Prolog element is a *fact*. A fact is a primitive Prolog element that expresses a relationship. For example,

```
father(joe,ed)
```

expresses the relationship that Joe is Ed's father. Relationships can have any number of participants. In the case of the father relationship there are two participants. The number of participants in a fact is called the **arity** of the fact. The arity of the father relationship is two.

Prolog facts are entered into the Prolog interpreter database. Like LISP, Prolog is an interpreted language. You can enter statements into the interpreter and they will be processed immediately. Let's consider a database of Prolog facts about a family:

1. `male(joe)`
2. `male(larry)`
3. `male(moe)`

4. `female(henrietta)`
5. `female(jackie)`
6. `female(joan)`
7. `female(marge)`
8. `female(lana)`
9. `father(joe,larry)`
10. `mother(joe,henrietta)`
11. `father(joan,larry)`
12. `mother(jackie,henrietta)`
13. `mother(lana,henrietta)`
14. `mother(henrietta,marge)`
15. `father(larry,moe)`

The facts are entered into the Prolog database in consultation mode. In this mode, Prolog programs can be loaded and facts can be added to the Prolog database. The facts can be read directly from a file or entered, one at a time. Once the facts are entered, **queries** can be entered against the database.

A query is another Prolog fact. When you enter a query into the Prolog interpreter, the interpreter responds **yes** when the query is true and **no** when the query is false. You can "ask" questions about the contents of the database. With our database we could ask

```
?- father(joe,larry).
```

to which the interpreter would respond **yes**. Likewise we could enter the query

```
?- father(joan,moe).
```

to which the interpreter would respond **no**.

Queries like these are certainly useful, but the true power of Prolog lies in the ability to embed variables into Prolog queries. Syntactically, a Prolog variable is a string beginning with a capital letter. Variables always begin with capital letters. No other Prolog element has this characteristic, so if you forget and name a relationship with an initial capital letter, you will get an error message from the Prolog interpreter. Likewise if you use a capital letter where a lowercase letter should have been used, the program probably won't work the way you expected it to work. Let's see how variables work in Prolog queries.

Suppose we made the following query to the Prolog interpreter:

```
?- father(X,moe).
```

In this query, **X** is a variable. When the Prolog interpreter tries to answer this query, it does so by looking for a fact in the database that matches the query, just as before. In this case, the matching process is different because the variable can match anything in the same position. Looking through the list of facts we find that the following fact matches this query.

```
father(larry,moe)
```

In the matching process X matches **larry**. We say that X is **bound** to **larry**.

Queries can have any number of variables, and queries can be written consisting of all variables, as in

```
?- father(X,Y).
```

In this case, several facts in the database match this query.

```
father(joe,larry)
father(joan,larry)
father(larry,moe)
```

The sequence of bindings are as follows:

```
X = joe; Y=larry
X=joan; Y=larry
X=larry; Y=moe
```

You can ask Prolog for the first set of bindings or ask for all of the bindings. Asking for all of the bindings means Prolog must **backtrack** and find another fact that matches the query.

Backtracking involves looking through the list of facts for a new fact that matches the query. The first matching fact is

```
father(joe,larry)
```

When Prolog backtracks, this fact is "checked off." The next matching fact is

```
father(joan,larry)
```

Facts are processed in the order in which they appear in the database. It is very important to remember this because it can sometimes explain a particular program behavior.

Prolog Rules

The ability to create databases of facts and query them is useful but could become unwieldy fairly rapidly if we could not express relationships in a different way. This is where Prolog rules come into play.

A Prolog rule consists of a left hand side (the relationship) and its definitions, the right hand side. Enough with the abstraction. Let's define a relationship for sister. Two persons are sisters if they have the same parent (father or mother) and both persons are females. We can write a rule expressing this relationship in Prolog.

```
sister(X,Y) :- father(X,Z), father(Y,Z), female(X),female(Y).
sister(X,Y) :- mother(X,Z), mother(Y,Z), female(X),female(Y).
```

The rules can be read as follows:

X is the sister of Y if the father of X is Z and the father of Y is Z and X is a female and Y is a female.

X is the sister of Y if the mother of X is Z and the mother of Y is Z and X is a female and Y is a female.

The symbol :- separates the left hand side of a rule from the right hand side of the rule and is read "if." The left hand side of the rule defines the name of the relationship and its arguments. The right hand side represents the code that defines the relationship. Facts are really rules with no right hand side. Another way to write a fact is:

```
fact :-.
```

which is read "fact if true."

Just how does a rule run? That is, what happens when a query activates a rule as opposed to a fact? As before, the best way to understand what happens is to see what happens. Consider the query

```
?- sister(jackie,laura).
```

The rule I will use is

```
sister(X,Y) :- mother(X,Z), mother(Y,Z), female(X),
        female(Y).
```

The query forces the binding of the variables **X** and **Y**. I can rewrite the rule based on the binding of **X** to **jackie** and the binding of **Y** to **laura**.

```
sister(jackie,laura) :-
    mother(jackie,Z),
    mother(laura,Z),
    female(jackie),
    female(laura).
```

The result of this query will be **yes** or **no**. When a rule participates in a query, in order for the rule-based query to be answered, it is necessary that all of the components of the right hand side of the rule be answered. In other words, each component of the right hand side of a rule becomes a query. In the case of the sister rule, four queries will have to be answered.

1. mother(jackie,Z)
2. mother(laura,Z)
3. female(jackie)
4. female(laura)

The first query, **mother(jackie,Z)**, asks, "Who is the mother of jackie?" Looking at the sequence of facts we see the fact

```
mother(jackie,henrietta)
```

This causes the variable **Z** to be bound in subsequent queries.

2. mother(laura,henrietta)
3. female(jackie)
4. female(laura)

When a variable gets a binding in a query, the binding remains in effect for the rest of the rule.

The second query, **mother(laura,henrietta)** is answered by fact number 13 in the fact list (p. 178). The existence of fact 13 continues the query. The remaining two queries of this rule, **(3) female(jackie)** and **(4) female(laura)** are in turn confirmed by facts (5) and (8). This completes all of the necessary queries of the sister rule and answers the query **yes**.

Prolog programs can become very complex, as rules may invoke other rules. Under these circumstances, backtracking will come into play. This is an important part of Prolog and occurs when an answer to a query does not precisely satisfy the query. Backtracking would occur to try to answer the query in a different way.

One of my favorite examples of a Prolog program is one that computes the factorial for an integer n. The definition of a factorial is a recursive one as follows:

$$f(n) = \begin{cases} n=0, \ f(n)=1 \\ n>0, \ f(n)=nf(n-1) \end{cases}$$

In a language like C, a function to implement this would be relatively straightforward.

Program Listing 4.3 C factorial function.

```
int f(n)
{
        if (n==0) return(1);
        return(n * f(n-1));
}
```

How would the same function be implemented in Prolog? It may seem that the C implementation would be appropriate. Try it yourself. It won't work. Actually the Prolog definition is very similar to the functional definition. As Prolog functions (called functors) only can return values through variable binding, we must construct our Prolog factorial function to make use of this characteristic.

Let's define a fact that yields the factorial of 0.

```
fact(0,1).
```

This fact is read, "the factorial of 0 is 1." This is the trivial case. The nontrivial case (the meat of the functor) is defined as follows:

```
fact(N,F) :-
        N1 is N - 1,
        fact(N1,F1),
        F is N * F1.
```

A couple of things about this rule. Notice that the assignment operator in Prolog is the operator **is**. The equals sign (=) is used as the equality operator. Also notice that new variables are always used on the left hand side of the **is** operator. To say **N is N - 1** makes no sense. It is a query that cannot be satisfied as it attempts to bind **N** to a new value **N - 1**. This is not possible. **N** is not **N - 1**.

The way this rule works is

1. Compute the value of $n - 1$.
2. Compute the factorial of $n - 1$.
3. Compute the factorial of n ($n \times n - 1$).

Eventually the recursion will stop when **N** is zero because the first factorial rule is **fact(0,1)**. At this time the recursion unwinds and produces the factorial. See if you can trace the operation of the Prolog factorial functor.

Representing How a Toaster Works in Prolog

To conclude my brief Prolog tutorial, I will show how a language like Prolog can be used to represent (simulate) the operation of a toaster. Part of this discussion consists of the representation, and the other part is a discussion of the engine that will interpret the representation.

My purpose in this section is to show how to represent the inner workings of a toaster using Prolog as the language to accomplish this. More generally though, we are building a model of the toaster. Eventually when we create the engine to make the toaster work, the model will operate just as a real toaster would operate. So in addition to showing the representation in Prolog, I will also be showing some of the model-building process.

To begin, I'll list the components of the toaster.

```
carriage
colorControlKnob
colorControlLever
heating element
keeper
keeperRelease
```

CHAPTER 4

```
keeperReleaseSwitch
keeperReleaseSwitchSpring
latch
lifterArm
liftKnob
liftLever
mainSwitch
piston
slideRod
thermostat
```

Next we want to discover the relationships between toaster components. I say discover because it is important to understand the relationships that make the toaster work. This aspect of creating the model, namely teasing out information about relationships is called **knowledge engineering**. Knowledge engineering is the process of representing knowledge in a computational system. Listed next are some of the relationships between toaster components. The relationships are italicized.

```
thermostat activates keeperReleaseSwitch
keeper holds latch
keeperRelease moves keeper
heatingElement affects thermostat
piston moves lifterArm
mainSwitch is part of carriage
lifterArm moves slideAssembly
slideAssembly moves carriage
liftKnob moves liftLever
liftLever moves slideAssembly
latch is a part of slideAssembly
```

If the set of relationships are sufficient for the purpose of modeling the toaster, it should be possible to use the relationships to describe the operation of the toaster. I will tackle this description in English first and defer the description using the relationship for a second refinement of this description.

@T = 1

Pushing down the lift knob moves the lift lever down. When the lift lever moves down, the slide assembly moves down. As the slide assembly moves down, the latch moves down with the slide assembly. When the slide assembly reaches its lower limit of travel, the latch engages with the keeper.

As the slide assembly moves down, the carriage moves down also. As the carriage moves down, the main switch moves down. At the lower limit of the carriage's travel, power is supplied to the main switch.

As the slide assembly moves down, the lifter arm moves down. When the lifter arm moves down, the piston is compressed.

@T = 2

With power supplied to the main switch, power is supplied to the heating elements. When power is supplied to the heating elements, the temperature of the elements begins to rise.

As the temperature of the heating elements rises, the thermostat deflects in the direction of the keeper release switch.

@T = 3

When the thermostat contacts the keeper release switch, the keeper release is activated. As the keeper release is activated, it moves the keeper in the release direction.

When the thermostat contacts the keeper release switch, the keeper release is activated. As the keeper release is activated, it moves the keeper in the release direction.

When the keeper is moved in the release direction, the latch is released. As the latch is released, the piston force is released. As the piston force is released, the lifter arm is moved in the up direction.

The lifter arm, moving in the up direction, pushes the slide assembly in the up direction. The slide assembly, moving in the up direction, pushes the carriage in the up direction.

When the carriage reaches the limit of its upper movement, the carriage stops moving. At the carriage's top movement limit, power is removed from the main switch. When power is removed from the main switch, the heating elements are inactivated.

The complexity of the representation depends on the requirements of granularity of the representation. For example, one way to represent the thermostat is as a series of discrete states, one state for its *at rest* or inactive state and the other for the activated state when the thermostat effects the keeper release switch. On the other hand, we might want to represent the operation of the thermostat as a function of the temperature being read by the thermostat. In the case of the toaster, we could devise a function for the distance between the thermostat and the keeper release switch based on the power applied to the toaster and the time that the heating elements remain on. For the sake of brevity and simplicity, I will use the discrete state representation. This could be changed if a more sophisticated approach is required in the simulation.

With this in mind, let's start working out more of the features of the model. We have a list of components and an English description of the operation of the toaster. To represent the operation of the toaster, we need to describe the behavior of the various components of the toaster. We can do this by associating with each component the **states** the components can achieve. A **state** is a particular position, orientation, or otherwise descriptive characteristic of the component that will change with the operation of the toaster. I will create a table listing each component and its associated state information. I'll begin the table with the carriage.

The **carriage** has two states at first glance. It can be in the down position or the up position. I will name these states **carriageDown** and **carriageUp** respectively. Thinking about this more, the **carriage** must travel to the up position and to the down position. These states will be called **carriageMovingDown** and **carriageMovingUp**. The first row of the component/state table is complete.

Component	State(s)
carriage	carriageDown
	carriageUp
	carriageMovingDown
	carriageMovingUp

Other components share in the movement kind of states. In fact, anything attached to the **carriage** will move in the same way as the carriage. An example of a component like this is the **lifterArm**.

Component	State(s)
carriage	carriageDown
	carriageUp
	carriageMovingDown
	carriageMovingUp
lifterArm	lifterArmDown
	lifterArmMovingDown
	lifterArmUp
	lifterArmMovingUp

A different kind of component is the **latch**. The **latch** has two states. When the **carriage** is in the down position, it is held down by the latch engaged in the keeper. When the **carriage** is up, the **latch** is disengaged. This is shown in the third row of the component state table

Component	State(s)
carriage	carriageDown
	carriageUp
	carriageMovingDown
	carriageMovingUp
lifterArm	lifterArmDown
	lifterArmMovingDown
	lifterArmUp
	lifterArmMovingUp
latch	engagedInKeepr
	disengagedInKeeper

I'll now fill in the remainder of this table. All of the entries were derived in a manner similar to deriving the states for the **carriage**, **lifterArm**, and **latch**.

Component	State(s)
carriage	carriageDown
	carriageUp
	carriageMovingDown
	carriageMovingUp
lifterArm	lifterArmDown
	lifterArmMovingDown
	lifterArmUp
	lifterArmMovingUp
latch	engagedInKeeper
	disengagedInKeeper
keeper	engaged
	disengaged
keeperRelease	off
	on
liftKnob	liftKnobUp
	liftKnobMovingUp
	liftKnobDown
	liftKnobMovingDown
liftLever	liftLeverUp
	liftLeverMovingUp
	liftLeverDown
	liftLeverMovingDown
heatingElementState	heating
	cooling
	off
heatingElement	heat0
	heat1
	heat2
	heat3

Component	State(s)
	heat4
	heat5
thermostat	deflect0
	deflect1
	deflect2
	deflect3
	deflect4
	deflect5
mainSwitch	upAndOff
	downAndOn
piston	compressed
	decompressed
colorControlKnob	color0
	color1
	color2
	color3
	color4
	color5
colorControlLever	color0
	color1
	color2
	color3
	color4
	color5
keeperReleaseSwitch	position0
	position1
	position2
	position3
	position4
	position5
	on
	off

Deriving Rules for the Operation of the Toaster

In this discussion of tools and how they might be used for creating intelligent tutoring systems, one step remains in the representation of the toaster. This step involves creating a series of rules that when completed, describe how the toaster operates. These rules and everything prior in this discussion constitute the model of the toaster. Although I might proceed directly to a discussion of the rules, I will first describe a tool for creating and running systems of rules.

Expert Systems and Expert System Languages

One of the real success stories of the field of artificial intelligence is the story of expert systems. If the field of artificial intelligence can point to any truly notable developments in its life, expert systems stand alone in this regard. Why is this so?

There are two reasons. First, expert systems are one of the few widespread examples of AI technology. Second, they represent an important and practical application of this technology. One would be hard put to find other examples of AI technology that have made as significant inroads to traditional systems as expert systems have made.

So why are these systems so prevalent and important? To begin, expert systems are an attempt to capture knowledge in an operational form. In the early 1980s when expert systems became a major part of artificial intelligence, it was apparent there needed to be a way to capture and codify expert decision-making knowledge. This kind of knowledge, expert knowledge, is extremely valuable because of the typically small number of experts in any one domain and because expert knowledge is typically accumulated through experience. Because there is a potential for losing expert knowledge over time (experts can die), a way to capture expert knowledge for perpetuity would certainly be beneficial to humanity in the long term. Expert systems are by no means panaceas for representing and capturing knowledge. To be sure, not all knowledge can be represented in this way. But as I said, expert systems are very useful.

What Is an Expert System?

An expert system encompasses two primary elements. The first of these is the expertise; the second is the system or engine processing the expertise. The system or engine processes expert system rules. Knowledge in the system is represented as a series of rules of predefined form. Conceptually, the engine and its related databases are shown in Figure 4.9.

In Figure 4.9, the expert system engine includes a pattern-matching device, short-term memory, and a knowledge base of rules. The engine provides the means to scan through the rules and short-term memory and, using pattern matching and conflict resolution, decide what to do.

The rules in an expert system make up its program but also make up its knowledge. Rules have two parts: an *antecedent* or *condition* and a *consequent* or *action*.

The **condition** of a rule consists of one or more tests. A **test** examines short-term memory and can verify or deny some specified condition. For example, suppose we want to know the relationship between several blocks.

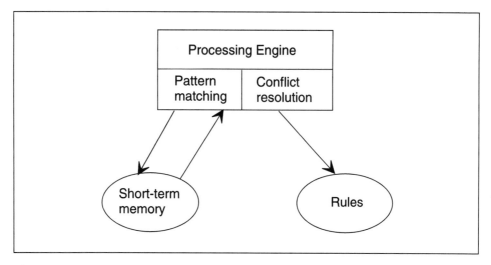

Figure 4.9 Expert system conceptual diagram.

Figure 4.10 A stack of blocks.

In short-term memory, we can represent the stack of blocks shown in Figure 4.10 as

ontop(block(a),block(b))
ontop(block(b),block(c))

A test could be formulated using a similar representation as

is(ontop(block(a),block(b)))

For this example, block *a* is on top of block *b* and the result of the test would be true.

If this test is embodied into a rule as the only condition in that rule, the resulting rule might look something like

if (if(ontop(block(a),block(b))),do something)

which brings the discussion to the other part of a rule, the **consequent** or **action** of the rule.

When the condition of a rule is true (all of its tests are true) then we say in expert system terminology that rule can **fire** or the rule can be **fired**. This means the consequent(s) or action(s) of a rule can be executed by the engine. Most typically, the consequent or action of a rule will make changes to short-term memory. Three kinds of changes are possible. Something can be added to short-term memory, something can be deleted from short-term memory, or some element of short-term memory can be modified. These three possibilities are depicted in Figure 4.11.

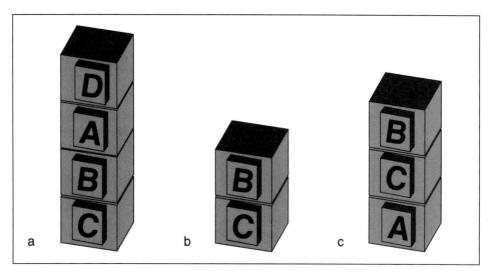

Figure 4.11 (a) Adding an element to short-term memory. (b) Deleting an element from short-term memory. (c) Modifying the contents of short-term memory.

Besides modifying short-term memory, rules may accomplish other tasks such as displaying information to a user of the system or requesting information from the user of the expert system, accessing other sources of information (performing I/O), and altering the way that the engine processes rules and data.

The basic algorithm for processing rules in an expert system is as follows:

while there are rules to fire do

begin

1. find one or more rules whose conditions are true (these are rules to be potentially fired)
2. if there is more than one rule that can be fired, select the best rule to fire
3. fire the rule

end

Step 1 is called the matching or pattern-matching phase of engine operation. It is called this because the condition represents a pattern to be matched against short-term memory. When a pattern (condition) in a rule matches some contents of short-term memory, the rule becomes a candidate to fire.

The second step, called **conflict resolution**, is the step when more than a single rule can be potentially fired and one rule is chosen to fire. Conflict resolution can be implemented in many ways. In one approach to selecting a rule to fire, the rules are ordered and maintained in the order in which they are to be fired. The first candidate in this order to be fired is fired when a conflict needs to be resolved. In another implementation, probabilities are used to select the best rule to fire—which rule, according to the probabilities, would yield the best results.

Once a rule is selected, it can be fired. This is step 3 of the operation of the engine. The engine will repeat this process until either (a) there are no more rules to be fired because no more rule conditions are true, or (b) the engine is explicitly halted by an action that stops the engine.

In a traditional expert system, a rule can only be fired once. Once fired, it can never be selected again as one potentially "fireable." Of course, it may be necessary to restore a rule's candidacy for firing for some reason. This might be handled by a specialized action included for this purpose.

Like Prolog, expert systems are tools for creating the intelligent aspects of multimedia systems. Expert systems can readily be created in languages like Prolog and LISP. There are also expert system shells that provide the engines without any rules. You supply the rules that are the expert knowledge in the system. To conclude this section, I will describe a simple language and environment for creating expert systems. The language is called Small-X.

A Small-X Tutorial

The Small-X language was designed as a means of constructing prototype expert systems. The language consists of a means of specifying a sequence of rules that will manipulate short-term memory.

In Small-X short-term memory can contain symbols, variables, numbers, strings, and simple lists. These short-term memory elements (STMEs) can be used to represent a multitude of different things. STMEs can be added to and removed from short-term memory and also modified in short-term memory. The basic form of a Small-X rule is

rule name if *conditions* [*rule value*] then *actions*

Rules may be given names. This is useful if you want to remember the purpose of a rule through its name or if you want to annotate the rule in some way. Even if you don't assign a name, a rule will be assigned a name.

A condition in a Small-X rule consists of one or more tests. In Small-X two types of tests can be specified. In one kind of test, you can check to see if a data object (symbol, integer, string, or list) is present in short-term memory. The other type of test, called a variable test, allows the value of a variable in short-term memory to be checked.

To test whether a data object is present in short-term memory, the condition is specified as an **IN-MEMORY** test. The condition is written as

```
IF IN-MEMORY(object) THEN ...
```

The object inside of the parentheses can be a

    real number

    integer

    string

    symbol

    variable

    list

    choice

Examples of these are:

```
IN-MEMORY(12.3)
IN-MEMORY(1)
IN-MEMORY('a string')
IN-MEMORY(cat)
```

```
IN-MEMORY(#sum)
IN-MEMORY([2 4 6])
```

It is also possible to determine if a data object is not in short-term memory. This is accomplished by prepending the keyword **NOT** to the condition as follows:

```
IF NOT IN-MEMORY(object)
```

The action part of a rule consists of one or more actions. Small-X actions support the capability to modify short-term memory and also other general functions like input and output, and variable assignment. A list of Small-X actions are shown in Table 4.1.

Rules to Make a Toaster Work

Small-X gives us a straightforward means to create a system of rules and test to see how those rules function. We will use Small-X to represent the operation of the toaster.

Table 4.1 Table of Small-X Actions

Action	Description
add	Add an object to short-term memory
remove	Remove an object from short-term memory
read	Read data into short-term memory
write	Write data from short-term memory
compute	Do simple short-term memory calculations
bind	Assign values to variables
unbind	Deassign a variable
halt	Stop the expert system engine
run	Run an external DOS program
reset	Reset a rule so it can be fired again
open	Open an external file
close	Close an external file
fire	Execute the actions of a rule directly
restrict	Restrict values that a variable can be assigned
modify	Modify a rule's conditional value

To begin formulating the necessary rules, I will list the variables we will need in the rules. The variables come directly from the toaster model I described earlier.

```
#carriage              #lifterArm           #mainSwitch
#latch                 #keeper              #piston
#keeperRelease         #liftKnob            #colorControlKnob
#liftLever             #heatingElement      #heatingElementState
#colorControlLevel     #thermostat          #slideAssembly
#keeperReleaseSwitch   #makeToast           #colorOfToast
```

To begin the simulation, we will have a rule that announces the system of rules. To accomplish this, we will make a rule whose condition will be the first one that is trivially true.

Program Listing 4.4 Introductory rule.

```
[intro] if not in-memory(dummy) then
{
       write clear
       write 'Toaster Simulation'
       write new-line
       write new-line
}
```

The symbol dummy will never be added to short-term memory; therefore, if this rule is the first of all of the rules, it will be the first one fired.

To make the toast, the lift knob is pushed down. To simulate the pushing down of the lift knob, we use a rule that asks if the user wants to make toast.

```
[makeToast] if not in-memory(#makeToast) then
            read 'Do you want to make toast?' #makeToast
```

If the user does not want to make toast, then there is no reason to run the simulation, so the inference engine should be halted.

```
[haltSimulation] if #makeToast = no then halt
```

To make toast, users will have to select the color of the toast. They can select one of light, medium light, medium, medium dark, or dark. The color knob will be set to the selected color.

```
[selectColor] if not in-memory(#colorOfToast) then
    read 'What color toast do you want?'
        #colorOfToast
```

Colors that can be entered are the ones listed. The color selection needs to be translated into settings for the components of the toaster.

```
[setColor1] if #colorOfToast = light then
    bind #colorControlKnob color1
[setColor2] if #colorOfToast = mediumLight then
    bind #colorControlKnob color2
[setColor3] if #colorOfToast = medium then
    bind #colorControlKnob color3
[setColor4] if #colorOfToast = mediumDark then
    bind #colorControlKnob color4
[setColor5] if #colorOfToast = dark then
    bind #colorControlKnob color5
```

When the color knob is set, the color lever follows. Rules for setting the color lever follow.

```
[setCCL1] if #colorControlKnob = color1 then
    bind #colorControlLever color1
[setCCL2] if #colorControlKnob = color2 then
    bind #colorControlLever color2
[setCCL3] if #colorControlKnob = color3 then
    bind #colorControlLever color3
[setCCL4] if #colorControlKnob = color4 then
    bind #colorControlLever color4
[setCCL5] if #colorControlKnob = color5 then
    bind #colorControlLever color5
```

If the user chooses to make toast, then the simulation can begin. When the simulation begins, variable initializations will occur, followed by the first step of the simulation—the lift knob begins moving down.

```
[start] if #makeToast = yes then
{
    bind #keeper disengaged
    bind #keeperRelease on
    bind #latch disenagagedIn Keeper
    bind #mainSwitch upAndOff
    bind #keeperReleaseSwitch position0
```

```
        bind #heatingElementState cool
        bind #heatingElement heat0
bind #liftKnob liftKnobMovingDown
}
```

When the lift knob moves down, the lift lever moves down with it.

```
[llmoveDown] if #liftKnob = liftKnobMovingDown then
        bind #liftLever liftLeverMovingDown
```

Several other elements move down with this motion. The following rules take care of this motion.

```
[cmoveDown] if #liftLever = liftLeverMovingDown then
        bind #carriage carriageMovingDown
[laMoveDown] if #liftLever = liftLeverMovingDown
        then bind #lifterArm lifterArmMovingDown
```

Eventually the lifter knob, lifter lever, and so on, will all reach the lower limit of their travel. All of the components in the moving down state will eventually reach the down state as specified in the next few rules.

```
[liftKnobDown] if #liftKnob = liftKnobMovingDown
        then bind #liftKnob liftKnobDown
[liftLeverDown] if #liftLever = liftLeverMovingDown
        then bind #liftLever liftLeverDown
[carriageDown] if #carriage = carriageMovingDown
        then bind #carriage carriageDown
[lifterArmDown] if #lifterArm = lifterArmMovingDown
        then bind #lifterArm lifterArmDown
```

Once the carriage is down, the keeper engages the latch to hold the carriage down. The piston becomes compressed (or in the case of a spring, it expands to its potential force state). The piston or spring will pull the carriage up when the toasting process is complete. When the carriage reaches its lower limit of travel, power is applied to the heating elements by way of the main switch.

```
[carriageDownActions] if #carriage = carriageDown
then {
        bind #piston compressed
        bind #latch engagedInKeeper
        bind #keeperRelease off
```

```
          bind #keeper engaged
          bind #mainSwitch downAndOn
          bind #heatingElement heat0
          bind #heatingElementState heating
}
```

With power applied to the heating elements, the elements will begin to warm.

```
[heat01] if #heatingElement = heat0 then
         bind #heatingElement heat1
```

When the temperature of the heating element changes, the thermostat is deflected. Likewise, all of the components related to the thermostat are also affected.

```
[thermostat01] if #heatingElement = heat1 and
               #heatingElementState = heating
         then bind #thermostat deflect1
```

The deflection of the thermostat moves the keeper release switch toward the color setting knob. The color setting knob controls the distance between the keeper release switch and the thermostat. Eventually the thermostat will push the keeper release switch activating the keeper release. When this occurs depends on the thermostat and the setting of the keeper release switch. The switch is set to the on position.

```
[krs1] if #thermostat = deflect1 and
           #keeperReleaseSwitch = position1
       then bind #keeperReleaseSwitch on
[krs2] if #thermostat = deflect2 and
           #keeperReleaseSwitch = position2
       then bind #keeperReleaseSwitch on
[krs3] if #thermostat = deflect3 and
           #keeperReleaseSwitch = position3
       then bind #keeperReleaseSwitch on
[krs4] if #thermostat = deflect4 and
           #keeperReleaseSwitch = position4
       then bind #keeperReleaseSwitch on
[krs5] if #thermostat = deflect5 and
           #keeperReleaseSwitch = position5
       then bind #keeperReleaseSwitch on
```

Once the keeper release switch is set to the on state, the release sequence begins. The rules for this appear next (before any additional rules for heating element temperature increase) to turn off the toaster at the soonest possible time when the toast reaches the desired color.

If the keeper release switch is turned on, the keeper release will turn on.

```
[krOn] if #keeperReleaseSwitch = on then
        bind #keeperRelease on
```

When the keeper release turns on, the latch becomes disengaged, allowing the piston to push the carriage to the up position.

```
[releaseLatch] if #keeperRelease = on then
        bind #latch disengagedInKeeper
[laMovingUp] if #latch = disengagedInKeeper and
        #piston = compressed
    then bind #lifterArm lifterArmMovingUp
[carriageMovingUp] if #lifterArm = lifterArmMovingUp
    then bind #carriage carriageMovingUp
```

Once the carriage begins to move up, the main power switch is turned off, power is removed from the elements, and they begin to cool. As they begin to cool, the thermostat returns to its original position.

```
[mainSwitchOff] if #carriage = carriageMovingUp then
{
        bind #mainSwitch mainSwitchOff
        bind #heatingElementState cooling
}
[lifterArmUp] if #liftArm = lifterArmMovingUp then
        bind #liftArm lifterArmUp
[carriageUp] if #liftArm = liftArmUp then
        bind #carriage carriageUp
```

The next sequence of rules takes care of cooling down the heating elements and resetting the deflection of the thermostat.

```
[he54] if #mainSwitch = mainSwitchOff and
        #heatingElement = heat5 and
        #heatingElementState = cooling then
    bind #heatingElement heat4
[t54] if #heatingElement = heat4 and
        #heatingElementState = cooling then
    bind #thermostat deflect4
```

```
[he43] if #mainSwitch = mainSwitchOff and
          #heatingElement = heat4 and
          #heatingElementState = cooling then
    bind #heatingElement heat3
[t43] if #heatingElement = heat3 and
          #heatingElementState = cooling then
    bind #thermostat deflect3
[he32] if #mainSwitch = mainSwitchOff and
          #heatingElement = heat3 and
          #heatingElementState = cooling then
    bind #heatingElement heat2
[t32] if #heatingElement = heat2 and
          #heatingElementState = cooling then
    bind #thermostat deflect2
[he21] if #mainSwitch = mainSwitchOff and
          #heatingElement = heat2 and
          #heatingElementState = cooling then
    bind #heatingElement heat1
[t21] if #heatingElement = heat1 and
          #heatingElementState = cooling then
    bind #thermostat deflect1
[he10] if #mainSwitch = mainSwitchOff and
          #heatingElement = heat1 and
          #heatingElementState = cooling then
    bind #heatingElement heat0
[t10] if #heatingElement = heat0 and
          #heatingElementState = cooling then
    bind #thermostat deflect0
```

When the carriage is in the up position, the toast is finished.

```
[toastFinished] if #carriage = carriageUp and
          #heatingElementState = cooling
    then bind #toast toastFinished
```

Once the heating element reaches **heat0**, the heating element is finished cooling.

```
[setStateOff] if #heatingElement = heat0 and
          #heatingElementState = cooling
    then bind #heatingElementState off
```

Now, the full cycle of actions to toast has been completed. All that remains is to complete the rules that take care of element heating. We deferred these until now so that the elements would not overheat before the toast was finished.

```
[he12] if #heatingElement = heat1 and
          #heatingElementState = heating then
       bind #heatingElement heat2
[t12]  if #heatingElementState = heating and
          #heatingElement = heat2 and
          #thermostat = deflect1 then
       bind #thermostat deflect2
[he23] if #heatingElement = heat2 and
          #heatingElementState = heating then
       bind #heatingElement heat3
[t23]  if #heatingElementState = heating and
          #heatingElement = heat3 and
          #thermostat = deflect2 then
       bind #thermostat deflect3
[he34] if #heatingElement = heat3 and
          #heatingElementState = heating then
       bind #heatingElement heat4
[t34]  if #heatingElementState = heating and
          #heatingElement = heat4 and
          #thermostat = deflect3 then
       bind #thermostat deflect4
[he45] if #heatingElement = heat4 and
          #heatingElementState = heating then
       bind #heatingElement heat5
[t45]  if #heatingElementState = heating and
          #heatingElement = heat5 and
          #thermostat = deflect4 then
       bind #thermostat deflect5
```

Chapter Summary

Tools for creating artificially intelligent applications consist of programming languages that support the development of symbolic applications. A symbolic application is a computer program that uses symbols (sequences of characters) as the basic means of representation. Symbolic computing represented a major step forward in computer use because it meant that computers could be something else besides huge number mills.

The LISP programming language, originally conceived of by John McCarthy, was one of the earliest languages for creating intelligent computer programs. LISP is a symbolic programming language because its most basic unit of data is the symbol. In LISP, symbols can be composed into lists and lists can be part of other lists. Structures of great complexity can be formulated using LISP lists. One of the most remarkable characteristics of the LISP programming language is its uniformity. Both data and program instructions share exactly the same notation. This means that a LISP program can manipulate itself. The idea of a self-modifying program was made legitimate by the LISP programming language.

Logic is used as a means to reason about the real world, and a second tool for creating intelligent applications is the Prolog programming language. Like LISP, the Prolog programming language manipulates symbols. Unlike LISP, Prolog is not a procedural language. Prolog accomplishes tasks by automatically proving statements made about collections of statements.

Prolog is an excellent tool for developing programs that can process and act upon new languages. It is a relatively simple matter in Prolog to construct a program to parse simple statements in the English language.

Another widely used class of tools for creating intelligent applications are expert system shells. An expert system is a computer program that mimics the reasoning processes of an expert. For example, we could have an expert system that can diagnose heart disease problems. Given the proper information such a system would be able to diagnose disease in the same way as an expert cardiologist would. An expert system consists of a means to reason and the knowledge. Without the knowledge, the reasoning engine by itself is called an expert system shell.

An expert system shell called Small-X is easy to learn and use, and facilitates the creation of small expert systems. By specifying a series of rules it is possible to construct models. For example, using Small-X we were able to construct a model that would simulate the operation of a toaster.

Suggested Reading

Abelson, Harold, Sussman, Gerald, and Sussman, Julie, *Structure and Interpretation of Computer Programs*, New York: McGraw-Hill, 1987.

Another book I recommend. This book teaches programming using the LISP language as a basis.

Clocksin, W., and Mellish, C., *Programming in Prolog*, New York: Springer-Verlag, 1981.

The Prolog Bible. This book is both a good introduction to the Prolog language and a good reference for the language. Most Prolog implementations use the definitions of the language contained in this book.

If you are interested in understanding how languages like Prolog evolved, read the following article by Alain Colmerauer and Phillipe Roussel. *The Proceedings of the History of Programming Languages Conference (HOPL-II),* in ACM Sigplan Notices Volume 28, Number 3, March 1993: *ACM*, New York.

Harmon, Paul, and King, David, *Expert Systems*, New York: John Wiley and Sons, Inc., 1985.

A very good introduction to expert systems. Although somewhat dated, this text gives an excellent overview of the technology and how it works.

Hayes-Roth, Frederick, Waterman, Donald, and Lenat, Douglas, *Building Expert Systems,* Reading, MA: Addison-Wesley, 1983.

A manual for creating expert systems.

McCorduck, Pamela, *Machines Who Think*, San Francisco: W. H. Freeman & Co., 1979.

A wonderful introduction to the history and people of artificial intelligence. Upon reading this book one gains a great insight into how and why the field of artificial intelligence evolved from its beginnings in the 1940s.

Steele, Guy, *Common LISP*, Bedford, MA: Digital Press, 1990.

This book should not be read by anyone faint of heart. This is the gospel according to LISP. It describes a function, statement, and nuance of the Common LISP language.

Winston, Patrick, *LISP,* Reading, MA: Addison-Wesley, 1984

A somewhat gentler introduction to LISP and its artificial intelligence.

CHAPTER 5

Knowledge Representation

Introduction

Let's suppose we have the amazing miniaturization machine that Isaac Asimov envisioned in the science fiction novel *Fantastic Voyage*, and let's suppose we could travel in a miniaturized state and see what the inside of our brain looked like and specifically see what the knowledge stored in our brains looked like. What would we see? What would it look like? If we could do this we might have a key to exactly how we could represent knowledge in a computer and also use that knowledge in programs we write, but there are some problems with this approach to figuring out what a brain does to represent knowledge.

Biological knowledge is stored in a much different way than digital knowledge, so ultimately whatever means of representation is used may not be appropriate for a digital computer. Of course a biological computer is another story, and this is what genetic programming and molecular automata are all about.

This introduction only scratches the surface of what knowledge representation is about. My claim (or rule) is this:

> If you want to make computers do intelligent things you need a way to represent knowledge and you need programs to operate on the knowledge.

The way people figure out how to represent knowledge is by empirical observation in terms of the problem-solving activities and other intelligent activities people do. Which brings me to the central purpose of this chapter—how can we represent knowledge to make intelligent systems?

Many Approaches for Many Reasons

What is the knowledge representation standard? This question is the same as, "What is the light bulb standard?" And the answer to both questions is none! So we can't say, *"This is the way that knowledge can be represented."*

Because there are so many approaches for as many reasons, we have a dilemma. Which one or two approaches do we use? How do we select a representation scheme? What criteria do we use? Even this decision process is not one that is clear cut. Whichever representation we choose will have positive and negative attributes that should be considered when selecting a representation. All this means is that (1) we will make a selection, and (2) others may be appropriate for your application.

Symbolic Representations

All the representations have one characteristic in common. They are *symbolic*. They use symbols as the main means to represent knowledge. A symbol can be literally anything that has a meaning defined in some context. In terms of knowledge representations, the most common kind of symbols are strings of letters, typically those that form words. In the context of the representation, the symbols will, be assigned meaning and be the primary entity of representation. Of course there is more to the story than just symbols.

---

*This sentence is written in italics meaning that some god of knowledge representation proclaimed what it will be. And in this case we cannot make this statement, since no god of knowledge representation has yet been recognized.

Semantic Networks

Introduction to Semantic Networks

Perhaps one of the most universal, widely known, and widely used knowledge representations is the semantic network. Semantic networks have evolved over the years to meet the demands of knowledge representation tasks, but for the most part the details that define semantic networks remain fundamentally the same.

Semantic networks are quite old in fact. John Sowa, in his book, *Principles of Semantic Networks*, describes the Tree of Porphyry. Porphyry was a Greek philosopher in the third century A.D. In the tree of Porphyry, a tree diagram is used to clarify and depict the relationships of Aristotle's categories. The tree is shown in Figure 5.1.

All of the features in modern semantic networks can be found in the Tree of Porphyry. There are a series of categories representing a most general category, SUBSTANCE, and more specific categories, BODY, LIVING, ..., HUMAN. An attribute is attached to each of the categories. SUBSTANCEs, for example, can be material (a kind of substance) or immaterial (another kind of substance). At the bottom of the tree are instances of a category. Plato, Socrates, and Aristotle are all individuals of the category HUMAN.

Semantic networks can be represented in many different ways. We could represent the relationships expressed in a semantic network in a formulalike notation. We could represent that an instance of HUMAN is Socrates with the formula,

HUMAN(Socrates).

The most common representation of a semantic network is in the form of a graph. A graph is a two-dimensional way of representing various things. Three kinds of entities make up a graph of a semantic network: nodes, edges, and labels.

A node is represented in a graph as an ellipse. Nodes are used to represent concepts in the graph. In the context of the Tree of Porphyry, SUBSTANCE, BODY, HUMAN, and so on, are examples of nodes in a graph. To denote a specific node, the node is labeled with a symbol.

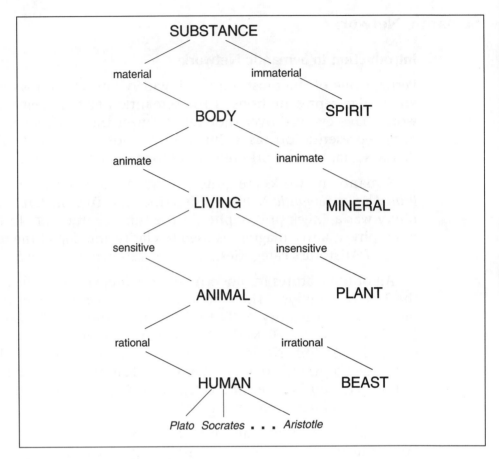

Figure 5.1 Tree of Porphyry.

To make the graph meaningful, nodes are connected with edges. An edge connects two nodes and is also labeled. An edge denotes a relationship between the nodes it connects. A relationship, an edge, can be directed or nondirected. If an edge is directed, then the relationship is a one-way relationship. For example, Plato is an instance of a HUMAN represented by the graph shown in Figure 5.2.

The relationship represented in this simple graph is directed. It states, an instance of a HUMAN is Plato, but it does not say the opposite, namely, a HUMAN is an instance of a Plato.

It is possible to use any symbols to label the edges of a graph representing a semantic net. In the development of semantic networks,

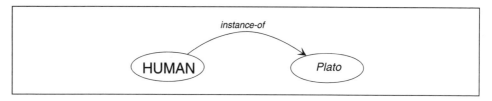

Figure 5.2 Example of a directed edge.

certain kinds of relationships have become standard. In the Tree of Porphyry, several of these standard relationships are represented. One of these relationships goes by different names, but examples of this relationship include *kind-of*, *is-a*, and *subtype-of*. We can say that a BODY is a *kind-of* SUBSTANCE or a BODY is a *subtype-of* SUBSTANCE.

Another kind of relationship shown in the Tree of Porphyry is the *instance-of* relationship. This relationship is used to connect examples or objects of a certain category to the category.

A very useful relationship is the *part-of* relationship. When we want to use a semantic network to represent an object and what it is made of, we can use the *part-of* relationship. For example, if we want to describe the make up of an automobile, we could use the *part-of* relationship as shown in the semantic network of Figure 5.3.

The *part-of* relationship is one of a family of related relationships. Included in this family are the relationships *connected-to*, which denotes the *part-of* relationship where parts are joined in some way, and *made-of*. When one concept is related to another by way of *made-of*, the relationship refers to the condition that one concept is inseparably part of another. For example, we can say that

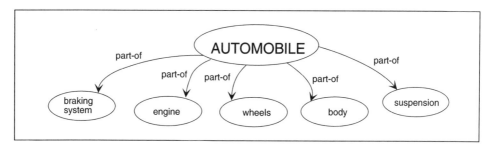

Figure 5.3 Semantic network representing an automobile and its parts.

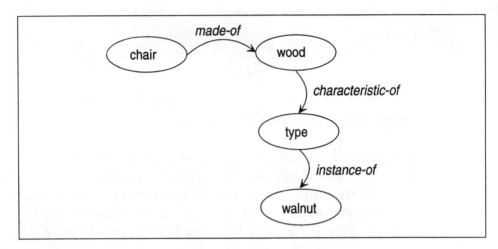

Figure 5.4 Semantic network representing a chair, what it is made of, and how a value of an attribute is represented.

a birthday cake is made of flour, yeast, sugar, chocolate, and icing. Once the cake is formed, it is not possible to return it to the components from which it was made.

Another relationship used the Tree of Porphyry: The *attribute-of* or *characteristics-of* relationship. This relationship is used to attach a node to another that represents a characteristic of the node. Let's take a moment to consider how this works. Suppose we have a semantic network describing a chair and the wood the chair is made of. Figure 5.4 shows an example of a semantic network describing the chair. It is important to distinguish the network shown in Figure 5.4 from the one in Figure 5.5.

In the semantic network shown in Figure 5.5, walnut is not the characteristic of wood but an instance of the characteristic. The chair can be made of different kinds of wood, so there needs to be some way to account for this in the network. Figure 5.4 shows the way to correctly represent a characteristic.

The difference between an instance and a class is very important. Instances refer to real world or specific examples of entities that are represented in the semantic. Representing a specific example of a concept represented in a semantic network, is accomplished by using an *instance-of* relationship.

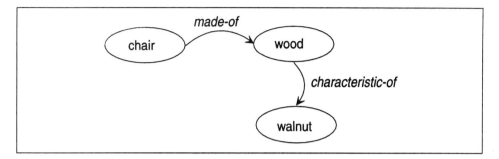

Figure 5.5 Semantic network representing a chair, but incorrectly representing the characteristic of the chair.

The relationships I have described so far are just the start of a set of useful relationships for semantic networks. In reality, when creating a semantic network, relationships are defined according to how the semantic network will be used. Perhaps the most important concept to keep in mind when creating a semantic network is to maintain consistency in what is being represented. Nodes should represent the same kinds of elements, and so should the relationships between nodes. If consistency is not maintained in its design, using the semantic network might prove to be very difficult.

Using Semantic Networks

Consider the semantic network of the toaster. It is shown in Figure 5.6. This semantic network represents several different kinds of relationships. These relationships are described in Table 5.1.

The definition of relationships is the key to how the semantic network can be used. The toaster semantic network was designed to simulate the workings of a toaster. How can we use the semantic network for this?

The power of the semantic network lies in its ability to carry out the reasoning operation called **inference**. Inference is an important part of human cognition. Some scientists believe it is a key reasoning mechanism. Consider the following situation.

While driving to work in the morning, you are listening to the morning travel report. Your commute is about 40 minutes, and it is

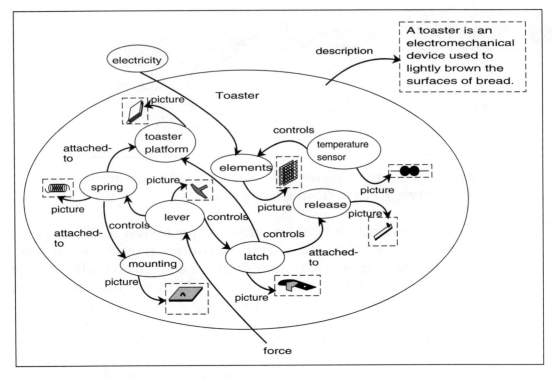

Figure 5.6 Semantic network for the toaster.

Table 5.1 Description of Relationships in the Toaster Semantic Network

Semantic Network Relationship	Description
Attached-to	Like the part-of relationship, except it specifies that one part is physically connected to another part. A point of attachment may be specified with this relationship.
Controls	A controls relationship is used when we want to show that when two controls are attached, one can control the other. The kind of control is included in the specification of this relationship.
Picture	This relationship connects a node to a graphic depiction of the node.

now about 8:00 A.M. You have an important meeting at 9:00 A.M, and you can't be late for the meeting. In the traffic report you hear there is an accident along the way of your current route, and there is a possible delay of as much as 30 minutes along this route. If you continue along the current route you will be late for your meeting (inference 1). It is important to be on time for that meeting, and if there is a delay caused by traffic, then seeking an alternate route would be a good idea (inference 2). If you need to seek an alternate route and there is a time limit, then consider an alternate route that meets the time requirements (inference 3).

Reasoning sequences like this, often subconscious and more complex, are typical of our reasoning process. This example shows what inference is all about. More generally, inference uses rules like,

if A then B
if B then C
If C then Y

.
.
.

if Y then Z

In terms of our toaster diagram we could have something like

if A is connected to B and if B is connected to C then we can infer that A is connected to C through B

A semantic network can easily be used to represent rules like the ones shown above. Such rules can be derived or extracted from the semantic network by **traversing** the network. Traversing is one of the important operations that can be carried out on a semantic network. When a semantic network is traversed, a place to start the traversal is chosen. This starting place is a node in the network. From this node, traversal consists of following the links to other nodes.

For example, suppose the node **lever** is selected as the starting node of the traversal. From this node, we can travel via the *controls* relationship to the latch node. At the latch node, we can travel to the toast platform. Based on this brief traversal we can infer that the lever controls the toast platform. This inference shows the power of semantic networks and also one of the main problems that arises when using them.

There are two instances in this network where the lever controls the toaster platform. In the case I just described, where the lever controls the latch, which in turn controls the toaster platform, the control refers to the toaster platform being secured by the latch when the lever is used to pull the toaster platform down. The lever pulling the toaster platform down is the second instance of the controls relationship between the lever and the toaster platform, and the more direct of the two. Both instances result in control of the toaster platform, but each has its own specific kind of control. When traversing the network and finding more than one instance of the same relationship between two nodes, care must be taken to understand the precise meaning of each instance of the relationship.

So far the networks I have shown contain static textual information. Nodes and edges in the semantic network are labeled with symbols. For simplicity the semantic networks were annotated with information that does not change, but there is no reason why the nodes and edges cannot also be labeled with more complex information. One possibility is to label edges and/or nodes with program code. For example, an edge could be labeled with a logical test. The test could be used to allow or deny access to a node during a traversal process. If the result of a test is true, then a traversal to the connected node is permitted. Figure 5.7 shows a sample semantic network with an edge labeled with a test.

The types of node and edge labels that can be used to annotate a semantic network can become very complex. For example, arriving

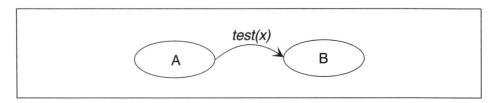

Figure 5.7 A part of a semantic network with an edge connecting two nodes labeled with a test.

at a node might cause a segment of code to be processed. The code could set variables, perform calculations, and access files.

Creating Your Own Semantic Networks

You usually create a semantic network for the purpose of creating a representation of a problem or process. Whether the entity being represented is conceptual (an idea) or concrete (a mechanism), the purpose of creating a semantic network–based representation is to be able to computationally manipulate this model.

To begin, it is important to consider exactly what is to be represented. If you want to represent a mechanism then you need to understand what part of that mechanism is going to be represented. Are individual components to be represented? Will the representation reflect the operation of the mechanism? These questions and others are also relevant for representing abstract entities.

The first step for creating a semantic network is to decide what you will be representing. The best way to do this is to make a list of the things you will represent. Suppose you want to represent a dictionary that will be part of a language tutoring system. In this dictionary you will want to represent the things contained in the following list.

word

part of speech for the word

sample sentences for the word

for verbs, various conjugations

definition

translation

In the semantic network I will design, the word will be the center of several nodes related to the word. Once you have this list, you then decide which of these things will be nodes and which will be edges connecting nodes. In the case of this dictionary, the nodes contain the data named by the edge. This may not be the case with other kinds of semantic networks. Figure 5.8 shows part of the dictionary semantic network.

218 CHAPTER 5

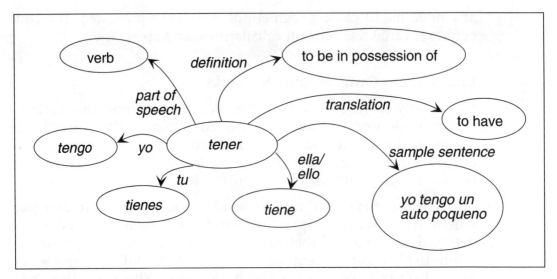

Figure 5.8 Semantic network dictionary entry for the Spanish verb *tener*.

I have already shown how a semantic network can be used for representing a mechanism (the toaster) and the more abstract dictionary entry semantic network. Semantic networks can also be used to represent taxonomies which are networks that represent how things are related to one another, and to represent processes.

A process can be represented by using nodes for steps or aspects of the process. For example, if a semantic network is being used to represent a manufacturing process, the nodes can denote each manufacturing step. Edges can be used to represent the means by which one manufacturing process step moves on to another step in the process.

Representing a Semantic Network

The next section describes a tool for creating semantic networks. This tool is a visual tool, so the construction of semantic networks is accomplished by placing nodes and connecting them with edges much as you would if you were to draw the semantic network on paper. This is the surface representation of a semantic network. How do you represent a semantic network programmatically?

node data	pointer to edge

Figure 5.9 Node structure.

To begin we will need two types of structures. One of these will be used to represent a node, the other an edge. A node will be represented with a structure containing two fields. One field will contain the data for the node and the other will be a pointer (or index) to an edge connector (another kind of structure). A node structure is shown in Figure 5.9.

An edge connector structure must serve three functions. First, it must connect a node to an adjacent node. Second, it may point to another edge connector structure and connect to another adjacent node, and third, it will contain the edge label for the edge. An edge connector structure is shown in Figure 5.10.

Together these structures can be used to represent arbitrarily complex semantic networks. In Figures 5.9 and 5.10, the data portions of the structures (node data and edge label) can also be complex structures. These portions of the structures can be pointers to other structures or pointers to code. To demonstrate how these structures are used to create a computational representation of a semantic network Figure 5.11 shows a representation of the dictionary entry semantic network.

A Tool for Creating Semantic Networks

To get you started with knowledge representation, I have created a tool that can be used to construct semantic networks. At the very least, this tool shows you (1) what is necessary to construct a tool for this purpose, (2) how this tool can be built, and (3) how to use

pointer to adjacent node	pointer to edge connector	edge label

Figure 5.10 Edge connector structure.

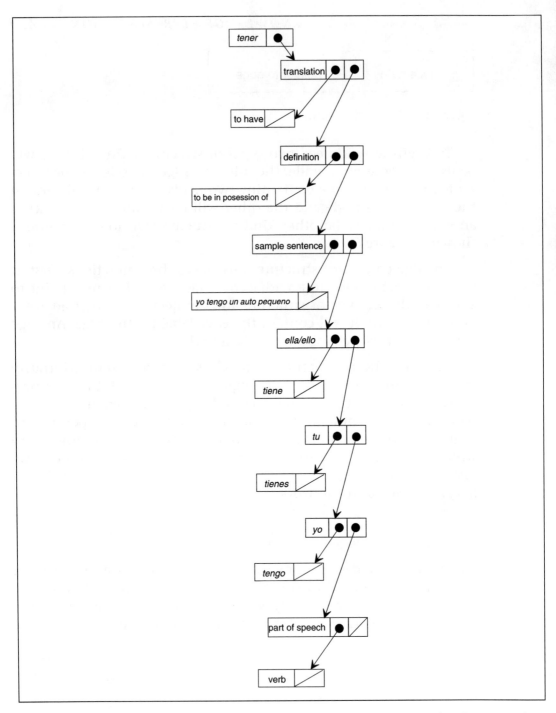

Figure 5.11 Semantic network representation for dictionary entry for the Spanish verb *tener*.

the tool once you have it. This section of the chapter is a functional specification and user manual all in one. Although the tool for creating semantic networks already exists on the CD-ROM included with this book, it's good to see how this tool was created.

Requirements for the Semantic Network Tool

As we said earlier, the easiest way to create a semantic network is with a tool allowing you to graphically create a semantic network. This approach gives you an important advantage of being able to see the semantic network as you design it. Since semantic networks can grow very complex, a visual representation will facilitate their construction.

As with any graphic user interface application, implementing a visual tool for constructing semantic networks is a complex task. The tool must be visually rich and allow you to create nodes, edges, and labels simply. As the network becomes more complex, the visual depiction must be updated to accurately represent the network as it grows and changes.

Let's consider some of the basic functions needed in our semantic network tool. Like most windows-based applications, the semantic network tool will allow you to open a semantic network file, create a new semantic network file, save a semantic network to a file with a specified name, and exit the semantic network tool. Two other major types of functions incorporated into the semantic network tool are those that manipulate nodes and those that manipulate edges. We also want to be able to create new nodes and new edges.

Creating a new node means that the graphic representation of the node is displayed and the internal representation for a node is created. This internal representation will be maintained throughout the life of the semantic network and will be saved in the semantic network file that can be created with the semantic network tool. The same is true for an edge. When an edge is created, the starting and ending nodes of the edge are specified, the node is drawn, and an internal structure is created for the edge. The previous section presented one possible internal representation (data structure) for nodes and edges. Our tool will use a slightly different representa-

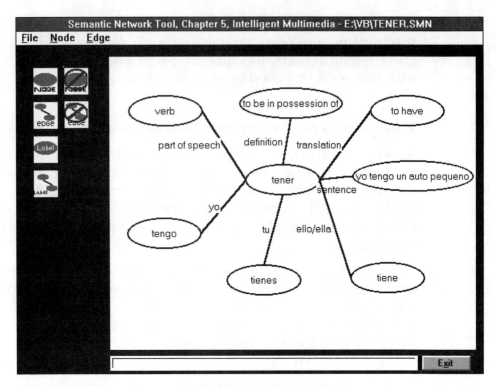

Figure 5.12 Semantic network tool interface.

tion. We will describe this representation shortly. For now, let's look at the interface for the semantic network tool shown in Figure 5.12.

The interface of the semantic network tool consists of a menu bar, several icon buttons, a drawing area, a message area, and an exit button. The menu bar at the top of the screen consists of three main pull-down menus: **File**, **Node**, and **Edge**.

The **File** pull-down menu includes the functions **Open**, **New**, **Save**, **Save As**, **About**, and **Exit**, as shown in Figure 5.13. The **Open** function will open an existing semantic network file, draw the network on the canvas (this is the large area in the interface), and create all of the internal structures representing the network. The **New** function erases the canvas and initializes all of the internal structures used to represent the semantic network. The **Save** function saves the contents of the internal representation of the semantic

KNOWLEDGE REPRESENTATION 223

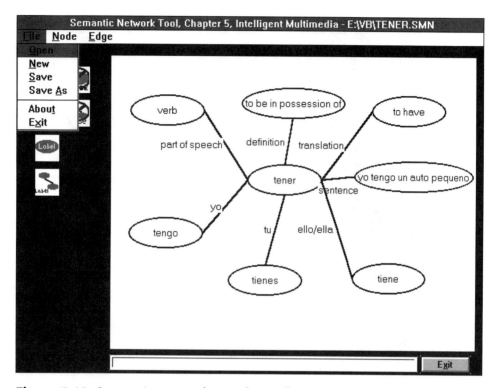

Figure 5.13 Semantic network interface **File** menu.

network to a file (either a previous opened file or a previously saved-as file). The **Save As** function allows you to specify the name of a file and then save the semantic network to the named file. As is typical of most Windows applications, the **About** function displays a window that describes the application and the **Exit** function closes the semantic network tool.

The icons on the left side of the interface give fast access to some of the functions manipulating nodes and edges. There are six icons in all: the node creation icon (🔵), the edge creation tool (🔗), the node label tool(🔵), the edge label tool(🔗), the delete node tool(🔵), and the delete edge tool(❌). The functions these icons initiate are duplicated in the **Node** and **Edge** pull-down menus. For example, the node creation icon creates a new unlabeled node and draws it on the semantic network canvas. Likewise, the edge cre-

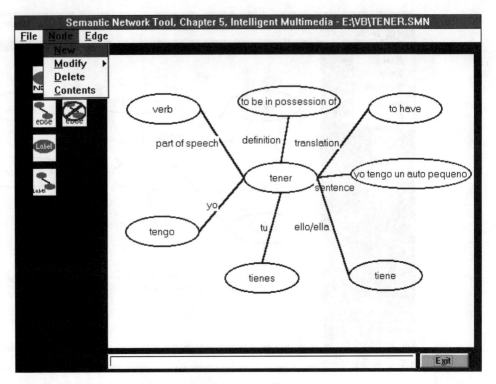

Figure 5.14 Semantic network interface **Node** menu.

ation tool allows you to select two nodes and create an edge between the nodes.

Figure 5.14 shows the **Node** pull-down menu and its associated functions. This menu duplicates the functions of the node icons described earlier. The **New** function creates a new unlabeled node and draws the node on the canvas. The **Modify** function allows you to change the position of the node on the canvas. (What should happen when the position of the node changes on the canvas?) The **Delete** function allows you to delete a node from the semantic network. The semantic network is redrawn. Finally, the **Contents** function allows you to label a node.

The **Modify** function of the **Node** menu allows you to change a node by moving it to another position or by changing the node's label. Selecting **Modify** produces another menu with two choices, **Modify Node** and **Modify Label**, as shown in Figure 5.15.

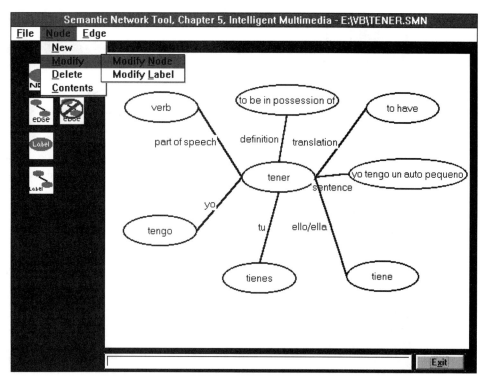

Figure 5.15 **Modify** function submenu functions.

Selecting **Modify Node** or **Modify Label** in this menu will allow you to select a node on the canvas. A list of nodes will be displayed, and you can select a node from the list. After selecting a node, you will be able to move and resize a node. The **Modify Label** selection from this menu will allow you to change the label of the node.

When you delete a node using the **Delete** selection of the **Node** menu, a node will be removed from the semantic network. Once a node is removed, there is a problem. Look at Figure 5.16. This figure shows a semantic network with a node partially deleted. The edges attached to the deleted node are hanging in space. When a node is deleted, all of the edges attached to it will also be deleted. Keep this in mind because you may find edges disappearing where you are not expecting them to disappear.

The tool must also redraw the network when something changes. In particular, if you move a node, the edges attached to it must also

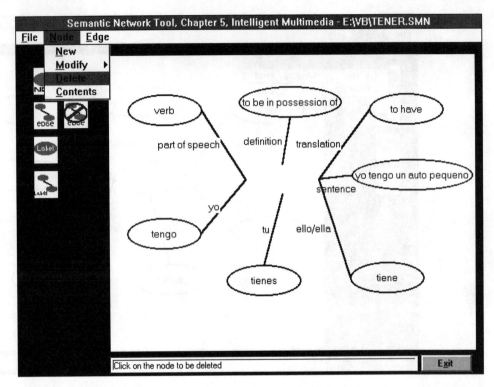

Figure 5.16 A semantic structure with a node deleted and corresponding edges left in place.

move (not to mention any labels associated with edges and nodes). Look at Figure 5.17. In this figure a node has been moved, but the edges have not yet been redrawn.

The **Edge** menu (Figure 5.18) includes the same basic functions as the **Node** menu. With this menu, you can connect two nodes with an edge, label an edge, and delete an edge. When you connect two nodes with an edge, you do so by clicking on the start node of the pair (where the edge is to begin) and the end node (where the edge will end). The semantic network tool will draw an edge between the nodes.

An edge is identified by clicking on or near the edge. The semantic network tool will identify the edge closest to the click. After this a label can be entered and the edge will be labeled with the specified label.

KNOWLEDGE REPRESENTATION 227

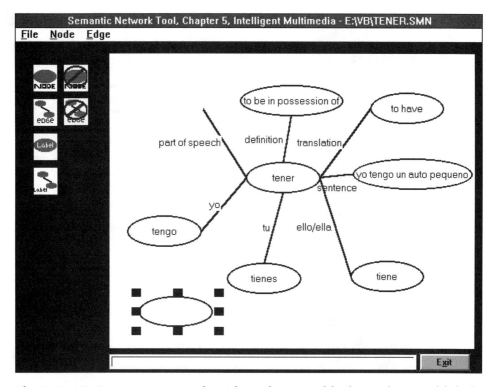

Figure 5.17 Semantic network with node moved before edges and labels are redrawn.

The **Delete** function removes an edge and its label from a semantic network. The semantic network will be redrawn and the removed edge will not appear in the revised drawing.

You can probably think of many other functions a semantic network tool could have. If you can't, you might want to reread this section to make sure you understand what the tool is doing. One example of a feature I did not include, but one you might consider, is what to do when the network grows too large to be displayed on the screen. Under these circumstances you might want to be able to scroll the semantic Network on the screen or zoom in and zoom out on a virtual canvas.

Another useful set of functions would be those appearing in an **Edit** menu. In this menu, you might include functions such as **Copy**, **Cut**, and **Paste**. These functions could be used to copy parts

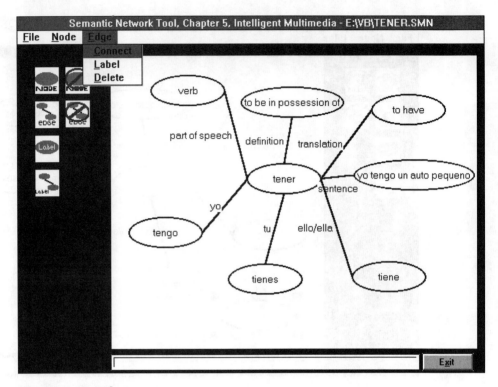

Figure 5.18 Edge menu.

of the network to the clipboard to paste into other places in the semantic network. I haven't implemented the **Edit** menu or scrolling canvas and leave these modifications to the reader.

Building the Semantic Network Tool

This section highlights some of the details of building the semantic network tool. The details of the interface are fairly straightforward. So, except where I think those details are interesting or important, I won't describe how the interface is implemented.

Internally, the semantic network is represented with two types of records, one used to represent nodes in the semantic network and the other used to represent edges in the semantic network. These two records are assembled into two tables, a node table and an edge table. The definition of the node record is:

```
Type nodeRecord
      label as String
      top as Integer
      left as Integer
      width as Integer
      height as Integer
      used as Integer
End Type
```

In this data structure, **label** contains the data contents of the node. As you will see later, a label could be replaced by a complex data structure containing much more information about the node.

The coordinates of the node on the canvas are **top**, **left**, **width**, and **height**. These coordinates are used when the node is drawn on the canvas and when it is moved. The **used** field indicates whether the record in the table is used. When a node is deleted, **used** will be set to indicate the record is free to be used for another node (set to "false").

The edge record, shown in Program Listing 5.1, consists of a **label** field, which will be used for the edge label data. The **startNode** and **endNode** fields contain index values specifying the starting node of the edge and the ending node of the edge. In a semantic network, the relationships between nodes are directed, and this is the reason for a starting point and ending point for an edge.

Program Listing 5.1 Edge record data structure.

```
Type edgeRecord
      label as String
      startNode as Integer
      endNode as Integer
      p1 as xy
      p2 as xy
      used as Integer
End Type

Type xy
      x as Integer
      y as Integer
End Type
```

The two fields **p1** and **p2** are used to record the position of the endpoint the edge. They are composite fields based on the *xy* structure, a data structure used to store *x* and *y* coordinates on the canvas. These coordinates are used when the label is placed. They are stored in the edge structure to avoid having to recompute the points when they are needed.

As before, the **used** field of the structure is set to "true" when the record contains a valid edge and "false" when it is deleted. The entry in the edge table will be used when a new edge is created.

Manipulating Nodes

One interesting feature of the semantic network tool is that nodes can be manipulated on the canvas. They can be moved and resized as needed. In graphic applications, graphic objects are represented with handles. These handles are usually rectangles used to "grab" the object. There are a couple of techniques I use to be able to accomplish this.

Besides being able to select a node for manipulation by way of the menu bar, you can also select nodes for manipulation by way of the canvas. If you click on a node or near a node in the canvas, code in the semantic network tool identifies the node clicked on. This is accomplished by a function named **findNodeBoundingPoint**. This function looks to see if the location of the MOUSE event, in this case a MOUSEDOWN event, is inside a node. If such a node is found, the index of the node in the node table is returned. Otherwise, if no node is found that encloses the point of the MOUSEDOWN event, the function returns a zero to indicate that no node was found that bounds the point.

When a node is found, the node and its handles follows the mouse. This is done easily by placing the predrawn node and associated handles on an invisible base called a frame. A frame is one of the controls in Visual Basic. The position of the frame is set to match the position of the mouse. As the position of the frame changes, so does the position of each of the elements contained on the frame. The frame behaves like a container—move the container and everything in the container moves also; make the container invisible and everything in the container becomes invisible.

Resizing a node occurs when one of the mouse handles is clicked. When this occurs, the size of the node changes as the mouse is moved. How the node will change depends upon which handle was clicked. Clicking a corner node and then dragging the mouse will change the height and width dimensions of the node. Clicking on a handle other than a corner handle results in a dimension change perpendicular to the direction of the side of the handle. Figure 5.19 shows how different handles affect the size of the node.

When resizing is finished, clicking on the handle again turns off the resizing "mode." The handles remain, and the node can still be moved. Clicking on the node again turns off the node manipulation and restores the canvas to an updated representation of the semantic network.

Drawing Edges

The actual drawing of edges could be handled in many different ways. One way would be to provide a drawing tool that allows a line to be drawn between nodes. The edge can be positioned with this sort of tool as needed. The responsibility of connecting two nodes is on the shoulders of the user. It is necessary when an edge is drawn that each end point of an edge touch a node. The computer could "fix up" any edge drawn, but this gives rise to another approach and the one I take.

Rather than choosing to draw a line between nodes, the user clicks on a pair of nodes. When the user clicks on the second node, an edge is automatically drawn between the pair of nodes. With this approach, the program needs to figure out where to draw the edge.

When you select the pair of nodes for which an edge is to be drawn, a line will be drawn between two points, one point on one node and one point on the other node. Which one point on each node should be selected? Figure 5.20 shows some of the possible points that could be chosen.

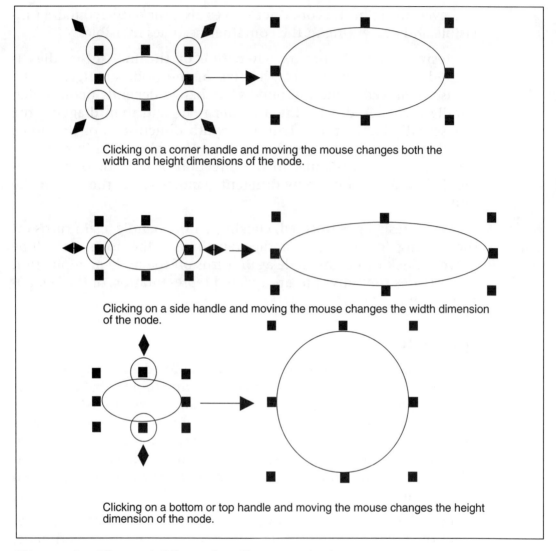

Figure 5.19 Effects of different handles on node dimensions.

Of the possibilities, the most acceptable is the last one in the figure. In the last drawing, the edge does not cross any node and it attaches the pair of nodes at their closest points. It would appear from Figure 5.20 that a good rule of thumb would be to connect the nodes at the points on each node that are closest to one another on the perimeter of the nodes.

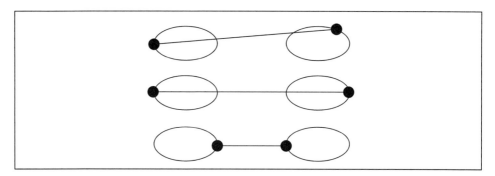

Figure 5.20 Possible edge connections.

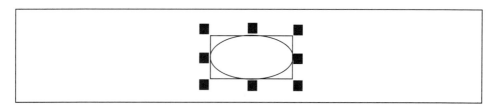

Figure 5.21 Node, boundary rectangle, and handles.

Each node is bounded by a rectangle. This same rectangle is the one on which the node handles reside. The boundary rectangle, node handles, and a typical node are shown in Figure 5.21. The boundary rectangle is drawn with a dotted line.

In order to facilitate the line drawing process, I use the bounding rectangle, and in particular four of the eight handles, to choose a point for the edge connection. Figure 5.22 shows the handles used for this purpose. The procedure calculates the closest points between nodes by looking to see which two of the eight node points

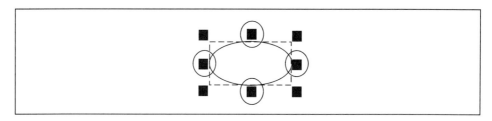

Figure 5.22 Handles used for edge connections.

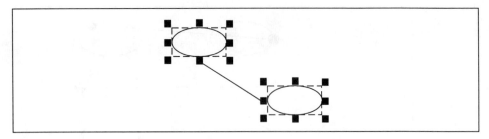

Figure 5.23 Closest handles of two nodes attached by an edge.

(four on each node) are closest to one another. These two points are the ones connected by an edge. Figure 5.23 shows two nodes, the handle points, and the two points selected for an edge.

When a node is modified by resizing the node or by moving it, the edges attached to that node will be left hanging and detached from the node. When the position and/or size of the node is fixed, all edges attached to the node are redrawn. This avoids having to redraw the edges every time the node moves.

Using the Semantic Network Tool

The last two sections have described quite a bit about the features of the semantic network tool and its internal workings. From this you can probably surmise how to use the tool. To complete this discussion fully, I will describe how the *tener* semantic network was created with the semantic network tool.

To create the *tener* semantic network, run the semantic network tool. When the tool starts, it will display a blank canvas. I'll start with the *tener* node and add all of the nodes belonging to the network.

1. To begin, click on the Node icon(). A node will appear in the top left hand corner of the canvas.
2. Click on the new node. The node will appear, but this time with its handles.
3. Drag the *tener* node (the new node) to the center of the canvas. Do this by moving the mouse. The node will follow the mouse.

KNOWLEDGE REPRESENTATION

4. When you have placed the node in the center of the canvas, click again. The handles will disappear. The node is now placed.
5. Now let's label the node. Click on the Node Label icon(●). If you look at the bottom of the display, you will see that the directions say to click on the node you wish to label.
6. Click on the node you just created. A dialog box is displayed. Type the label **tener** and click on the **OK** button in the dialog box. You will notice when you do this, the label will be written into the node. This completes the *tener* node.
7. Click on the Node icon (●) to create the next node. A new node will appear at the upper left hand corner of the canvas again.
8. Click on the second new node. Move it a short distance to the 11 o'clock position off of the *tener* node.
9. Click on the new node to fix its position.
10. Now let's label this node. Click on the Node Label icon(●), and click on the new node. This will be the one you will label.
11. Enter the label **verb** in the dialog box. Click on the **OK** button in the dialog box.

The remaining six nodes are created similarly. You can create these to complete the semantic network. Now I will create an edge so you can see how this is done.

1. To create an edge, click on the Edge icon(●).
2. The instructions at the bottom of the screen tell you to click on the node where the edge will begin. Click on the *tener* node.
3. Now the instructions at the bottom of the screen say to click on the node where the edge ends. Click on the node labeled **verb**.
4. When you have done this, the edge is drawn. Now we will label the edge.
5. Click on the Edge Label icon(●).
6. As the instructions indicate, now click on (or near) the edge you want to label. Click on or near the edge between the *tener* node and the **verb** node.

7. A label dialog box appears. Enter the label **part of speech**. Click on the **OK** button. The edge label will be written on the canvas near the edge.

Do the same for the remaining edges in the *tener* semantic network. Once the network is complete, you can save it by selecting the **File** menu **Save** function.

Logic Representations

Introduction to Logic Representations

One of the more interesting features of representation is that there are many different ways to represent the same things. Semantic networks are only one possible means of representing knowledge. Like semantic networks, logic remains one of the primary means of representing knowledge. This is attributable to several characteristics of logical representation. Logical representation affords us a mathematically grounded means of representation. All of the mechanisms of logic are available to manipulate the representation. Second, there are computer-based means to manipulate logical representations. This comes in the form of a programming language named Prolog. For the most part, this discussion will be about a logical representation in the form of Prolog language statements.

A logical representation can be used to represent the same kinds of entities that can be represented in a semantic network. To demonstrate this ability to express, here is the *tener* semantic network represented in a logical formalism.

```
partOfSpeech(tener,verb)
yo(tener,tengo)
tu(tener,tienes)
ello(tener,tiene)
ella(tener,tiene)
sentence(tener,yo tengo un pequeno auto)
translation(tener,to have)
definition(tener,to be in possession of)
```

Sometimes when a representation changes from a visual representation to a mathematical one, all comprehension is lost, but the representation shown here is fairly straightforward. Consider that each of the lines is a sentence in the language of logic. Each line expresses one of the relationships expressed in the semantic network.

Just as a sentence in English has a form and a structure, so do the sentences in our logical language. In this case each sentence expresses a relationship—part of speech, *yo* form of the verb, *tu* form of the verb, *ello* form of the verb, and so on. To separate the name of the relationship from the participants of the relationship, the participants are enclosed in parentheses. The participants are separated by commas. In this case, the first participant in each of the sentences is the word for which the relationship is specified, *tener*. The second participant is called the value of the relationship. The sentences represent facts in the logical representation. Together they represent a logical database.

Facts in a logical database are very useful. They can be used to prove things. To understand this, let's create a database of facts about a family. We want to express relationships like father and mother. We use the notation

```
mother(X,Y)
```

to say that **X** is the mother of **Y** and

```
father(X,Y)
```

to say that **X** is the father of **Y**. Now we are ready to specify a database about our hypothetical family.

```
father(mark,david)
father(david,jack)
father(david,june)
father(mark,clem)
mother(daisy,clem)
mother(mary,jack)
mother(mary,june)
father(jim,mary)
father(jim,zelda)
mother(zelda,alice)
mother(zelda,arlene)
```

We could go on like this, but I am sure you are getting the idea of how to create a database of father and mother relationships describing a family. A list of facts like these can be pretty useful. We can determine whether a relationship is true of false. For example, we can ask whether the question, is Daisy the mother of Clem? To ask this question, we construct a query that looks a lot like a fact. In other words, the query is

```
mother(daisy,clem)
```

In order to answer this query it is necessary to use the machinery of logic. We will call this machinery a **proof engine**. This engine takes facts in a logical language and proves whether the facts are true or false. Without getting too technical, the process of proving involves a mechanical process of manipulating the fact to resolve whether it is true or false.

To accomplish this, the type of proof engine used is quite famous, and although it is not really important to remember, the type of engine used is a **resolution theorem prover**.

To prove a statement in a logical language, we show that the opposite of the statement is inconsistent with other statements in the logical database. The opposite of a statement in a logical language is called the **negation** of the statement. The opposite of the statement,

```
mother(daisy,clem)
```

is

```
~mother(daisy,clem)
```

The symbol ~ is the symbol for negation. If **~mother(daisy,clem)** is inconsistent with other fact(s) in the logical database, then we know **mother(daisy,clem)** is true (and consistent) with the statements in the logical database. For this database it is fairly easy to prove that **~mother(daisy,clem)** is inconsistent with one or more facts in the database. If a fact is inconsistent with one or more in a logical database then it should be possible to locate a fact that states the opposite of the fact we are trying to show is inconsistent. In other words, if F is a fact in a database, ~F cannot also be part of the database as this would be a contradiction—thus the inconsistency. Likewise, if a database contains a ~F statement, it also cannot contain a statement F because that would also be a contradiction.

In our logical database we are looking for a fact that matches **mother(daisy,clem)** exactly. In other words, such a fact would match symbol for symbol everything in the fact. Looking at the list of facts,

```
father(mark,david)
father(david,jack)
father(david,june)
father(mark,clem)
mother(daisy,clem)
mother(mary,jack)
mother(mary,june)
father(jim,mary)
father(jim,zelda)
mother(zelda,alice)
mother(zelda,arlene)
```

we find a match. Therefore, with respect to this logical database, ~**mother(daisy,clem)** is a contradiction and inconsistent. We have shown **mother(daisy,clem)** is a true relationship.

Being able to verify a fact in a database is one aspect of the usefulness of the logical formalism. We can make some changes and additions to increase the versatility of the logical representation. First, we can add variables to these queries and facts. By adding variables to queries, we can ask the question, "Who is Jack's father?" This question can be asked by the query

```
father(X,jack)
```

Variables are represented as capital letters or symbols with first letters that are a capital letter. A query with one or more variables is answered by the same process as a query with no variables. The difference is that the variable X can match any first participant in a father relationship. In this case the second participant must match some second participant in the facts in the database. In this case, the fact that matches is

```
father(david,jack),
```

In this case, the **X** matches **david**, and the meaning of the resulting relationship is "David is the father of Jack." Adding variables makes the logical representation more useful.

One more modification can be made to make the logical representation quite powerful, and equivalent in expressiveness to semantic networks. If we wanted to, we could add more facts to the database representing relationships such as grandfather, grandmother, aunt, uncle, and others. Given the information we have, wouldn't this new information be redundant? After all, for example, if two people share the same father or mother, we know they are siblings. If a rule that defines siblings can be specified, this would be all that would be needed for our logical representation to be complete.

In fact, such a rule could be formulated. Two rules to express the sibling relationship are

```
sibling(X,Y) :- father(Z,X),father(Z,Y),X<>Y.
sibling(X,Y) :- mother(Z,X),mother(Z,Y),X<>Y.
```

The first rule reads, "X is the sibling of Y if Z is the father of X and Z is the father of Y." Likewise, the second rule reads, "X is the sibling of Y is Z is the mother of X and Z is the mother of Y."

Several new elements of notation appear in these rules. The symbol **:-** is read "if." It divides the left hand side (the conclusion of the rule) of a rule from the right-hand side of a rule (the conditions of the rule). For the conclusions of a rule to be true, all of the conditions of a rule must be true. Let's see how this works.

Suppose we want to find the sibling of Jack. In other words, "Who is the sibling of Jack?" or,

```
sibling(X,jack)
```

Looking at the database of facts, we see there are no facts that directly match this query, but there are two rules whose left hand side matches this query. If the left hand side of a rule matches a query then the goal is to prove all of the elements on the right-hand side of a rule. Let's try the first of the two rules.

```
sibling(X,Y) :- father(Z,X),father(Z,Y),X<>Y.
```

The query **sibling(X,jack)** matches the left hand side of this rule and causes some of the variables in the rule to "take on" a value. The rule now looks like this:

```
sibling(X,jack) :- father(Z,X),father(Z,jack),X<>jack.
```

To prove this rule, and to concurrently determine the sibling of Jack it is necessary to determine

1. What Z is a father of X [**father(Z,X)**].
2. What Z is a father of Jack [**father(Z,jack)**].
3. What X is not Jack.

When all three of these elements have been proven, we will know who is the sibling of Jack.

Looking at the database, we can see that the first match for **father (Z,X)** is **father(mark,david)**.

```
father(mark,david)
father(david,jack)
father(david,june)
father(mark,clem)
mother(daisy,clem)
mother(mary,jack)
mother(mary,june)
father(jim,mary)
father(jim,zelda)
mother(zelda,alice)
mother(zelda,arlene)
```

Once we prove the first fact, we go on and try to prove the next fact in the rule. The three facts in the rule are

```
father(Z,X)
father(Z,jack)
X <> jack
```

When we prove the first element of the rule with **father (mark,david)**, the elements of the rule change, as certain of the variables are now "filled in." The new set of elements is

```
father(mark,david)  proven
father(mark,jack)
david <> jack
```

Looking through the facts, we look for a fact that matches the query **father(mark,jack)**. There is no fact, so we cannot prove this query, and it is necessary to go back and try the first query again. This means that the set of things to prove goes back to their original state.

```
father(Z,X)
father(Z,jack)
X <> jack
```

Since we tried the first fact in the logical database, and this fact did not work, we now look for the next fact that matches **father (Z,X)**.

```
father(mark,david)
father(david,jack)
father(david,june)
father(mark,clem)
mother(daisy,clem)
mother(mary,jack)
mother(mary,june)
father(jim,mary)
father(jim,zelda)
mother(zelda,alice)
mother(zelda,arlene)
```

In this case, the next fact to match is **father(david,jack)**. The elements change appropriately.

```
father(david,jack)  proven
father(david,jack)
jack <> jack
```

Now we proceed to prove the next element, **father(david,jack)**.

```
father(mark,david)
father(david,jack)
father(david,june)
father(mark,clem)
mother(daisy,clem)
mother(mary,jack)
mother(mary,june)
father(jim,mary)
father(jim,zelda)
mother(zelda,alice)
mother(zelda,arlene)
```

There is a fact that matches, so the second element is "proven."

```
father(david,jack)  proven
father(david,jack)  proven
jack <> jack
```

KNOWLEDGE REPRESENTATION

The next element is specified as **jack <> jack**. This may seem a little confusing. This last element comes from the term in the rule **X<>Y**. The purpose of this element of the rule is to ensure that we are not saying that a person is his or her own sibling. In this case, the two facts used to prove the first two elements of the rule are the same, so the rule cannot be proven. This is because **jack <> jack** is false. This means it is necessary to go back and look for another fact in the database that matches the query **father(Z,X)**. We are at the starting gate again.

```
father(Z,X)
father(Z,jack)
X <> jack
```

Considering the database of facts, we see that the next fact that matches is **father(david,june)**.

```
father(mark,david)
father(david,jack)
father(david,june)
father(mark,clem)
mother(daisy,clem)
mother(mary,jack)
mother(mary,june)
father(jim,mary)
father(jim,zelda)
mother(zelda,alice)
mother(zelda,arlene)
```

Again, the elements are modified accordingly, based on the use of this fact.

```
father(david,june) proven
father(david,jack)
june <> jack
```

We proceed to try to prove the next element, **father(david, jack)**. There is a fact that matches this element, so we can proceed to prove the third element of the rule.

```
father(david,june) proven
father(david,jack) proven
june <> jack
```

The element, **june <> jack** is true, so the complete rule has been proven. June is the sibling of Jack. Or, in the logical notation, **sibling(june,jack)**.

By way of this lengthy description, I have shown how one relatively simple rule is processed. Rules can be combined to create more complex descriptions. Rules are very important to the descriptive power of a logical representation. All of the elements of the logical representation have been described.

Using Logic Representations

It may not be entirely obvious how this representation can be used. Let's consider the following example. There are three components in our wooga machine. A diagram of the wooga machine is shown in Figure 5.24. The behavior of this machine is described by the following rules.

If the input to component A is a 1+ then the output from component A is a 1.

If the input to component A is a 1– then the output from component A is a 0.

If the input to component A is a 0+ then the output from component A is a 2.

If the input to component A is a 0– then the output from component A is a 3.

If the input to component B is a 1 then the output from component B is a 0.

If the input to component B is a 2 then the output from component B is a 0.

If the input to component B is a 3 then the output from component B is a 0.

If the input to component B is a 0 then the output from component B is a 1.

If the input to component C is a 0 then the output from component C is a +.

If the input to component C is a 1 then the output from component C is a –.

KNOWLEDGE REPRESENTATION 245

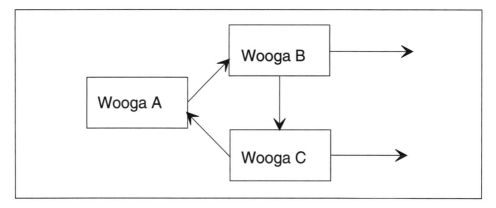

Figure 5.24 Wooga machine.

We want to use the logic-based representation to represent the wooga machine. What is it that we want to represent? We want to represent the relationships between wooga components. In this representation, we will want to represent how components are connected to one another. In a relationship between components some of these relationships will express inputs from one component to another and others will express outputs from one component to another. Outputs are attached to inputs. We will represent connected components with facts that look like

```
connected(X,Y)
```

to specify that **X** is connected to **Y**. The following sequence of facts represents the connections between components.

```
connected(woogaA,woogaB)
connected(woogaB,woogaC)
connected(woogaC,woogaA)
```

In addition to representing the connections between components, it is a good idea to represent the inputs and outputs of the machine:

```
input(woogaA)
output(woogaB)
output(woogaC)
```

In general, since any complex component may have more than one input or output, each will have to be identified. This is not necessary for the wooga machine, but is important to remember for more complex machines.

The last elements of the wooga machine we need to represent are the relationships between inputs and outputs. That is, for each device in the machine, when that device or component is given a certain input (or input configuration for a device with more than one input), we represent what the output of the device will be. In the case of a component with more than one output, we would represent the relationship between each input configuration and each output of the component. The relationship between inputs and outputs of a component are represented with the **io** fact. Here is an example of an **io** fact.

```
io(woogaA,input(woogaA(1),woogaC(+)),output(woogaA(1)))
```

In this relationship there are two participants: the input participant and the output participant. Each of these is an element representing a relationship. The input and output relationships can have any number of participants. The number of participants is determined by the number of inputs and outputs for the components represented in the **io** relationship. The remaining **io** relationships for the wooga machine are

- r1. `io(woogaA,input(woogaA(1),woogaC(-)), output(woogaA(0)))`
- r2. `io(woogaA,input(woogaA(0),woogaC(+)), output(woogaA(2)))`
- r3. `io(woogaA,input(woogaA(0),woogaC(-)), output(woogaA(3)))`
- r4. `io(woogaB,input(woogaB(1)),output(woogaB(0)))`
- r5. `io(woogaB,input(woogaB(2)),output(woogaB(0)))`
- r6. `io(woogaB,input(woogaB(3)),output(woogaB(0)))`
- r7. `io(woogaB,input(woogaB(0)),output(woogaB(1)))`
- r8. `io(woogaC,input(woogaC(0)),output(woogaC(+)))`
- r9. `io(woogaC,input(woogaC(1)),output(woogaC(-)))`

We want to be able to run this representation. That means we want to supply it with values and see how the various components change. Of course if this were a real device, we might see some activity as a result of our supplying one or more values to the device. If the device were a faucet, and the value of the input was to turn the faucet on, the activity we would see is water running. How can we run the wooga machine?

To do this, we need to supply some "real" input to the wooga machine. The starting device, **woogaA**, will be supplied with some initial inputs.

```
input(woogaA,woogaA(1),woogaC(-1))
```

With this input specification, the device can be run. To run the device, we locate a rule that matches the input and asserts* the output of the rule.

Looking through the rules, we try to find the device for which the input specification supplies input. In this example, the device is **woogaA**. Rules **r1** through **r4** all pertain to **woogaA**. The input to **woogaA** (as specified in the input specification) is **woogaA(1)** and **woogaC(–)**. Looking through the rules, we see that **r1**'s input specification (the input elements of the rule), match the supplied inputs. For this rule, we can determine the output of **woogaA**. With these inputs, the output from **woogaA** is 0. The output of **woogaA** is connected to **woogaB**. We know this from the series of connected relationships, and specifically the connected relationship, **connected (woogaA, woogaB)**.

Once we know the next device or devices in the sequence we can look for an **io** rule that applies to the input configuration. In this case, four **io** rules are relevant to **woogaB**. The input supplied to **woogaB** is 0. Rule **r8** is the relevant rule. The output from this rule, and the device is **woogaB(1)**. Looking again at the connected relationships, we see that **woogaB** is connected to **woogaC**. The input supplied to **woogaC** from **woogaB** is a **1**. Rule **r10** is the relevant rule for this input. In this rule, the output from **woogaC** is a **–**. Now, **woogaC** is connected to **woogaA**. This output (–) will be supplied to **woogaA** as input. Since the input to **woogaA** remained the same (it

---

*The word assert has a technical meaning from its use in the Prolog programming language. When we assert a fact we mean that we add that fact to all of the facts that we know about.

did not change from the original input specification), there will be no change in the output of the wooga machine.

Although the wooga device is a simple one, it suffices to show how a device like this might be represented in a logic representation and how that representation can be used. Later, when I describe the model for the Toaster Tutor, you will see a more complex representation based in the same representation scheme. Our purpose in this section was to show how a logic representation could be used for this purpose.

Representation Structure

Introduction to Frames

Like most things, representation schemes have evolved since the first representations were formulated. Although not new, frames are a fundamental means for representing knowledge. Many of the features found in present-day knowledge representations can be traced back to the frame representation.

Originally conceived by Marvin Minsky in 1972, the frame representation was formulated as a means to describe how humans might represent and use knowledge. As you might imagine, the original description of the representation was very abstract. The concretization of the frame structure took form very quickly.

In many ways a frame represents a record. Like a record, a frame consists of fieldlike components. These components contain data. Unlike a record containing fields, the elements of a frame are slots, facets, and data. Frames are more stratified than records. The fields of a record are most similar to the slots of a frame, but this is where the similarity ends.

A frame can have one or more slots. Each slot contains a particular kind of data. For example, if a frame describes an object, then a slot would describe a characteristic of the object. If the frame represents a chair, then a slot might represent the number of legs attached to the chair.

A facet is used to represent a characteristic of a slot. This may be a little confusing, as fields do not usually have characteristics, only values. In fact, the most basic kind of facet a slot can have is the value facet. The value facet is the facet of a slot used to hold the data for the slot. In the case of our chair example, the value facet of the number-of-legs slot (each slot has a name), may be four (4) for a particular kind of chair.

We need to stop for a moment and consider an important aspect of representation. In general we want to represent descriptions of things and things themselves. In other words, some frames describe kinds of chairs, whereas other frames describe specific chairs, such as the chair I am now sitting on or the chair on the outside patio that seats two people. When a frame describes a specific real world object*, the frame is called an *instance frame*. The object described must be a specific one, and not a class of objects.

Frames describing classes of objects, prototypical objects, or object descriptions, and that do not refer to specific objects are sometimes called *prototype frames*, *generic frames*, or *class frames*.

Why is this an important distinction? In the first case, this distinction mimics what we know about the real world—namely, that there are objects and that these objects can be grouped into classes of objects and in turn, classes might be grouped into larger classes. By organizing objects into classes, we have a way to describe objects. For example, when we say chair, we have a general idea of what a chair is. In this context, the word "chair" does not refer to a single chair but to a class of objects with a certain set of characteristics. If we know something is a chair and we see its characteristics, then we only need to note those characteristics that differ from those of our general class of chairs. For example, we might have as a subset of the most general class of chairs, chairs that can be found in the kitchen. Since there might be more than one of these, we can describe a kitchen chair as a class, and distinguish instances of kitchen chairs (each chair) by position, orientation, color, markings, and so on. These characteristics (among others) will distinguish specific instances of chairs. Figure 5.25 shows how a specific instance of a chair fits into more and more general classes of objects.

---

*We use the term "real world" object in the most general and abstract sense because we want to include things like chairs and baseballs, which are tangible objects, and also ideas and concepts, which are not tangible objects, but objects, nonetheless.

250　CHAPTER 5

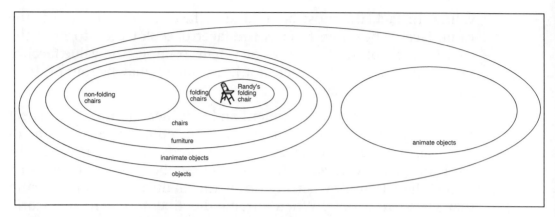

Figure 5.25 An object hierarchy for my folding chair.

In Figure 5.25, I have chosen several ever more general classes to show how a chair might relate to more general classes. Although there is no standard organization to this hierarchy, classes must be chosen with care so as to represent more general concepts than the classes or objects they contain, and so that the classes and their organization represent some aspect of their relationships to the real world.

Now it might seem simpler to have one frame for describing each and every possible chair, for example, a frame for Randy's folding chair, a frame for Matthew's rocking chair, a frame for Adriana's doll chair, and so on. After all, why bother to create this complex representation of classes when we can quite simply create frames for each specific chair object. The same question could be posed about our minds and how we represent objects and their relationships. Think about how you "represent" the idea of the chair you are sitting on (if you are sitting on a chair). Do you represent the chair as a completely independent entity or does the chair draw its characteristics from more and more general information? Upon reflection, you will probably find that the characteristics of the chair are based on characteristics of chairs and other objects. This is nothing but an economical way to accomplish representing things like chair objects—after all why repeat information when it does not have to be repeated? This idea of sharing information from more and more general classes of information is called *inheritance*.

If you have ever done any object-oriented programming, you know that inheritance, the ability in a programming language to define one data structure and have a second different data structure inherit characteristics from the first data structure is one of the most important aspects of this kind of programming. In programming languages like Smalltalk and C++, new data structures are constructed from existing data structures. In C++ and Smalltalk, the term "data structures" refers not only to structures in storage but also to the functions and operations that manipulate these structures.

The ability to construct new data structures in this way represents an advance in programming because it no longer becomes necessary to repeat definitions in a computer program. One uses an existing structure and adds to it or makes modifications to it. Object-oriented programming provides a more economical and efficient way to write programs.

In the context of frames, inheritance means one frame can inherit information from another frame. This does not happen automatically—a special slot is needed for this purpose. There are different names for this slot, but I will use the one originating from the original definition of frames, the AKO or a-kind-of slot.

If you think about semantic networks, links between nodes were created by attaching one node to another by way of an edge. An AKO slot represents an edge between frames. Instead of a graphical representation (an arrow-tipped line), frames are connected by naming one frame in another's AKO slot.

An AKO slot creates a class relationship between two frames. When we say that frame A is a-kind-of frame B, we are saying frame A is in the same class as frame B and also that frame A inherits all of frame B's slots and facets. Let's see how this works. Table 5.2 shows a general frame for chairs. The slots, facets, and values of those facets suggest one possible way of describing chairs and are *not* meant to represent the only way to describe chairs.

Before I continue to describe a frame related to the generic class chair frame shown in Table 5.2 several comments about this frame may help you to understand it. As I mentioned, frames are orga-

Table 5.2 Generic Class Frame for Chair

frame:

slot	name	facet	value	genericClassChair
slot	type	facet	value	class
slot	AKO	facet	value	furniture
slot	optional-part-of	facet	value	legs
				seat
slot	construction	facet	value	on-top-of(seat,legs)
slot	optional-construction	facet	value	attached-to(back,seat)
slot	number-of-legs	facet	default	4
slot	number-of-seat	facet	default	1
slot	number-of-back	facet	default	0
slot	purpose-of	facet	default	sitting

nized into slots, facets, and values, with the most basic being the slot/facet/value triplet. Another kind of useful facet is the default facet.

As the name implies, the default facet is a slot facet that supplies default information. In other words, this facet is present when there is a need to supply a typical value for a slot in the event that an instance of a frame has no value for a specific slot. In the frame in Table 5.2, there are several slots with default values. For example, if a chair frame does not have a specification of the number of legs attached to a chair, by way of the default facet of the number-of-legs slot we assume the chair will have four legs. Just as when we think about something, we can fill in the blanks with typical or familiar information, we can do the same in a frame with the default facet of a slot.

Let's understand how a default slot might be used. Consider the frame shown in Table 5.3.

This frame is a definition of a stool. Notice that this frame contains a different set of slots than the more general chair frame. Some of the slots are entirely missing and there are some new slots.

Table 5.3 Stool Type of Chair, a Kind of Chair Frame

frame:

slot	name	facet	value	stoolChair
slot	type	facet	value	class
slot	AKO	facet	value	genericClassChair
slot	part-of	facet	value	seat
				legs
slot	shape-of-part	facet	default	(seat,round)

Because the **stoolChair** frame is a-kind-of **genericClassChair**, it will inherit slots from the **genericClassChair** frame. Slots inherited include number-of-legs, construction, optional-part-of, number-of-seat, number-of-back, and purpose. This means that when an access is made to the **stoolFrame** and the slot accessed is the number-of-legs frame, the value returned will be 4. This value comes by way of the a-kind-of slot in the **stoolFrame** that names the **genericClassFrame** and its kind.

So far, the frames shown in Tables 5.2 and 5.3 are class-type frames. Another type of frame is an instance frame. It is important

Table 5.4 Instance Frame for Kitchen Chair

frame:

slot	name	facet	value	kitchenChair
slot	type	facet	value	instance
slot	AKO	facet	value	genericClassChair
slot	instance-id	facet	value	chair0001
slot	shape-of-part	facet	default	(seat,square)
slot	number-of-back	facet	value	1
slot	construction	facet	value	attached-to(back,seat)
slot	made-of	facet	value	wood
slot	position	facet	value	at(kitchenTable0007)
slot	occupied-by	facet	value	matt0341

to distinguish these two types of frame because class frames do not represent real-world instances of objects, whereas instance frame are used to represent instances of objects. The next frame, shown in Table 5.4, depicts an instance frame for a chair.

An instance frame is distinguished from a class frame by its type slot and several other slots. Each instance frame has associated with it a unique identification. In this case, the identification for this chair instance is chair0001. This instance also has a position associated with it, has someone who occupies it, and is composed of wood. Instances can also inherit information from the class slot by way of the AKO slot. This **kitchenChair** frame, for example, has four legs because it inherits this slot information from its related class frame, **genericClassChair**.

Using Frames

Frame Functions

Frames are particularly useful for representing real world objects, animate or inanimate. There are a basic set of functions for creating and manipulating frames. From this basic set, others may be created depending on your application. For now, I'll describe how to create them, access, and modify them. These functions were defined in the original specification of the Frame Representation Language (FRL).

assertFrame A frame can be created "all at once" with the **assertFrame** function. With this function, frame slots, slot facets, and their associated values can be specified as arguments to the function, and the function will create a frame structure. The structure will be created in frame memory.* The **assertFrame** function is called with the arguments

```
assertFrame frameName frameSlot1 frameSlot2 ... frameSlotn
```

---

*For now, we consider the functions without regard to their implementation. We assume that when a frame function is run, it will access a memory location that contains frames. Frame memory will be a global memory area accessible by all frame functions.

KNOWLEDGE REPRESENTATION

Each of the **frameSlots** has the basic structure

```
slotName(slotFacet1 slotFacet2 ... slotFacetm)
```

The **slotFacets** of the structure are constructed as

```
facetName(facetValue)
```

Although the arguments to this function can become complex, this function is the most efficient way to create a frame in one operation. Here is how a call to **assertFrame** can be used to create the **kitchenChair** frame.

```
assertFrame chair0001
     name(value(kitchenChair))
     type(value(instance))
     ako(value(genericClassChair))
     instance-id(value(chair0001))
     number-of-back(value(1))
     construction(value(attached-to(back,seat)))
     made-of(value(wood))
     position(value(at(kitchenTable0007)))
     occupied-by(value(mat0341))
```

putFrame The **putFrame** function is used to write information into frames. Specifically, **putFrame** allows you to add slots, facets, and values to any frame. Whereas **assertFrame** creates a complete frame, **putFrame** is used to add a single entry to a frame. Before **putFrame** can be used, a frame must exist in the frame database. The function **putFrame** has several different forms.

F1. `putFrame frame-name slot-name`

F2. `putFrame frame-name slot-name facet-name`

F3. `putFrame frame-name slot-name facet-name value`

As you can see from these forms, it is possible to create a frame entry for just a slot (**putFrame** form F1), a slot and a facet (**putFrame** form F2), and a slot, a facet, and a value (**putFrame** form F3). Let's suppose for example we wanted to add a slot named **number-of-legs** to frame **chair0001**. We want to specify a default facet whose value is 4. To create this slot/facet/value combination we use the following **putFrame** operation.

```
putFrame chair0001 number-of-legs default 4
```

getFrame The **getFrame** function is the operation used to access information contained in a frame. The **getFrame** operation not only can access information in a named frame but also make use of a-kind-of and default slots. For this discussion we will assume a particular access protocol, but keep in mind other protocols are possible.

An access protocol defines how information is retrieved from the frame database. For our version of **getFrame**, the protocol followed is

1. Access named frame.
2. Access a-kind-of chain.
3. Access default slot.

In other words, when you use **getFrame** to access information in a frame, it will first look for the data in the named frame (this is the frame named in the **getFrame** operation). If no data is found in the named frame, we look at the a-kind-of slot (if one exists in the frame) and go and visit the a-kind-of linked frame. An attempt is made to access the slot/facet/value triple in the a-kind-of linked frame. If the requested information is found, it is returned. Otherwise, we look in the a-kind-of linked frame (first jump) to another a-kind-of link. If one is found, we go to visit this frame and look for the slot/facet/value triple. You can think of the frames as a chain being linked together by the a-kind-of slots. We continue in this way, tracing a path along the a-kind-of slots until the requested data are found. Eventually we might come to the end of the a-kind-of chain. If we reach the frame at the end of the chain and still have not found the requested data, the search begins again at the named frame, this time looking for a default facet for the same named slot. If the requested data are found in the default slot, it will be returned. If no data are found, the a-kind-of slot is accessed and a search is made along the a-kind-of chain looking in the frame/slot/default triple for the requested information. Figure 5.26 shows the **getFrame** access protocol.

It is sometimes convenient to define three related but slightly different **getFrame** operations. In some cases, it is desirable to restrict the nature of the search through the frames. For this reason, three variants of the **getFrame** operation are **getFrameImmediate**, **getFrameAKOOnly**, **getFrameDefaultOnly**.

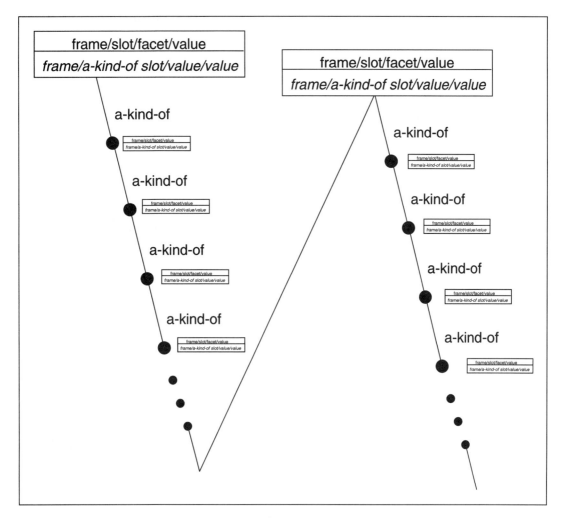

Figure 5.26 Diagrammatic depiction of **getFrame** access protocol.

getFrameImmediate This operation only looks in the named frame/slot/facet triple for the desired information. No other accesses are made to the frame database. If no data is found, an empty or **NIL** value is returned. Otherwise the desired data is returned.

getFrameAKOOnly As the name of this operation implies, **getFrameAKOOnly** will first access the named frame/slot/facet triple. If the requested information is not found in this frame, then the a-kind-of chain is searched for the requested information. If the end of the a-kind-of chain is reached and the requested data is not found, an empty or **NIL** value is returned.

getFrameDefaultOnly This operation looks in the named frame/slot/facet triple for the desired information, and if that is not found it searches the a-kind-of chain looking in the default facet of the frame/slot pair. If no data are found, an empty or **NIL** value is returned.

eraseFrame It is sometimes useful to expunge a frame from the frame memory. The **eraseFrame** function serves this purpose. When a frame is removed from the frame memory, no part of it is available for any operation. Care should be taken when removing a frame, especially if the frame is part of an a-kind-of chain. Removing a frame that is connected to another via the a-kind-of slot will effectively break the a-kind-of chain. The erase operation has no provision to fix the chain if it is broken. The form of this operation is

```
eraseFrame frame
```

In this operation **frame** is name of the frame that will be erased from frame memory.

frameRemovePart Parts of a frame can be removed with the **frameRemovePart** operation. Like the **putFrame** operation, the **frameRemovePart** operation has several variations that can be used. The forms of these variations are

F1. `frameRemovePart frame`

F2. `frameRemovePart frame slot`

F3. `frameRemovePart frame slot facet`

F4. `frameRemovePart frame slot facet value`

Form F1 carries out the same operation as **eraseFrame**. The complete frame is removed from the frame memory.

Form F2 removes only the slot in the named frame. All information contained in the slot (all slot facets and values) is removed from the frame. If the slot being removed is an a-kind-of slot, then care must be taken in removing this slot, as its removal may break an a-kind-of chain.

Form F3 deletes a named frame/slot/facet triple. All of the values of the facet are deleted from the frame. Care must be taken when this form of the **removeFramePart** operation is used, as it may damage and a-kind-of chain if the slot being modified is an a-kind-of slot.

The last form of the **removeFramePart** operation, F4, deletes a specific value in a frame/slot/facet triple. All other values in the frame/slot/facet triple are left intact. If the slot is an a-kind-of slot and the value being deleted is the only value in the frame/slot/facet triple, then deleting this frame/slot/facet triple will break this a-kind-of chain.

isAKO Sometimes it is useful to determine if one frame is a-kind-of another frame. The **isAKO** (is a-kind-of ?) is a predicate function (returns true and false) indicating whether one frame is a kind of another. The form of this operation is

```
isAKO frameA frameB
```

This operation is read, "Is frameA a-kind-of frameB?"

frameSlots The **frameSlots** operation is used to access a frame and return a list containing the names of the slots in that frame. The form of this operation is

```
frameSlots frame
```

where **frame** is the name of the frame whose slot list will be returned.

These ten operations are the basis of those used for creating and manipulating frames. In this discussion these operations are represented as they might be used in a programming language. Although this is one way to create and manipulate frames, it is cumbersome, so in the next section a tool for creating frames is described. Underlying this tool are the operations I described in this section.

A Tool for Creating Frames

The previous section described operations necessary to manipulate frames. This section describes the Frame Tool, included on the CD-ROM with this book, for creating and manipulating a database of frames. As with all the tools described in this book, the tool can be extended by the reader (source code is included). The Frame Tool implements most of the basic functions required for building databases of frames.

Figure 5.27 shows the basic Frame Tool interface. From this screen all frame operations are selected and executed. The icon buttons down the center of the screen provide quick access to the basic frame manipulation functions. These include creating a new frame database, opening an existing frame database, drawing and displaying the frame hierarchy, drawing and displaying frame relation-

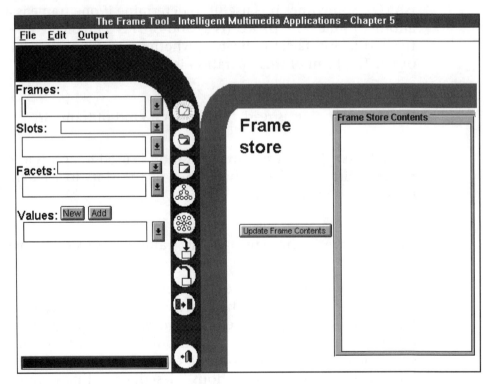

Figure 5.27 Main Frame Tool screen.

KNOWLEDGE REPRESENTATION

ships, writing frame information, and deleting frame information. To the left of the icon buttons are a series of fields for specifying frame contents. To the right of the icon buttons is an accumulated list of the frame database. As you will see, you can use the list to rapidly access different frames, slots, facets, and values in the frame database.

Creating a New Frame Database

A new frame database is created by clicking on the ◎ or by pulling down the **File** menu and clicking on the **New** option as shown in Figure 5.28. Clicking on **New** or the ◎ icon causes a new file dialog box to be displayed. Enter the name of the new frame database into this dialog box and click **OK**. The new database dialog box is shown in Figure 5.29.

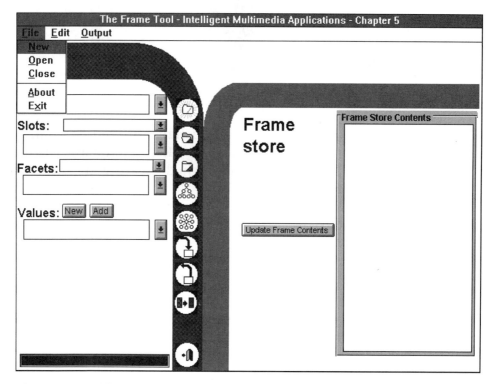

Figure 5.28 File pull-down menu—new frame database option.

262 CHAPTER 5

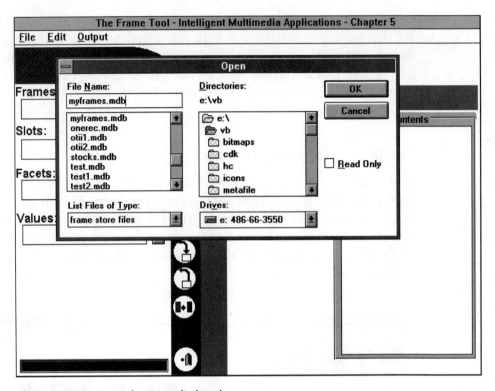

Figure 5.29 New frames dialog box.

Notice that in Figure 5.29, I have entered the database name **myframes.mdb**. After you click **OK** the database will be created. When the Frame Tool has finished creating the new database, a database create message is displayed as shown in Figure 5.30. After a database has been created, you can then proceed to enter frames into the database.

Opening an Existing Frame Database

An existing database can be opened by clicking the ▣ or by clicking on the **Open** option in the **File** pull-down menu. When you click on either of these, a dialog box appears for you to specify the frame database to open as shown in Figure 5.31.

Enter or select the name of the frame database to open and click the **OK** button. This will cause the Frame Tool to open the selected

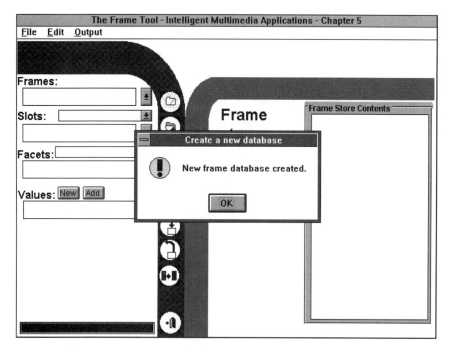

Figure 5.30 New database created message.

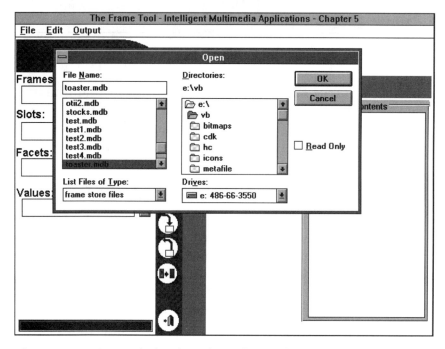

Figure 5.31 Open dialog box for a frame database.

264 CHAPTER 5

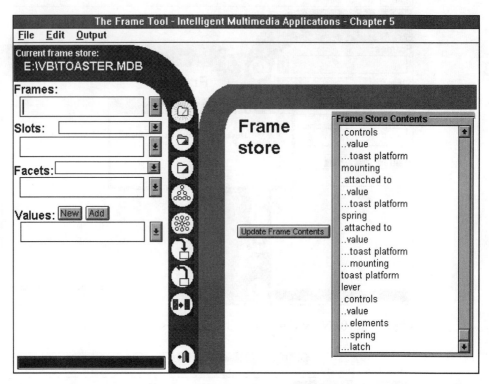

Figure 5.32 An example of an open database display.

database. Once the database is open you can manipulate the frames contained in it. If a database is opened successfully, then the frames list (on the right-hand side of the Frame Tool display) is filled in. An open database display is shown in Figure 5.32.

Entering and Accessing Frames with the Frame Tool

When a new frame database has been created or an existing one opened, a Frame Tool user can add to or modify the database of frames. Entering new frame components is accomplished with the fields on the left hand side of the Frame Tool screen and also with a special value entry window that appears on the right-hand side of the Frame Tool Screen when needed.

On the left hand side of the screen are four fields with pull-down menus. These are shown in Figure 5.33. Each of these four fields can

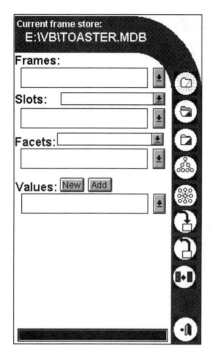

Figure 5.33 Frame element entry fields.

be used to enter frame elements. The first field is for specifying the name of a new frame. The second field is used to name slots belonging to the frame. The third field is for specifying facets of the slot, and the last field is for entering the value of the facet (if any).

Each of the fields contains one or more pull-down menus associated with it, as indicated by the down arrows to the right of each field. The pull-down menus are provided for rapid access to frame, slot, facet, and value elements. For example, clicking on the pull-down menu next to the frames field displays a list of all of the frames in the database as shown in Figure 5.34.

The database I have loaded happens to contain a set of frames that represent a toaster. As you can see, the **Frames:** field pull-down menu contains a list of frames in the database. Suppose you wanted to edit a particular frame. You would do so by clicking the name of the frame you want to edit. This frame name will be entered into the frame name field. Likewise, once a frame is selected you either

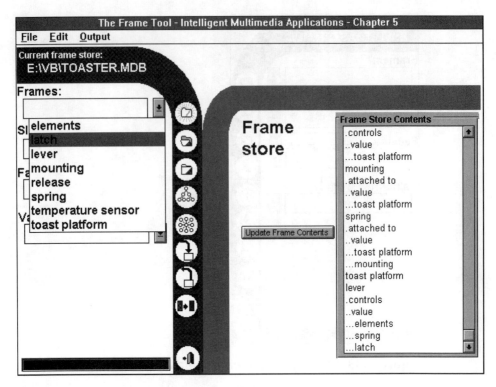

Figure 5.34 Frame element pull-down menu.

enter a slot name or click on the **Slots:** field pull-down menu. The **Slots:** field pull-down menu to the right of the **Slots:** field contains a list of newly entered slots belonging to the frame. The pull-down menu above the **Slots:** field lists slots belonging to all frames in the frame database. As before, you can select a slot name or enter a new slot name.

The **Facets:** field is like the **Slots:** field because it also has two pull-down menus. In this case, the pull down to the right of the **Facets:** field lists newly entered facets belonging to the specified slot, and the pull-down menu on the right of the **Facets:** field lists all facets belonging to all slots in the frame database.

Names of frames, slots, and facets are all entered by selecting a name from the pull-down menus or by entering the name directly in the **Frames:**, **Slots:**, or **Facets:** fields. Values are entered in a

KNOWLEDGE REPRESENTATION 267

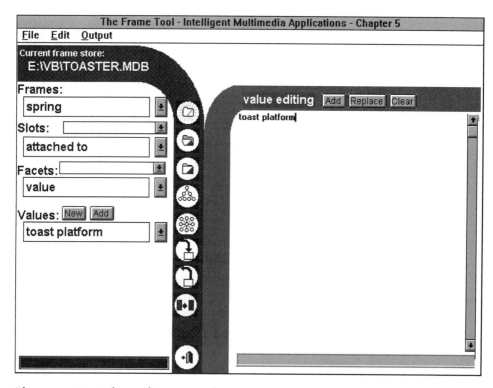

Figure 5.35 Value editing window.

slightly different way. The **Values:** field also has a pull-down menu associated with it, so you can see values that have been entered for frames in the frame database. If you select a value from the pull-down menu or click the **New** button above the **Values:** field, the screen changes so the right-hand side contains an editing box for values. This is shown in Figure 5.35.

The **value editing** window is an area on the right-hand side of the screen where you can enter and edit values. In this window you can enter whatever will be the value corresponding to the frame, slot, and facet. On top of the window are three buttons: **Add**, **Replace**, and **Clear**.

To add a value to a frame, after a value has been entered into the **value editing** window, click the **Add** button. Facets can have more than one value, so adding a value to a facet with existing values causes the value to be appended to the existing values in the frame.

You can also replace a facet value. If you click on the **Replace** button and the facet has a single value, it will be replaced with the newly entered value. If a facet has more than one value, the value present in the **Values:** field will be replaced.

The **Clear** button removes the **value editing** window and redisplays the frame database contents list.

Navigating Through the Frame Database

One way to navigate through the frame database is to use the fields and pull-down menus. A complete view of the database is also provided in the frame contents list shown in Figure 5.36. This is a listing of all frames, slots, facets, and values in the frame database. They are arranged by frame, with slots, facets, and values listed under the frame. The type of entry is denoted by the number of periods that precede the entry.

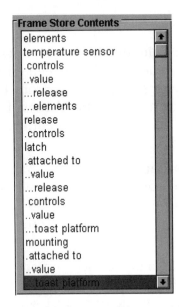

Figure 5.36 Frame contents list.

Number of Periods	Denotes
0	frame
1	slot
2	facet
3	value

In the frame contents list, you can click any entry. Doing so will set the fields on the left hand side of the screen. For instance, if you click on a frame name, the **Frames:** field will be set to this frame name. Clicking on a slot will set the **Slots:** name field and the **Frames:** field (the frame to which the slot belongs). Likewise, clicking on a facet in the frame contents list sets the **Facets:**, **Slots:**, and **Frames:** fields. The **Slots:** field is set to the name of the slot to which the facet belongs, and the frame name is set to the name of the frame to which the facet and slot belong. Clicking the **Values:** field has a similar effect—in this case facet, slot, and frame fields will be set. The value entry window will display the value selected in the frame contents list. Figure 5.37 shows the frame **latch** selected in the frame contents list. The frame name **latch** is also displayed in the frame field.

Closing a Frame Database

You can close a frame database by clicking the ▣ icon. Closing a database writes all updates and additions to the database. Once a database is closed, you can no longer access the frames contained in it. You must open the database again if you want to add any frames or make any changes to frames in the database. A frame database can also be closed by clicking the **File** menu and clicking the Close option in this menu.

Showing the Frame Hierarchy

When you specify frames in a frame database, it is sometimes useful to view the contents of the full database as a hierarchy. The hierarchy is rooted at a node representing the entire frame database. De-

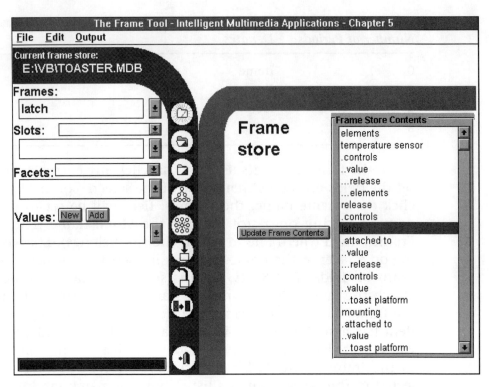

Figure 5.37 Selecting the "latch" frame in the frame contents list.

scending from the root node is an edge connecting the root to a node for each frame in the database. Each frame may have one or more slots. For each slot belonging to a frame, there is a node and an edge connecting the frame to the slot node. Likewise, each slot can have zero or more facets. A node will be drawn for each facet, and an edge connects these to the slot to which they belong. Values are drawn and connected to their parent facets in the same way. Figure 5.38 shows the toaster frames database drawn as a hierarchy.

You will notice in Figure 5.38 that the node labels overlap one another. Depending on the number of frames, slots, facets, and values, this may occur to a greater or a lesser extent. The hierarchy is always drawn to fit on one screen. To facilitate reading the node labels, each of the nodes can be clicked. Clicking on a node opens a window with the node label displayed in the window. The node label display is shown in Figure 5.39.

KNOWLEDGE REPRESENTATION 271

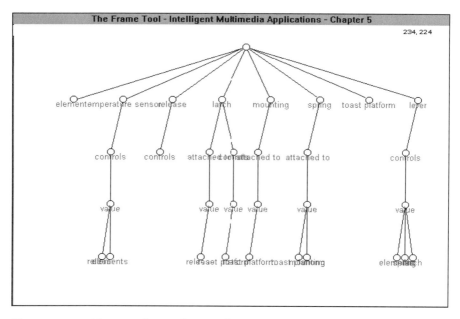

Figure 5.38 Toaster frame hierarchy.

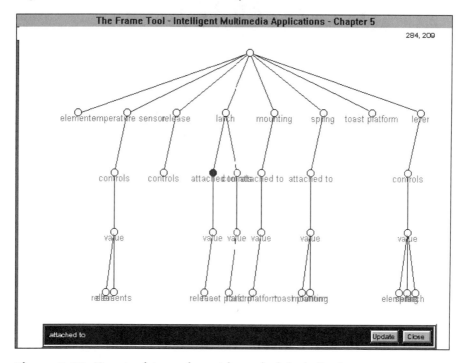

Figure 5.39 Toaster hierarchy with node label display.

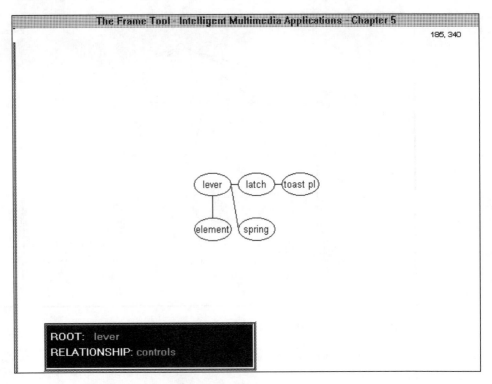

Figure 5.40 Visual representation of frame relationships with other frames.

The node label window contains two buttons, an **Update** button and a **Close** button. The **Close** button removes the node label window from the display. The **Update** button allows the value of the node to be modified. To display the frame database hierarchy click on the ▦ icon.

Showing Frame Relationships

A second visual representation of the frame database shows the relationship between frames using slot values and slot names as the basis for the representation. Figure 5.40 depicts an example of this representation.

The visual representation shown in Figure 5.40 is created by first clicking on the ▦ icon. When you click on the ▦ icon with the

KNOWLEDGE REPRESENTATION 273

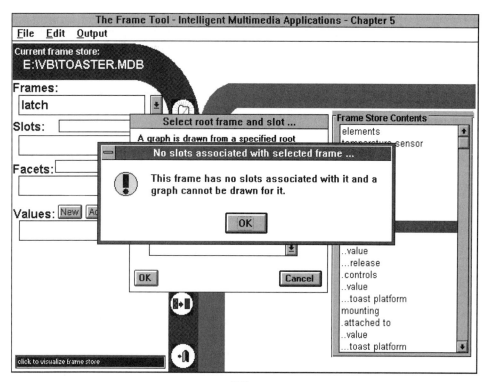

Figure 5.41 Result of clicking the ⚙ icon with the toaster database open.

toaster frame database open, the display changes as shown in Figure 5.41. The message box displayed contains the message

This frame has no slots associated with it and a graph cannot be drawn for it.

This message is displayed because the first frame in the frame database has no slots and a graph can only be drawn when a frame has one or more slots. Why is this so?

Graphs are drawn by determining how a frame is related to another through a slot. In other words, frames can be used to represent semantic networks by using the slots of the frames to represent relationships (the edges of a semantic network) and slot values to name other frames (the nodes in a semantic network). Consider the frames shown in Figure 5.42.

lever frame	latch frame	carriage frame
....	....	....
....	....	....
....	....	....
slot: name	....	slot: name
facet: value	....	facet: value
value: lever	slot: name	value: carriage
slot controls	facet: value	....
facet: value	value: latch	....
value: latch	slot controls	....
....	facet: value	....
....	value: carriage	....
....	....	....

Figure 5.42 Lever, latch, and carriage frames.

Figure 5.42 shows three frames: lever, latch, and carriage. The lever and latch frames have a controls slot that names another frame among the three frames. Although it requires some imagination, you can see how the frames shown in the figure represent a semantic network. If we were to draw this network using *controls* as the relationship between nodes, the result would be the semantic network shown in Figure 5.43.

The ✲ icon analyzes frames in the frame database in just the same way. By specifying a root frame and a relationship (the name of a slot), the graph function produces a graph. Consider Figure 5.44. In this display I have specified **latch** as the root of the graph and **controls** as the slot. The resulting graph is shown in Figure 5.45.

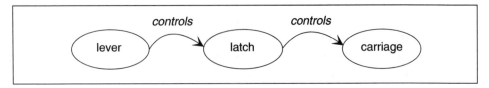

Figure 5.43 Semantic network representation of lever, latch, and carriage frames.

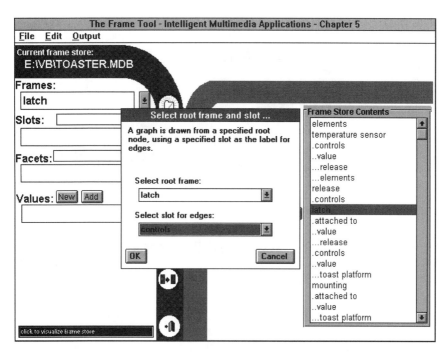

Figure 5.44 Example of specification of frame and relationship.

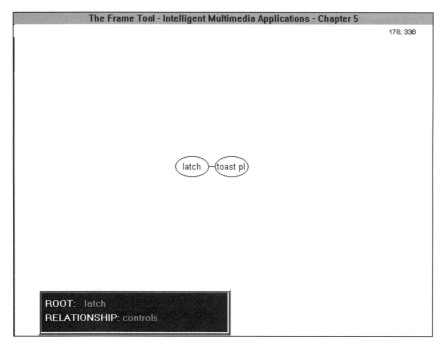

Figure 5.45 Graph of latch and controls relationship.

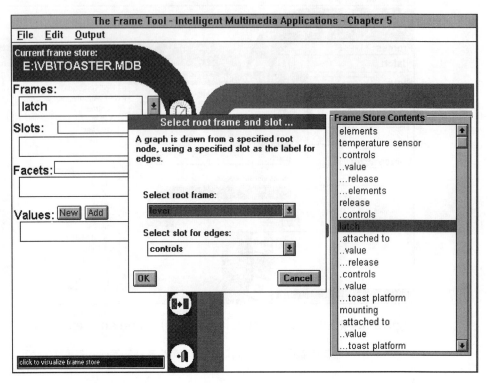

Figure 5.46 Specifying lever and controls as the graphing input.

As a more complex example, I will enter **lever** as the root of the graph, and **controls** as the relationship as shown in Figure 5.46. The resulting graph is shown in Figure 5.47.

Saving a Frame Element

The 💾 icon is used to save frames in the database. When you enter frames, slots, facets, and values, they will not be stored unless you click this icon. If a frame, frame and slot, or frame, slot, and facet are already part of the database, they will not be stored again in the frame database. If a frame, slot, facet, and value are saved, the value will only be stored if it is not already part of the database unless the value is explicitly replaced in the **value editing** window. Also, no frame or frame element can be saved unless a database is open.

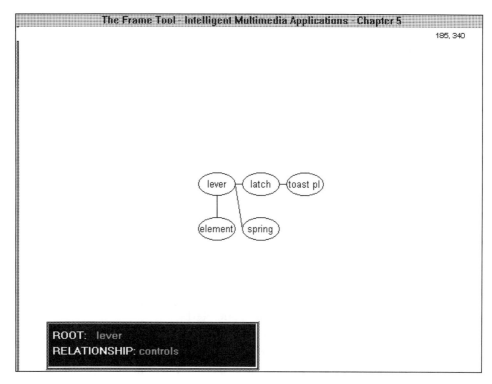

Figure 5.47 Lever/controls graph.

Deleting a Frame Element

A frame element can be deleted from the database by clicking on the icon. To delete an element from the frame database, a frame, a frame and slot, a frame, slot, and facet, or a frame, slot, facet, and value must be selected. Deletion in a frame database is somewhat complex, as deleting a particular element may result in more than that element being deleted. Table 5.5 specifies what is deleted when a particular element is deleted in a frame database. As you can see, what you delete determines what is deleted. If you think of the frame as a container, then when the frame is deleted, everything in it will also be deleted. A slot contains facets and values. Deleting a slot deletes the slots and values it contains. The same is true for facets.

Table 5.5 Frame Elements Affected by Deletion

Delete what:	What is deleted:
frame slot facet value	Only the specified frame, slot, facet, and value are deleted.
frame slot facet	The frame, slot, and facet are deleted. All values associated with the frame, slots, and facet are also deleted.
frame slot	The frame and slot are deleted. Any facet associated with the frame and slot are also deleted. All values associated with any deleted facet are also deleted.
frame	The frame is deleted. All slots associated with the frame are deleted. All facets associated with any deleted slots are deleted. All values associated with any deleted facets are deleted.

Copying a Frame

Frequently a frame is needed that is similar to another already present in the database. The copy icon (▣) is provided for just this purpose. When you click the copy icon, a dialog box is displayed that allows you to select a frame to copy and the name of the new frame that will be created as a copy. The dialog box is shown in Figure 5.48.

Let's make a copy of the lever frame. Click the copy icon. Select the lever frame as the source to copy. In the field provided, enter the name **lever2** (the name of the copy of the frame). The dialog box at this point is shown in Figure 5.49. Now click the **OK** button. The copy dialog box disappears. When the copy operation is completed, the frame contents list is updated. There is now a **lever** frame and a **lever2** frame. Note that the **lever2** frame has the same slots, facets, and values as the **lever** frame. The updated contents list is shown in Figure 5.50.

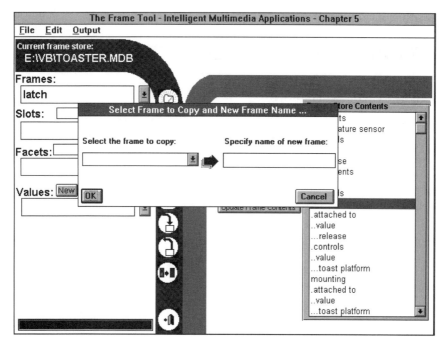

Figure 5.48 Frame copy dialog box.

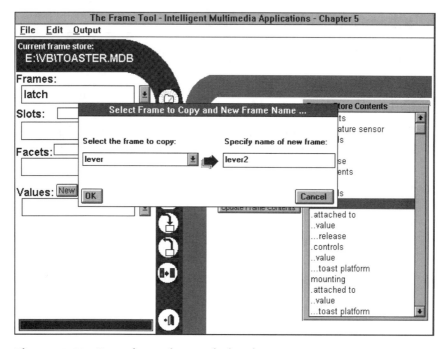

Figure 5.49 Copy lever frame dialog box.

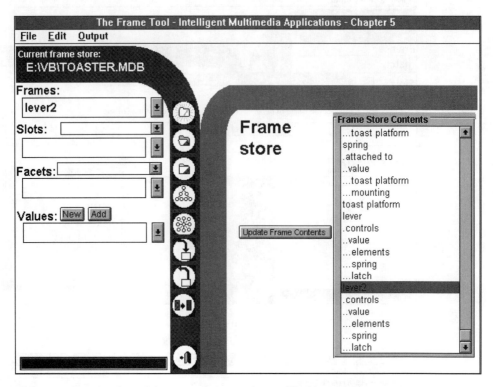

Figure 5.50 Updated frame contents list with **lever2** frame.

Outputting the Frame Database

The Frame Tool maintains the database of frames for manipulation. Using functions that are part of the Frame Tool, a Visual Basic application could be written to use the frames in a frame database. It is also useful to be able to output the database in several forms. The **Output** menu selection is provided for just this reason. Figure 5.51 shows the output selections available in the Frame Tool. Four selections are available: **Lisp**, **Prolog**, **Rules**, and **Text**. As the selections imply, choosing **Lisp** will produce a LISP representation of the contents of the frame database. An example of a LISP output of the toaster frame database is

```
(temperature_sensor(controls(value("release"))))
(temperature_sensor(controls(value("elements"))))
(latch(attached_to(value("release"))))
```

KNOWLEDGE REPRESENTATION 281

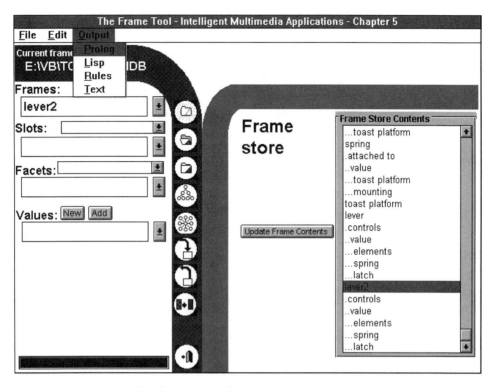

Figure 5.51 Frame Tool output selection.

```
(latch(controls(value("toast platform"))))
(mounting(attached_to(value("toast platform"))))
(spring(attached_to(value("toast platform"))))
(spring(attached_to(value("mounting"))))
(lever(controls(value("elements"))))
(lever(controls(value("spring"))))
(lever(controls(value("latch"))))
```

A Prolog representation is available by selecting the **Prolog** option of the output menu. An example of Prolog output is

```
temperature_sensor(controls(value('release'))).
temperature_sensor(controls(value('elements'))).
latch(attached_to(value('release'))).
latch(controls(value('toast platform'))).
mounting(attached_to(value('toast platform'))).
spring(attached_to(value('toast platform'))).
spring(attached_to(value('mounting'))).
```

```
lever(controls(value('elements'))).
lever(controls(value('spring'))).
lever(controls(value('latch'))).
```

The rules output produced by the Frame Tool creates rules for the Small-X interpreter. The idea underlying the rules is that they create short-term memory entries representing frame elements. An example of the **Rules** output of the Frame Tool is

- if #frame = temperature_sensor and #slot = controls and #facet = value then bind #value 'release'
- if #frame = temperature_sensor and #slot = controls and #facet = value then bind #value 'elements'
- if #frame = latch and #slot = attached_to and #facet = value then bind #value 'release'
- if #frame = latch and #slot = controls and #facet = value then bind #value 'toast platform'
- if #frame = mounting and #slot = attached_to and #facet = value then bind #value 'toast platform'
- if #frame = spring and #slot = attached_to and #facet = value then bind #value 'toast platform'
- if #frame = spring and #slot = attached_to and #facet = value then bind #value 'mounting'
- if #frame = lever and #slot = controls and #facet = value then bind #value 'elements'
- if #frame = lever and #slot = controls and #facet = value then bind #value 'spring'
- if #frame = lever and #slot = controls and #facet = value then bind #value 'latch'

The last output option is a text file. An example of the Frame Tool's text output of a frame database is

```
Frame:     temperature sensor
Slot:      controls
Facet:     value
Value:     release

Frame:     temperature sensor
Slot:      controls
Facet:     value
Value:     elements
```

```
Frame:    latch
Slot:     attached to
Facet:    value
Value:    release

Frame:    latch
Slot:     controls
Facet:    value
Value:    toast platform

Frame:    mounting
Slot:     attached to
Facet:    value
Value:    toast platform

Frame:    spring
Slot:     attached to
Facet:    value
Value:    toast platform

Frame:    spring
Slot:     attached to
Facet:    value
Value:    mounting

Frame:    lever
Slot:     controls
Facet:    value
Value:    elements

Frame:    lever
Slot:     controls
Facet:    value
Value:    spring

Frame:    lever
Slot:     controls
Facet:    value
Value:    latch
```

A Problem For The Reader

The Frame Tool can be used to produce databases consisting of frames. The semantic network tool can be used to produce semantic network representations of knowledge. Can these two tools be married in some way? This problem is left to the reader.

Chapter Summary

This chapter scratched the surface of knowledge representation. The concept of symbolic representation was described and serves as the basis for any knowledge representation that we devise. A symbolic representation also forms the basis for programs we might write to process knowledge representation. A knowledge representation is a kind of data structure that uses symbols as a means to represent objects, concepts, and processes.

Two kinds of knowledge representation schemes described in this chapter were semantic networks and logic representations. Although these two do not make up the universe of knowledge representation, they do represent several important aspects of knowledge representation schemes.

As a structure from which many others were devised, semantic networks serve as a foundation of knowledge representation structures. Physically, semantic networks are a graph—nodes connected by edges. Conceptually, the nodes represent entities such as concepts, objects, and processes, and the edges represent relationships between these. Semantic networks can be used to represent many different kinds of phenomena. In the context of intelligent multimedia, semantic networks are a good representation for the models we will construct. The section about semantic networks concluded with a description of a tool that can be used to construct semantic networks. The tool is based on a graphical interface that allows nodes and edges to be drawn on a canvas.

Logical representations of knowledge are also a classic means of representation. One of the benefits of using a logical representation is that there is a computing mechanism built around logical representation in the form of a programming language named Prolog. By constructing a logical representation in the form of a Prolog program, the representation can be run by a computer.

The remaining sections of this chapter described a data structure called a frame and defined many of the operations associated with this data structure. Frames, like logic representation, can be used to construct semantic networks. A frame is a data structure consisting of physical entities named frames, slots, facets, and values. A frame can be thought of as a container that holds slots, facets, and values. An important aspect of frames is that they implement inheritance—one frame can inherit slots, facets, and values from another frame.

The end of this chapter presents the Frame Tool, a tool for constructing databases of frames. The Frame Tool allows for the creation and modification of frames and also can visually represent the contents of the frame database.

There is quite a bit more I could have described about knowledge representation in this chapter. I have only touched the surface to provide an introduction to the topic. The idea of representing knowledge is both fascinating and daunting and remains one of the most salient in all of Artificial Intelligence. The brain seems to have an uncanny ability to represent and compute using an extremely complex chemical and biological representation scheme. I have tried to do the same, albeit with a much simpler system to represent some of what the brain represents so readily.

Suggested Reading

Barr, Avron, and Feigenbaum, Edward, *The Handbook of Artificial Intelligence*. Menlo Park, CA: William Kaufmann, 1981.

This is a tome in the real sense, as it presently consists of four volumes, and spans the complete field of Artificial Intelligence. As a reference and a historical reference, it is invaluable.

Davis, Ernest, *Representations of Commonsense Knowledge*. San Mateo, CA: Morgan Kaufmann, 1990.

An interesting text about representing commonsense knowledge that goes into much more depth about the topic.

Sousa, John, *Principles of Semantic Networks*, San Mateo, CA: Morgan Kaufmann, 1991.

Contains a series of classic and comtemporary papers about Semantic networks. It is a good reference on the subject.

Winston, Patrick, ed. *The Psychology of Computer Vision*. New York: McGraw-Hill, 1975.

Contains the original description of frames by Minsky, Marvin, "A Framework for Representing Knowledge." Minsky is one of the founding fathers of Artificial Intelligence.

CHAPTER 6

Models

Introduction

Models are wonderful things. With a model you can explore things that otherwise might be impossible to explore. For example, a model of a jet aircraft made from plastic, if sufficiently detailed and accurate, can allow children and adults to see almost first hand what the aircraft looks like, what equipment it has, and so on.

Models make movies possible. After all, if a spaceship like the *Enterprise* had to be actually built for the "Star Trek" series, we might never have had the television show, because building an actual spaceship of this kind would have been too expensive.

Models are also extremely useful for testing and understanding ideas. In medical research, models are frequently used to postulate theories about biological mechanisms and how they work. Useful drugs could not be formulated without a very sophisticated modeling process.

Intelligent multimedia systems also make use of models. You have already seen some formulation of a model of a toaster. There are other models that will be part of the Toaster Tutor—a model of the student and a model of the instructor. This chapter describes what is meant by a model and shows some examples of typical models in systems like the Toaster Tutor.

For the most part this chapter focuses on models of mechanisms. There is a great deal of interest in how we can create accurate and effective models of common mechanisms so that we can better understand them. In particular I will focus on mechanisms like the toaster, which consists of tangible elements like a thermostat and a color setting knob. The same kinds of concepts for modeling can also be applied to mechanisms that are not mechanical or even tangible. For example, we can devise a model of problem solving. Later in this chapter I will show how a model like this can be represented.

Introducing Models

A model is something that copies the characteristics of a real world object, process, or concept. It may copy physical characteristics as do the plastic model kits that can be purchased at toy stores and assembled. The model may look like a jet fighter aircraft, but in reality it has no bombs that will explode when dropped. It is a visual model of the real object.

Other kinds of models may copy other characteristics of their real world counterparts. For example, we may want to create a model of a new automobile to see how the automobile will operate. The advantage of creating a model is that it will be less expensive than creating the real thing. It will also be safer if it is a model that operates by remote control. If the design is unsafe, this may be discovered without injuring anyone. The issue of expense and safety are key reasons to create models. In the case of a toaster, expense certainly isn't an issue (new toasters can be had for about $15) but safety is. You could get burnt from the heating element or suffer electrocution if you forget to unplug the toaster and touch the wrong wires, so a model of a toaster for our tutor would be a good idea from the standpoint of safety.

A model is an abstract representation of some mechanism. It is abstract in the sense that it does not really exist, it is something we will create in the boundaries of a computer program. A mechanism need not mean something mechanical or electronic. We could model something as nonconcrete as a thought process. Keep in mind that a model is a representation of some mechanism.

To construct a model for a mechanism, the mechanism must be decomposable. This means the mechanism you elect to model should have identifiable parts that comprise the mechanism. Without getting overly recursive, a model consists of submodels, smaller mechanisms to be modeled. Eventually the decomposition of model into components will result in things that are not decomposable (at least you have decided the decomposition is sufficient for your purposes). These nondecomposable components are those that make up the model.

The behavior of a model is described by the behavior of the components of the model. The behavior of components of the model is defined by the intercomponent and intracomponent behavior. Intercomponent behavior is a description of how components interact with one another. In the toaster an example of intercomponent behavior is the interaction between the keeper and the keeper release. Intracomponent behavior is behavior that can be defined for a component. For example, the keeper release has associated with it two states: engaged and disengaged. These states are part of the intracomponent behavior of the keeper release.

Why Models?

The ability of human beings to reason about complex mechanisms appears to be closely related to their ability to create mental models of the mechanisms. It is not practical for humans who have to repair or use very complex devices such as jet aircraft to maintain a complete model of the device in their heads—there is just too much to remember at once. Just a single subsystem of a jet aircraft may have 500 components with various connections. Humans seem to be able to engage with systems in an extremely competent fashion. How can this be?

A very useful approach to dealing with complex systems is to partition or chunk the system into smaller and manageable pieces. An interesting idea in this regard is the notion of *autonomous objects* as defined by Williams, Hollan, and Stevens. An autonomous object is "a mental object with an explicit representation of state." Since an autonomous object must behave in the context of the mechanism to which it belongs, some kind of behavior should be defined for it. A convenient way to accomplish this is through a set of rules and parameters describing the behavior of the object. A model, then, is a collection of connected autonomous objects

To better understand the modeling process, I will present an example from deKleer and Brown, who share the view that complex devices are constructed from "combinations of simpler devices." Consider the model for a door buzzer shown in Figure 6.1 and its related description:

"The clapper-switch of the buzzer closes, which causes the coil to conduct a current thereby generating an electromagnetic field which in turn pulls the clapper arm away from the switch contact, thereby opening the switch, which shuts off the magnetic field, allowing the clapper arm to return to its closed position, which starts the process over again." (deKleer and Brown, pg. 156, *see suggested reading*)

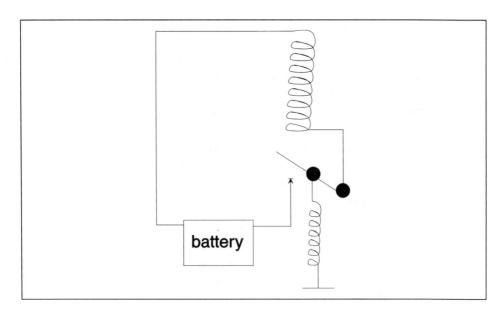

Figure 6.1 Buzzer diagram.

Several aspects of creating a model are defined by deKleer and Brown: device topology, envisioning, the causal model, and running the causal model.

The device topology consists of the definition of how components are connected to or otherwise relate to one another. Another way of thinking of the device topology is as the way a device is assembled from its component parts.

Envisioning is the process of trying to discover what a device does, given its topology. This means looking at the components and their connections and inferring the function of the device. Although it is an important process in general, the process of envisioning for our purposes is also important for understanding how parts of a mechanism function. The same inferencing process that can be applied to the whole device can also be applied to subsections of the device.

In any device the connections and relations between components that make up the device define the operation of the device. This aspect of the model is the causal model that describes how one component affects another in the model.

Our ability to reason about a mechanism is based on our ability to operate the mechanism in our minds. What we are really doing when we operate a mechanism in our minds is to run the model of the mechanism so as to elicit from it some desired behaviors.

Qualitative and Quantitative Models

The models we present in this book are called qualitative models. A qualitative model is one based on the characteristics and attributes of the entity being modeled. A quantitative model is also based on the characteristics and attributes of the entity being modeled. The difference is in how the characteristics and attributes are being treated in the model.

The next section describes the steps needed to create a model of a mechanism—specifically, the door buzzer used in earlier examples in this chapter. This model can be constructed by treating the entity in one of two ways: qualitatively or quantitatively. A quantitative model of the buzzer would describe it with the precise mathematics that define the physics of the device. For example, there are mathematical formulas defining how strong an electromagnetic field produced by a coil is. To properly engineer the buzzer, I would need this information. The field could not be too strong or too weak, as either situation would keep the buzzer from operating properly.

Most of the models presented in this book are qualitative as opposed to quantitative. The relationships are described by way of the qualities of the entity's parts as opposed to mathematical descriptions of how they operate. Whereas in a quantitative model it is important to define the field strength of the electromagnetic coil, in a qualitative model it is only necessary to describe what it does and under what conditions it does what it does. In the qualitative model in the next section the coil is described in terms of current being applied to it and then attracting the clapper away from the switch.

Humans seem to use qualitative reasoning quite a bit in their everyday encounters with the world. What's more, the skill of qualitative modeling seems to be learned at a very young age. After all, most kids can understand fairly well when it is safe or not safe to cross a street when a car is approaching. If the car is very far away, the car is traveling fairly slow, and the street to cross is less than a certain width, then it is probably safe to cross the street. This decision-making process is an example of qualitative modeling in the real world.

A Mini-How-To Guide

The initial step of the model-building process is to decide what to model. Let's use the buzzer example once more to specify how a model can be constructed. The diagram representing the buzzer is shown again in Figure 6.2. This time all of the components in the diagram have been labeled. We want to construct a model for the buzzer so that we can eventually use the model to simulate the buzzer. This section describes the steps needed to create this model.

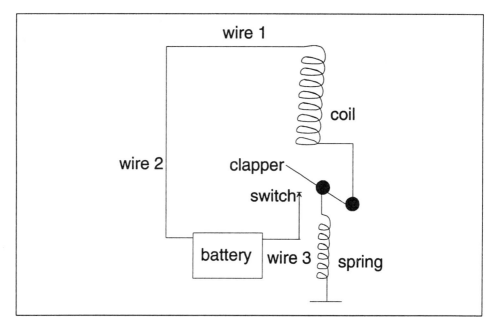

Figure 6.2 Buzzer diagram.

Step 1: What are the Components in the Mechanism?

The first step of this process is to identify the components of the mechanism you have decided to model. The buzzer consists of the following components.

1. Coil.
2. Clapper.
3. Battery.
4. Spring.
5. Switch.
6. Wire 1.
7. Wire 2.
8. Wire 3.

Step 2: Identify Which Components Represent Sub-components of the Mechanism and Which Represent Connections between Mechanisms

In the buzzer I have identified the connections between components explicitly as wire 1, wire 2, and wire 3. In general it is a good idea to identify the connections between components explicitly. In some cases there may not be an explicit connection—one component may somehow affect another. For example, the thermostat in the toaster is not connected to anything, yet there is a relationship between the thermostat and the keeper release switch. In the buzzer there is a similar relationship between the switch and the coil—the coil affects the switch through its electromagnetic action—although there is no actual connection between these components. It is important to identify both physical connections and effectual relationships like the one in the buzzer and the one described in the toaster.

The subcomponents of the buzzer are

1. Coil.
2. Clapper.
3. Battery.
4. Spring.
5. Switch.

With the components identified we can begin construction of the model. The diagram shown in Figure 6.3 displays each of the components in the model.

Step 3: Identify the Relationships between Components in the Model

In this step of the process we identify the physical connections between the components. How is one component connected to another? Is the component unidirectional or bidirectional? In the buzzer all of the connections are bidirectional. We can identify the following connections in the buzzer.

1. The battery is connected to the coil.

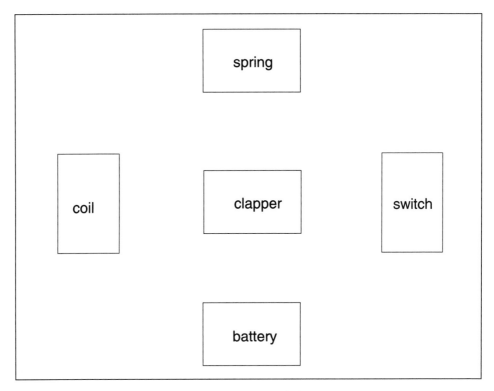

Figure 6.3 Components in the buzzer model.

2. The coil is connected to the clapper.
3. The spring is connected to the clapper.
4. The battery is connected to the switch.

These relationships are represented in Figure 6.4.

Step 4: Identify Implicit Relationships in the Mechanism

As I mentioned, some subcomponents in a mechanism affect one another without being connected. In the buzzer the implicit connection is the relationship between the clapper and the switch. When the clapper makes contact with the switch, the current flows through the coil and causes the clapper to move away from the switch contact. The implicit relationships in the buzzer are specified as:

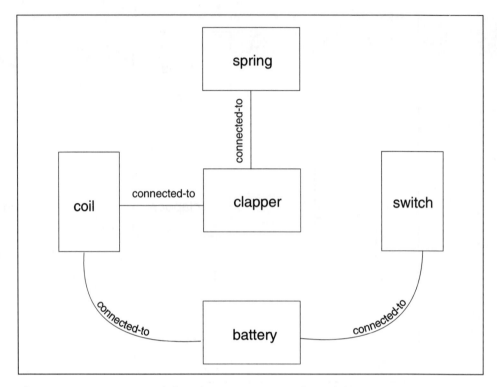

Figure 6.4 Buzzer model with connection relationships.

1. The clapper affects the switch.
2. The coil affects the clapper.

and are represented in Figure 6.5. The second implicit relationship defines how the clapper is affected by the coil as a result of the electromagnetic field created by the current applied to the coil.

Step 5: Specify the Rules of Operation of the Model

The rules for the operation of each component in the model must be written. To accomplish this it is necessary to identify the states a component can obtain. For example, the coil has two states: ON and OFF. The component operation for each of the components in the buzzer is defined as follows.

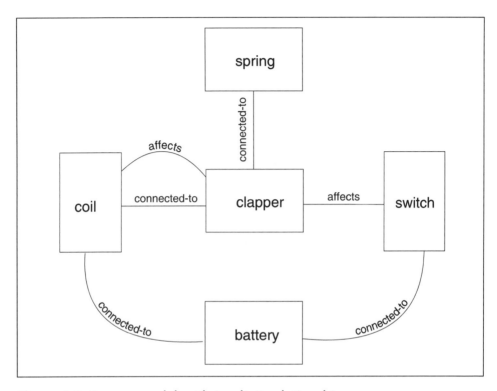

Figure 6.5 Buzzer model with implicit relationships.

1. *Coil.*
   - state: on / off
   - electromagneticField: on / off
2. *Spring.*
   - state: expanded / compressed
3. *Battery.*
   - state: on
   - current: on / off
4. *Clapper.*
   - state: up / down

5. *Switch.*
    state: on
                                off

Once the component operation is defined in terms of state variables and the values that can be obtained, rules can be written describing the operation of the buzzer.

1. *Coil rules.*

   If the current is on then the coil is on.

   If the current is off then the coil is off.

   If the coil is on then the clapper is up.

   If the coil is off then the clapper is down.

2. *Spring rules.*

   If the spring is expanded then the clapper is down.

3. *Battery rules.*

4. *Clapper rules.*

   If the current is on and the clapper is down, then the switch is on and the spring is compressed.

   If the battery is on and the clapper is up, then the switch is off and the spring is expanded.

5. *Switch rules.*

   If the switch is on and the battery is on, then current is on.

   If the switch is off and the battery is on, then current is off.

Step 6: Test the model

Having created the model we need to know if the model will work, so the last step in the process of model creation is the test of the model. This is accomplished by using the rules of the model in an appropriate sequence to simulate the actions and activity of the model.

To begin testing the model, let's organize the rules a little differently. I will assign a label to each rule so I can easily identify a rule when I need it. I will also remove the rule headings (coil rules, switch rules, etc.) because these groupings are not needed for us to test the model. The set of rules with these modifications are as follows:

R1 If the current is on then the coil is on.
R2 If the current is off then the coil is off.
R3 If the coil is on then the clapper is up.
R4 If the coil is off then the clapper is down.
R5 If the spring is expanded then the clapper is down.
R6 If the battery is on and the clapper is down, then the switch is on and the spring is compressed.
R7 If the battery is on and the clapper is up, then the switch is off and the spring is expanded.
R8 If the switch is on and the battery is on, then current is on.
R9 If the switch is off and the battery is on, then current is off.

Next we need to define the initial state of the bell. Think of the bell at the front door of a house. When there is no one to press the bell button, you don't hear the bell because the bell is not actuated. The bell is in a resting state.

In the resting state I can say the following about the bell:

The switch is off.

The coil is off.

The clapper is down.

The battery is on.

Now a friendly delivery person comes to the door and presses the bell button, and the bell is not at rest any longer. How does our model respond to this new condition? At the instant when the switch is depressed, the bell is in this state:

The switch is on.

The coil is off.

The clapper is down.

The battery is on.

Of course I am simulating the bell sequentially—the activation of the bell occurs very rapidly. When the switch is on, rule R8

If the switch is on and the battery is on, then current is on.

comes into play. The state of the buzzer now looks like this:

The switch is on.
The coil is off.
The clapper is down.
The battery is on.
The current is on.

Once the current is on things begin to happen in the buzzer. Looking at our rules we can see that the current affects the coil by way of rule R1:

If the current is on then the coil is on.

Rule R1 changes the state again, which will enable another rule to be activated. After rule R1 is applied, the current state of the buzzer is

The switch is on.
The coil is on.
The clapper is down.
The battery is on.
The current is on.

Once the coil is on, this affects the clapper by exerting an electromagnetic pull on the clapper. Rule R3

If the coil is on then the clapper is up.

changes the state of the clapper to this:

The switch is on.
The coil is on.
The clapper is up.
The battery is on.
The current is on.

Now the clapper is up. Once the clapper moves up, current is no longer on because the movement of the clapper breaks the circuit, so the clapper has clapped and now it has to return to its resting position. Rule R7

If the battery is on and the clapper is up, then the switch is off and the spring is expanded.

makes the appropriate changes to the state of the buzzer. The state of the buzzer will be this:

The switch is off.
The coil is on.
The clapper is up.
The battery is on.
The current is on.
The spring is expanded.

Now it makes sense that if the switch is off, current is not flowing in the buzzer. Rule R9

If the switch is off and the battery is on, then current is off.

takes care of this state change. The new state of the buzzer will be this:

The switch is off.
The coil is on.
The clapper is up.
The battery is on.
The current is off.
The spring is expanded.

No current means the coil is no longer operating. Rule R2 takes care of this, and the resulting state will be

The switch is off.
The coil is off.
The clapper is up.
The battery is on.
The current is on.
The spring is expanded.

Now the spring is expanded, which means it is exerting a pull on the clapper.

The change in state of the clapper due to the spring is caused by rule R5:

If the spring is expanded then the clapper is down.

Changing the position of the clapper results in the following state change.

The switch is off.
The coil is off.
The clapper is down.
The battery is on.
The current is on.
The spring is expanded.

The last rule to be activated starts the whole process over again beginning with Rule R8. Rule R6

If the battery is on and the clapper is down, then the switch is on and the spring is compressed,

activates the switch. This causes the new state change

The switch is on.
The coil is off.
The clapper is up.
The battery is on.
The current is on.
The spring is expanded.

Model Examples

Model construction can be daunting if you are doing it for the first time, because model construction also involves the process of devising a representation for a mechanism or a process. It is always useful to see examples to understand how models can be constructed. This section describes several different examples of models and their associated representations.

PROUST

Among intelligent tutors, PROUST (Soloway) is a classic example. The purpose of PROUST was to tutor students learning PASCAL for the first time in the solution and construction of writing simple PAS-

CAL programs. I like to think of PROUST as a kind of semantic debugger. A semantic debugger is one that understands what a program is supposed to do and assists the programmer with achieving the intended goal of the program.

PROUST models consist of a highly detailed description of what a program does. For example, if the program is supposed to compute the average of a sequence of numbers then PROUST's description will represent how this is accomplished.

To model the programming process we need to represent PASCAL programs in such a way that what is represented reflects what the program does and how it does what it does. Conceptually, the modeling problem becomes one of (a) defining what is important about PASCAL programs and (b) defining a language used to describe those important aspects. The modeling problem is represented in Figure 6.6

The language used for modeling program behavior is the same as the language used for specifying the program features as depicted in Figure 6.6. The large triangle in the figure represents the program that processes the language used to describe the program and program features. The outcome of this processing (processing the description language) is an assessment of the student's program. PROUST is the program that processes the description languages and is represented by the triangle in Figure 6.6. Let's consider what a PROUST model might look like.

First it is necessary to define a program. Since the programs PROUST can process are fairly simple, it is possible to succinctly represent these programs as a series of goals necessary to achieve the ultimate goal of the program. In other words, a program can be defined as a goal itself and in turn can be defined by smaller goals that together will accomplish the goal of the program.

Let's first assume the solution we desire from a student has the following algorithmic form:

1. Set a variable representing the SUM to 0.
2. Set a variable representing a sentinel to –99999.
3. Set a variable representing a count to 0.
4. Loop.

a. Read an input value into a variable—call it INVAL.
b. If INVAL is equal to the sentinel value then exit the loop.
c. Add the contents of INVAL to SUM.
d. Increment the count.
5. If any data was input (count > 0) then compute the average (SUM/count).

This algorithmic representation of the desired PASCAL program can be specified as a description of the following subgoals.

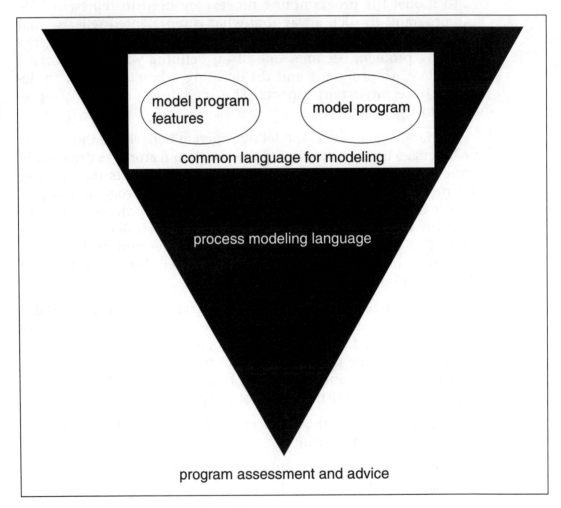

Figure 6.6 Conceptual representation of PROUST representation.

Defining program AVERAGE

1. Initialize variables.
   Define a sentinel.
   Define a counter.
   Define a sum.
2. Read data until a sentinel is encountered.
3. Compute average.

As you can see, three subgoals define the program AVERAGE. This only defines a top most description of the program. Now we can go a step further by defining what is meant by a particular subgoal.

The types of constructs used in simple programs tend to be similar. That is to say, novice program assignments may include a subgoal of reading data into a program. There are many ways to accomplish this, but a group of novices would only use a limited range of potential ways to get data into a program. With this in mind it is possible to create a library of these methods that can be referred to and used. For example, the subgoal "Read data until a sentinel is encountered." could be part of a description of subgoals that are called "Read data into program."

The next part of the model identifies these various kinds of "data-getting" processes. It does so by assigning names to them (which will be used to identify actual descriptions of processes), and also by defining what the process needs (input variables) and what the process produces (output variables). An example of such a definition is

Define a process called "Sentinel Controlled Input."

Description: This process is used to obtain multiple data items. It accomplishes this by reading data from an input source until a special value is read, at which point the process of reading data terminates.

Process form: sentinel-controlled input INVAL SENTINELVAL

Process uses: This process will use two variables, a variable to hold the data item read and a variable to hold the special sentinel value.

Prototype processes:

1. Check for sentinel, process, read, loop.
2. Check for sentinel, read, process, while.
3. Check for sentinel, read, process, repeat.
4. Check for sentinel, process, read, repeat.
5. Fake counter-based loop.

The subgoal definition specifies several important characteristics of the subgoal. The process form defines the way the process is referred to in descriptions (i.e., "sentinel-controlled input") and also the parameters of the process, an input value (INVAL), and a sentinel value (SENTINELVAL). The process uses section of the definition defines the role for the process parameters. Finally, the prototype processes section specifies all input process that can be called a sentinel-based input process. The remainder of this model defines specific processes.

Specific processes must be defined for a PASCAL program to be analyzed and reformulated into the language of the model. When we define how a particular goal can be carried out, a so-called plan, we can identify whether a programmer has accomplished the necessary goals and subgoals for the program.

A plan definition specifies a process. The plan definition includes a kind of template that defines what the process code should look like with place holders for the variables that a student actually uses in a program. An example of a template is

```
subgoal INPUT INVAL
WHILE INVAL <> SENTINELVAL
BEGIN
  ...
  SUBGOAL INPUT INVAL
END
```

This looks more like PASCAL code than what we have seen in the model so far. This is because the template is used to identify actual code. The model represents the code by identifying portions of the code that fulfill program subgoals. By identifying these sections, the semantic debugger can accomplish two tasks. It can "know" if a student wrote the code for a particular subgoal, and it can comment on whether the approach to writing the code used by the student was correct.

A Process-Oriented Model

Whereas the purpose of PROUST was to examine the result of a process and give advice about it, another possible kind of tutoring involves instruction in a process. As a possible tutoring domain, consider the VCR programming process and how we might model that process.

Early VCRs were notoriously difficult to program because the functionality was not yet implemented using a microprocessor (these were still too expensive to use when VCRs first appeared). The programming process for early VCRs was usually implemented with a series of switches on the control panel. The fortunate evolution of VCRs has changed the programming process from using a series of switches to following a series of on-screen menus. Even so, early VCRs provide a good example of a different kinds of model that can be used as part of an intelligent tutor. The VCR example and the following discussion are derived from the work of Mark and Greer.

If we wish to model a process, we can do so with something called a state diagram. A state diagram is represented as a graph; a series of labeled nodes connected by directed edges. A directed edge is one that is tipped with an arrow to indicate the direction of the connection (the from- and to- nodes). Processes like programming a VCR or cooking your favorite recipe can readily be represented by a state diagram.

In the case of VCR programming, we can identify the following major steps of the process.

1. Turn on power to the VCR.
2. Select a program (to be used to set the VCR).
3. Select the channel.
4. Select the day.

5. Set the start time.
6. Set the end time.
7. Set record mode.
8. Insert a tape.

As in the case of the PROUST model, each of these major steps could have zero or more substeps. For example, setting the start time and the end time involves setting the hour and minute.

To model this with a state diagram, we could create one node for each of the steps of the process and connect the nodes with edges that specify the conditions for proceeding to the next step (next node) of the process. An example of a state diagram for VCR programming is shown in Figure 6.7. Looking at Figure 6.7 we can see all of the major steps of the VCR programming process and the criteria for transition from one step to the next. Of course both the steps of the programming process and the criteria necessary to transit from one state to the next can consist of any number of substeps.

A model such as the one shown in Figure 6.7 can be used for several purposes in an intelligent multimedia tutor. If the tutor is to provide an instructional sequence of the steps in the process, then a state-based model can be used as the basis for the instructional sequence. On the other hand, if it is necessary to observe and compare a student's VCR programming process with the actual VCR programming process, then the state-based model supplies a means to monitor student actions during a simulated process and give directives or feedback when the student goes astray of the actual process.

Another useful model that is part of the Mark and Greer system is the dictionary of bugs. The dictionary of bugs can be used to identify a problem or potential problem a student might be having. Many intelligent tutors have a catalog like this to assist the process of assessing student actions and also to provide instruction. In the case of the VCR tutor, this information consists of a name of a bug and a description of what the bug might be. For example, one potential bug is called "random thrashing," and is described as "unsystematic search (apparently random selection of buttons)." Another

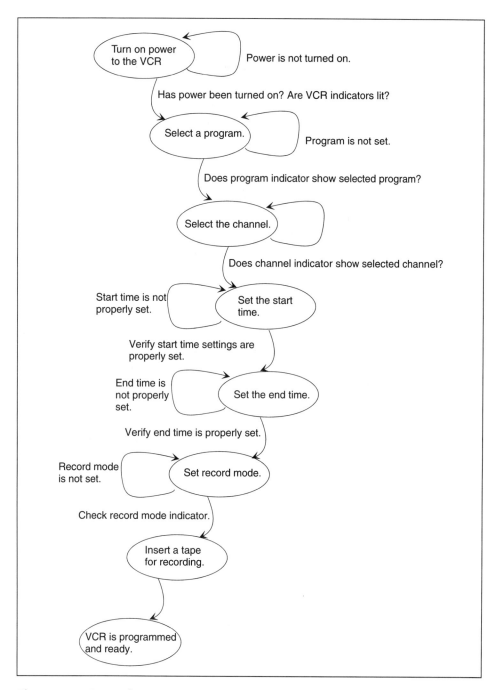

Figure 6.7 State diagram representing VCR programming process.

potential bug is, "ignore power." This bug is described as "trying to set the VCR without turning on the power of the VCR."

With sufficient knowledge, a catalog of bugs can be formulated by an expert. Another way to formulate a bug catalog is to have people program a VCR and to record the kinds of mistakes they make. This was the procedure used by Mark and Greer for their VCR tutor.

Knowledge, Metaknowledge, Meta-metaknowledge

There are models of mechanism, models of problem solving, student models, and instructional models. All of these are ground or base models in the sense that they operate on entities in the domain. For example, in Chapter 7 you will see that the student model operates by examining student actions on the model of the toaster. Another kind of model is a model of the models or a metamodel.

Suppose we have our three basic models in an intelligent tutor: the mechanism or domain model, the student model, and the instructional model. Now let's define a set of rules defining when and how the domain, student, and instructional model are used. These rules constitute a metamodel in the sense that they control the ground models and their associated rules. Think of the metamodel as having the ability to activate and deactivate the ground models. The relationship between the ground and metamodel is shown in Figure 6.8.

What kinds of rules can we expect in a metamodel? Consider the following:

> The student has completed the present topic, but the tutor has little confidence in its assessment of the student's knowledge of the present topic.

> The tutor will now question the student about a variety of topics.

This rule, an example from the Meno-tutor, is a metarule. It controls the operation of the tutor as opposed to controlling the operation of a specific model. This rule may cause the tutor to obtain a

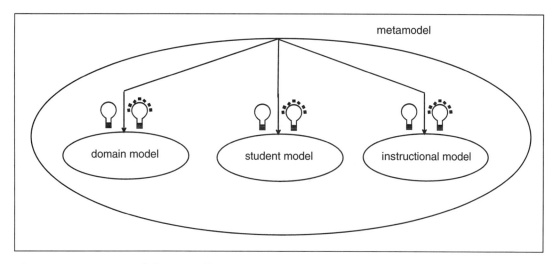

Figure 6.8 Metamodel controlling ground models.

list of related topics from the domain model and then use the instructional model to ask questions about the topic. The answers to the question are analyzed by the student model, which in turn may cause other metatype rules to be called into play.

A More Complete Toaster

The previous chapters showed a preliminary model of the toaster by way of constructing a series of rules that would simulate an operating toaster. For our purposes in the Toaster Tutor we need to create a model for the toaster representing when the toaster is operating and when the toaster is not operating. Using the process developed in the mini-how-to guide we will develop a complete model for the toaster. So far I have only modeled the operating aspects of devices. In the toaster model I will model both operating and nonoperating states of the toaster.

Step 1: What are the Components of the Mechanism?

The diagram shown in Figure 6.9 will be used to carry out the first step of the model-building process. In this diagram all of the com-

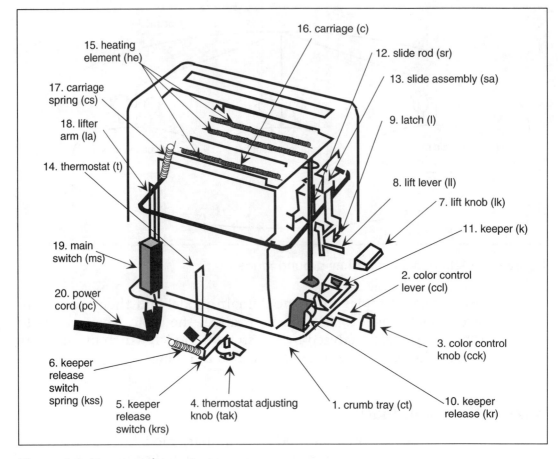

Figure 6.9 Toaster schematic.

ponents are shown and labeled. Diagrams like the one shown in Figure 6.9 are good sources for the construction of models. Based on this diagram we can identify the subcomponents, which actually make up the toaster. The list following each component has a "long name," one that precisely names the subcomponent, and also a "short name," one that will be used when we write rules for the components. The short names are enclosed in parentheses.

1. crumb tray (ct)
2. color control lever (ccl)
3. color control knob (cck)

4. thermostat adjusting knob (tak)
5. keeper release switch (krs)
6. keeper release switch spring (kss)
7. lift knob (lk)
8. lift lever (ll)
9. latch (l)
10. keeper release (kr)
11. keeper (k)
12. slide rod (sl)
13. slide assembly (sa)
14. thermostat (t)
15. heating element (he)
16. carriage (c)
17. piston (or carriage spring) (p) (cs)
18. lifter arm (la)
19. main switch (ms)
20. power cord (pc)
21. toast* (t)

Step 2: Identify Which Components Represent Subcomponents of the Mechanism and Which Represent Connections between Mechanisms

In this list of components, none of the components represents an explicit connection between components. This does not mean there are not entities that connect one component to the next. We just have not identified them at this stage. In more complex devices, the number of connections can be overwhelming, and it is better to wait until step 3 of the model building process to define the relationships between components in the model. The model diagram at the end of step 2 is shown in Figure 6.10.

---

*Toast is not really an element of the toaster, but we need it for the simulation of the toaster.

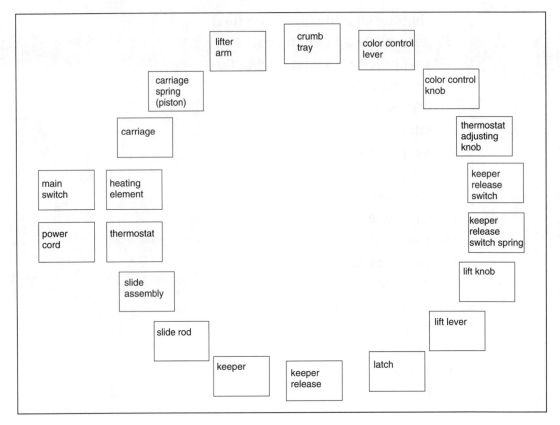

Figure 6.10 Toaster model, step 1 diagram.

Steps 3 and 4: Identify Relationships between Components in the Model

Now we proceed to identify the relationships between components in the model. There are two kinds of relationships we want to identify—the same two types of relationships that were used in the model of the buzzer. These are the connected-to relationship and the affects (or controls) relationship. A good way to do this is to make a table whose rows and columns are labeled with the names of the components as shown in Table 6.1.

If a component is related to another because the component is connected to it, I will write a "c" in the cell. If a component is related to another by the affected relationship, I will write an "a" in

Table 6.1 Table of Component Relationships (not yet completed)

	ct	ccl	cck	tak	krs	lk	ll	l	kr	k	sl	sa	t	he	c	cs	la	ms	pc
Crumb tray																			
Color control lever																			
Color control knob																			
Thermostat adjusting knob																			
Keeper release switch																			
Keeper release switch spring																			
Lift knob																			
Lift lever																			
Latch																			
Keeper release																			
Keeper																			
Slide rod																			
Slide assembly																			
Thermostat																			
Heating element																			
Carriage																			
Carriage spring																			
Lifter arm																			
Main switch																			
Power cord																			

the cell. Finally, if two components are not related (have no physical or affecting relationship), then the cell of the table will be left blank. For example, the lift knob is connected to the lift lever. A "c" would be inserted in the table at the intersection of the row containing the component lift knob and the column containing the lift lever (ll). The row and column of the components and the inserted indicator are shown shaded in Table 6.2.

Table 6.3 shows the completed table of component relationships. To complete this table, I used the toaster diagram shown in

316 CHAPTER 6

Table 6.2 Relationship Table Showing Lift Knob and Level Relationship

	ct	ccl	cck	tak	krs	lk	ll	l	kr	k	sl	sa	t	he	c	cs	la	ms	pc
Crumb tray																			
Color control lever																			
Color control knob																			
Thermostat adjusting knob																			
Keeper release switch																			
Keeper release switch spring																			
Lift knob							c												
Lift lever																			
Latch																			
Keeper release																			
Keeper																			
Slide rod																			
Slide assembly																			
Thermostat																			
Heating element																			
Carriage																			
Carriage spring																			
Lifter arm																			
Main switch																			
Power cord																			

Figure 6.9 to guide the specification of connected and related components. Using the information contained in this table, I can revise the diagrammatic view of the model to include these relationships. The result is shown in Figure 6.11.

Step 5: Specify the Rules of Operation of the Model

We have the model components and the relationships between these components. We know which components affect other com-

Table 6.3 Complete Table of Component Relationships

	ct	ccl	cck	tak	krs	lk	ll	l	kr	k	sl	sa	t	he	c	cs	la	ms	pc
Crumb tray																			
Color control lever				c															
Color control knob		c																	
Thermostat adjusting knob					a														
Keeper release switch								c											
Keeper release switch spring																			
Lift knob							c												
Lift lever										c									
Latch												c							
Keeper release										a									
Keeper									a										
Slide rod															c				
Slide assembly															c				
Thermostat					a														
Heating element																			
Carriage																			
Carriage spring																	c		
Lifter arm														c					
Main switch														a	c				
Power cord																		a	

ponents in the model. Now we can describe the operation of the toaster. To do so I will follow the same process as that used for the buzzer model. First I will list the characteristics of each of the components. These characteristics represent variables describing the state of toaster components, and together they describe the state of the toaster.

For example, the color control knob is used to select the color of the toast. The color control knob can be set to white (no color), very light brown, light brown, brown, medium dark brown, and

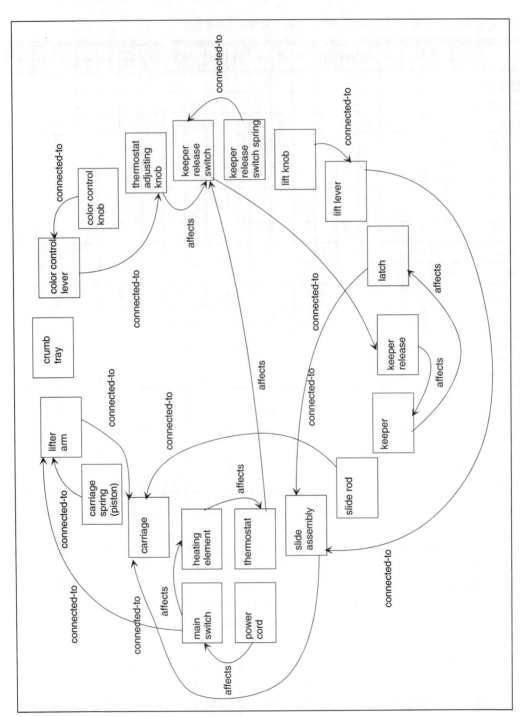

Figure 6.11 Model showing components and relationships.

dark brown. These color settings are used throughout the model of the toaster. For convenience, in the toaster model the colors will be named color$x$, where color$x$ is defined as follows:

color0	white (no color)
color1	very light brown
color2	light brown
color3	brown
color4	medium dark brown
color5	dark brown

Because the color control knob is connected to the color control lever, we know the color control lever can obtain the same values as the color control knob. In some cases the connected component will transform the values in some way. In other cases the connected component will use the values directly. Because the color control lever is connected to the color control knob, the lever will obtain the same values as the color control knob—it does not perform any transformation on its input. Therefore, the color control lever will have exactly the same values as the color control knob. Table 6.4 shows the characteristics of each of the components in the model.

Model Rules

The remainder of this section consists of defining the rules that will define the operation of the model. Each set of rules is based on a relationship between two components in the model and depends on whether the components are connected or whether one component affects another component. Rules also depend on the function of the component and whether the component can be made defective. The rules that follow have listed the relationship upon which the rules are based, the rules for that relationship, and some annotation when clarification about the purpose of a rule seems appropriate.

Relation: Lift knob is connected to the lift lever.

R1. If the lift knob is down then the lift lever is down.
R2. If the lift knob is up then the lift lever is up.

Table 6.4 Component Characteristics

Component	Characteristic	Values	Notes
Crumb tray			
Color control knob	color setting	color0, color1, color2, color3, color4, color5	
Color control lever	color setting	color0, color1, color2, color3, color4, color5	
Thermostat adjusting knob	color setting	color0, color1, color2, color3, color4, color5	
Keeper release switch	position	position0, position1, position2, position3, position4, position5	The thermostat adjusting knob moves the keeper release switch to a position so that the toaster will turn off when the toast has reached the desired color. The color settings are directly related to the position settings.
	state	on, off	
	OK	yes, no	The ok characteristic provides for the need to make a component defective. By setting the ok characteristic to 'no', different model rules will take effect, which will cause the model to behave differently.
Keeper release switch spring	position	position0, position1, position2, position3, position4, position5	
Lift knob	position	up, down	
Lift lever	position	up, down	
Latch	state	engaged, disengaged	
Keeper release	state	releasing, stationary	
Keeper	state	engaged, disengaged	
Slide rod			
Slide assembly	state	up, down	
Thermostat	deflection	deflect0, deflect1, deflect2, deflect3, deflect4, deflect5	The thermostat is affected by the heating of the elements. As the elements heat, the thermostat bends. We call this a deflection. The hotter the elements, the more bend. The deflection value is related to the color setting and the position characteristic.

Table 6.4 Component Characteristics (*Continued*)

Component	Characteristic	Values	Notes
	OK	yes, tooquick, tooslow, no	The thermostat is special in that it can be defective, but also defective in certain ways. For example, the thermostat may turn off the toaster too soon, in which case the toast will be consistently lighter than desired. The 'tooquick' setting of ok allows the model to simulate this defective state of the toaster.
Heating element	state	on, off	
	temperature	temperature0, temperature1, temperature2, temperature3, temperature4, temperature5, temperature6	
	OK	yes, no	
Carriage	state	up, down	
Piston	state	up, down	
	OK	yes, no	
Carriage spring	state	compressed, expanded	As an alternative to a piston, a toaster may have a carriage spring that serves the same purpose as the piston.
	OK	yes, no	
Lifter arm	state	up, down	
Main switch	state	on, off	
Power cord	state	attached, detached	
Toast	state	up, down	
	color	color0, color1, color2, color3, color4, color5, burnt	

Comments: When the lift knob is moved, the lift lever will also be moved because of the connected relationship of these components. A more precise simulation may model the travel of the lift knob from its starting position to its ending position. For our purposes, these rules are sufficient. In these rules and those that follow you will see that mechanically connected components in general transfer movement from one component to another. This gives rise to similar rules in the model.

Relation: Lift lever is connected to the slide assembly.

R3. If the lift lever is down then the slide assembly is down.

R4. If the lift lever is up then the slide assembly is up.

Relation: Slide assembly is connected to the lifter arm.

R5. If the slide assembly is down then the lifter arm is down.

R6. If the slide assembly is up then the lifter arm is up.

Relation: Lifter arm is connected to the carriage.

R7. If the lifter arm is down then the carriage is down.

R8. If the lifter arm is up then the carriage is up.

Relation: Lifter arm is connected to the piston (or carriage spring).

R9. If the lifter arm is down and the piston is OK, then the piston is compressed.

R9d. If the lifter arm is down and the piston is not OK, then the piston is decompressed.

R10. If the lifter arm is up and the piston is OK, then the piston is decompressed.

Comments: Rules R9, R9d, and R10 are the first example of a set of rules including a rule for a defective component. Notice that each of these rules checks to see if the piston is OK. If the piston is OK, then it operates as expected in conjunction with the lifter arm. If, on the other hand, the piston is not OK, then the lifter arm will not effect the piston. Under these circumstances when the toast is finished, at the end of the toasting cycle, the toast will not pop up.

Relation: Latch is connected to the slide assembly.

R11e. If the slide assembly is down then the latch is engaged.

R11d. If the slide assembly is up then the latch is disengaged.

Relation: Main switch is connected to the lifter arm.

R12. If the lifter arm is down then the main switch is on.

R13. If the lifter arm is up then the main switch is off.

Relation: Heating element is affected by the main switch.

R14. If the main switch is attached to power then the heating elements are on.

R15. If the main switch is detached from power then the heating elements are off.

Component: Keeper release switch affects the keeper release.

R16. If the keeper release switch is on then the keeper release switch is releasing.

Relation: Keeper release affects the keeper.

R17. If the keeper release is releasing then the keeper is disengaged.

Component: Heating elements.

R18. If the heating elements are on and the heating elements are OK and the heating elements are at temperature 0, then the heating elements are at temperature 1.

R19a. If the heating elements are on and the heating elements are OK and the heating elements are at temperature 1, then the heating elements are at temperature 2.

R19b. If the heating elements are on and the heating elements are OK and the heating elements are at temperature 2, then the heating elements are at temperature 3.

R20. If the heating elements are on and the heating elements are OK and the heating elements are at temperature 3, then the heating elements are at temperature 4.

R21. If the heating elements are on and the heating elements are OK and the heating elements are at temperature 4, then the heating elements are at temperature 5.

R22. If the heating elements are on and the heating elements are OK and the heating elements are at temperature 5, then the heating elements are at temperature 6.

Comments: R18 through R22 represent the first set of rules controlling the operation of a component that changes over time. The heating elements "heat up" as power is applied from the main switch. In this model, the heating of the heating elements is modeled discretely from temperature to temperature. True heating elements do not work like this. Heating is a more gradual process. This discrete representation will suit our needs in the model of the toaster.

There are a couple of specific features to note about rules R18 through R22. First, even though the components of the toaster have a maximum color of 5, a maximum position of 5, and so on, the heating elements can reach a temperature of 6. This is necessary to allow the toaster to burn the toast in case some component of the toaster is not functioning properly.

Another characteristic of these rules is that they check to make sure the heating elements are functioning properly by testing OK. There are no defective rules corresponding to the OK rules because the defective rules are implicit. If the heating elements are not operating properly, then no one of rule R18 through R22 will take effect, and therefore the elements will not heat as expected. In some cases, as in this one, a set of defective rules will not be necessary.

Relation: Heating elements affect thermostat (heating).

- R23. If the heating elements are at temperature 0 and the thermostat is OK, then the thermostat is at deflect 0.
- R23d2. If the heating elements are at temperature 0 and the thermostat is deflecting too quickly, then the thermostat is at deflect 2.
- R24. If the heating elements are at temperature 1 and the thermostat is OK, then the thermostat is at deflect 1.
- R24d1. If the heating elements are at temperature 1 and the thermostat is not OK, then the thermostat is at deflect 0.
- R24d2. If the heating elements are at temperature 1 and the thermostat is deflecting too quickly, then the thermostat is at deflect 3.
- R24d3. If the heating elements are at temperature 1 and the thermostat is deflecting too slowly, then the thermostat is at deflect 1.

R25. If the heating elements are at temperature 2 and the thermostat is OK, then the thermostat is at deflect 2.

R25d1. If the heating elements are at temperature 2 and the thermostat is not OK, then the thermostat is at deflect 0.

R25d2. If the heating elements are at temperature 2 and the thermostat is deflecting too quickly, then the thermostat is at deflect 4.

R25d3. If the heating elements are at temperature 1 and the thermostat is deflecting too slowly, then the thermostat is at deflect 2.

R26. If the heating elements are at temperature 3 and the thermostat is OK, then the thermostat is at deflect 3.

R26d1. If the heating elements are at temperature 3 and the thermostat is not OK, then the thermostat is at deflect 0.

R26d2. If the heating elements are at temperature 3 and the thermostat is deflecting too quickly, then the thermostat is at deflect 5.

R26d3. If the heating elements are at temperature 2 and the thermostat is deflecting too slowly, then the thermostat is at deflect 2.

R27. If the heating elements are at temperature 4 and the thermostat is OK, then the thermostat is at deflect 4.

R27d1. If the heating elements are at temperature 4 and the thermostat is not OK, then the thermostat is at deflect 0.

R27d2. If the heating elements are at temperature 4 and the thermostat is deflecting too quickly, then the thermostat is at deflect 6.

R27d3. If the heating elements are at temperature 2 and the thermostat is deflecting too slowly, then the thermostat is at deflect 3.

R28. If the heating elements are at temperature 5 and the thermostat is OK, then the thermostat is at deflect 5.

R28d1. If the heating elements are at temperature 5 and the thermostat is not OK, then the thermostat is at deflect 0.

R28d2. If the heating elements are at temperature 5 and the thermostat is deflecting too quickly, then the thermostat is at deflect 6.

R28d3. If the heating elements are at temperature 3 and the thermostat is deflecting too slowly, then the thermostat is at deflect 3.

Comments: Among all of the rules in the toaster model, those governing the operation of the thermostat are the most complex. Rules R23 through R28d3 represent a whole palette of operational possibilities for the thermostat. The reason I chose to do this was to give some diversity to how a particular component can become defective. The thermostat is a nice component for this because its operation is controlled by the heating of the elements. I have elected not only to allow the thermostat to be defective, but also allow it to heat too quickly or heat too slowly. This gives rise to four rules for each possible temperature of the heating elements: one for proper operating, another for operating too slowly, another for deflection occurring too quickly, and the last for the defective thermostat.

Relation: Thermostat adjustment affects keeper release switch.

R29. If the thermostat adjustment knob is at color 0 then the keeper release switch is at position 0.

R30. If the thermostat adjustment knob is at color 1 then the keeper release switch is at position 1.

R31. If the thermostat adjustment knob is at color 2 then the keeper release switch is at position 2.

R32. If the thermostat adjustment knob is at color 3 then the keeper release switch is at position 3.

R33. If the thermostat adjustment knob is at color 4 then the keeper release switch is at position 4.

R34. If the thermostat adjustment knob is at color 5 then the keeper release switch is at position 5.

Relation: Thermostat affects keeper release switch.

R35. If the keeper release switch is OK and the keeper release switch is at position 0 and the thermostat is at deflect 0, then the keeper release switch is on.

R35d. If the keeper release switch is not OK and the keeper release switch is at position 0 and the thermostat is at deflect 0, then the keeper release switch is off.

R36. If the keeper release switch is OK and the keeper release switch is at position 1 and the thermostat is at deflect 1, then the keeper release switch is on.

R36d. If the keeper release switch is not OK and the keeper release switch is at position 1 and the thermostat is at deflect 1, then the keeper release switch is off.

R37. If the keeper release switch is OK and the keeper release switch is at position 2 and the thermostat is at deflect 2, then the keeper release switch is on.

R37d. If the keeper release switch is not OK and the keeper release switch is at position 2 and the thermostat is at deflect 2, then the keeper release switch is off.

R38. If the keeper release switch is OK and the keeper release switch is at position 3 and the thermostat is at deflect 3, then the keeper release switch is on.

R38d. If the keeper release switch is not OK and the keeper release switch is at position 3 and the thermostat is at deflect 3, then the keeper release switch is off.

R39. If the keeper release switch is OK and the keeper release switch is at position 4 and the thermostat is at deflect 4, then the keeper release switch is on.

R39d. If the keeper release switch is not OK and the keeper release switch is at position 4 and the thermostat is at deflect 4, then the keeper release switch is off.

R40. If the keeper release switch is OK and the keeper release switch is at position 5 and the thermostat is at deflect 5, then the keeper release switch is on.

R40. If the keeper release switch is not OK and the keeper release switch is at position 5 and the thermostat is at deflect 5, then the keeper release switch is off.

Relation: Heating elements affect thermostat (cooling).

R41. If the heating elements are off and the heating elements are at temperature 5, then the heating elements are at temperature 4.

R42. If the heating elements are off and the heating elements are at temperature 4, then the heating elements are at temperature 3.

R43. If the heating elements are off and the heating elements are at temperature 3, then the heating elements are at temperature 2.

R44. If the heating elements are off and the heating elements are at temperature 2, then the heating elements are at temperature 1.

R45. If the heating elements are off and the heating elements are at temperature 1, then the heating elements are at temperature 0.

Comments: When power is removed from the heating elements as a result of the carriage returning to the up position, the heating elements will undergo a cooling process. These rules are specified for just this purpose—to allow the elements to cool.

Relation: Piston is connected to the lifter arm (carriage spring is compressed).

R46. If the piston is OK and the piston is down and the keeper release is releasing and the keeper is disengaged, then the lifter arm is up and the piston is up.

R46. (alternate) If the carriage spring is OK and the carriage spring is compressed and the keeper release is releasing and the keeper is disengaged, then the lifter arm is up and the carriage spring is expanded.

R46d. If the piston is not OK and the piston is down and the keeper release is releasing and the keeper is disengaged, then the lifter arm is down and the piston is down.

R46d. (alternate) If the carriage spring is not OK and the carriage spring is compressed and the keeper release is releasing and the keeper is disengaged, then the lifter arm is down and the carriage spring is compressed.

Relation: Heating elements affect toast.

R47. If the heating elements are at temperature 6 then the toast is burnt.

R48f. The heating elements are at temperature 0 then the toast is at color 0.

R49. If the heating elements are at temperature 1 then the toast is at color 1.

R50. If the heating elements are at temperature 2 then the toast is at color 2.

R51. If the heating elements are at temperature 3 then the toast is at color 3.

R52. If the heating elements are at temperature 4 then the toast is at color 4.

R53. If the heating elements are at temperature 5 then the toast is at color 5.

Relation: Carriage affects toast.

R54. If the carriage is down then the toast is down.

R55. If the carriage is up then the toast is up.

Relation: Color control knob is connected to the color control lever.

R56. If the color control knob is set to color 0 then the color control lever is at color 0.

R57. If the color control knob is set to color 1 then the color control lever is at color 1.

R58. If the color control knob is set to color 2 then the color control lever is at color 2.

R59. If the color control knob is set to color 3 then the color control lever is at color 3.

R60. If the color control knob is set to color 4 then the color control lever is at color 4.

R61. If the color control knob is set to color 5 then the color control lever is at color 5.

Relation: Color control lever is connected to the thermostat adjusting knob.

R62. If the color control lever is set to color 0 then the thermostat adjusting knob is set to color 0.

R63. If the color control lever is set to color 1 then the thermostat adjusting knob is set to color 1.

R64. If the color control lever is set to color 2 then the thermostat adjusting knob is set to color 2.

R65. If the color control lever is set to color 3 then the thermostat adjusting knob is set to color 3.

R66. If the color control lever is set to color 4 then the thermostat adjusting knob is set to color 4.

R67. If the color control lever is set to color 5 then the thermostat adjusting knob is set to color 5.

Step 6: Test the Model

But will it work? Here is where we prove the model out. The toaster model is significantly more complex than the buzzer model, and a complete test of the model would require far more space than is available here, so I will do a partial test and leave the remainder of the test as an exercise for the reader.

Before starting, let's do some preparation that will simplify the process of tracing the state of the model, the state of components in the model, and the rules that will be invoked as the model is run.

To keep track of the components of the model as the model runs we will use a table containing five columns. The first column will be used to hold the component name. The second and third columns of the table will contain a characteristic for the component and its current value. The fourth column will contain a single row that names a rule applying to the configuration in the first, second, and third column, and the fifth column contains any change in characteristic value caused by applying the rule. The starting state table, before anything is "done" to the toaster is shown in Table 6.5.

The first step of the testing process is to set the toaster to a new state that would begin the toasting process. With a real toaster this is accomplished by setting the desired toast color and by pushing down the lift knob. Table 6.6 shows the new state table.

With the lift knob in the down position, we can now start to look for rules applying to the current state of the toaster. We can apply rule R1 to the current state of the toaster, as shown in Table 6.7 Tables 6.8 through 6.12 continue the process of applying rules to the current state of the toaster.

Table 6.5 Toaster Model Initial State

Component	Characteristic	Value	Applied Rule	New Value
Crumb tray				
Color control lever	color setting	color0		
Color control knob	color setting	color0		
Thermostat adjusting knob	color setting	color0		
Keeper release switch	position	position0		
	state	off		
	OK	yes		
Keeper release switch spring	position	position0		
Lift knob	position	up		
Lift lever	position	up		
Latch	state	disengaged		
Keeper release	state	stationary		
Keeper	state	disengaged		
Slide assembly	state	up		
Thermostat	deflection	deflect0		
	OK	yes		
Heating element	state	off		
	OK	yes		
Carriage	state	up		
Piston	state	up		
	OK	yes		
Carriage spring	state	compressed		
	OK	yes		
Lifter arm	state	up		
Main switch	state	off		
Power cord	state	detached		
Toast	state	up		
	color	color0		

Table 6.6 Starting the Toaster Model

Component	Characteristic	Value	Applied Rule	New Value
Crumb tray				
Color control lever	color setting	color0		
Color control knob	color setting	color3		
Thermostat adjusting knob	color setting	color0		
Keeper release switch	position	position0		
	state	off		
	OK	yes		
Keeper release switch spring	position	position0		
Lift knob	position	down		
Lift lever	position	up		
Latch	state	disengaged		
Keeper release	state	stationary		
Keeper	state	disengaged		
Slide assembly	state	up		
Thermostat	deflection	deflect0		
	OK	yes		
Heating element	state	off		
	OK	yes		
Carriage	state	up		
Piston	state	up		
	OK	yes		
Carriage spring	state	compressed		
	OK	yes		
Lifter arm	state	up		
Main switch	state	off		
Power cord	state	detached		
Toast	state	up		
	color	color0		

MODELS

Table 6.7 Propagating the Lift Knob State to the Lift Lever State by Way of R1

Component	Characteristic	Value	Applied Rule	New Value
Crumb tray				
Color control lever	color setting	color0		
Color control knob	color setting	color3		
Thermostat adjusting knob	color setting	color0		
Keeper release switch	position	position0		
	state	off		
	OK	yes		
Keeper release switch spring	position	position0		
Lift knob	position	down	R1	
Lift lever	position	up		down
Latch	state	disengaged		
Keeper release	state	stationary		
Keeper	state	disengaged		
Slide assembly	state	up		
Thermostat	deflection	deflect0		
	OK	yes		
Heating element	state	off		
	OK	yes		
Carriage	state	up		
Piston	state	up		
	OK	yes		
Carriage spring	state	compressed		
	OK	yes		
Lifter arm	state	up		
Main switch	state	off		
Power cord	state	detached		
Toast	state	up		
	color	color0		

Table 6.8 Propagate the Lift Lever Down State to the Slide Assembly by Way of R3

Component	Characteristic	Value	Applied Rule	New Value
Crumb tray				
Color control lever	color setting	color0		
Color control knob	color setting	color3		
Thermostat adjusting knob	color setting	color0		
Keeper release switch	position	position0		
	state	off		
	OK	yes		
Keeper release switch spring	position	position0		
Lift knob	position	down		
Lift lever	position	down	R3	
Latch	state	disengaged		
Keeper release	state	stationary		
Keeper	state	disengaged		
Slide assembly	state	up		down
Thermostat	deflection	deflect0		
	OK	yes		
Heating element	state	off		
	OK	yes		
Carriage	state	up		
Piston	state	up		
	OK	yes		
Carriage spring	state	compressed		
	OK	yes		
Lifter arm	state	up		
Main switch	state	off		
Power cord	state	detached		
Toast	state	up		
	color	color0		

Table 6.9 Propagate the Down State of the Slide Assembly to Lifter Arm by Way of R5

Component	Characteristic	Value	Applied Rule	New Value
Crumb tray				
Color control lever	color setting	color0		
Color control knob	color setting	color3		
Thermostat adjusting knob	color setting	color0		
Keeper release switch	position	position0		
	state	off		
	OK	yes		
Keeper release switch spring	position	position0		
Lift knob	position	down		
Lift lever	position	down		
Latch	state	disengaged		
Keeper release	state	stationary		
Keeper	state	disengaged		
Slide assembly	state	down	R5	
Thermostat	deflection	deflect0		
	OK	yes		
Heating element	state	off		
	OK	yes		
Carriage	state	up		
Piston	state	up		
	OK	yes		
Carriage spring	state	compressed		
	OK	yes		
Lifter arm	state	up		down
Main switch	state	off		
Power cord	state	detached		
Toast	state	up		
	color	color0		

Table 6.10 Propagate the Down State of the Lifter Arm to Carriage Spring by Way of R9

Component	Characteristic	Value	Applied Rule	New Value
Crumb tray				
Color control lever	color setting	color0		
Color control knob	color setting	color3		
Thermostat adjusting knob	color setting	color0		
Keeper release switch	position	position0		
	state	off		
	OK	yes		
Keeper release switch spring	position	position0		
Lift knob	position	down		
Lift lever	position	down		
Latch	state	disengaged		
Keeper release	state	stationary		
Keeper	state	disengaged		
Slide assembly	state	down		
Thermostat	deflection	deflect0		
	OK	yes		
Heating element	state	off		
	OK	yes		
Carriage	state	up		
Piston	state	up		
	OK	yes		
Carriage spring	state	compressed		expanded
	OK	yes		
Lifter arm	state	down	R9	
Main switch	state	on		
Power cord	state	detached		
Toast	state	up		
	color	color0		

Table 6.11 Propagate the Down State of the Lifter Arm to the Main Switch by Way of R12

Component	Characteristic	Value	Applied Rule	New Value
Crumb tray				
Color control lever	color setting	color0		
Color control knob	color setting	color3		
Thermostat adjusting knob	color setting	color0		
Keeper release switch	position	position0		
	state	off		
	OK	yes		
Keeper release switch spring	position	position0		
Lift knob	position	down		
Lift lever	position	down		
Latch	state	disengaged		
Keeper release	state	stationary		
Keeper	state	disengaged		
Slide assembly	state	down		
Thermostat	deflection	deflect0		
	OK	yes		
Heating element	state	off		
	OK	yes		
Carriage	state	up		
Piston	state	up		
	OK	yes		
Carriage spring	state	expanded		
	OK	yes		
Lifter arm	state	down	R12	
Main switch	state	off		on
Power cord	state	detached		
Toast	state	up		
	color	color0		

Table 6.12 Propagate the State of the Main Switch to the Heating Element by Way of R14

Component	Characteristic	Value	Applied Rule	New Value
Crumb tray				
Color control lever	color setting	color0		
Color control knob	color setting	color3		
Thermostat adjusting knob	color setting	color0		
Keeper release switch	position	position0		
	state	off		
	OK	yes		
Keeper release switch spring	position	position0		
Lift knob	position	down		
Lift lever	position	down		
Latch	state	disengaged		
Keeper release	state	stationary		
Keeper	state	disengaged		
Slide assembly	state	down		
Thermostat	deflection	deflect0		
	OK	yes		
Heating element	state	off	on	
	OK	yes		
Carriage	state	up		
Piston	state	up		
	OK	yes		
Carriage spring	state	expanded		
	OK	yes		
Lifter arm	state	down		
Main switch	state	on		R14
Power cord	state	detached		
Toast	state	up		
	color	color0		

The state of the toaster shown in Table 6.12 represents the point at which the elements begin to heat. When the elements begin to heat, the rules controlling element heating (R18–R22) cause the elements to heat to the desired temperature. This is controlled by the setting of the color control knob. The test of the rules proceeds in this fashion until the toast is returned to the up position and the toast is the desired color.

Chapter Summary

A model is a copy of a real world object, mechanism, or concept. Models give us a way to reason about and manipulate complex entities when it may be too costly or dangerous to manipulate the real version of the object or mechanism. For example, jet pilots are frequently trained by piloting aircraft simulators. A simulator is one kind of complex model.

Models can be constructed that are very precise replicas of their real world counterparts. These models may be based on quantitative descriptions of the mechanism. Models can also be constructed using qualitative properties. A qualitative property is one that describes some aspect of a model with a descriptive word or phrase.

Models are constructed by examining a mechanism or process to decompose it into smaller parts. In the case of the toaster the parts consist of the components of the toaster that enable it to perform its function. These parts include the heating elements, thermostat, and temperature controls. The level of decomposition depends on the intended use of the model. If we were to need to model the activity of the thermostat, then it would be necessary to decompose the thermostat into a set of parts that would describe its operation.

Models can be devised that simulate complex problem-solving processes like programming. Other models can be devised to simulate processes like programming a VCR. Models represent a kind of knowledge. In this case the knowledge describes some object, mechanism, or process. It is also possible to create models that manipulate knowledge. These models contain metaknowledge.

Six steps can be identified for creating a model. First, identify the components of the mechanism or process. Second, distinguish between components and relationships between components in the mechanism. The third and fourth steps require that the relationships of the model be identified. In step 5 the rules that define the operation of the model are specified, and in the sixth step of constructing the model, the model is tested to ensure that it works as expected.

Suggested Reading

Barr, Avron, and Feigenbaum, Edward, *Handbook of Artificial Intelligence*, Menlo Park, CA: William Kaufmann, 1981. William Kaufmann, 4 vols.

An invaluable source of information about artificial intelligence methods and research.

Faltings, Boi, and Struss, Peter, *Qualitative Physics*, Cambridge: MIT Press, 1992.

Qualitative physics attempts to formalize the way humans informally reason about physical systems.

Gentner, Dedre, and Stevens, Albert L. eds., Mental Models, Hillsdale, NJ: Lawrence Erlbaum, 1983.

A good source of information about mental models. Contains various papers about how people reason.

Kearsley, Greg, *Artificial Intelligence and Instruction*, Reading, MA: Addison-Wesley, 1987.

This text contains descriptions of significant intelligent tutoring systems (like PROUST) and also covers topics about authoring systems for intelligent tutors.

Psotka, Joseph, Massey, L., and Mutter, Sharon, *Intelligent Tutoring Systems Lesson Learned*,. Hillsdale, NJ: Lawrence Erlbaum, 1988.

Another source of information about intelligent tutors.

A discussion of a tutor for UCR operation is described in a paper by Mary A. Mark and Jim E. Greer. This paper describes the necessary analysis required to create the tutor. The paper is available as ARIES Research Report 91-7. ARIES laboratory, Department of Computer Science, University of Saskatchewan, Saskatoon, Saskatchewan, 1991 or on the Internet at URL: ftp://ftp.cs.usask.ca/pub/aries/papers /mark-jls.ps.

CHAPTER 7

A Toaster Tutor

Introduction

My first intelligent tutor project was to implement an intelligent tutoring system to teach mechanics who work on jet aircraft how to repair one of the subsystems of a particular aircraft. The subsystem was quite complex, encompassing more than 500 distinct components. After finishing this tutor, one of the things I often joked about was that the same ideas I used to create the aircraft tutor could be used to create any other tutor—including a tutor for a toaster. So what better example to begin with then to develop an intelligent multimedia tutor for a toaster?

There are several reasons why I have chosen a toaster as an example of a complete intelligent multimedia system. First, the tutoring domain represents an important class of intelligent multimedia programs. As multimedia becomes more sophisticated, we will see more and more intelligent tutoring programs that act as teachers and teacher's assistants for many different subjects. The toaster tutor is an example of a significant application of intelligence and multimedia.

Second, toasters are very common household appliances. Most people have seen a toaster and know what they do. As you have seen in earlier chapters, a toaster has a limited number of components and can be understood by most people. A toaster is not the simplest device I could have chosen. The mechanism encompasses both mechanical and electric aspects.

This chapter shows how a series of intelligent components can be linked together to create a tutoring program. Because this chapter presents the application in its entirety, I will present the design and development of the Toaster Tutor from a top-down perspective. First, I will specify some goals for the system, then from these goals I will define the major components of the system, and so on.

Just What Is an Intelligent Tutor?

There is a long history of computer-based systems developed for the purpose of "teaching." I use quotes because, although they were developed for this purpose, their effectiveness in this regard is certainly open for debate. There are quite a few acronyms for these systems—CBI, for computer-based instruction; CBT, for computer-based training; CAI, for computer-assisted instruction; and ITS, for intelligent tutoring system. This chapter focuses on ITS.

CBI, CBT, and CAI all have one thing in common. They present information in a static fashion. Although these systems may engage the student by means of exercises, they are not dynamic in the sense of allowing students to learn what they need to learn when they need to learn it and, in some cases, how they need to learn it. In other words, as a rule CBI, CBT, and CAI systems do not make judgments about students while they are in the instruction process. In this sense, they are passive teachers.

ITSs, on the other hand, are much more interactive and dynamic. An ITS is a computer program that attempts to impart information to a learner in the same way(s) a real teacher would impart the information. The ITS tries to provide feedback to the learner, diagnose problems the learner may have, and adjust the presentation of information as needed based on the learner's progress through the instruction. I like to call this the Teacher-in-a-Box. In essence, an ITS attempts to simulate some of the activities of a real teacher.

As with most things in Artificial Intelligence, this might seem like a very ambitious goal. I certainly don't claim this can be accomplished in any way that would make you believe the computer was a teacher, but the computer can behave in some ways like a teacher.

Consider this chapter to be about developing an intelligent multimedia application whose goal is to behave something like a teacher. The true purpose of this chapter is to show how intelligent components can be used in conjunction with multimedia tools to create our rudimentary Teacher-in-a-Box.

The Tutoring Domain

Whether we want to create a traditional CBI course or a complex ITS, we have to select a *domain of instruction*. A domain of instruction is the subject matter we are trying to teach. In its simplest form, a domain of instruction could be something like addition or subtraction. A more complex domain might be teaching a foreign language. Domains may also be multilevel in the sense that we are giving instruction about a specific concrete domain, and simultaneously giving instruction about a more abstract domain. An example would be teaching how to solve algebra word problems (the concrete domain) and problem solving (the abstract domain).

For our domain of instruction, I have selected a particular task, repairing a toaster. This is the concrete domain. At a more abstract level, the domain of instruction is how to problem solve in the domain of repair. That is to say, given something is broken, how do we go about repairing it?

I chose the example of a toaster for our domain of instruction for several reasons. First, the toaster is simple enough for everyone to understand. Everyone has seen a toaster (I hope), and the things that can go wrong with a toaster are fairly obvious. A toaster is also inexpensive; I bought the one I will be using for this tutor for about $15. If I cannot reassemble the toaster correctly (after I break it a couple of times), I can go out and get another. For these reasons it seems like a good domain of instruction for our tutor.

The basic idea of the Toaster Tutor is as follows: In the tutor you will be presented with a broken toaster. You will be given the symptoms the toaster is exhibiting, and you will be asked to make repairs to the toaster. To make repairs you will be able to fix various parts of the toaster, replace parts, and check to see how the toaster is working.

Now That We Know What It Is, What Do We Want It to Do?

Now you know more or less what an intelligent tutor is, and you more or less know what we want our Toaster Tutor to do, so the question is now, What exactly will the Toaster Tutor do? And, what exactly does a Toaster Tutor look like? I'll start the description of the Toaster Tutor by developing some sample drawings of the screens we will use to interact with the Toaster Tutor. These screens will be the basis for a definition of the components that will make up the tutor.

Tutor Design

Story Board

The opening screen introduces the tutoring program. Our opening screen will do just this and give access to the rest of the Toaster Tutor. It will look something like Figure 7.1.

The Toaster Tutor consists of several distinct areas a student can navigate through. These are represented in the story board screen shown in Figure 7.2. You can see that the tutor consists of a toaster tutorial, a problem-solving tutorial, a toaster operational reference library, and the part of the intelligent tutor that deals directly with fixing a broken toaster.

The toaster tutorial allows a student to review the basic principles of an operational toaster. This includes descriptions of how a toaster makes toast and how the components of a toaster participate together to carry out a toaster's function.

The problem-solving tutorial is a presentation of some of the basic ideas about problem solving. It is meant to be a reference to help the student with problem-solving strategies.

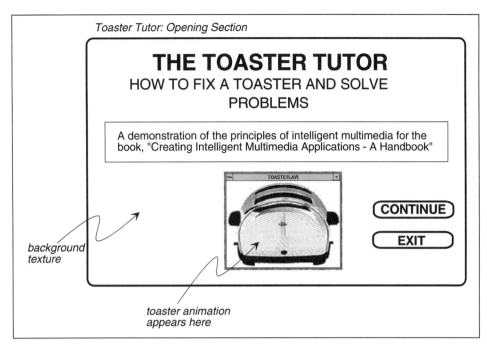

Figure 7.1 Toaster Tutor story board opening screen.

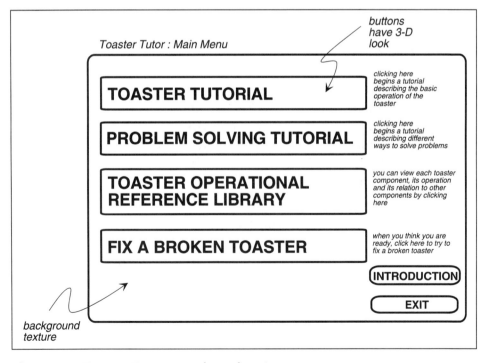

Figure 7.2 Toaster Tutor story board main menu.

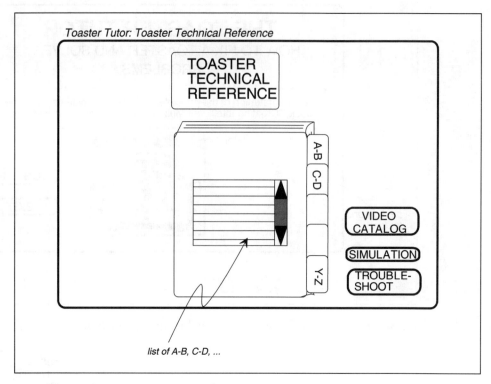

Figure 7.3 Topmost interface view of Toaster Tutor technical reference.

A toaster reference is included in the intelligent tutor to give the student a reference to the toaster. The reference contains descriptions of the operation of various toaster components including small movies showing the operation of the component. In addition, this section includes a troubleshooting guide that can also be referenced. Students using the tutor can access this reference while troubleshooting a broken toaster, the last part of the Toaster Tutor.

The toaster tutorial technical reference consists of several different screens allowing access to the information contained in the knowledge base about toasters and how they operate. The topmost view of access to the Toaster Tutor technical reference is shown in Figure 7.3.

Access to the components of the toaster is provided through the tabbed booklet shown in Figure 7.3. The list in the center of the booklet lists all components in the specified letter range. Clicking

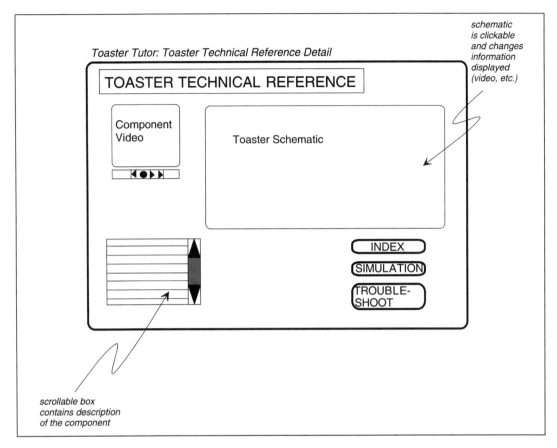

Figure 7.4 Toaster Tutor technical reference detailed view.

on a component in this list causes a display like the one shown in Figure 7.4, the technical reference detail. In this display, the complete toaster schematic is shown with the selected component highlighted to show its relationship to other components in the toaster. Also, the video of the toaster component is available along with a text description of the component.

An alternative way to access individual components, is the catalog view of components. The catalog view of components is shown in Figure 7.5. In this view, a student can select a particular component and play the video of that component. Double clicking on a component in the catalog will display detailed information about the component.

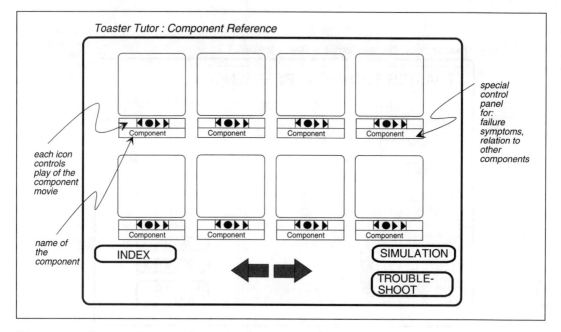

Figure 7.5 Toaster Tutor technical reference, video component catalog.

In simulation mode, the student is given the ability to fix a broken toaster. The simulation interface is depicted in Figure 7.6. In this screen, a toaster in disrepair is presented to the student in the **Situation** frame, and the student is given tools in the rest of screen to fix the toaster.

Fixing the toaster includes doing things like examining components of the toaster, and repairing them as required. These two operations are selected by the **Toaster Component Map** and the **Repair** button, respectively. A student can also access the troubleshooting guide and the toaster technical reference from the simulation screen.

Clicking on the **Advice** button provides the student with some assistance during the repair process.

The toaster troubleshooting guide is depicted in Figure 7.7. This screen gives the student assistance in determining the problem with the toaster by specifically listing potential problems. The student can select a problem and subsequently view a list of components re-

A TOASTER TUTOR 351

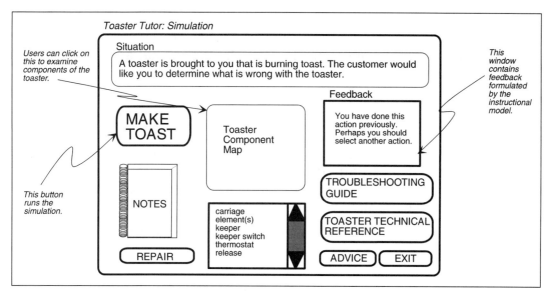

Figure 7.6 Toaster simulation screen.

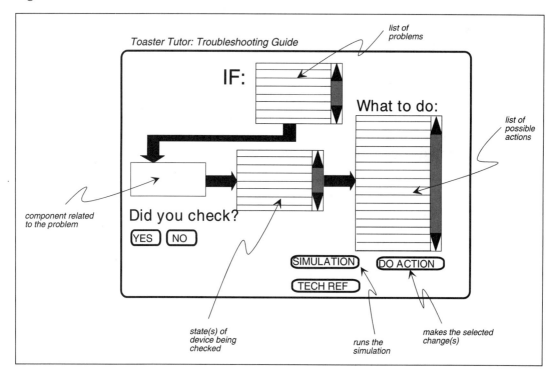

Figure 7.7 Toaster Tutor troubleshooting guide.

lated to the problems. For example, suppose the problem with the toaster is that the toast is always burnt. Components that are related to this problem may include the thermostat and the color setting lever.

Choosing a particular device causes the state of that device to be displayed and also a list of possible actions for the component. A student can select an action and cause the action to be "done." Sometimes this means a component will be replaced. Other times this might mean an adjustment will be done. In either case, after the adjustment or repair the simulation can be run again to determine if the problem with the toaster was resolved.

As you can see, a key element of the Toaster Tutor is its ability to simulate a toaster, to allow it to be "repaired", and to let the user examine the effects of the repair or adjustment. This concludes this part of the discussion about the story board. One thing to keep in mind is that the story board represents a rough sketch of what the application will look like in order for the application be created. Elements of the program may change. Sometimes this happens because of things that happen when a system, application or program is being implemented from a story board. For example, during the implementation process, you may decide a particular button is not needed or should be moved. Figures 7.8 through 7.14 show the screens of the toaster tutor. Notice that in some cases the screens are different from the story board screens and in other cases they have remained the same as they were in the story board.

Now let's consider how data will flow through the toaster simulation. Figure 7.15 shows this flow. The proposed simulation display is shown again in Figure 7.16.

At the top of the display you can see a box titled **Situation**. This is the starting point for the student. The situation gives information about the state of the broken toaster. The student decides how to proceed to fix the problem. Figure 7.15 depicts the process of troubleshooting the toaster using the tutor.

A student can perform several different steps in the repair process such as inspecting components of the toaster. The inspection consists of visually examining a component to see if anything

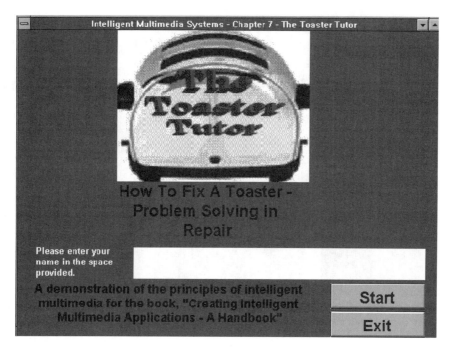

Figure 7.8 Toaster Tutor opening screen.

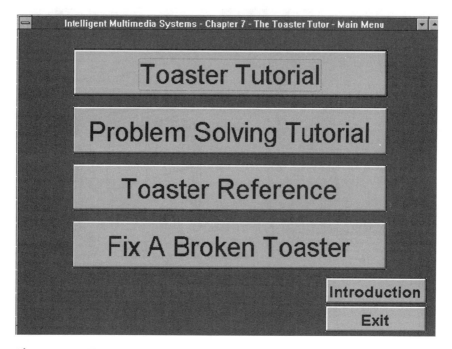

Figure 7.9 Toaster Tutor main menu.

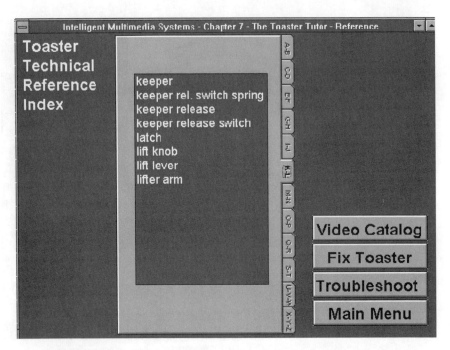

Figure 7.10 Toaster Tutor Technical Reference screen.

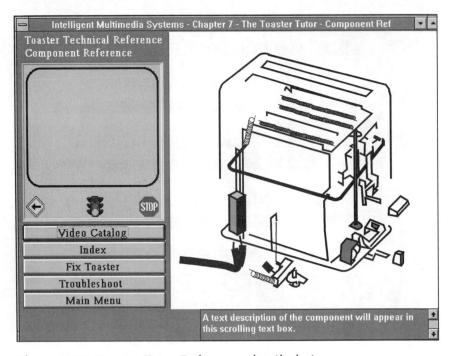

Figure 7.11 Toaster Tutor Reference detailed view.

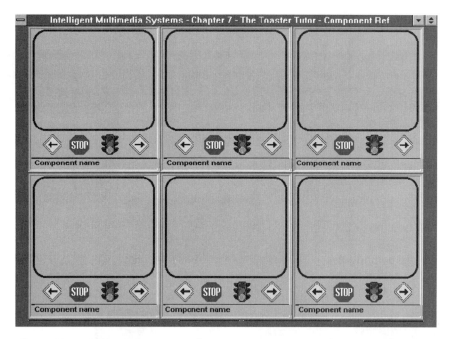

Figure 7.12 Toaster Tutor Video Component Catalog screen.

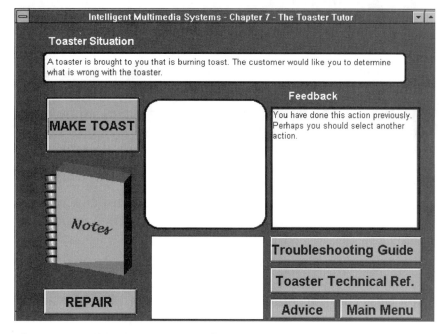

Figure 7.13 Toaster Tutor Simulation screen.

355

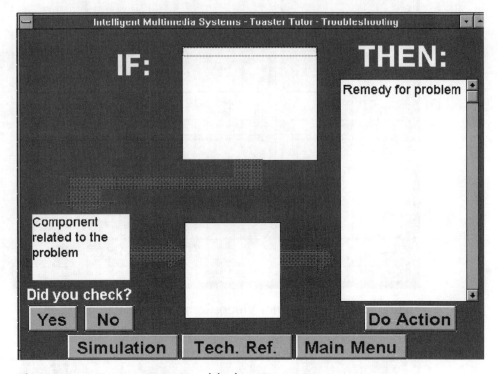

Figure 7.14 Toaster Tutor Troubleshooting screen.

is wrong with the component, replacing or repairing any component, or disassembling a component.

Usually, the results of an action are evaluated by the student attempting to make toast. The Make Toast button in Figure 7.16 runs the simulation to determine if the action the student performed had any effect on the toaster. If the toaster is repaired, the student need not do anything else—the goal of the simulation has been attained. If the toaster is not repaired, the student may continue by choosing to examine or repair some other component of the toaster.

The notebook icon is provided so that the student can make notes about the state of the toaster, the state of the problem-solving process, and the components of the toaster. These notes do not play a role in the tutor's analysis of the student's knowledge. The notebook is provided as a convenience to the student.

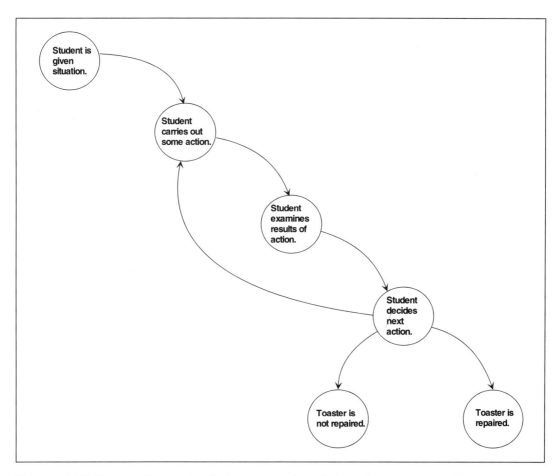

Figure 7.15 Toaster Tutor simulation control and data flow (version 1).

While problem solving it is useful to take notes. Students can click on the notebook and write whatever it is they want to remember about their simulated repair session.

Figure 7.15 shows the flow of control through the Toaster Tutor from the perspective of the student. Figure 7.17 adds some detail to this view—it adds the perspective of the tutoring program. When the student performs an action, the three models underlying the tutor will receive the action and subsequently analyze the action in terms of their responsibilities. In other words, the toaster model will analyze the action in terms of how it affects the toaster. Likewise, the stu-

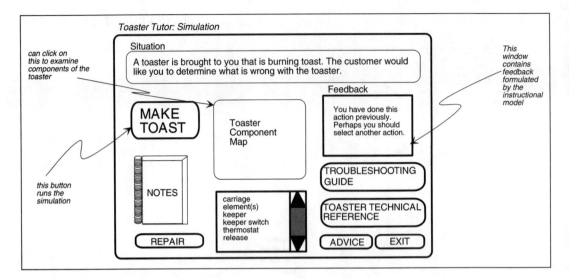

Figure 7.16 Toaster simulation screen.

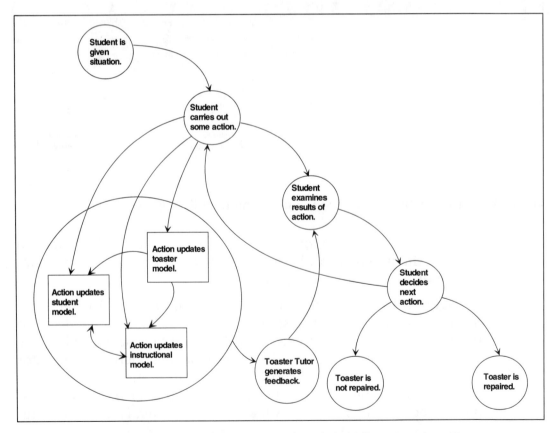

Figure 7.17 Toaster Tutor simulation control and data flow (version 2).

dent model will assess the action in terms of attempting to determine what the student knows about the toaster. The instructional model examines the action (and information provided by the student mode) to determine what instruction, if any, should be given.

The toaster model is responsible for maintaining the current state of the toaster. An action may cause the model to be modified, and this in turn may cause the behavior of the toaster to change when the simulation (Make Toast) is run.

Actions are also analyzed by the student model. The student model is a record of what the student knows. A student action tells us some things about what a student knows. A sequence of student actions may tell us more. The student model consists of two components: one that records and analyzes the student action and one that comprises the student model. The model will be updated by this analysis component.

The instructional model uses information in the student model to determine whether and what kind of feedback will be given by the system. For example, the student model keeps track of repetition actions such as examining the same component more than once. In this case, the instructional model may give some feedback. The feedback may suggest some alternate action or some remedial action. This feedback is presented in the feedback window of the simulation display.

How It Works

Figure 7.18 shows a miniature collection of the screens described in the previous section. I want to use these screens as a road map to describe how a student might move through the system. This description represents another part of the story board, namely the flow through the various parts of the tutor.

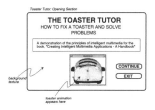

When the students starts a session at the tutor, the opening screen is displayed. At this time, the student is asked to enter his or her name. The tutor keeps track of the problems that a student has solved in the past and tries not to give the student the same prob-

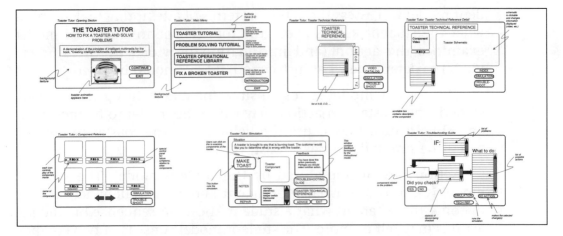

Figure 7.18 Tutor road map screens.

lem twice in a row. The tutor also maintains a record of students' actions as they solve other problems presented by the system. These actions are used to formulate new assessments about student knowledge and the kinds of instruction that might be offered. After the student enters his or her name, he or she can click the **Continue** button or the **Exit** button. Clicking the **Continue** button will take the student to the main menu of the tutor.

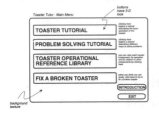

The main menu screen contains six buttons for the student to select. Students can view a tutorial describing how a toaster works, view another tutorial about problem solving, or access specific information about the toaster by clicking on the **Toaster Operational Reference Library** button. In this screen they can also do some problem solving by clicking the **Fix A Broken Toaster** button.

If students are unfamiliar with the toaster and its various parts, they may view an introduction to the toaster tutor by clicking the **Introduction** button. They may also exit the program at this time by clicking the **Exit** button.

Let's consider what happens when the student elects to fix a broken toaster.

The Simulation

When the student clicks the **Fix A Broken Toaster** button, he or she leaves the main menu screen and enters the toaster simulation section of the program. In this section, the student is able to perform several different kinds of activities based on the information given at the top of the screen.

The text at the top of the screen presents the problem the student is expected to solve. In order to solve the problem students are able to examine various parts of the toaster and determine the status of the parts selected. This is accomplished by clicking on the menu of toaster components. A component can also be repaired. The student is able to accomplish this by clicking on the **Repair** button. A repair affects only the selected component.

Once a component is repaired or there is a change to the toaster, the student may opt to try out the newly repaired toaster. To try out a potentially repaired toaster the student will click on the **Make Toast** button. This runs the model of the toaster. The result of the run is read by the tutor and is used to give the student feedback about the state of the toaster. For example, if the toaster successfully made toast because of the student's action(s), then this will be part of the information produced by the toaster model for the toaster tutor.

Clicking on the **Make Toast** or the **Repair** button results in feedback to the student. This appears in the feedback display on the right side of the simulation screen. The feedback is produced by the instructional model in conjunction with the student and toaster models, and several types of feedback may be given. For example, suggestions about how to proceed with the problem-solving process may be given in the feedback window. After the toaster model run, the feedback window will display the state of the toast[*]—finished, burnt, unfinished, and so on.

---

[*]One could also envision multimedia feedback showing burning toast, finished toast, or the toast never appearing from the toaster.

The process of determining the problem is an iterative one. The student will inspect a particular component. After inspection and consideration, the student will select an action. The action can be to repair the component, examine the troubleshooting guide, examine the toaster technical reference, seek advice, or perhaps write down some notes.

The **Troubleshooting Guide** button gives the student access to the visual troubleshooting guide. Basically this guide contains some of the information contained in troubleshooting guides for toasters. A student can also carry out actions in the toaster from the troubleshooting guide. Access to the troubleshooting guide is recorded as a student action, and a student's activity is also recorded while in this guide. Because activity here can affect the state of the broken toaster, it is important to monitor the activities of the student. One of the goals for this tutor is to encourage the student to solve problems independently; therefore, if the student is always using the troubleshooting guide, the instructional model will provide some feedback to the student to make less use of the troubleshooting guide.

The **Toaster Technical Reference** button will allow the student to access information about each of the components of the toaster. No actions can be taken from the guide—a student must return to the simulation in order to carry out further actions.

Clicking the **Advice** button will sometimes provide some additional information to the student about the problem or about the current state of the toaster. Sometimes no advice will be available. Advice will appear in the feedback window.

In the center of the simulation display is a component map of the toaster. This is provided as another means to access information about the components in the toaster. Clicking on the various components in this window will display the same information in the feedback window given when a component in the component list is selected.

The Troubleshooting Guide

The troubleshooting guide gives the student visual access to information about troubleshooting various problems that could occur in

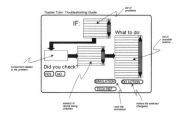

a toaster. The troubleshooting guide is by no means comprehensive (as is the case in more complex situations), and students may not find the exact solution they are looking for in this guide. The guide is organized as several text windows and lists.

The topmost list of the troubleshooting guide display lists some potential problem symptoms. Each selection is a brief description of a problem that could be encountered with the toaster. Clicking on a particular problem causes the "Did you check?" window to display a component that could be involved in the problem. Students can click the **YES** button to indicate they have checked the component or the **NO** button to indicate they haven't. Doing so causes the information about the component to be displayed in the state window (to the right of the "Did you check?" window). For this component, a list of possible actions is listed in the "What to do:" list. A student can select something to do from this list, and by clicking the **Do Action** button, can have it done to the toaster.

The **Simulation** button is provided so the student can click on it to return to the simulation screen. Likewise, the **Tech Ref** button is provided to give the student access to the toaster component technical reference.

Toaster Technical Reference

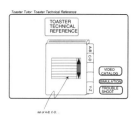

Three screens make up the toaster technical reference. The first screen consists of an alphabetical list of toaster components organized in a tabbed book. Clicking on the pair of letters in the tabs gives a list of components beginning with those letters. To see information about a particular component, click on the component in the list.

If a student knows the name of the component, then the alphabetical list is a quick way to get information about the component, but if a student is new to the internal workings of a toaster, the second means to access information about a component is through the video catalog. Access to the video catalog is gained by clicking the **video catalog** button.

In addition to the video catalog, the simulation and troubleshooting functions are available from the technical reference by clicking the corresponding buttons.

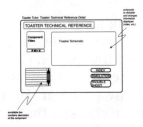

Information presented about a toaster component consists of three elements. One of these is a description of the component and how it functions in the toaster; a second is a video sequence for the component; and the third is the component map showing the location of the component in the mechanism.

The video player has the usual controls: play, stop, forward, and rewind. The video can be played as desired by the student.

Access to the index of the technical reference is provided by the **Index** button. Likewise, the simulation and troubleshooting functions are accessed by the **Simulation** and **Troubleshoot** buttons respectively.

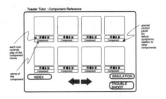

The video catalog is another view of the components that make up the toaster. Each of the windows displays one of the components in the toaster and also has its own set of player controls. Since there are more components than windows, two buttons are provided to page forward and backward among the video sequences of the toaster components. The left arrow moves back a page of components and the right arrow moves forward a page of components. Access to the simulation and troubleshooting functions of the tutor is also provided from this screen.

Tutor Models

Chapter 6 described in detail what a model is and how it can be created. The Toaster Tutor consists of three models that communicate

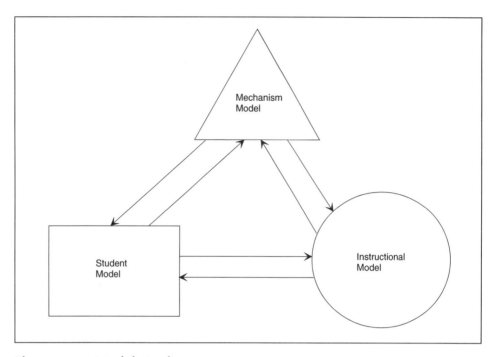

Figure 7.19 Models in the Toaster Tutor.

with one another. These are shown in Figure 7.19 and are called the domain or mechanism model, the student model, and the instructional model.

I have already discussed the mechanism model in Chapter 6 and earlier. A student using the tutor will interact with this model to manipulate the toaster. The student model and the instructional model differ from the mechanism model in what they model.

In the student model we represent what the student knows. For the Toaster Tutor we will model, among other things, what the student knows about the toaster. We could represent the knowledge in the student model (what the student knows about the toaster) in the same way as the mechanism is modeled because one of the things we want to know is specifically what the student knows or does not know about the toaster. As you will see in the section discussing the student model, we are interested in modeling not only what the student knows about the toaster but also what the student knows about solving problems. The mechanism model and the student actions on the mechanism model can be analyzed by a series of rules to make assessments about student knowledge.

Just as the student model captures student actions on the mechanism model, the instructional model examines changes in the student model to decide when to intervene and give instruction to the student. For example, the instructional model examines the student model and sees that the student, after a series of actions, does not get closer to fixing the toaster. The instructional model gives help to the students so they are able to repair the toaster. The instructional model is described in more detail later in this chapter.

Student Model

Student Model

What do we want the student to know about the toaster? What kinds of things should a student know in order to repair a broken toaster? At one level a student must know how a toaster works. The parts and components of the toaster are the things that make a toaster work. So at one level, a student must know the following:

- What the components are
- How the components operate
- How the components interrelate
- How the toaster operates

If a student elects to examine a particular component, then we assume the student knows something about the component. Given the context of the problem, the selection of a component is a kind of confirmation or disconfirmation that the student understands what the component does and how it relates to the operation of the toaster. For example, let's say the problem with the toaster is that the toaster platform never pops up. Once down, it stays down. When the toast is finished, it will burn unless removed. Suppose a student examines and or replaces the heating elements in an attempt to fix the problem. What does this tell us about what the student understands about how the toaster operates? Figure 7.20 might

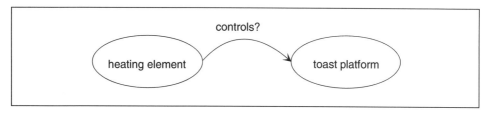

Figure 7.20 Preliminary student model using heating element action as a basis for the model.

represent a rough sketch of what we may have learned about what the student knows about the toaster and how it operates.

Every time the student checks, manipulates, or examines a component, this tells us something about what the student knows or does not know about the toaster. To make inferences about what the student knows, it is necessary to make assumptions about the meaning of student actions. If this seems complex, you are right—it is the crux of the problem of developing a student model. Let's develop some rules of how we might assess student actions.

Rule 1: Assessing a Student's Understanding of the Mechanism Through a Single Student Action

A student performs an action x on a component y. In the mechanism, component z is the problem. Figure 7.21 contains an abstract model of this device. As the first step in constructing the student model, we could create a connection between the y component and the z component as shown in Figure 7.22 by the dotted line relationship.

When we add this relationship we immediately see that it does not contradict other relationships in the mechanism model. To make this assessment, we can determine if there is a path in the mechanism model from the point or element of examination, in this case element y, to the problem element z. For the mechanism shown in Figures 7.21 and 7.22, the path via the controls relationship is y controls c, c controls b, and b controls z. We say a student-proposed relationship (proposed by student's action on the model) subsumes a set of model relationships if there is a path in the model

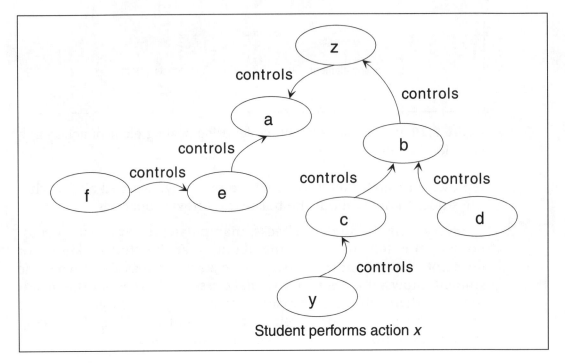

Figure 7.21 The *xy* mechanism.

as described earlier. Some terminology will make this easier to understand.

Let's call the cause of the problem the *target*. The target is what the student needs to find in the diagnosis procedure. What the student examines we will call the *source*. Between the source and target in the model, there may be components connecting the source and target elements. We will call these elements *path elements*. For an element to be a path element, there must be a relationship between the path elements in the direction of source to target, and each path element must be connected to another.

Suppose $p_1, p_2, ..., p_n$ are potential path elements. In order for the p_k's to be path elements, there must be a relationship from the source s to p_1. Likewise, p_1 and p_2 must be connected by some relationship r. There must also be a path from p_2 to p_n by way of the relationship r. Finally, p_n must be related to the target by way of

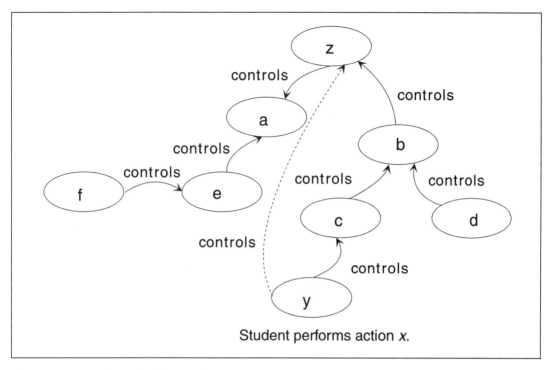

Figure 7.22 Inferred relationship.

relationship r. Under these conditions, the set of p_k's are path elements (as opposed to potential path elements). Also, under these circumstances, the path from source s to target t by way of relationship r subsumes the path in the model from source s to target t (a definition we will need).

Let's consider another situation. Look at Figure 7.23. This figure shows a new element that the student chooses to examine. The potential path elements in Figure 7.23 are f, e, and a. If the path from source w to target z subsumes the path consisting of the path elements, then we must be able to construct a path via the controls relationship from the source w to the target z through the path elements. There is a path from w to f via controls and a path from e to a via controls. The last required path is from e to a via controls or through other path elements in the mechanism. The only relationship that exists is from z to a via controls. Hence, the path from

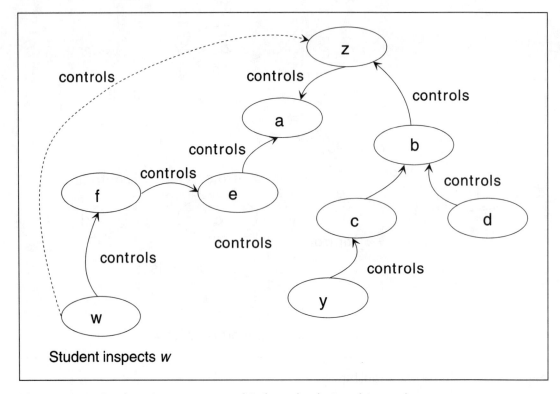

Figure 7.23 Student inspects *w* and inferred relationship *z*, the target.

source *w* to target *z* does not subsume a path in the mechanism because there is no path consisting of elements in the mechanism. The inferred path is a contradiction to the operation of the mechanism.

Expressing assessment Rule 1 in terms of this subsumption analysis, we have the following:

> If the inferred path from source *x* (the point of examination or manipulation) subsumes a sequence of path elements from source *x* to target *y* then there is evidence supporting student knowledge of the inferred path in the mechanism.

Likewise, if the inferred path from the source *x* to the target *y* does not subsume a path of path elements, then there is evidence not supporting student knowledge of the inferred path in the mechanism.

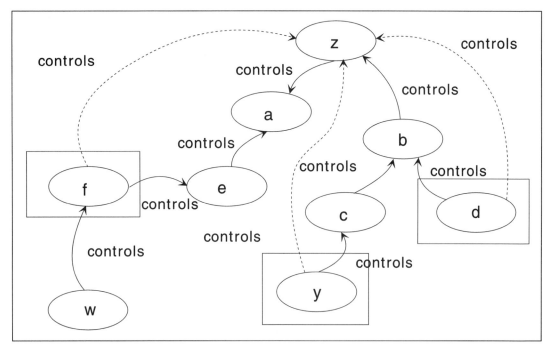

Figure 7.24 Possible next actions after examining element w.

Rule 2: Assessing a Student's Understanding of the Mechanism Through a Series of Actions

As a student continues to manipulate the toaster and its components, we can make additional assessments about a student's knowledge. Consider Figure 7.24 where the student has initially examined w. What might the student do next and how could we assess the next action in the context of the first action?

Although a student could choose any component next, let's assume that, after some feedback about component w, the student chooses component f, component y, or component d as the next selected component. We can think about these selections in the context of Rule 1. We can also decide whether the student's action moves closer or farther from the target (a sort of hot-potato/cold-potato game). In other words, is the student moving closer to the solution to the problem or farther away from the solution—determining what is wrong with the mechanism.

Consider the selection of *f* as the next action by the student. In terms of physical distance to the target, component *f* is closer to target *z* than component *w*. We have already determined that *w* resulted in a negative assessment of the student's knowledge. Rule 1 applied to this source adds more negative evidence about the student's knowledge of the mechanism.

Component *y* is physically further from target *z* than component *f*, but, unlike component *f*, the inferred path from the source *y* to the target *z* does subsume a set of path elements. Because of this, it will add positive evidence about the student's knowledge about the mechanism. Since the evidence shifts positively, *y* is closer to target *z* than component *f*.

Finally, consider component *d*. It is similar to component *y* in terms of the subsumption rule. Physically it is also closer to target *z*, adding evidence about the student's knowledge of the mechanism.

Rule 2 can be stated as follows:

If an action examines a component that is closer to the target in terms of physical distance and evidence, then there is positive evidence that the student has knowledge of the mechanism. Likewise, if an action examines a component that is physically more distant and is adding negative evidence to the assessment of a student's knowledge about the mechanism, then there is negative evidence that the student has knowledge of the mechanism.

Rule 3: Assessing a Student's Problem-Solving Process—Divide and Conquer

Rules 1 and 2 were used to assess whether the student has knowledge about the mechanism. Now let's consider a different kind of knowledge—namely, the kind of knowledge the student is using to diagnose or solve the problem in the mechanism. Suppose we have the type of mechanism shown in Figure 7.25.

The problem is in element *g*, as indicated by the square enclosing this component. The symptom is in component *a*, which is enclosed by a triangle. Observe that this mechanism can be easily divided into three parts based on the apparent paths in the mechanism as shown in Figure 7.25. The vertical dotted lines show how

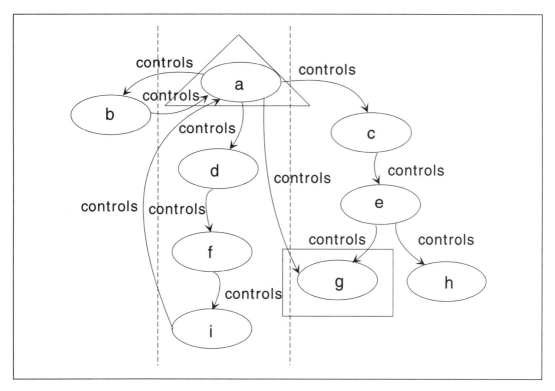

Figure 7.25 A divisible mechanism.

the mechanism can be divided. Since the problem is in g, one strategy the student might follow is to eliminate complete paths in the mechanism to localize where the problem may be. If the student examines one component in each path of the mechanism (as defined by the dotted lines), there may be evidence the student is using an elimination strategy, sometimes called divide and conquer, to solve the problem they are presently working on. The divide and conquer approach is a good one for mechanisms that can be partitioned like the one shown in Figure 7.25. Rule 3 can be stated as follows:

> If there is evidence that a student is using a divide and conquer approach to problem solving, then there is increased evidence that the student has understanding of some problem-solving methodology.

We can only assume a student is using this methodology. But how can we make a judgment like this?

To make this determination, we must look at a sequence of student actions. To minimize the degree of assumption, we should examine the sequence of actions only after the number of actions equals the number of apparent paths in the mechanism. In the case of Figure 7.25, the magic number is three, since there are three apparent paths in this mechanism. After three actions we look at the sequence of actions to see if the components that are examined are from each apparent path. Preferably, the last component examined should be the one containing the problem being sought. In Figure 7.24, these preferred components would be b, i, and g or h.

I have set a minimum number of actions for which Rule 3 will be in effect, but when is it appropriate not to consider Rule 3 any longer? One way to set a maximum number of actions is to say that Rule 3 can no longer be used if some other strategy is being used. For example, the next rule, Rule 4, determines if the student is using a sequential problem-solving strategy. A sequential strategy could be used after a divide and conquer strategy, but it could also be used from the start of the problem-solving process. If an alternative problem-solving strategy is being used, we could not consider divide and conquer as the strategy being used by the student.

The divide and conquer strategy is one that would be used at or near the beginning of a problem-solving session. In the case of Figure 7.25, with the limited number of paths in the mechanism, it would make sense to use divide and conquer at the very beginning of the problem-solving process. Thus, Rule 3 should be used when the third action has been taken by the student, but not after this, as the probability that a divide and conquer strategy was being used becomes very small given the nature of the mechanism.

Rule 4: Assessing a Student's Problem-solving Strategy—Sequential Analysis

As was mentioned in previous paragraphs, a sequential strategy is one a student might also use. A sequential strategy could be useful to diagnose a problem when the number of components in the mechanism are limited. In other cases, a methodology like divide and conquer may be more cost effective (i.e., it takes less time to di-

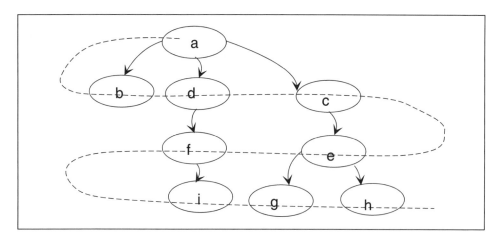

Figure 7.26 A breadthwise sequential search pattern.

agnose the problem). Several kinds of sequential search patterns can be identified. Three examples of these are shown in Figures 7.26, 7.27, and 7.28.

The dotted lines in Figures 7.26, 7.27, and 7.28 represent the sequence of components examined by the student. In all three fig-

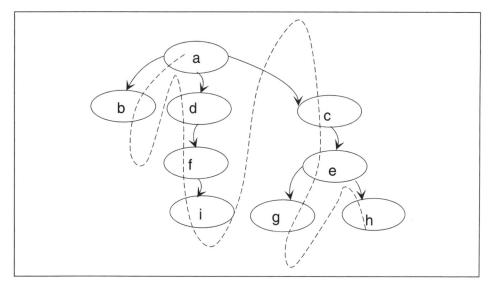

Figure 7.27 A depthwise sequential search pattern.

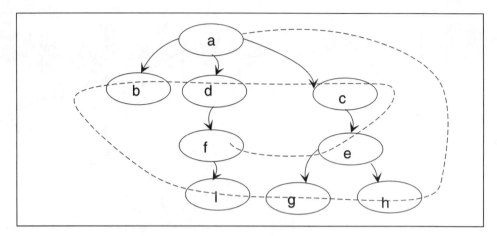

Figure 7.28 A spiralwise sequential search pattern.

ures, the starting component is arbitrary. The starting component will of course depend on the student's knowledge of the mechanism. Rule 4 is defined in terms of the possible paths shown in the figures:

> If a student's sequence of actions follows a breadthwise, depthwise, or spiralwise path through the mechanism, then there is evidence that the student is using a sequential strategy to diagnose the problem.

Rule 5: Assessing Student Knowledge of Components

It is important the student know about the various components of the toaster. Therefore, as the student carries out actions the tutor will record the components that are manipulated in the actions.

From the rules I have described so far, this seems obvious. In order to make the kinds of assessment we have described, the tutor must record the component involved in the student's action. In each case, it is not only the component used in assessing an action, it is actually a combination of the component and its relationship to other components and the cause of the problem. This brings us to the present problem—how do we know if a student knows about a particular component?

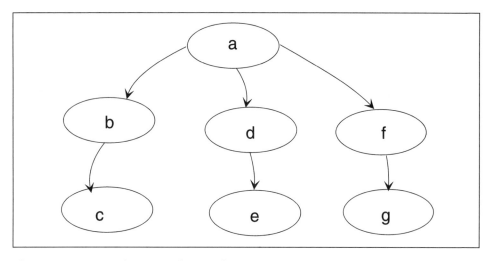

Figure 7.29 Another simple mechanism.

Figure 7.29 shows another mechanism. The student examines component *b*. By itself, this action does not mean too much. But suppose that following the examination of *b* the student examines *a* and *c* as the next actions. The order in which *a* and *c* are examined does not matter—what matters is the sequence of actions is either

Examine b.
Examine a.
Examine c.

or

Examine b.
Examine c.
Examine a.

This sequence is important for the following reason. If the student knows something about component b, then a sensible thing to do would be to look at all of the immediate components connected to it. Why does this make sense?

If a student suspects a particular component and does not know if the component is the cause of the problem, then it would make sense to look at the components that feed component *b* and the components that are fed by component b. Let's call the components that feed component b the *sources* to b and the components fed by b the *sinks* for b. Our notation for sources is $b_{source x}$ where x is the label of the source component and likewise $b_{sink y}$ where y is the sink of b.

If all b_{source}'s are operating properly then their state should be expected for properly operating components. Likewise, by examining $b_{sink y}$ we can tell if these components are in an expected state. If not, then it is possible component b is not operating correctly. So, by examining $b_{source x}$ and $b_{sink y}$ the student is showing some understanding about component b and its relationship to other components in the mechanism.

In Figure 7.29, component d presents a different problem in that it has no sources and two sinks. In this case, examining the sinks are critical because if either sink is not operating properly this will point to component d as the potential culprit.

The remaining situation is represented by component f, which has no sinks, but two sources. In this case, checking component f tells us whether it is operating properly and also whether the sources are operating properly. Given this analysis, Rule 5 can be stated as follows:

> If a student examines a component x and then in sequence examines the sources of the component ($X_{source a}$) and the sinks ($X_{sink b}$) then there is evidence that the student has some understanding of component x and its relation to other components.

Rule 6: Assessing Student Use of the Troubleshooting Guide

As the student learns more about the toaster and the way it works, we would expect the use of aids like the troubleshooting guide to diminish. Using the troubleshooting guide is not necessarily a bad thing—in fact, in some cases it is a very good thing to do. Given our goals for the Toaster Tutor, we would like the student to become less dependent on specific information about the toaster and more reliant on a general ability to solve problems.

The assessment of student use of the troubleshooting guide occurs over time from session to session. We can carry out the assessment by looking at the number of times the troubleshooting guide is used from tutoring session to tutoring session. As a percentage of the total number of actions, the number of times the troubleshooting guide is used should follow a downward trend. Rule 6 may be stated as follows:

> If the number of times that the student uses the troubleshooting guide follows a downward trend over time, then there is evidence that the student's knowledge of problem solving and the toaster is increasing over time.

Rule 7: Assessing Student Repetitive Actions

Sometimes, in the middle of solving a problem, we find ourselves in the middle of a desert. We decide to strike out to find water. Before doing so we mark the place we have been so we know we have been there and proceed to walk for what seems like hours. After this time we come upon a marker left by someone. It is our marker. We set out in a different direction and also return to this marker. We are traveling in circles. In problem solving this will occur when we find ourselves doing the same things again and again. It could be the same step over and over again or it could be a sequence of steps.

The student model keeps track of whether a student is doing one or more actions in the following ways. We keep a record of each action that is performed by a student. Along with the record, we also keep a count for the particular action. For the action to be repetitive, the number of times the student carries out the action must exceed a specified threshold.

A more serious repetitive action is when the student repeats a sequence of steps. Under these circumstances, the student will carry out some series of actions and then start with the first of these and repeat them again. In the record of actions we can determine if one action has been repeated or a sequence of actions has been repeated. Consider how we might accomplish this.

A student carries out the following sequence of actions to diagnose the problem in the toaster. The actions are labeled A, B, C, and so on:

A B C E F

At this point the student has checked several components. Now the next action is an A-type action, giving the sequence

A B C E F A

When the student chooses to do action A again, the count for this action is incremented, but we don't have evidence yet that the student is carrying out a repetitive action. The next action is a B action:

A B C E F A B

Now we have more evidence the pattern of actions is repeating itself. The next action refutes the possibility (at this point) that the student is repeating actions:

A B C E F A B G

Later in the sequence of actions, the student carries out the sequence of actions

C E F

The complete action sequence now looks like,

A B C E F . . . C E F

and the same sequence is repeated again.

A B C E F . . . C E F C E F

Now the sequence of actions C E F has been repeated three times, and the student does not appear to be closer to a solution, so we might assess at this time that the student is repeating actions.

Rule 7 is stated as follows:

a. If the count associated with the performance of any action is over a specified threshold then there is evidence that the student is repeating actions.

b. If a sequence of actions results in an identifiable pattern of actions then there is evidence that the student is repeating actions.

Instructional Model

A More Precise Definition

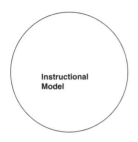

The purpose of the instructional model in an intelligent tutor in general and in the Toaster Tutor specifically is to give instruction. The instructional model is a representation of the method or methods we will use in the tutor to provide information to the student. The model can be as simple as one based on the idea that it is a useful thing to tell students whether they are right or wrong, or it can be more complex—directing the student during a learning process and making adjustments in the direction as a student progresses.

Instructional modeling has received attention in the literature because it is important that an intelligent tutor, or any instructional system for that matter, be well founded in its instructional methodology. For example, a tutoring program might have, as its formal basis, a Socratic dialog that describes how a learning dialog will take place. One system that employed such a methodology, a system for tutoring students about the causes for rainfall, was called WHY.

In a practical sense we have the following problem to solve in constructing an instructional model. The student is manipulating the domain/mechanism model and the student model is making inferences about these manipulations. The instructional model must make use of both of these kinds of data to provide useful information to the student. The relationship is depicted in Figure 7.30.

Figure 7.30 shows the relationship between the student, the mechanism model, and the instructional model. For the instructional model to provide useful feedback to the student, it must be able to use the information produced by the student model. In their most general form we have to answer the following questions in order to define the operation of the instructional model.

When should instruction be given?

What kinds of instruction should be given?

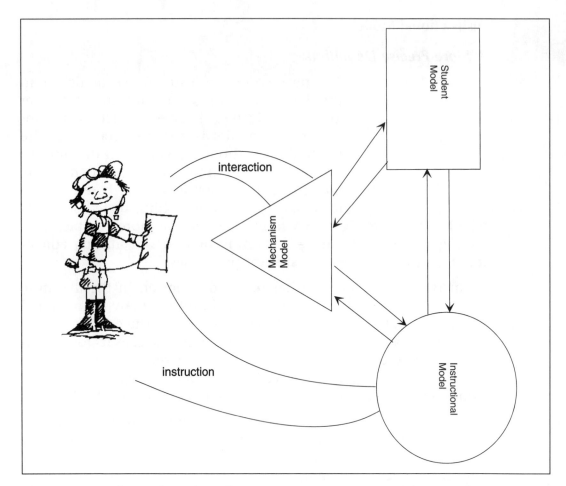

Figure 7.30 Relationship of intelligent tutoring systems models to student.

To answer these questions we must consider the kinds of data produced by the student model. So far, the section defining the student model only described the rules that are used to analyze the actions taken by a student. A task that still remains is to define how this information will be represented. In other words, we still need to define the data that will feed the rules in the instructional model.

The preceding section described a student model containing seven rules. The rules can be roughly classified as shown in Table 7.1. The partitioning of the rules into three categories allows the in-

Table 7.1 Student Model Rule Classifications

Rule	Description	Classification
R1	Infer knowledge of the toaster mechanism from a single action.	mechanism knowledge
R2	Infer knowledge of the toaster mechanism from a series of actions.	mechanism knowledge
R3	Is the student using a divide and conquer problem-solving strategy?	problem-solving knowledge
R4	Is the student using a sequential problem-solving strategy?	problem-solving knowledge
R5	Does the student understand components?	component knowledge
R6	Is the student using the troubleshooting guide?	problem-solving knowledge
R7	Is the student performing repetitive actions?	mechanism knowledge/ problem-solving knowledge

structional model to address three distinct kinds of knowledge and assist students with these kinds of knowledge while they are interacting with the tutor. As Table 7.2 shows, tutoring or instructional strategy can be organized around these classifications.

This organization of student model rules and their relation to instruction assumes that these three kinds of knowledge are important in the process of diagnosing and repairing the toaster. Of

Table 7.2 Summary of Student Model Rule-Based Instructional Strategy

Rule(s)	Classification	Instruction and Feedback
R5	component knowledge	Provide the student with instruction about the function of a specific component.
R1, R2	mechanism knowledge	Provide the student with instruction about how the mechanism works and the relationship between components.
R3, R4, R6, R7	problem-solving knowledge	Provide the student with instruction about problem-solving methods that would be useful.

course, other kinds of knowledge might be appropriate for other kinds of domains and problems.

The data produced by the student model are only indicative of what a student may know about the three areas we have defined. For example, data from the student model might indicate that a student has little or no knowledge about components in the toaster. The student model data should be interpreted as meaning there is only a possibility of this observation being true. Based on the idea that the data from the student model is an indication of the possibility of a particular problem, we can formulate the following instructional model tutoring rules.

INSTRUCTIONAL MODEL RULE R1—COMPONENT KNOWLEDGE

If the student model indicates there is a possibility the student has a deficit of component knowledge and the assessment is above a specified threshold, then provide first-level instruction to the student about the relevant components.

If the student model indicates there is a possibility the student has a deficit of component knowledge and the assessment is above a second specified threshold, then provide second-level instruction to the student about the relevant components.

INSTRUCTIONAL MODEL RULE R2—MECHANISM KNOWLEDGE

If the student model indicates there is a possibility the student has a deficit of mechanism knowledge and the assessment is above a specified threshold, then provide first-level instruction to the student about the relevant portions of the mechanism.

If the student model indicates there is a possibility the student has a deficit of mechanism knowledge and the assessment is above a specified second threshold, then provide second-level instruction to the student about the relevant portions of the mechanism.

INSTRUCTIONAL MODEL RULE R3—PROBLEM-SOLVING KNOWLEDGE

If the student model indicates there is a possibility the student is problem solving using a sequential approach to problem solving and the assessment is above a specified threshold, then provide instruction to the student about alternative methods of problem solving.

If the student model indicates there is a possibility the student is problem solving by continuously referring to the technical reference and the assessment is above a specified threshold, then provide instruction to the student about using the technical reference manual less.

If the student model indicates that there is a possibility that the student is performing repetitive actions and that the assessment is above a specified threshold, then provide instruction to the student about trying different actions to avoid repeating the same actions.

The concept of assessment built into the three instructional model rules gives us a way to build a bridge between the student model and the instructional model and is also a way to have some control over when feedback is given to a student. By varying the individual instructional thresholds we can change when the instructional model will provide instruction.

As the student model runs, it keeps track of evidence for or against the kinds of knowledge and skills the student should exhibit while using the tutor to fix the toaster. One possibility for structuring the tracking process is a scoreboard where evidence is accumulated for a particular knowledge or skill. A prototype of the student model score board is shown in Table 7.3.

The SIMSB (Student/Instructional Model Score Board) consists of several columns governing the action of the instructional model. The column labeled "Skill or Component" names the skill as defined by the classification or the component to which the table row applies. The "Type" column identifies whether the table row defines a skill or a component. All components are defined by rule R5, the component knowledge rule. Skills are defined by the other rules de-

Table 7.3 Student/Instructional Model Score Board (SIMSB)

Skill or Component	Type	Relevant Rule	Score	Threshold 1	Threshold 2	Target
Color control lever	component	R5		−2	−4	
Color control knob	component	R5		−2	−4	
Thermostat adjusting knob	component	R5		−2	−4	
Keeper release switch	component	R5		−2	−4	
Keeper release switch spring	component	R5		−2	−4	
Lift knob	component	R5		−2	−4	
Lift lever	component	R5		−2	−4	
Latch	component	R5		−2	−4	
Keeper release	component	R5		−2	−4	
Keeper	component	R5		−2	−4	
Slide rod	component	R5		−2	−4	
Slide assembly	component	R5		−2	−4	
Thermostat	component	R5		−2	−4	
Heating element	component	R5		−2	−4	
Carriage	component	R5		−2	−4	
Carriage spring	component	R5		−2	−4	
Lifter arm	component	R5		−2	−4	
Main switch	component	R5		−2	−4	
Power cord	component	R5		−2	−4	
Mechanism knowledge	skill	R1		−3	−5	
Mechanism knowledge	skill	R2		−3	−5	
Problem-solving knowledge	skill	R3			−5	
Problem-solving knowledge	skill	R4		3	5	
Problem-solving knowledge	skill	R6			5	
Problem-solving knowledge	skill	R7		3	5	

fined for the student model. The "Score" column will contain the actual assessment as calculated by the student model. The scores are signed integer values. All assessment scores are initially set to zero.

A negative assessment score indicates a lack of evidence that the student has particular knowledge—the more negative, the greater the possibility. A positive score indicates there is evidence that the student has knowledge of the component or skill—the more positive the assessment score, the greater the possibility the student has knowledge of the skill or component.

Assessment scores are computed by considering the outcome of each student model rule. If a student model rule indicates a student has a particular knowledge or skill, then the appropriate assessment score will be incremented by one. On the other hand, if a relevant student model rule does not indicate knowledge of the related skill of component, then the appropriate assessment will be decremented by one.

Each SIMSB row has two threshold entries, threshold 1 and threshold 2. In some cases, a skill or component will have only a single threshold defined for it. When an assessment score reaches a specified threshold, the instructional model will provide instruction to the student. If the assessment score reaches the first threshold, a preliminary type of feedback will be given to the student. After preliminary feedback is given, the assessment score can improve or worsen. If it worsens and reaches the second threshold, a more detailed kind of feedback will be given. When an assessment score reaches the second threshold it will be reset to zero.

For components I have specified the first threshold to be −2 and the second threshold to be −4. For mechanism knowledge the thresholds are −3 and −5 respectively. An assessment score threshold (second threshold only) is specified as −5 for rule R3—an assessment of whether the student is using a divide and conquer problem-solving strategy. The remaining assessment score thresholds are set at 3 for the first threshold and 5 for the second or only threshold. Why are these particular values chosen?

As was mentioned earlier, the threshold values for giving feedback are used to tune the tutor so that feedback will be given at appropriate times. These values can be adjusted as needed. A few comments may be useful in giving you some insight on how they might be selected.

If feedback should be given when the student is performing actions contrary to solving a problem, then a threshold should be set to a negative number. The more negative the number, the more chances the student will have to pursue a possibly incorrect problem-solving strategy. For components I have chosen −2 and −4 for the two thresholds because I don't want a student to stray too far in manipulating components that might be irrelevant to the problem at hand. The choice of −2 as the first threshold represents two chances to manipulate a component before the first type of feedback is given by the tutor. To reach the second level of feedback, another two chances are given by setting the second threshold to −4. These choices seem like reasonable ones for components of the toaster.

I chose −3 and −5 for skill thresholds to provide the student more time to show the possibility of knowledge of the skill and to give the tutor more time to accumulate evidence about the skill. These thresholds may be set higher if more evidence must be accumulated before feedback can be given about a particular skill.

A positive assessment is based on a student's demonstration of a particular piece of knowledge or skill. In the case of rules R4, R6, and R7, we want to give feedback when there is evidence a student may be using or showing the skill associated with the rule. For example, the purpose of rule R7 is to keep track of repetitive operations carried out by the student. If the student is doing the same action again and again or is looping through several actions, it makes sense to give some feedback. For rule R7 I have set the first threshold at 3 and the second threshold at 5. My interpretation of an assessment score of 3 is that a student will have repeated the same action several times and needs some basic feedback to this effect.

Another question deserving some discussion concerns the kinds of feedback the tutor will give. Since I have stratified the feedback into two classes by way of the assessment score thresholds, two kinds of feedback will have to be defined.

Table 7.4 First Threshold Feedback

Rule	Type	Feedback	Variable
R5	component	Are you sure that you understand the purpose or function of component C? Perhaps you should refer to the technical reference.	C
R1	mechanism	This component (C) may not be a good one to examine for this problem.	C
R2	mechanism	Does this component relate to the symptoms that the toaster is exhibiting? Check to make sure.	
R3	problem solving—divide and conquer	You might want to try a different approach to diagnosing the toaster problem.	
R4	problem solving—sequential	Although using a sequential approach to diagnosing the toaster problem may eventually be effective, it can also be time-consuming. Consider another approach to diagnosing the toaster problem.	
R6	problem solving—troubleshooting guide	Try to solve the problem by using the troubleshooting guide less. This will help you develop your own troubleshooting skills.	
R7	problem solving—repetition	Some of the actions that you have done recently, have already been done. Make sure you are carrying out the actions you need to diagnose the problem.	

Conceptually all feedback at the first threshold will be simple, a sentence or two at most attempting to provide some useful information to the student. The kinds of feedback given can also be adjusted, although this is a more complex change. Table 7.4 shows a table defining first-level feedback given to the student.

The second-level feedback, that given when the student's assessment score reaches the second threshold, is more detailed than the first level of feedback. When the student reaches the second threshold, he or she will be given specific information about the component, skill, or actions rather than a more general comment. Because the feedback is more detailed, it will make more use of information contained in the models of the toaster tutor. Table 7.5 defines second-level feedback for each of the kinds of rules used in the instructional model.

Table 7.5 Second Threshold Feedback

Rule	Type	Feedback	Procedure
R5	component	Perhaps some additional information about component C would be helpful. Component(s) I are connected or effect component C and component C effects component(s) O.	Collect the inputs and outputs of component C, assign to variables C, I, and O respectively, and generate feedback.
R1	mechanism	Can you name the components that may be related to the present problem with the toaster? If you can, select the components from the list provided below.	Accept selections from the student and check these selections using the model and the problem target. Give the student feedback. When a student has identified the correct components he or she can continue diagnosing the problem. Also include an answer button so the student can obtain the answer *after* making at least one attempt at the exercise.
R2	mechanism	The components of this toaster relevant to the problem are: (list of components).	Gather and display the components along the path relevant to the problem.
R3	problem solving—divide and conquer	See first-level feedback.	
R4	problem solving—sequential	Divide and conquer might be another approach to use to diagnose this problem. Toaster components can be divided into groups, and if you think a problem can only occur with components in one of the groups, all other groups of components can be eliminated from consideration.	Show the classification view of toaster components.
R6	problem solving—technical reference	see first-level feedback.	
R7	problem solving—repetitive actions	The following actions have been repeated. Make sure that this is what you intended to do.	From the action log, display the repeated or sequence of repeated actions.

Simulating the Simulation

This section heading may seem to be from the department of redundant departments, but consider that we still don't know if any of this will work. It makes sense to try to test the mechanism, student, and instructional models. We could do this by writing the all of the programs necessary to implement the models, but this would be very time-consuming, and we may find out during the implementation process that some part of our design does not function the way we need it to. In this section I will start a low-tech paper and pencil-based test of Toaster Tutor so we can watch how it will function.

Here is the problem we have to diagnose:

Customer: When I try to make toast, the toast goes down okay, but it never comes up when it is finished and this usually means that the toast burns.

Now we can go ahead to figure out what is wrong with the toaster. Before doing this, as part of our preparation for the simulation let's consider the relevant paths in the model which are important to consider for rules R1 and R2. The component/relationship diagram of the toaster is shown in Figure 7.31.

Now, as a student we normally would not know what is wrong with the toaster, but for the sake of this simulation of the simulation we need to know this so we can do some preparation for the system. As we are playing the role of the student and the Toaster Tutor, the tutor will know the problem causing the toaster to malfunction.

The problem with this toaster is that the carriage spring has become disconnected from the lifter arm, so the lifter arm cannot lift the carriage when the toast is finished. When we look at Figure 7.31, there might be two paths a student could possibly pursue to diagnose this problem. We will call one of these paths the "thermostat system," and the other path the "carriage movement system." In the context of the component/relation diagram, the thermostat system is shown in Figure 7.32(a) and the subdiagram showing just the components in this path are shown in Figure 7.32(b). Likewise Figure 7.33(a) shows the carriage movement system in the context of the component/relation diagram and Figure 7.33(b) shows just the components of this system.

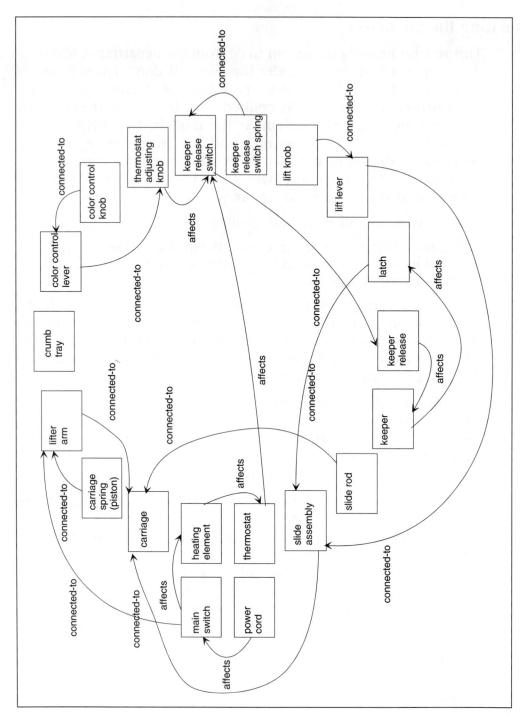

Figure 7.31 Component/relation diagram of the toaster.

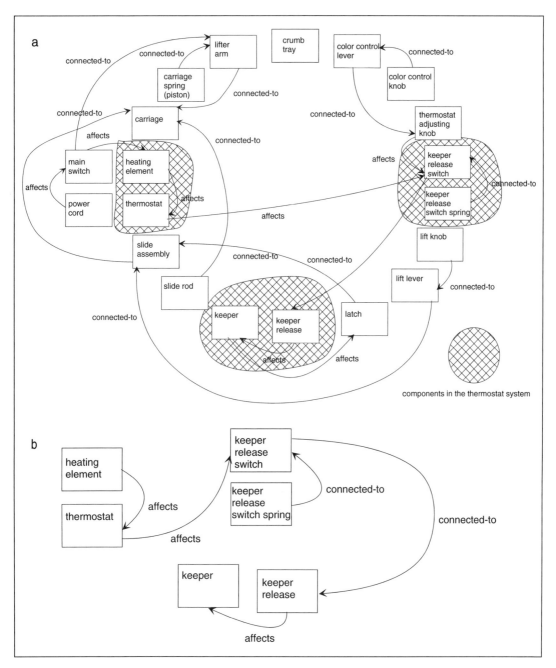

Figure 7.32 (a) Thermostat system in the context of the component/relation diagram. **(b)** Thermostat system component/relation diagram.

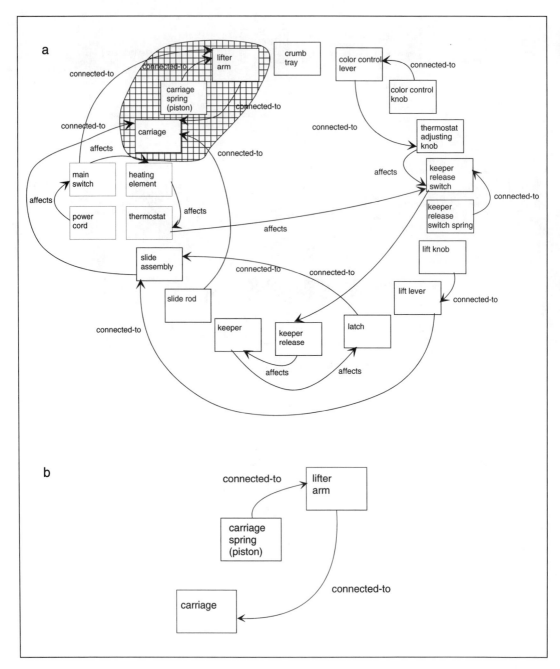

Figure 7.33 (**a**) Carriage movement system in the context of the component/relation diagram. (**b**) Carriage movement system component/relation diagram.

The SIMSB will be used to keep track of the assessment scores. The initial SIMSB for this problem is shown in Table 7.6. You can see in Table 7.6 that all of the assessment scores have been initialized to 0 and the target component (the component causing the problem) has been identified.

Using the simulation the first thing to do would be to make some toast. The student does this and then begins examining some of the components in the toaster. The action log, shown here, contains the single action, "make toast."

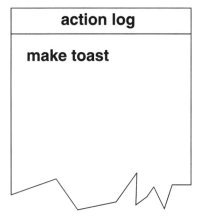

The student examines the state of the lift knob.

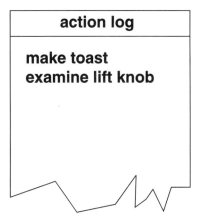

Table 7.6 Initialized SIMSB for the Simulation of the Simulation Problem

Skill or Component	Type	Relevant Rule	Score	Threshold 1	Threshold 2	Target
Color control lever	component	R5	0	−2	−4	
Color control knob	component	R5	0	−2	−4	
Thermostat adjusting knob	component	R5	0	−2	−4	
Keeper release switch	component	R5	0	−2	−4	
Keeper release switch spring	component	R5	0	−2	−4	
Lift knob	component	R5	0	−2	−4	
Lift lever	component	R5	0	−2	−4	
Latch	component	R5	0	−2	−4	
Keeper release	component	R5	0	−2	−4	
Keeper	component	R5	0	−2	−4	
Slide rod	component	R5	0	−2	−4	
Slide assembly	component	R5	0	−2	−4	
Thermostat	component	R5	0	−2	−4	
Heating element	component	R5	0	−2	−4	
Carriage	component	R5	0	−2	−4	
Carriage spring	component	R5	0	−2	−4	X
Lifter arm	component	R5	0	−2	−4	
Main switch	component	R5	0	−2	−4	
Power cord	component	R5	0	−2	−4	
Mechanism knowledge	skill	R1	0	−2	−5	
Mechanism knowledge	skill	R2	0	−3	−5	
Problem-solving knowledge	skill	R3	0		−5	
Problem-solving knowledge	skill	R4	0	3	5	
Problem-solving knowledge	skill	R6	0		5	
Problem-solving knowledge	skill	R7	0	3	5	

The state of the lift knob is down. At this point, the tutor will check to see if any of the student model rules apply. There is no path from the lift knob to the carriage spring, so we decrement the rule R1 assessment score.

Skill or Component	Type	Relevant Rule	Score	Threshold 1	Threshold 2	Target
mechanism knowledge	skill	R1	−1	−2*	−5	

*For the simulation of the simulation this threshold has been modified so that we can show how feedback will be given.

Since this is the first action, rule R2 does not apply yet. Rules R3 and R4 also do not apply because there are too few actions. Rule R5 applies, but only to note that this component was inspected. If the next component is one related to the lift knob, rule R5 may be able to add information to the student model. Rule R6 is not relevant (the student has not referred to the technical reference), and rule R7 does not apply because no actions have been repeated.

Once all of the student model rules have analyzed the action, the instructional model analyzes the state of the SIMSB. If any of the assessment scores are at the threshold, the instructional model gives feedback to the student. No score exceeds the threshold, so the instructional model does not give any feedback in this cycle.

In the next cycle, the student examines the lift lever and sees that the state of the lift lever is also down.

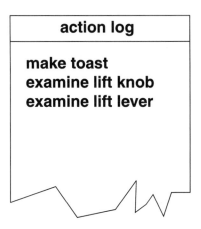

As the lift lever is also not on the path to the target component, rule R1 causes the rule R1 assessment score to be decremented again.

Skill or Component	Type	Relevant Rule	Score	Threshold 1	Threshold 2	Target
mechanism knowledge	skill	R1	−2	−2*	−5	

*For the simulation of the simulation this threshold has been modified so that we can show how feedback will be given.

Because the lift lever is not on the path to the target the student is no closer to the target, so rule R2 has no effect on the assessment score. This action does not cause rule R3 to make any change to its assessment score because there is no clear evidence the student is using a divide and conquer problem-solving approach. However, Rule R4 does change its assessment score. Since the student has examined a second component connected to the first component examined, he or she may be following a sequential problem-solving procedure. This causes the rule R4 assessment score to be incremented by 1.

Skill or Component	Type	Relevant Rule	Score	Threshold 1	Threshold 2	Target
problem-solving knowledge	skill	R4	1	3	5	

Since the lift lever is connected to the lift knob and since the lift knob has no other components connected to it, there is a possibility the student understands the relationship between the lift knob and the lift lever. Rule R5 increments the assessment score associated with the lift knob.

Skill or Component	Type	Relevant Rule	Score	Threshold 1	Threshold 2	Target
lift knob	component	R5	1	−2	−4	

The technical reference has not been referenced, and rule R6 does not change the corresponding assessment score. Rule R7 is also not relevant because no actions have been repeated.

The student model has been updated in this cycle and the instructional model examines the assessment scores. The rule R1 assessment score has reached a feedback threshold. The feedback given is

"The component lift lever may not be a good component to examine for this problem."

Paying attention to this feedback, our student chooses to examine another component in the toaster.

The student reasons, based on the given feedback, that there might be something wrong with the thermostat or components related to it. The student chooses to examine the thermostat as the next action.

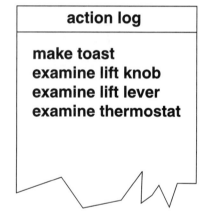

The thermostat's state is deflect 0, which means the thermostat is in its initial (start) state. The thermostat is not on the path to the target, so rule R1's assessment is decremented again.

Skill or Component	Type	Relevant Rule	Score	Threshold 1	Threshold 2	Target
mechanism knowledge	skill	R1	−3	−2*	−5	

*For the simulation of the simulation this threshold has been modified so that we can show how feedback will be given.

Again, this action does not put the student any closer to the solution, so rule R2's assessment score does not change in this action cycle. This action may indicate that a student is using a strategy other than a sequential one and may in fact be using a divide and conquer strategy. Rule R3's assessment score is incremented.

Skill or Component	Type	Relevant Rule	Score	Threshold 1	Threshold 2	Target
problem-solving knowledge	skill	R3	1		–5	

The student may be using a different problem-solving strategy (other than a sequential one), so rule R4's assessment score is decremented because there is now less evidence the student is using a sequential strategy.

Skill or Component	Type	Relevant Rule	Score	Threshold 1	Threshold 2	Target
problem-solving knowledge	skill	R4	0	3	5	

Rule R5 does not cause a change to the assessment score associated with component knowledge of the thermostat because the student has not examined any of the components connected or related to the thermostat. The technical reference still has not been used, so there is no assessment score change for rule R6's assessment. Rule R7 does not change its assessment score because no action has been repeated. The instructional model examines the SIMSB and determines in this action cycle that no additional feedback needs to be given.

Chapter Summary

This chapter has described the major parts of an intelligent tutor, how they are designed, and how they can be implemented. The chapter focused on three important aspects of developing an intelligent tutor—the overall interface to the tutor, the student model and instructional model implementations, and a "low-tech" test (paper and pencil) of the system as it is running.

I designed the intelligent tutor by story board. This was done by drawing a series of screen mock-ups defining the main features of the intelligent tutor. The design of each mock-up screen entailed defining the purpose of the screen and also how it related to the other mock-up screens. When the story board is complete, it can be used to assemble the actual screens to be used in the intelligent tutor. The actual screens for the Toaster Tutor are shown at the end of the section describing the story board.

Following the story board, I describe the student model. An important part of defining the student model is working out the rules that will operate to make assessments on student progress throughout the tutoring process. The section about the student model describes seven rules that will collect information to assess what the student knows about components in the toaster, about mechanisms in the toaster, and about problem-solving skills. The rules are based on the model of the toaster that is manipulated by the student, and they are defined in detail.

Next, the instructional model was defined. The purpose of the instructional model is to give feedback to the student that might help in the learning/problem-solving process. The instructional model uses information provided by the student model and makes decisions about when and what kinds of feedback to give the student. The instructional model uses the SIMSB to decide when and how to give feedback.

The chapter ended with a partial test of the system to show how the mechanism model, student model, and instructional model function together to create an operational tutor. A defective toaster was provided to a hypothetical student and the student performed several diagnostic steps on the toaster. The operation of the various models was demonstrated.

Suggested Reading

Barr, Avron, and Feigenbaum, Edward, *Handbook of Artificial Intelligence*, Menlo Park, CA: William Kaufmann, 1981.

In general, a good source for historical information about intelligent tutors.

Kearsley, Greg, *Artificial Intelligence and Instruction*, Reading, MA: Addison-Wesley, 1987.

Another source of information about intelligent tutors. Although these readings do not go into the detail presented in this chapter, the reader can gain some understanding of the various approaches to constructing student and instructional models.

CHAPTER 8

Natural Language Processing and Intelligent Multimedia

Introduction

The last chapter presented an example of intelligent multimedia that used expert systems to provide the "intelligence." The rules written for the mechanism, student, and instructional models comprise the expert systems implemented with video sequences, graphics, and the now fairly common mouse-based interface—the "point-and-click" interface.

Although artificial, mouse-based interfaces have made the computer easier to use. People did not start out life using a pointing device to communicate though. People use *language* to communicate.

The capability for computers to understand language has long been a desire of computer scientists. At first glance, the problem seems very simple, and in the 1950s it was seen in a simple and solvable light, but scientists quickly learned that the ability of humans to process language is one of the most complex cognitive tasks that people can do.

The last chapter more or less identified expert systems as an important aspect of artificial intelligence to create richer and more powerful multimedia systems. This chapter considers natural language processing in the same context—namely a way to make intelligent multimedia systems more powerful.

When we say natural language processing, exactly what do we mean? Simply put, natural language processing is getting computers to understand written or spoken language. But what do we mean by understand? What does it mean for a computer to understand natural language?

The answer to this question deserves great philosophical consideration. In fact, it has received this consideration, so you should be aware that there is no easy answer to the question of what it means for a computer to understand language. It is possible to formulate an answer by constraining the context in which the question is answered.

My own view of this is a very pragmatic one. We use programming languages, artificial and highly specialized languages, to communicate with computers. Our communication consists of instructions to the computer that cause it to "do things" for us. The kinds of things we have computers do vary, but in all cases the computer carries out some desired behavior. We need artificial languages because we have not yet achieved the ability to have a computer understand English. English or artificial language, the goal is the same: to have the computer carry out some desired behavior.

When a computer carries out the instructions in a language like C or LISP, we can say that the computer understands the instructions written in the program. In fact, if a computer can carry out the instructions in a program then the programmer understands the meaning or semantics of the language and can specify this meaning in the appropriate form (a computer program) to the computer.

If a computer understands English (spoken or written), then it can carry out the instructions specified in the English. This is what we mean by "understanding" as it is used in the rest of this chapter.

Multimedia and Natural Language Processing

The beginning of this chapter mentioned that mouse-based interfaces are only one possibility in the spectrum of potential interfaces. Another alternative is natural language. The purpose of this chapter is twofold: first, to describe how natural language is processed; second, to describe some potential applications for multimedia and natural language processing.

Most obviously natural language processing could replace or augment a mouse-based interface, but there are other possibilities. In this chapter, the first use for natural language processing will be one that creates illustrations from sentences that are presented to the application. Although this is an extremely complex application and our presentation will only scratch the surface, it represents the potential for natural language processing in conjunction with multimedia.

The second application uses natural language processing to interact with a student in the context of a tutor. The tutor is largely hypothetical, but the use of natural language processing in it is not. Rather than use natural language processing for the interface alone, the tutor uses natural language processing as a means to make assessments of the student's knowledge of language.

The next section gives a technical introduction to natural language processing. Following this, the application examples will be discussed.

Natural Language Processing—The Details

Two things can be said about natural language processing: There are lots of approaches, and no one has solved the problem completely. The information given here represents one approach to natural language processing. Throughout this section I will be reminding you of this because a different approach to natural language processing may be appropriate for an application that you have in mind.

A language is described by a grammar. The grammar we learned in grade school is an example of a grammar that expresses the rules of English in English. In order to get a computer to process language, a more formal representation of a grammar is needed. Formal grammars fill this requirement of a more formal means to describe a language.

A grammar consists of four parts: a special symbol called the start symbol, a set of symbols called the nonterminals, another set of symbols called the terminals, and a set of rules that define how the language is written. These rules are called rewrite or production rules. An example of a grammar is

- P1. S → NP VP
- P2. NP → Art N
- P3. NP → N
- P4. VP → V NP
- P5. Art → the
- P6. Art → a
- P7. N → dog
- P8. N → cat
- P9. N → boy
- P10. N → girl
- P11. V → plays
- P12. V → sees
- P13. V → walks
- P14. V → likes

Start symbol = S
Nonterminals = {S, NP, VP, N, V, Art}
Terminals = {the, a, dog, cat, boy, girl, play, sees, walks}

Sentences that can be written according to this grammar include

The dog sees the girl.
A boy walks a dog.
The girl likes a boy.

and also sentences like

The dog walks a girl.

The cat plays a girl.

How do we know these sentences are allowed by this grammar? If a sentence is part of a language specified by some grammar, then the sentence can be derived using the grammar. The process of derivation entails transforming the start symbol of the grammar into the sentence. The transformation is accomplished using the rules in the grammar.

A derivation begins using the start symbol

S

and locating any rules in the grammar that applies to this symbol. A rule consists of three parts. A left hand side, the symbol →, and the right hand side.

left hand side → right hand side
S → NP VP

A rule applies in a derivation step if the left hand side of the rule matches some symbol in the derivation string. In this case the derivation string is S and the rule that applies is

S → NP VP

In the case where more than one rule applies it is necessary to select the correct rule. The rule

S → NP VP

is called a production or a rewrite rule because it says that the symbol S can be replaced by the symbols NP and VP. In a derivation this would look like

S ⇒ NP VP

The special symbol ⇒ is read "derives." The symbol → is read "rewrites."

The sequence of symbols NP VP is an intermediate form of the derivation because it contains only nonterminal symbols. A derivation is complete when the string contains only symbols from the set of terminals. If no such string can be derived, then the sentence is not part of the language.

Consider the sentence

A boy walks a dog.

The derivation begins with the start symbol S. The only production that is relevant is P1.

$\quad$ S $\Rightarrow$ NP VP

Now we look for rules that allow NP to be rewritten. There are two of these, P2 and P3.

P2. NP → Art N

P3. NP → N

The phrase "a boy" gives away which rule to use—P2. NP is rewritten according to P2.

$\quad$ S $\quad\Rightarrow$ NP VP
$\quad\quad\quad\Rightarrow$ Art N VP

The sentence begins with the word "a", so the next rule we choose is P6 to rewrite the symbol Art.

$\quad$ S $\quad\Rightarrow$ NP VP
$\quad\quad\quad\Rightarrow$ Art N VP
$\quad\quad\quad\Rightarrow$ a N VP

Notice now that the last derivation contains one terminal and two nonterminals. The derivation is not yet complete because the nonterminal symbols are still present. More rewriting needs to be done.

The symbol N is the next candidate to be rewritten. The word in the sentence is "boy" so the relevant rule is P9.

$\quad$ S $\quad\Rightarrow$ NP VP
$\quad\quad\quad\Rightarrow$ Art N VP
$\quad\quad\quad\Rightarrow$ a N VP
$\quad\quad\quad\Rightarrow$ a boy VP

Next the symbol VP is rewritten using rule P4.

S   ⇒ NP VP
    ⇒ Art N VP
    ⇒ a N VP
    ⇒ a boy VP
    ⇒ a boy V NP

The sentence uses the word "walks" and the rule that applies at this stage of the derivation is P13.

S   ⇒ NP VP
    ⇒ Art N VP
    ⇒ a N VP
    ⇒ a boy VP
    ⇒ a boy V NP
    ⇒ a boy walks NP

The remaining nonterminal to be rewritten is NP and the phrase remaining in the sentence that has not been considered is "a dog." Rule P2 applies again.

S   ⇒ NP VP
    ⇒ Art N VP
    ⇒ a N VP
    ⇒ a boy VP
    ⇒ a boy V NP
    ⇒ a boy walks NP
    ⇒ a boy walks Art N

The article in the sentence is "a" and the next rewrite rule to be applied is P6.

S   ⇒ NP VP
    ⇒ Art N VP
    ⇒ a N VP
    ⇒ a boy VP

⇒ a boy V NP

⇒ a boy walks NP

⇒ a boy walks Art N

⇒ a boy walks a N

One more rule application and the sentence will be completely derived. The last word in the sentence is "dog" and rule P7 applies.

S   ⇒ NP VP

⇒ Art N VP

⇒ a N VP

⇒ a boy VP

⇒ a boy V NP

⇒ a boy walks NP

⇒ a boy walks Art N

⇒ a boy walks a N

⇒ a boy walks a dog.

The derivation is now complete because there are no more non-terminal symbols to rewrite and also because the derived sentence exactly matches the sentence that we set out to derive.

Another way to represent the derivation process is in the form of a tree. The tree for the example sentence is shown in Figure 8.1.

What happens when a sentence cannot be derived? For example, consider the sentence fragment

walk a boy

The derivation begins in the same way as the previous derivation.

S   ⇒ NP VP

and proceeds just as before:

S   ⇒ NP VP

⇒ Art N VP

Since we cannot rewrite Art or N any further, we rewrite VP:

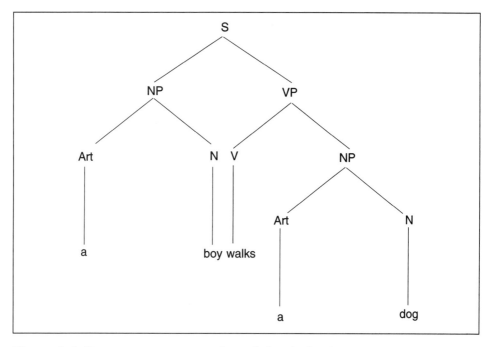

Figure 8.1 Parse tree representation of the derivation.

        S   ⇒ NP VP
           ⇒ Art N VP
           ⇒ Art N V NP

V can be rewritten with rule P13.

        S   ⇒ NP VP
           ⇒ Art N VP
           ⇒ Art N V NP
           ⇒ Art N walks NP

and with rule P2, NP can be rewritten:

        S   ⇒ NP VP
           ⇒ Art N VP
           ⇒ Art N V NP
           ⇒ Art N walks NP
           ⇒ Art N walks Art N

The symbol Art is rewritten with rule P6.

$$\begin{aligned} S &\Rightarrow NP\ VP \\ &\Rightarrow Art\ N\ VP \\ &\Rightarrow Art\ N\ V\ NP \\ &\Rightarrow Art\ N\ walks\ NP \\ &\Rightarrow Art\ N\ walks\ Art\ N \\ &\Rightarrow Art\ N\ walks\ a\ N \end{aligned}$$

And the symbol N is rewritten with rule P7.

$$\begin{aligned} S &\Rightarrow NP\ VP \\ &\Rightarrow Art\ N\ VP \\ &\Rightarrow Art\ N\ V\ NP \\ &\Rightarrow Art\ N\ walks\ NP \\ &\Rightarrow Art\ N\ walks\ Art\ N \\ &\Rightarrow Art\ N\ walks\ a\ N \\ &\Rightarrow Art\ N\ walks\ a\ dog \end{aligned}$$

No more rewriting can be done in this derivation and we are left with the sentential form,

Art N walks a dog

A sentential form is an intermediate string in the derivation. When a sentential form has terminals and nonterminals and no additional derivation steps can be performed, the sentence is not part of the language defined by the grammar.

How do we fix this problem? That is, how do we fix the problem that the sentence or sentence fragment is not part of the language this grammar defines. In the case of the fragment, "walks a dog," we may not want the phrase to be part of the language, but in other cases we may, and this is one of the places where grammar writing becomes tricky. How do you write rules in a grammar so that one rule does not have to be written for each and every sentence that can be written in the language? As you might imagine, if you were to try to write a rule per sentence for English, the number of rules that you would have to write would be huge. Part of the problem with writing a grammar is how to come up with the right set of rules that describe the language you are trying to describe.

The process of creating a derivation is called parsing. We can write a computer program to accomplish this feat also. I will describe one way to automate the parsing process, but keep in mind that there are other ways to accomplish the same task. The kind of parser I will describe is called an augmented transition network or ATN.

An ATN is represented in the form of a graph. Like other graphs, this one consists of nodes and edges with labels for the nodes and edges. The graph that represents the ATN specifies how a sentence in a language is derived or parsed. In this way, the ATN parser is carrying out the parsing process according to the grammar for the language. Figures 8.2 and 8.3 show an ATN for a small but useful part of the English language.

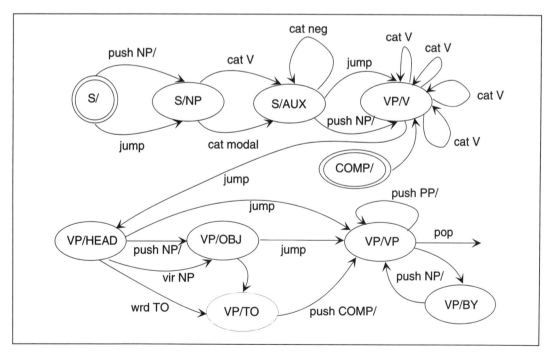

Figure 8.2 ATN parser for a subset of English (part 1) (Bates, 1978, p. 207).

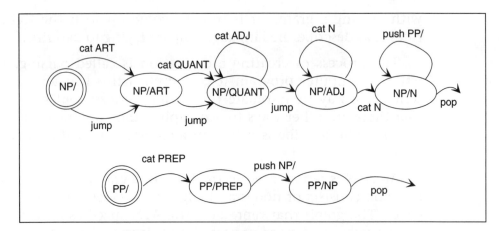

Figure 8.3 ATN parser for a subset of English (part 2) (Bates, 1978, p. 193).

The ATNs shown in Figures 8.2 and 8.3 represent a mechanism to parse a significant subset of English sentences. ATNs represent an alternative representation of a grammar. In fact, if you look closely at the ATN, you will notice similarities between it and a grammar.

Remember that the derivation process used rewrite rules to modify sentential forms until a sentence was achieved. An ATN implicitly represents the derivation process. It accomplishes this by processing an input sentence according to the instructions specified in the graph. Let's consider the sample sentence we used before, but this time we will parse the sentence with the ATNs shown in Figures 8.2 and 8.3. The sentence was

A boy walks a dog.

In an ATN, nodes of the graph represent state of the ATN. For example, the first state encountered in the graph is state S/. This state label, S/, means that we are about to process a sentence. State S/ is shown in Figure 8.4.

Two edges connect state S/ to state S/NP: the push NP/ edge and the jump edge. These labels specify what can be done at this point in the parsing process. If we want to move to the next state we can either

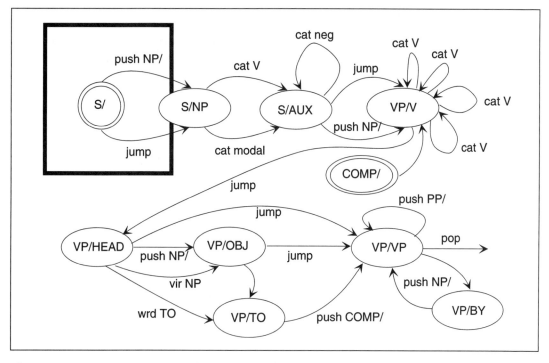

Figure 8.4 Sentence ATN with state S/ highlighted.

1. go and process an NP, or
2. jump to the next state without processing anything.

The push instruction calls a new ATN into play. In this case, the ATN is the NP ATN shown in Figure 8.5.

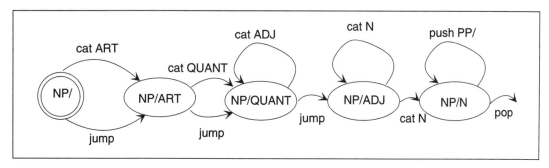

Figure 8.5 NP ATN.

At this point our choices are to

1. read an article (specified by the edge labeled cat ART), or
2. jump to the NP/ART state.

The input string contains the word "A," so we read in an article and remember this for later. Every time we process a particular element of a sentence we will save it in a variable. In this case, the article is saved in a variable named "ART." By processing an article, we have moved to state NP/ART. Our choices are now to

1. process a quantifier, or
2. jump.

The next word in the sentence is "boy," so we choose to jump to the next state (the sentence contains no quantifiers).

In state NP/ADJ we can process a noun. The next word is a noun (boy), so we advance to state NP/N. Also, the word "boy" is stored in a variable named N. Notice that there is another push operation occurring here. This operation pushes the PP/ ATN shown in Figure 8.6.

The PP/ state expects a preposition, but the next word in the sentence is "walks" and is not a preposition. At this point we return from the PP ATN with no prepositional phrase. When we do this, we also return from the NP ATN with the following result.

(NP (Art a) (N boy))

Now we are back at state NP/N and the variable NP contains the value shown, that is, the value returned from the NP ATN.

At S/NP, two possible actions can take place:

1. cat V, or
2. cat modal.

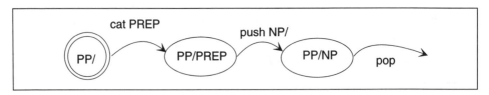

Figure 8.6 ATN to process prepositional phrases.

Because the next word in the sentence is "walks," we take the cat V edge and save the word "walks" in a variable named V. We are now in state S/AUX. In S/AUX there are three possible actions:

1. accept a negative word (like not), or
2. jump to VP/V, or
3. push NP/.

Since the ATN has processed a verb on its way to S/AUX, the next phrase is "a dog," a noun phrase. The most obvious action would be to push NP/. If we do this and we return to state VP/V, we can jump to VP/HEAD, jump to VP/V, and out of the ATN. But in this case the structure we get from the parser is

(S (NP (Art a) (N boy) (VP (V walks)
(RMOD (NP (Art a) (N dog))))

where the noun phrase is called a right modifier of the verb. This is not correct, so from S/AUX we take a different action—number 2, jump to VP/V. In VP/V we will push NP/ and process the noun phrase, "a boy." After completing the ATN processing, the parse of the sentence is

(S (NP (Art a) (N boy)) (VP (V walks)
(NP (Art a) (N dog))))

The ATNs shown in Figures 8.2 and 8.3 do not show the details of how the structure shown here is created. The actual ATN is represented as a programming language:

Program Listing 8.1 ATN code.

```
(define-grammar
   '(start
       (xpush s/ t
           (cond ($lexstate (abort)))
           'parse-found))
    '(s/
       (xpush np/ (npstart)
           (setr subj ^)
           (setrq type dcl)
           (to s/np))
       (xjump s/np t
```

(continues)

Program Listing 8.1 ATN code. (*Continued*)

```
              (setrq type q)))

  '(s/np
         (xcat v (xgetf tns)
               (setr v ^)
               (setr tns
                     (buildq (tns =) (xgetf tns)))
               (setr pncode (xgetf pncode))
               (to s/aux))
         (xcat modal t
               (setr modal (buildq ((modal ^))))
               (setr tns (buildq (tns =)
                                 (xgetf tns)))
               (to s/aux)))

  '(s/aux
         (xcat neg (nullr neg)
               (setrq neg (neg))
               (cond ((equal (get (getr v) 'lex) 'do)
                      (setrq v nil)))
               (to s/aux))
         (xjump vp/v t)
         (xpush np/ (nullr subj)
               (setr subj ^)
               (to vp/v)))

  '(vp/v
         (xcat v (and (xgetf pastpart)
                      (equal (get (getr v) 'lex) 'be))
               (hold (getr subj))
               (setrq subj (np (pro someone)))
               (setr agflag t)
               (setr v ^)
               (to vp/v))
         (xcat v (and (xgetf pastpart)
                      (equal (get (getr v) 'lex) 'have))
               (addr tns 'perfect)
               (setr v ^)
               (to vp/v))
         (xcat v (and (xgetf untensed)
                      (getr modal)
                      (nullr v))
```

```
                    (setr v ^)
                    (to vp/v))
            (xcat v (and (xgetf prespart)
                         (equal (get (getr v) 'lex) 'be))
                    (addr tns 'progressive)
                    (setr v ^)
                    (to vp/v))
            (xjump vp/head t
                    (cond ((or (getr modal)
                               (getr neg))
                           (setr aux
                                 (buildq (($@ aux + +)) modal
neg))))))

    '(vp/head
        (xpush np/ (and (xgetf trans (getr v)) (npstart))
                (setr obj ^)
                (to vp/obj))
        (xjump vp/vp (xgetf intrans (getr v)))
        (xvir np (xgetf trans (getr v))
                (setr obj ^)
                (to vp/obj))
        (xwrd to (and (xgetf scomp (getr v))
                      (nullr agflag))
                (setr specialsubj (getr subj))
                (to vp/to)))

    '(vp/obj
        (xwrd to (xgetf scomp (getr v))
                (setr specialsubj (getr obj))
                (to vp/to))
        (xjump vp/vp t))

    '(vp/vp
        (xpush pp/ (ppstart)
                (addr vmods ^)
                (to vp/vp))
        (xwrd by (getr agflag)
                (setr agflag nil)
                (to vp/by))
        (xpop (cond ((getr obj)
                     (buildq (s + + + ($@ + (vp (v +) +) +))
                             type subj tns aux v obj vmods))
```

(continues)

ProProgram Listing 8.1 ATN code. (*Continued*)

```
                        (t (buildq (s + + + ($@ + (vp (v +)) +))
                                    type subj tns aux v vmods)))
                 t))

'(vp/by
     (xpush np/ t
           (setr subj ^)
           (to vp/vp)))

'(vp/to
     (xpush comp/ t
           (<sendr subj (getr specialsubj))
           (<sendr tns (getr tns))
           (<sendrq type comp)
           (setr obj ^)
           (to vp/vp)))

'(comp/
     (xcat v (xgetf untensed)
           (setr v ^)
           (to vp/v)))

'(np/
     (xcat art t
           (setr art (buildq ((art ^))))
           (to np/art))
     (xjump np/art t))

'(np/adj
     (xcat n t
           (setr n ^)
           (setr nu (xgetf number))
           (to np/n))
     (xcat pro t
           (setr n ^)
           (setr nu (xgetf number))
           (to np/n))
     (xcat adj t
           (addl adjs (buildq (adj (np (n ^) (nu =)))
                               (xgetf number)))
           (to np/adj)))
```

```
'(np/art
    (xcat quant t
        (setr quant (buildq ((quant ^))))
        (to np/quant))
    (xjump np/quant t))

'(np/quant
    (xcat adj t
        (addr adjs (buildq ($@ adj = (^))
                            (xgetf degree)))
        (to np/quant))
    (xjump np/adj t))

'(np/n
    (xpush pp/ (ppstart)
        (addl nmods ^)
        (to np/n))
    (xwrd and t
        (setr savenp (append (getr savenp)
                        (buildq ($@ np + + + ((N +)) ((nu +)) +)
                                        art quant adjs n nu nmods)))
        (to np/))
    (xpop (append (list '(cnj and))
            (list (getr savenp))
            (list
                (buildq ($@ np + + + ((N +)) ((nu +)) +)
                                art quant adjs n nu nmods)))
            (getr savenp))
    (xpop (buildq ($@ np + + + ((N +)) ((nu +)) +)
            art quant adjs n nu nmods)
        (detagree)))

'(pp/
    (xcat prep t
        (setr prep ^)
        (to pp/prep)))

'(pp/prep
```

(continues)

Program Listing 8.1 ATN code. (*Continued*)

```
              (xpush np/ (npstart)
                       (setr np ^)
                       (to pp/np)))

     '(pp/np
         (xpop (buildq (pp (prep +) +)
                        prep np)
                t))
     )

(defun ppstart ()
  (member 'prep (xgetf cat)))

(defun npstart ()
  (or (member 'n (xgetf cat))
      (member 'pro (xgetf cat))
      (member 'art (xgetf cat))
      (member 'adj (xgetf cat))))

(defun detagree ()
  (cond
    ((null (getr art)) t)
    ((equal (xgetf number (getr n)) '(sg/pl)) t)
    (t (equal (xgetf number (getr n))
              (xgetf number (cadar (getr art))))))))
```

The language follows the structure of the ATN fairly closely, with the important ability to output the structures like the one shown earlier. The ATN program outputs a parse structure similar to the ones shown earlier, but in a flattened form using parentheses to specify relationships between various phrases in a sentence. Figure 8.7 shows how the parenthesized parse structure related to the tree-based parse structure.

Now that we can process a sentence with an ATN, what can we do with the output of the process? The structure output by an ATN (according to the grammar specified) is only one possible output. Others are possible. One useful representation gives us a more structured picture of the meaning of a sentence.

NATURAL LANGUAGE PROCESSING AND INTELLIGENT MULTIMEDIA 423

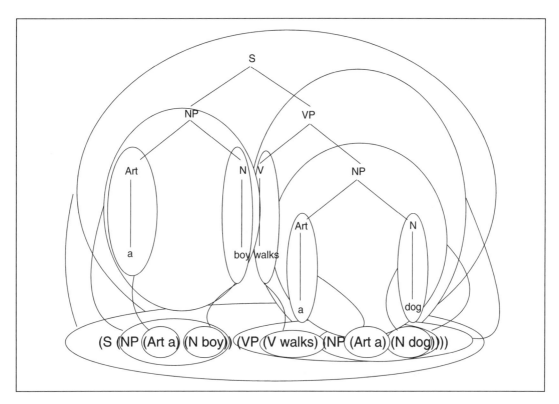

Figure 8.7 Relationship of parse tree to flattened parser representation.

Let's say that a verb plays a central role in a sentence (actually sentences would be pretty boring without verbs). As we learned in grammar school, a verb expresses activity in a sentence. The other parts of a sentence are participants for the verb. In other words, the verb needs the other parts of the sentence to work in the sentence, and these parts play important roles with the verb. Consider the sample sentence

A boy walks a dog.

In this sentence the verb expresses an event that is taking place. The event is called walking. In walking, there is usually someone who is walking, and in this particular sense the activity of walking is associated with something being walked. So in this sentence, we could call the boy an agent and the dog a patient or object of the activity. The structure we can construct might look something like

$$walk_{event}(boy_{agent}, dog_{patient})$$

This alternative representation is one that expresses the meaning of the sentence more readily than the structures produced by the parser. One way to produce this meaning representation is to have the parser produce it. Another way to construct the representation is to carry out a transformation on the parse structure produced by the parser. How would a transformation like this be accomplished?

To accomplish this it is necessary to have two new databases that will be used in the transformation process. The first of these two databases is a list of possible characterizations of words. In the example given, "event", "agent", and "patient" are characterizations. An example of one possible set of characterizations is

accompaniment	instrument
activity	location
abstract-destination	manner
after	mental-object
agent	object
abstract-location	patient
abstract-source	possessed-by
attribute	quantity
before	reason
comparison	recipient
destination	source
direction	state
event	subject
force	time-location
goal	time-span

Remember that in the first grammar described (Figure 8.1) there were rewrite rules like

N → dog

Table 8.1 Lexicon for Simple Grammar (Figure 8.1)

Word	Part of Speech
the	art
a	art
dog	N
cat	N
boy	N
girl	N
plays	V
sees	V
walks	V
likes	V

In the ATN there were edges labeled

cat N

This edge label checks to see if the present word is classified as a noun. The rewrite rule specifies exactly this information. Instead of writing one rule for each possible word classification, we can use a table that contains classifications, such as whether the word is a noun or a verb. These classifications are called "parts of speech." The rewrite rules that classify terminal strings can be respecified as in Table 8.1. This table is called a lexicon.

We can extend this lexicon to contain other characterizations. Specifically, we can also include in the lexicon word roles as assigned from the list shown earlier. The result is shown in Table 8.2.

If we want to construct the verb-based meaning representation commonly called a logical form or a proposition, then there must be more information in the lexicon. In order to create the logical form, entries in the lexicon must specify how they might play a part in a propositional representation. For example, for verbs, the lexicon must have templates representing the structures that can be produced for each verb. For example, "walks" has the following template associated with it.

$$walks_{event}(X_{agent}, Y_{patient})$$

Table 8.2 Lexicon with Role Characterizations

Word	Part of Speech	Role
the	art	—
a	art	—
dog	N	agent, patient, subject
cat	N	agent, patient, subject
boy	N	agent, patient, subject
girl	N	agent, patient, subject
plays	V	event
sees	V	event
walks	V	event
likes	V	mental event

In this template, the letters X and Y represent variables that will be filled in when the parse structure is transformed into the propositional representation. In the parse structure the two elements that have been classified in the lexicon are boy and dog. Here "boy" can be classified as agent, object, patient, or subject. Because the boy is doing the action, the most likely classification is as an agent. Thus we have

$$\text{walks}_{event}(\text{boy}_{agent}, Y_{patient})$$

The dog, on the other hand, is being walked and is the patient in this activity. In the lexicon a dog can be a patient so the resulting proposition is

$$\text{walks}_{event}(\text{boy}_{agent}, \text{dog}_{patient})$$

To make this explanation as brief as possible, I have glossed over an important aspect of the process—namely, how the word "boy" becomes an agent and how "dog" becomes a patient. This is a very complex process, and I will give one possible approach to making the assignments. In general a variety of techniques are necessary to accomplish this.

Along with a template like,

$$\text{walk}_{event}(X_{agent}, Y_{patient})$$

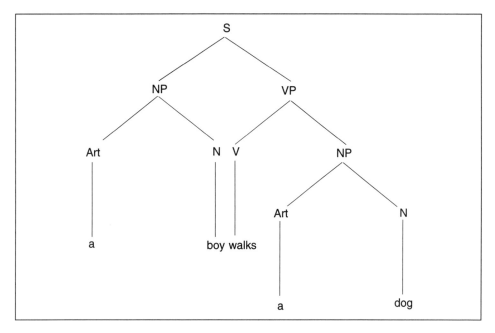

Figure 8.8 Parse tree (again) for sentence "A boy walks a dog."

it is possible to create rules that choose parts of the parse tree that can be used to fill in the template. Consider the parse tree for the sentence shown in Figure 8.8.

In general, an agent could be the noun in the subject position of the sentence. In the tree shown in Figure 8.8 it is possible to identify the path to the noun in this position. The path is shown in Figure 8.9.

Suppose that we create a pattern from this path. The pattern would specify the relationship between the path and the template for the proposition. In this case, the path pattern would be

(S, NP, N, X)

We could use a pattern like this to traverse the tree and assign a value to the variable X. The pattern has the meaning:

1. Start at S.
2. Travel to a node labeled NP.
3. Travel to a node labeled N.
4. Travel to the next node and assign the contents of this node to label X.

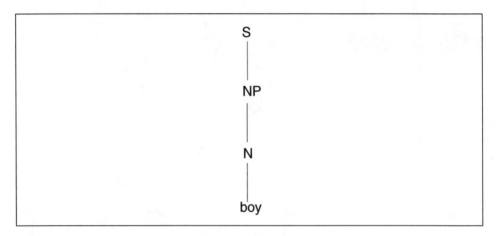

Figure 8.9 Path to possible agent noun.

In the context of the path pattern and the parse tree, X would be assigned the value "boy." Likewise, a pattern can be specified for the patient in the proposition template. Patients are usually in the object position of the parse tree following the verb. A path for this position is shown in Figure 8.10.

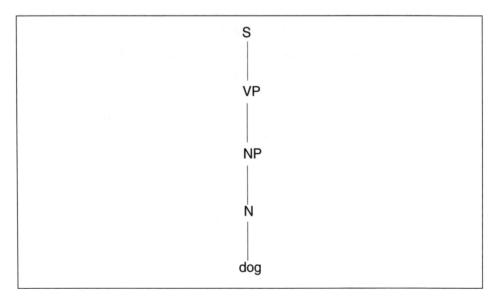

Figure 8.10 Path to possible patient noun.

The related pattern would be

(S, VP, NP, N, Y)

The lexicon table can be augmented with path patterns to define how template variables are assigned according to the roles they might play. A revised lexicon showing some of the path patterns and proposition templates is shown in Table 8.3.

Table 8.3 Lexicon Extended with Proposition Templates and Path Patterns

Word	Part of Speech	Role	Template	Path Patterns
the	art	—	—	—
a	art	—	—	—
dog	N	agent	—	—
		patient	—	—
		subject	—	—
cat	N	agent	—	—
		patient	—	—
		subject	—	—
boy	N	agent	—	—
		patient	—	—
		subject	—	—
girl	N	agent	—	—
		patient	—	—
		subject	—	—
plays	V	event	$\text{plays}_{event}(X_{agent}, Y_{object})$	agent: (S,NP,N,X)
				object: (S,VP,NP,N,Y)
sees	V	event	$\text{sees}_{event}(X_{agent}, Y_{patient})$	agent: (S,NP,N,X)
				patient: (S,VP,NP,N,Y)
walks	V	event	$\text{walks}_{event}(X_{agent}, Y_{patient})$	agent: (S,NP,N,X)
				patient: (S,VP,NP,N,Y)
likes	V	mental-event	$\text{likes}_{mental\text{-}event}(X_{agent}, Y_{patient})$	agent: (S,NP,N,X)
				patient: (S,VP,NP,N,Y)

Propositions Are the Key

Key to the applications that I will describe is the use of the propositions. In general, both the automatic illustrator and the tutor for Spanish use propositions as the means by which they make decisions. The approach that will be used is depicted in Figure 8.11.

In an application, the input from the application will be parsed and then transformed into a proposition. The application will include a database of propositions. In this database, each proposition will be associated with one or more actions. The action(s) specify what to do if the proposition created from the input sentence to the system matches one of those in the database. The action(s) can be as simple as to return success when a proposition is found in a series

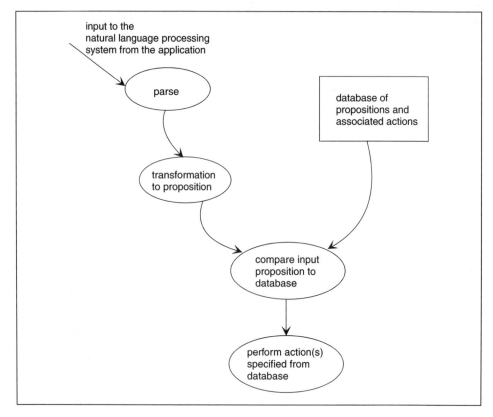

Figure 8.11 Use of propositions in an application.

of operations for creating an illustration. The next sections describe two hypothetical applications in more detail.

Application Example 1—An Automatic Illustrator

The purpose of the automatic illustrator is to create illustrations from natural language expressions. For example, suppose we present the sentence, "The man went fishing in a boat," to the automatic illustrator. We would expect something close to the illustration shown in Figure 8.12 to be created.

An automatic illustration system could be used to automatically create large numbers of illustrations

In any multimedia application, one of the most time-consuming activities is the creation of graphics used as the basis of the multimedia application. In an intelligent tutor or other application we may also want to produce illustrations as part of exercises that are given, and since we want the exercises to change, the illustrations will naturally have to change.

The automatic illustrator accepts sentences. The sentences can be written in any language. The illustrator requires an analyzer for

Figure 8.12 Desired illustration for the sentence "The man went fishing in a boat."

Figure 8.13 Illustration for the sentence "Joan and John attend a university."

the natural language that will be accepted and processed by the automatic illustrator.

Here is what an automatic illustrator will do. We will give the automatic illustrator a sentence such as

Joan and John attend a university.

and the illustrator will produce the illustration depicted in Figure 8.13.

Consider what it would take to create this simple illustration. Looking at the illustration we can see that it is composed of several different elements. There is a picture of a "Joan," one of a "John," and one of a stately looking building we could envision being called a university. Also, there are some other elements in this illustration. To fill in the image, making it more interesting, there are some trees and a path from the foreground to the university building. Besides these elements, there is also the issue of placement. How do we decide where to place elements of the illustration? Is there some way to decide how this can be done?

Elements of the Automatic Illustrator

The task of creating an illustration can be broken down into the following steps.

1. Parse the sentence.
2. Create a proposition for the parse structure of the sentence.
3. In the proposition database, find the proposition constructed for the input sentence. This retrieval will provide a series of instructions that can be used to assemble the illustration.
4. Execute the instructions to assemble the illustration.

Two problems need to be solved. The first is what the instructions contained in the proposition database used by the automatic illustrator will look like; the second is how the images will be maintained so that they can be used to create the necessary composite images.

I suggest two approaches to what the instructions retrieved from the proposition database might look like. The first approach to this problem allows the computer to do more work and the instructions to do less. In this context the instructions consist of a list of images that are to be retrieved and used to construct the composite image. For example, in the case of the sentence, "Joan and John attend a university," the images returned are shown in Figure 8.14.

Based on Figure 8.14, the list of images that are associated with "John and Joan attend a university." would be

university (building)
joan (person, female)
john (person, male)
trees
grass

The illustrator would take this list and construct a composite image. It would accomplish this with a set of placement rules like

People should be placed in front of buildings.

and

People should be placed so that they do not overlap.

and

An attempt should be made to position the people in the foreground.

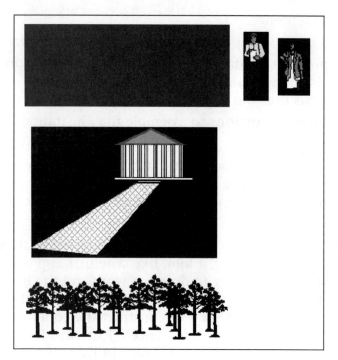

Figure 8.14 Pictures used to create illustration for "John and Joan attend a university."

The second approach to creating an illustration from instructions that are retrieved from the proposition database is to have the instructions specify where the component images are placed. Under this approach the system does not have to be smart about this, it only has to follow directions. The first approach has the advantage that it tries to avoid overlap, but for this reason it is significantly more complex to create. The second approach would be significantly easier to create but might result in a need to edit the images after they are composed.

The next problem that needs to be solved is where and how the images used by the automatic illustrator will be stored. To retrieve a picture or a graphic of a university for example, there must be a specification of where the image is and that it is an image of a university. The next part of this discussion introduces the idea of an image library.

Picture and Image Library Utility

Figure 8.14 shows all of the pictures that are used in the composite illustration for the sentence "John and Joan attend a university." These are the pictures that will need to be stored in the picture database and indexed in such a way that they can be retrieved and used to create a composite picture. Now the problem to solve is how to store these pictures so that they can be assembled in the manner described.

There are several approaches to solving this problem. For example, we could find a database that is capable of storing both picture data, like that shown in the illustration, and also text and numerical data. This would mean that all of the information about the pictures would be kept in one place and be accessed from that one place.

Still another possibility is to make use of an existing database program and write some program functions that will allow a picture to be stored in that database as typical data. This is a good way to avoid the expense of purchasing a new database specifically for images of your project. The disadvantage of doing this is that retrieval might be slow, as it might be necessary to reread the picture from the database and create a file so that some other program can load the image.

Yet another possibility, and the one I am going to take is to make use of an existing database, and store the picture outside of that database. In this case I will conveniently store the image on a Visual Basic form in a picture array. Why do this?

As long as we can efficiently get access to the images, and as long as Visual Basic provides us with this nice technique for storing them directly on a form, why not use it? By using a picture array we can gain access to the image through its index. Since it may also be necessary to store a mask of the image, we can store the pairs of images in adjacent picture element cells. If the picture library grows too large and we run out of memory, then we can shuffle forms containing pictures in and out as they are required by the programs we write. The next task is to decide what the database that describes the pictures will contain.

Since we are storing pictures, it makes sense to include a field that contains a *name* for the picture. This is a piece of identifying information and only serves that purpose. It will not be used, for instance, by the part of the illustrator that extracts pictures from the database. Other important information is the index of the picture in the picture array and the index of the mask for the picture. Although I said that pictures could reside in adjacent cells, this might not happen, so I will plan for this possibility by including a field for this purpose.

Next, I will want to keep the dimensions of the picture in the database. This allows for simple retrieval of this information. I will store the width and the height of the picture in pixels and in twips (the measure used by Visual Basic). I also want to classify the image into one of several major categories. This will be one of the factors that control how the illustrator eventually places the image in the illustration.

In addition to classifying an image into one of several major categories, we also want to specify the necessary information for extracting an image. This categorization will consist of a list of words that describe a particular picture. These words (or phrases) should relate directly to the vocabulary of sentences to be illustrated. A match between one of these word entries and a word in a sentence will cause the image to included in the illustration built by the illustrator. Since there may be more than a single word or phrase that describes the picture, a separate table in the database will be used to store this information. A summary of the fields that will be used to describe a picture is

- Name of the image
- Index of the image in the picture array
- Index of the mask of the image in the picture array
- Width of the image in pixels
- Height of the image in pixels
- Width of the image in twips
- Height of the image in twips
- Classification of the image
- Content descriptions for extraction

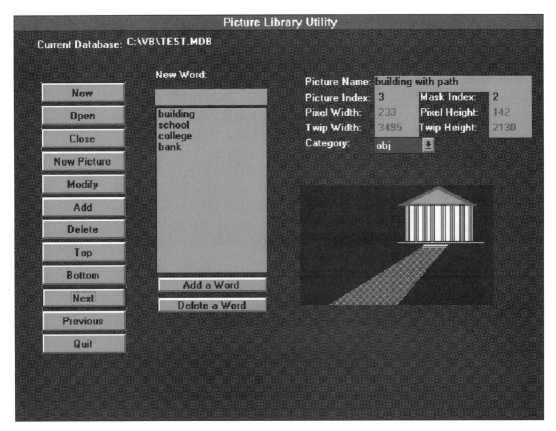

Figure 8.15 Picture/image library utility.

The picture database will be maintained by a utility specifically for this purpose. It can be used to add information to, modify information in, or delete information from the image database. Figure 8.15 shows a picture of the interface for the image database utility. The Picture/image library (PILL) utility is used to maintain information about the pictures that can be used by the automatic illustrator. The automatic illustrator will extract information from this database in order to make decisions about how to assemble illustrations.

PILL is controlled by a panel of buttons, a small area for data input, and a section of the screen for displaying the graphic image associated with the data entered in the data entry fields. The button panel, shown in Figure 8.16 includes all of the basic functions to manipulate the picture database.

Figure 8.16 PILL button panel.

In the PILL control panel, the functions **New**, **Open**, and **Close** are used to create a new picture database, open an existing database, and close an opened database, respectively. When **Open** or **Close** is clicked, a dialog box is displayed that requires the user to enter a file name.

The remainder of the buttons (other than **Quit**) are used to manipulate and control picture data entry into the database. The **New Picture** button clears the various fields of the form, allowing for entry of new picture data. The **Add** button, when clicked, saves data entered onto the form into the open picture database. **Modify** is used to make changes to data in the picture database. Picture data

Figure 8.17 Image data entry area.

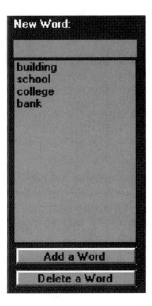

Figure 8.18 Image classification data entry.

can be deleted with the **Delete** button. The remaining keys are used to view the contents of the picture database. **Top** and **Bottom** move to the beginning and end of the picture database, respectively, and **Next** and **Previous** move from one record to another in the forward and reverse directions. Besides the button controls, there are two other important areas on the PILL interface. These are the data entry area (Figure 8.17) and the word list entry area (Figure 8.18). The latter has two buttons that allow an image in the database to be classified. As shown in Figure 8.18 an image can be classified with any words or phrases deemed useful/appropriate for referring to the image. Classifications can be added and deleted as necessary.

Application Example 2—A Foreign Language Tutor Named *Habla*

This section describes the second potential multimedia application of natural language processing. The application is a tutor for Spanish that presents Spanish passages and asks questions about these passages. The natural language processing is applied to student responses to the questions.

Before describing the application, I want to take a little time to discuss the issue of pedagogy. Until now I have avoided any discussion of this topic, but in the case of *Habla*, some mention of this is relevant. Although this book is about implementing applications, pedagogic considerations are of particular importance in a system that will be used in an educational context.

Pedagogy

Pedagogy is about how to assemble information so that students can effectively learn the information. In this context, pedagogy is a methodology closely related to the process of instructional design. Instructional design is just the process of creating courses for students. The discipline of instructional design is well established and researched, and there is an abundance of information about instructional design to draw upon.

A practical discussion of the subject of instructional design can be found in *Making Instruction Work*, by Robert Mager. A practical book about instructional design is germane to our discussion for two reasons. From a practical standpoint, the chances of being a multimedia implementer and an instructional designer at the same time are very small, so any approach we select must be a practical one so that we are able to apply it to our task.

Another reason for selecting this source of material for instructional design, as opposed to others, is that the procedure for creating instruction is defined as a step by step procedure. This is particularly important because it eliminates confusion with the process and allows us to focus on the subject matter of the instruction.

In reading the material about instructional design, one will find that for the most part it represents good common sense about how to structure information so that it can be effectively presented to the student. As with any problem, the first step is to define the problem. In this case, the problem is to clearly define what it is we want to teach the student, or more generally to specify what information we want to impart to the student. Once the problem has been defined, we can set out to solve the problem. In the context of instructional design, this means structuring the information for the student. In terms of *Habla*, let's consider what this means. The passage that follows, is the first passage *Habla* presents to a student. For the non–Spanish speakers among you, I have also provided an English translation of the passage.

Enrique es español. Él es amigo de María. Ellos son muy buenos amigos. María es de los Estados Unidos. El apellido de Enrique es Pereda. El appellido de María es Jackson.

Enrique y María son alumnos de Colegio Buenavista. Ellos son alumnos muy buenos y muy inteligentes. Hay muchos alumnos en el colegio. (Tardy, 1990, p. 3).

English translation:

Enrique is Spanish. He is Maria's friend. They are very good friends. Maria is from the United States. Enrique's last name is Pereda. Maria's last name is Jackson.

Enrique and Maria are students of Buenavista College. They are very good students and very intelligent. There are many students in the college.

In *Making Instruction Work*, (1988, p.6) Mager identifies seven steps of instructional strategy:

1. Determine that there is a need for instruction.
2. Describe what the instruction should accomplish, deriving these objectives from the world in which the student will be expected to function.
3. Determine which of these objectives students have already accomplished.
4. Develop, try out, and revise instruction that will fill the gap between what students can already do and what they need to be able to do.
5. Implement the instruction.
6. Find out how well the instruction worked.
7. Improve the instruction.

This list of steps represents a grand plan for creating instruction. Each of these steps relates to one of four phases in the instructional design process: performance analysis, development, implementation, and improvement.

In the performance analysis phase, we determine what the instruction will be about. The goal of this phase is to determine what people know, in order to know what needs to be taught. This may seem an obvious step in the process, but consider how often you have attended a class where an instructor presented information that you already know. To carry out the performance analysis, Mager defined several stages in the process.

In the first stage of the performance analysis, we examine the task(s) for which the instruction is being created. If the student was doing the task(s), what would he or she be doing? Think about what this means for reading Spanish passages like the sample passage shown. When students read a passage, they should be able to understand the passage.

We want the student to be able to read and understand a passage in Spanish. What does this mean? What does it mean for a student to read a passage in another language? What does it mean for a student to understand the passage? The word "read" and the word "understand" are abstract terms. For us to create instruction that will facilitate student accomplishment of these tasks, we need to be able to define what these terms mean in concepts that are not abstract. When we define what it means to *read* and *understand* a passage in Spanish, we define the goals for the instruction. The goal analysis is the next stage of the performance analysis.

A goal analysis is used to define what students will have to do when they are able to read a Spanish passage, and what students will have to do when they understand a passage. To read a Spanish passage, a student will have to know how to recognize words. This includes the knowledge of how letters go together to form words and how the words form sentences. Understanding a sentence requires a student to know what individual words of the sentence means, and how the words go together to form a sentence. This goal really includes two subgoals. One of these is knowing the rules for assembling words into sentences—the rules of grammar. The other subgoal is knowing what the words assembled into a sentence mean. Table 8.4 shows a summary of the task and goal analyses.

Table 8.4 Results of the Task and Goal Analysis

Task Analysis	Goal Analysis
Read and understand a Spanish passage	Recognize words in a sentence
	Know how words form a sentence
	Know meaning of each word
	Know meaning of sentence from words that form sentence

In a full performance analysis, there are several more stages. These include a description of the target population, the students who will be given the instruction. Instruction written for a population of second graders will differ from instruction written for a high school student. Likewise, instruction written for a student of Spanish having one year of classroom Spanish instruction will differ from instruction written for a student having had little or no classroom Spanish. Understanding who the target audience of the instruction is, can result in more effective and appropriate instruction.

The remaining stages of the performance analysis include defining the objectives of the instruction—namely, what you expect the students to know when they are finished with the instruction. This specification of what is expected of a student upon completion of the instruction is in the form of a hierarchy. The hierarchy represents the sequence or ordering of the presentation of skills in the instruction. For example, since the *Habla* tutor will present a series of passages to be read, it makes sense that as the sequence progresses, the passages become more demanding. The first passage (shown earlier) is relatively simple, offering few new words and few new syntactic constructions. As we progress through the passages, the vocabulary becomes more complex, as do the passages. This amounts to saying that the initial skills learned will include understanding simple sentences, with one or two words per sentence of the passage. Later, there might be five to seven new words per sentence and sentences will be more complex. In specific passages, there may be other kinds of things that we want the student to learn. This too would be part of the skills hierarchy.

Finally, it is important as part of the performance analysis to specify the prerequisites for the instruction. For students to be able to understand the instruction and learn new concepts from it, they must have some set of skills prior to taking the new instruction. For reading Spanish passages, this might include a certain knowledge of Spanish vocabulary, a basic understanding of simple Spanish sentences, and an understanding of certain verb conjugations.

Instruction Development Phase

Once you know everything about what you need to teach, the next step in the instructional design process is to create the material to teach. This phase usually occurs without any knowledge about what to teach because it is always tempting to put pen to paper before thinking about what might be written. The performance analysis phase is an important phase because it represents the thinking before the writing.

Just as in the performance analysis phase, Mager defines several stages in the instructional development phase. These stages include developing criterion tests, determining what the relevant practice will be, deriving the content of the instruction, determining the delivery system for the instruction, developing modules in the instruction, sequencing the modules of the instruction, and (often forgotten, but very important) trying the instruction out.*

A criterion test is way to determine if a student is grasping a particular concept, task, or skill in the instruction. Criterion tasks can take many different forms. They can be large or small. They can be continuous throughout an instructional sequence. They can be given at particular points in the instruction. We are most familiar with the last of these: tests given at particular times in an instructional sequence by the names of midterm and final examinations. Although an economical form of test for a typical classroom and a typical instructor, one or two examinations across a long sequence

---

*The various stages of the performance analysis and instructional development are not all required. In fact, some thought should be given to selecting which are most appropriate for the instruction that you plan to develop.

of instruction may not serve to verify that a student has, in fact, learned the important concepts, ideas, and techniques presented in the instruction. More frequent and shorter assessments may be given to provide continuous feedback to the student.

For our Spanish passage, what sorts of criterion tests may we give? In the teaching of reading and understanding of Spanish passages, we would like to verify whether the students (a) understand the vocabulary of the passages, (b) understand the sentence structure, and (c) understand the meaning of the sentences. To verify that they have been learning these skills, we can provide small tests that ask students to fill in missing words in a sentence, to match a word with the meaning of the word in two lists, to complete a sentence, to translate a sentence, and to write a passage that mimics the contents of the passage they just read. What's more, we can make sure that a student is retaining the instruction by making the questions of the tests cumulative, so that a question may be about the passage just read, or about some passage read previously.

The relevant practice consists of exercises that the student can use to practice the concepts presented in the instruction. One type of practice may be very similar to the content of the tests that are given. Other kinds of practice may also be devised. For example, to ensure that students understand the content of the passage, we could ask them to annotate a series of illustrations based on the passage. Other exercises could involve specific words or word types, such as verbs.

Content development involves the creation of the teaching material. It is distinguished from module development in that development of the content does not presuppose any organizational structure. The development of content involves providing a student with the necessary information to achieve the various goals of the instruction. If, for instance, I would like students to increase their Spanish vocabulary by ten words for each passage that they read, I must ensure that there are ten new words in each passage. On the other hand, if I want students to be able to understand certain sentence structures, then I must make sure that the sentence structures are part of the passages, and that I explain them. Of course, I may not want to be so specific about how I am going to achieve my goals, and may take a more implicit approach by giving passages that have certain features that I want the student to be able to understand.

The selection of a delivery system is a particularly important element of this discussion because our delivery system is going to be a computer. The passages, exercise, and feedback will all be presented by computer. Using a computer for delivery imposes certain requirements and limitations. For example, one thing that I can do using a computer-based delivery system is to illustrate the passages. Using computer graphics, and animation, I can illustrate each sentence in the passage, so even if students do not have a good understanding of the vocabulary, they can still be on their way to learning it by virtue of pictures.

I can also give feedback to a student when tests and exercises are given. If I give a simple multiple choice test, I can grade this test immediately and present a grade to the student. If students need remediation in a particular concept or area, I can provide this remediation by "sending" them to additional exercises. Computer-based delivery offers a wider spectrum of presentation possibilities.

The development of modules entails structuring the modules according to the goals of the instruction. Each module, or more specifically each related group of instruction, is assembled together to address one goal of the instruction. A student could be forced to achieve a certain performance level for a particular goal before proceeding to the next goal.

How the modules and lessons within modules are presented is determined by the sequencing of modules. It is desirable, for example, to order the modules from less complex material to more complex material. It is also desirable to structure the modules so as to combine related pieces of information in the instructional presentation so that a student is not confused by seemingly unrelated information in the instruction.

After modules have been created and sequenced, it is an excellent idea to try out the instruction. Find some willing volunteers and run through the new instruction with them. This could provide invaluable feedback and make the instruction that much more effective. If the instruction is delivered by computer, then it is absolutely necessary for the instruction, which will be software, to be "tried out." Such trying out could be a very effective test for the software that delivers the instruction, and also point out other deficiencies in the instruction. Earlier I indicated that some of the stages in the process of instruction design were optional, depending on the needs for the instruction.

Implementation and Improvement Phase

Once the instruction has been prepared and tried out, it is ready to be delivered. Computer delivery of instruction means that the system can be distributed on disks or installed on student computers. To achieve improvement of the instruction, it will be necessary for the instructor to monitor student performance and also student reception of the instruction. This can be accomplished in a computer-delivered instruction directly, by including as part of that instruction, a multiple choice evaluation. The responses to the multiple choice evaluation are recorded and can be reviewed or analyzed at an appropriate time during the instruction.

A Proposed Description of Habla

Habla's intended purpose is to provide a tutoring environment for reading Spanish passages. The tutor will present a passage to the student and then present one of two kinds of exercises to the student. A simple passage is

> *Enrique es español. Él es amigo de María. Ellos son muy buenos amigos. María es de los Estados Unidos. El apellido de Enrique es Pereda. El appellido de María es Jackson.*
>
> *Enrique y María son alumnos de Colegio Buenavista. Ellos son alumnos muy buenos y muy inteligentes. Hay muchos alumnos en el colegio.*
> (Tardy, 1990, p. 3).

One kind of exercise that will be given for passages are questions about the passage. After students read a passage they will be presented with a series of questions. One of the questions that might be given for the passage is

Que es el apellido de Enrique?

The answer to this question is

El apellido de Enrique es Perada.

For this question, the answer is derived directly from the passage.

The answer produced by the student can be processed by the natural language processing mechanism I described earlier. Consider what this response would look like in propositional form:

$$is_{relation}(apellido_{feature}, Enrique_{subject}, Perada_{value})$$

When a student enters a response to a question, the response would be transformed into its proposition and judged against propositions that are stored in a database used by the tutor. It is possible to check both the correctness of the complete answer and also whether any part of a response is incorrect.

The second type of exercise given makes use of the automatic illustrator and natural language processing of responses. For this type of exercise, the automatic illustrator is used to create an illustration from an arbitrary sentence. The illustration is shown to the student, who is asked to write a sentence that describes it. The student written caption for the illustration should be derived from the passage. Depending on the sentence chosen for illustration, the natural language processing component produces a proposition for the sentence and is also used to produce a proposition for the student caption of the illustration. The two propositions are compared, and feedback is given based on the results of the comparison of propositions. The processing that takes place is summarized in Figure 8.19.

Chapter Summary

This chapter described natural language processing as another kind of intelligence that can be used in multimedia applications. Natural language processing is the capability of a computer to accept spoken or written language as input and to process the input language for

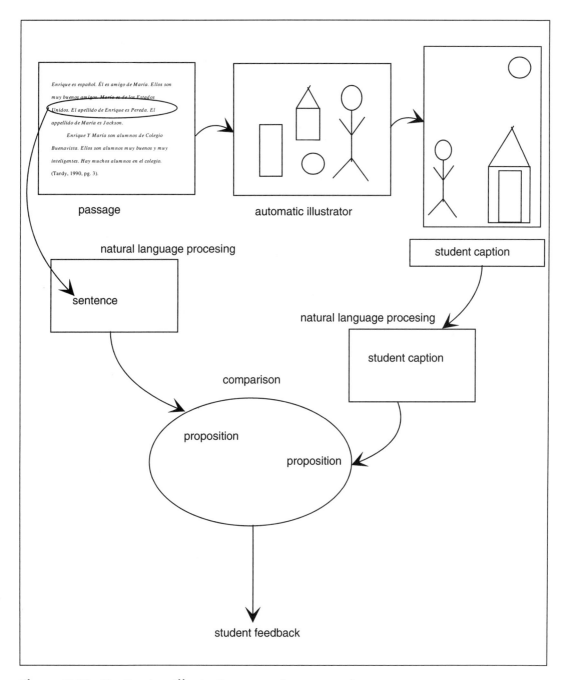

Figure 8.19 Captioning illustration exercise processing.

understanding. We defined understanding as the ability of the computer to carry out the desired behavior as stated in the natural language. This makes the idea of a computer understanding something more tangible.

Natural language is described by a grammar and formal grammars have been developed for this purpose. A grammar consists of a special symbol called the start symbol, a set of terminals, a set of nonterminals, and a set of rules that define how a language is written. This is called the syntax of the language. A sentence is part of a language if a derivation can be constructed for the sentence using the grammar for the language.

A mechanism to process a grammar is called an augmented transition network or ATN. An ATN is represented by a graph that specifies, according to a grammar, how a language is processed and how a structure can be built for a sentence in a language. ATNs are one approach to processing natural language in this way.

The grammar representation, noun phrase, verb phrase, and so on is just one the representations that can be constructed for a language. A useful alternative representation is the proposition. A propositional representation uses the verb in the sentence as the keystone and all other parts of the sentence as participants. A proposition is a concise representation of the meaning of a sentence in a language.

Propositions can be the basis for natural language processing in multimedia applications that use natural language. Two potential applications were described. The first of these, the Automatic Illustrator, used natural language to produce illustrations from sentences that were presented to it. The images for these illustrations were maintained in an image database, and a utility called PILL was described to maintain these images.

A second potential application, a tutor for the Spanish language, was described that uses natural language processing to analyze the meaning of responses to questions about a passage.

The use of natural language processing as part of multimedia applications could greatly enrich the interactions of people using those applications. Although complex, the use of the techniques may have great benefit to the application.

Suggested Reading

Allen, James, *Natural Language Processing*, 2nd ed., Redwood City, CA: Benjamin Cummings, 1995.

My favorite book about natural language processing describes all of the relevant issues about natural language processing and presents techniques for implementing this kind of processing. It is well written but it is also not for the beginner.

Mager, Robert, *Making Instruction Work*, Belmont: David S. Lake, 1988.

Mager's book about instructional design is an excellent and concise treatment of the subject. It is not a long book, but I found it to be thorough in its treatment of the subject of instructional design. Presently this book is out of print, but you may still be able to find it in a library.

Although an older article, "The Theory and Practice of Augmented Transition Network Grammar" by Madeline Bates is well worth reading. It is one of the best and most concise descriptions of ATNs I have ever read. This paper is contained in *Lecture Notes in Computer Sciences, No. 63, Natural Language Commmunication with Computers*, Springer-Verlag, New York, 1978.

The passage in Spanish used in this chapter can be found in *Easy Spanish Reader, A Three Part Text for Beginning Students* written by William T. Tardy and published by Natural Textbook Co., Lincolnwood, IL, 1990.

CHAPTER 9

The Future of Intelligent Multimedia

What Does the Future Hold for Intelligent Multimedia?

Well, there you have it. I have described some aspects of multimedia and artificial intelligence and have shown how to bring these together into functional systems. To recap, my goal for this book had two parts: first, to practically describe how to construct intelligent multimedia systems, and second, to recount my experiences with implementing systems such as these.

To be sure, the systems I am suggesting be implemented by merging the tools of multimedia and the tools of artificial intelligence are at the frontier of programs and systems that can be written at the present time. I make this statement because there are very few commercial examples of intelligent multimedia systems. As a general rule, the current family of edutainment-based CD-ROMs, although interesting in terms of interactivity, are limited in terms of their ability to make any intelligent decisions about the interactions that go on. This statement, may incur quite a bit of disagreement (and wrath) because artificial intelligence is a lot like meat in a fast food hamburger—everyone says they have it but it is quite another thing when you ask them to show you where the artificial intelligence is.

If intelligent multimedia systems are in the future, what is in the future of intelligent multimedia systems? What other kinds of technologies might we expect to see/use in intelligent multimedia systems? This chapter briefly discusses some of these so the reader can gain a perspective of the frontier of the frontier.

I have selected four areas to discuss in this chapter. They were selected because when I look into my crystal ball, I see these things prominently displayed. These things are neural nets, genetic programming, virtual reality, and the Internet. Of course I could have selected from many topics out in front of the cutting edge, but these four represent to me important ones for the present topic.

Advances in Artificial Intelligence

In this book the intelligent tutor and the other artificial intelligence I have presented are all symbolically based. This means representation schemes are all founded on symbols used to represent ideas, concepts, and real world objects. The rules written for the Toaster Tutor name parts of the toaster to create the operation of the toaster. Symbolic representation is not the only means of representing knowledge. In particular I would like to suggest some alternatives to the reasoning and representation mechanisms described in this book. Although these alternatives are not new, they are novel in the context of intelligent multimedia systems.

Neural Nets

The reasoning components in the rule-based systems implementing the decision-making processes in the Toaster Tutor are symbolically based as stated in the previous paragraph. Those decision-making processes look at the state of the toaster or the state of the student's knowledge and perform actions based on these states. It is possible the same decision-making processes could be implemented using a different approach to reasoning.

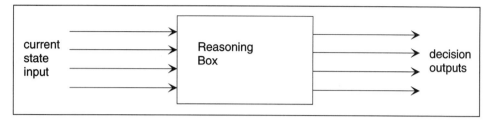

Figure 9.1 Reasoning box.

Our inputs to the reasoning engines (toaster model, student model, and instructional model) are various state variables such as the position of the carriage and the position of the thermostat. In some ways, the reasoning engines are a processing box that accepts the current state as input and outputs a decision about the state. Such a mechanism is shown in Figure 9.1.

Let's suppose our reasoning box operates as follows: We supply the box with inputs and outputs. That is to say, we tell the reasoning box not only the input but also the output we expect, given some input. We do this with lots of sets of inputs and outputs. As each input and output is supplied to the reasoning mechanism, the mechanism reconfigures itself so that the inputs produce the desired output. In other words, the reasoning mechanism learns how to compute outputs from its inputs. Is there a device that could produce such a result? It turns out we can look to our own brains for the answer to this question.

The human brain is made of cells called neurons and cells that connect neurons to one another called axons. Neurons and axons work electrochemically, but the basic idea is this: Each and every neuron in the brain is connected to many other neurons via axons. Electrochemical signals are passed from neuron to neuron. When a neuron receives enough of a signal from its connected neighbors, it will fire and send a signal to neurons connected to it. How signals are passed around is only partially understood in terms of what they mean. Nevertheless the model of computation gives rise to what are called artificial neural networks (ANNs).

An ANN is electrical as opposed to electrochemical. The devices that make up this network are like neurons, although not as general

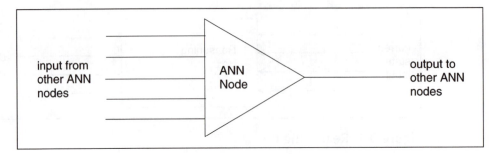

Figure 9.2 Pictorial representation of an ANN node.

or powerful. Because an ANN is an electrical network, each node is connected to one or more other nodes via electrical connections (wire). A node in the ANN receives electrical input from its neighbors and fires when the electrical input is above a certain electrical threshold. A node can be pictorially represented as shown in Figure 9.2.

For the network to learn like the brain it is necessary to incorporate a kind of adjustability into each node. We accomplish this in two ways. First, we can control node firing by defining a function that controls when and how the node will fire. For example, a node could have a linear firing profile as shown in Figure 9.3(a) or a discontinuous firing profile (binary) as shown in Figure 9.3(b).

The other aspect of the adjustability of the ANN nodes is the weights attached to inputs. The weights are values that are com-

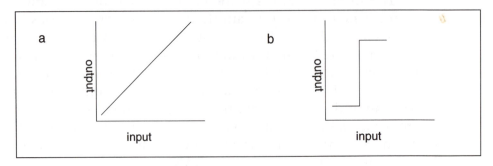

Figure 9.3 (a) Linear threshold firing function. (b) Binary threshold firing function.

bined with the actual input value to modify how a particular input affects the ANN node. For an ANN to compute a particular output from a particular input configuration, it is necessary to readjust the weights of each of the inputs.

Earlier I described a process by which we could supply state information to the reasoning mechanism and have it be able to compute an output. An ANN has two modes: a learning or training mode and an operational or running mode. In the training mode, inputs and outputs are supplied to the ANN and the weights are adjusted so that the inputs produce the desired output. In the operational or running mode, the ANN is provided input and produces output—the weights remain constant in operational mode.

How could an ANN be used in an intelligent multimedia system? I will use the intelligent tutor as an example of when we might use an ANN as a means of creating a reasoning engine. Consider an intelligent tutor tutoring in the domain of arithmetic—specifically subtraction. We could write a symbolic model of subtraction containing rules for "figuring out" when a particular result (as computed by a student) is correct or incorrect. Another way to accomplish this is to create an ANN trained to recognize when a result is correct or incorrect. To accomplish this we need to construct an appropriate ANN with the appropriate number of nodes and connections connecting the nodes. The ANN would serve as the model of the subtraction mechanism.

Likewise, if we wanted to simulate a toaster we might consider representing the toaster as a series of ANNs, each of which represents a component of the toaster. To understand how this might be accomplished, let's consider a problem and how we would represent that problem for an ANN.

The Towers of Hanoi puzzle can be described as follows: There is a wooden platform with three pegs. The pegs are numbered 1, 2, and 3 and shown in Figure 9.4. The puzzle begins with four disks arranged from largest on the bottom to smallest on the top on tower 1. The initial state of the puzzle is shown in Figure 9.5. The object of the puzzle is to transfer the disks from the first tower to the last tower using tower 2 as a place to temporarily store disks, by

458 CHAPTER 9

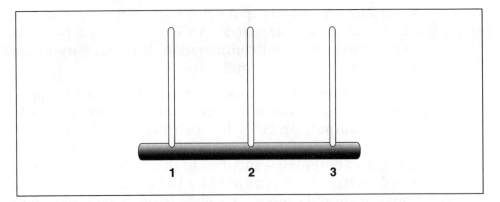

Figure 9.4 "Towers" of Towers of Hanoi puzzle.

never placing a larger disk on a smaller disk, and by only moving one disk at a time. The solution to the puzzle is a sequence of moves that upon completion of the last move will result in the puzzle configuration shown in Figure 9.6.

If we want an artificial neural network to solve the Towers of Hanoi puzzle then we must do two things. First, a representation of the puzzle must be devised; second, the ANN must be trained.

Our representation is as follows. A puzzle is represented as two 12-bit binary numbers. Each 12-bit number is divided into three groups of four bits. Each group of four bits represents a tower of the puzzle, and each bit of a group of four bits represents the disks on

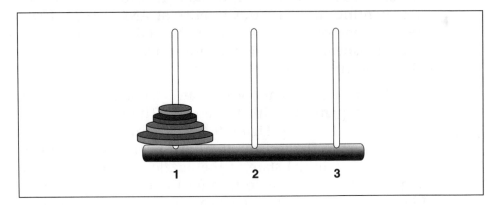

Figure 9.5 Initial state of the Towers of Hanoi puzzle.

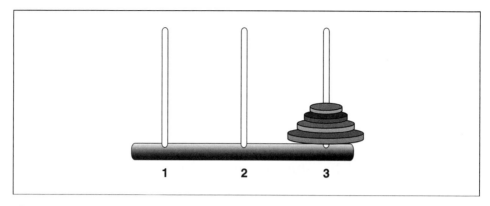

Figure 9.6 "Winning" configuration of the Towers of Hanoi puzzle.

the tower. The first bit of each group of four bits represents the smallest disk, the second bit represents the second smallest disk, and so on. The configuration shown in Figures 9.6 and 9.7 would be represented by the following 12-bit numbers.

0 0 0 0   0 0 0 0   1 1 1 1   0 0 0 1   1 0 0 0   0 1 1 0

The second 12-bit number represents the state of the puzzle after a disk has been moved. You can think of both 12-bit numbers as representing the from- and to- state in single move in the puzzle.

Designing the topology of an ANN is more art than science. By topology we mean the number of nodes in the ANN and how the nodes are connected. Knowing how to arrange nodes in an ANN de-

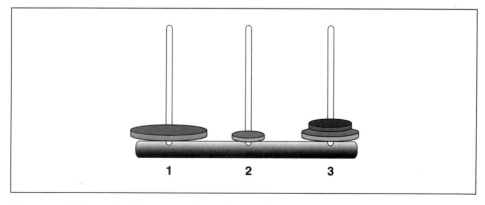

Figure 9.7 Sample Tower of Hanoi configuration.

pends on the types of nodes used and a knowledge of how they will interact. It is typical that several different configurations are tried before one that is acceptable is discovered.

An ANN is typically constructed from several layers. A layer is a grouping of nodes serving a purpose in the ANN. One layer is used to process input, another to produce the output, and there is also a layer that carries out the processing between the input and output layers—called the hidden layer. A possible configuration of nodes might look like the one shown in Figure 9.8.

Getting back to our original purpose, designing an ANN as a part of an intelligent tutoring system, I have already described two possible applications for ANNs in the context of intelligent tutoring. One of these was in a tutor for subtraction and the other was to model the operation of a toaster. In general, an ANN could replace any model in the intelligent tutoring system. This would include mechanism models and student and instructional models. ANNs might be better for the student and instructional models (human activi-

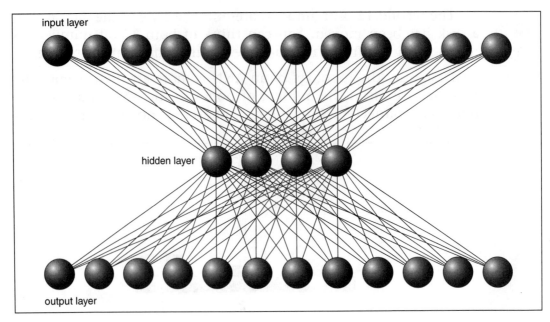

Figure 9.8 Potential artificial neural network configuration for the Towers of Hanoi puzzle.

ties) as opposed to a mechanism like the toaster. The key is in the representation used by the ANN to process data.

Think back to the rules used in the student model to draw a conclusion about how the student was problem solving. An ANN might be designed for the same purpose. Suppose we wanted to create an ANN that would be able to tell us whether a student was using a divide and conquer approach as opposed to a sequential approach to problem solving. We might design an ANN consisting of an input layer to process several pieces of information and output one of two pieces of information. The output layer for our hypothetical ANN would consist of two nodes: one to indicate a sequential problem-solving approach and the other to specify a divide and conquer approach to problem solving. So far the ANN I have designed is shown in Figure 9.9.

The input layer of the student model ANN would consist of several clusters of nodes. One cluster of nodes would represent the component involved in the current activity. This would be represented by one node for every possible component in the toaster. A second group of nodes would be used to represent the history of actions. In other words, we would want to supply as input to the ANN some information about what the student has done so far. Since ANNs only remember what their training was about and have no memory from processing one set of data to another, we will have to supply this. Part of this representation of nodes (the history) must also be the order in which the history occurred. We would view the nodes in this cluster as pairs of nodes. In a pair, one node is used to represent the component and another the order in the history. Another cluster of nodes will be used to represent the last decision made by the ANN. This cluster will consist of two nodes one for sequential problem solving and the other for divide and conquer problem solving. The student model ANN with input layer is shown in Figure 9.10.

The remaining layer to be defined in this ANN is the hidden layer. This is the layer that must combine the input from all available nodes and produce output to the two decision nodes. I envision a hidden layer containing one node for each of the nodes in the input layer and also that each node in the input layer is con-

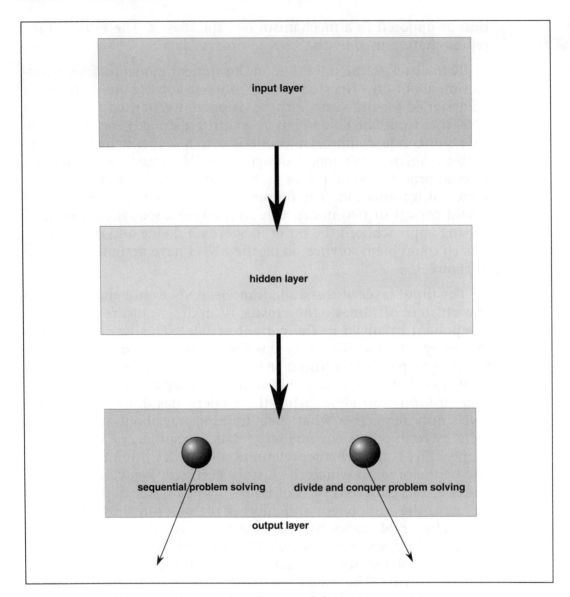

Figure 9.9 Preliminary design of student model ANN.

nected to all nodes in the hidden layer. Likewise, each node in the hidden layer is connected to each of the nodes in the output layer. The resulting ANN is shown in Figure 9.11. The design shown is a preliminary one; until it is trained and tested, we won't know how

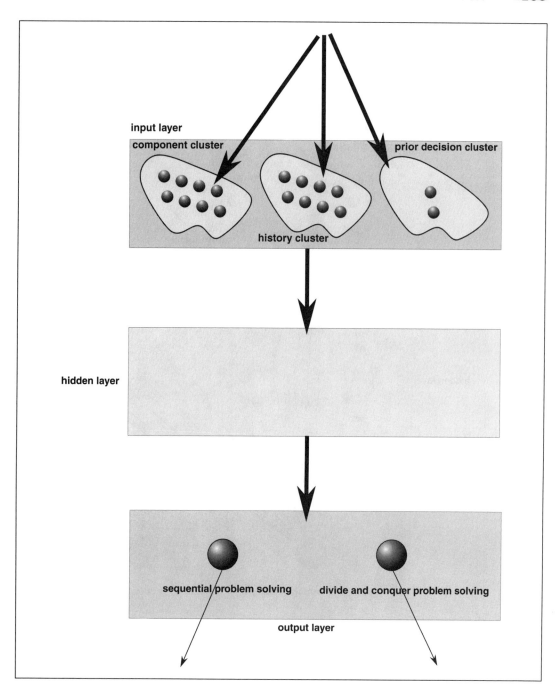

Figure 9.10 Student model ANN with input layer.

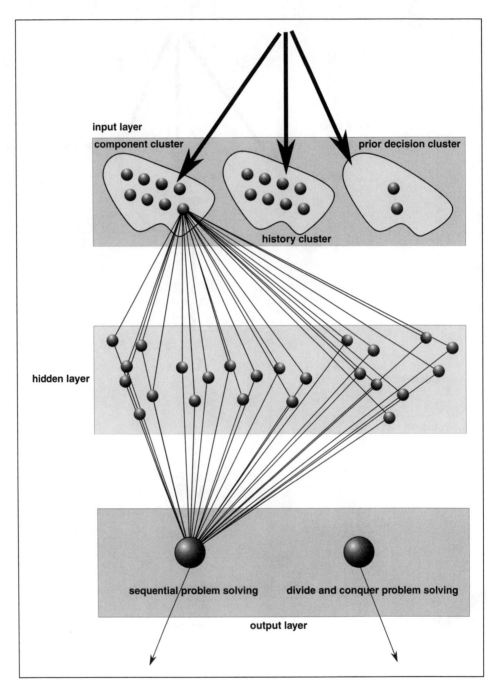

Figure 9.11 Complete student model ANN.

it will perform. Nevertheless, it represents a starting point for an ANN-based student model design.

I consider ANNs to be an important part of the future of intelligent multimedia because, in conjunction with traditional symbolic systems, the combination may prove to be an extremely powerful method to create complex models. This remains an important research question.

Genetic Programming

Another interesting development and departure from traditional symbolic approaches in artificial intelligence is genetic programming. Like artificial neural networks, genetic programming uses a natural phenomenon as a basis and attempts to find a best solution to a problem. The methodology is based on the theory of evolution and the Darwinian theory of survival of the fittest.

Deoxyribonucleic acid (DNA) is an encoding of information defining the composition of cells. When any cell reproduces, chromosomes containing the DNA encodings combine so as to produce another encoding for the new cell. Some of the many characteristics of the cell may be exactly the same as those of the parent cell. Invariably some of the characteristics will be different. The differences may be good or bad. What we mean by good or bad is whether a particular characteristic adds to or takes away from the cell's ability to survive. The nice thing about this process is it works by itself—the creation of new cells with new characteristics goes on as part of the life process. Now the question is, "How can this be applied to programming and eventually intelligent multimedia?"

Like artificial neural networks and symbolic systems, genetic programming can be classified under the general rubric of artificial intelligence because this methodology is typically employed to solve problems for which solutions have long been sought using traditional artificial intelligence. Furthermore, genetic programming can be roughly classified as a sort of automatic programming, as I will describe shortly, and automatic programming (having a computer program itself) has been a part of the research agenda of artificial intelligence.

The relevance of genetic programming to artificial intelligence in general and to intelligent multimedia specifically has to do with whether computers will ever be able to solve problems by themselves. Given a fast enough computer with a program to generate all of the solutions to a particular problem and the ability to locate the correct solution, the answer to this question would be yes. As long as the number of potential solutions to some problems are so large that it is difficult to conceive of the number of solutions, this is not a viable alternative to problem solving.*

Genetic programming offers an alternative to brute force search. It says the following: Produce some solutions to a problem and see which ones are good. Select a pair of these and allow them to trade some characteristics and then see how this new offspring performs. The process starts over with the new mutated solutions. Let's take a closer look at a general procedure for genetic programming. (The following discussion was drawn from a book by John R. Koza titled, *Genetic Programming, On the Programming of Computers by Means of Natural Selection*. I consider this book one of the handbooks of the subject, an important addition to anyone's library interested in genetic programming.)

A Description of the Traditional Genetic Algorithm

1. Create an initial population

    The traditional genetic algorithm (TGA) begins with producing a group of potential solutions to the current problem (CP). The CP is the entity to which the genetic algorithm is applied. For example, the population may consist of a series of programs representing ones that are able to perform a specific task. This initial set of programs will be used to create the eventual solution to the problem.

---

*The present state of the art in computer processing power is still not yet sufficient to be fast enough to search huge search spaces. Of course with the evolution of processing power (doubling every 18 months), it may not be too long before brute force methods like this may truly be a viable approach to problem solving.

2. Are we finished?

   If we look at the set of solutions we have produced, do we find one that meets our needs? If so, then we can stop here.

3. For each solution in the population, compute its fitness.

   There must be some way to know whether a solution meets our criteria for success. This may be a simple measure or a complex analysis, but it is necessary to have in order to carry out the genetic algorithm process. In the real world the evaluation of fitness is carried out by the survival or demise of the biological entity.

4. Using the evaluations of step 3, select a subset of the population.

   This subset will be used to create new solutions through the genetic process. The subset selection will be based on the fitness criteria. The resulting subset may have in it only "better" solutions, or some mix of solutions dependent on the criteria for section.

5. Copy characteristic(s) from one solution in the selected subset to another. Add the resulting solutions to the population.

   This is called the cross-over step. It creates new offspring by trading characteristics from one offspring to another.

6. Go back to step 2 and evaluate the population.

   After the new population is created with the new offspring, iterate through the new generation (the selected subset and new offspring).

What in the world will a solution look like using this algorithm? Remember, in the case of ANNs it was necessary to find a representation for the problem we would apply to the network. Since the nodes of ANNs are devices accepting essentially numeric data, the encoding must also be numeric. The genetic algorithm requires the same encoding of a problem into a numeric representation. For example, if a problem and its solution can be posed as a binary vector, the representation is well suited for genetic programming.

As you might imagine, finding an appropriate representation is tricky because the procedure does not care about what is in the solution it produces. When the offspring are produced they may be completely invalid. In constructing the representation for a problem the formulation should try to avoid the possibility of bad solutions. This might be very difficult to actually accomplish.

Consider again the Towers of Hanoi problem. How would we represent this problem as a genetic programming problem? We might try to use the same representation used for the ANN, but immediately the potential for incorrect solutions can be seen because if we trade features of a solution (in this case the sequence of moves), incorrect moves might be produced as offspring. Rather than use the same representation we adopt a different representation eliminating the possibility for bad offspring.

In the revised formulation we represent how one disk is moved to another. In this representation we use the following encoding scheme:

Code	Move	Description
1	(Min,Max)	Move the smallest ring on top of the largest ring.
2	(Min,Med)	Move the smallest ring on top of the medium ring.
3	(Med,Max)	Move the medium ring on top of the largest ring.

The largest ring is relative—it is the largest on the tower. In this way, the representation is independent of a particular configuration. The following example (from Margarita, 1993, p. 25) shows how a chromosome can be encoded.

Move #	1	2	3	4	5
State 1 2 3	1 2 3	2 3 1	3 1 2	1 2 3	1 3 2
Assignment	m M M	= m M M	m = = M	m m M	= m = M
Move	(m,M)	(=,M)	(m,=)	(m,=)	(=,M)
Encoding	1	3	2	2	3

In this table, the row labeled "State" represents the state of the three towers. The state is represented by three columns underneath each cell in the row labeled "Move #." The first column represents the first tower of the puzzle, the second column, the second tower, and so on. The disks are labeled 1 to 3 from smallest to largest respectively. The row labeled "Assignment" contains the letter assignments of each of the columns. Columns not containing any disks are labeled with an "M." The first move, (m,M) represents a move of the smallest disk (signified by an m) to the largest disk (signified by an M)—in this case the first empty tower. This yields the configuration shown in the Move #2 column. The row labeled "Encoding" transforms the move (m,M) to its corresponding code. Based on the series of moves shown in the table, the chromosome would be encoded as:

1 3 2 2 3

Now I am going to make a leap and ask you to leap with me. How can genetic programs be used in intelligent multimedia? The strengths of genetic approaches to problem solving lie in the adaptability of these approaches and in their generality. As long as an appropriate representation scheme can be devised, the genetic algorithm can be applied. Just as for ANNs, genetic programming may lend itself well for application to the modeling tasks that are part of the intelligent tutoring program we presented.

Along other lines, consider our discussion in Chapter 8 about the program performing layout of the graphic objects retrieved from the multimedia database. The approach taken here was to divide the available space on which the graphics were placed into a grid and then attempt to place the graphic objects on cells of this grid. This was accomplished using a series of simple rules. A genetic program could provide an alternate solution to this problem. Suppose the layout is described to the genetic program as a binary matrix and suppose our criterion for fitness was minimum overlap. We could use the binary matrix as the representation by stringing these into a long sequence of bits. Then after a set of offspring was produced we could re-evaluate the bit string by reassembling it into a matrix and by applying the evaluation criteria. Of course, the evaluation criteria could be made more complex.

Another application for genetic programming as applied to the intelligent tutor would be to create a genetic program that could determine the best way to solve the problem given to the student using the tutor. One could envision sending the output of the genetic program to a natural language generator to produce English explanations of how to approach the problem-solving process or to give remedial advice as determined by the instructional model. The Toaster Tutor described in Chapter 7 does not have a built-in capability to troubleshoot itself in the sense of being able to solve the problems that it presents to a student. This capability would add to the tutorial capability of the Toaster Tutor specifically and intelligent tutors in general.

Advances in Multimedia

We need to keep a careful watch on the advances in multimedia because these will also profoundly affect the development of new kinds of intelligent multimedia. For example, the wide-scale acceptance of CD-ROMs has made it possible to distribute applications consisting of large amounts of program and content material. Without a medium like this, applications would have to be delivered on multiple disks. Typical users would not be too happy if they had to load an application consisting of 200 disks. CD-ROM also seems to be evolving at the present time. For example, several manufacturers have joined to develop a standard for a very high density CD-ROM. Other manufacturers believe that the CD-ROM media is only a temporary stopover toward a smaller and higher-capacity media. This has significant implications in the development of highly sophisticated applications and their distribution.

I could discuss many different developments in this section on the frontiers of multimedia, but I have selected two that I believe are among the most significant. Both of these selections represent alternative methods of computing. They deviate from the traditional and will have significant impact on the future of multimedia and related applications.

Virtual Reality and Environments

In theater there is the concept of "suspension of disbelief." This concept has to do with the idea that when you watch a play or a show on television, you are willing to forgo the traditional questions about the possibility of what you are seeing and believe, for the time of the presentation, in the presentation. If you see a character appear out of nowhere, you believe in the context of the presentation that this is actually happening. When you leave the context of the theater, if you saw an event like someone appearing out of nowhere you would tend to disbelieve the reality of this event.

The Toaster Tutor asks you to suspend your disbelief while you are using it. It does so by assuming you believe the process you are about to undertake is very much like the real process of toaster repair. For the Toaster Tutor the suspension of disbelief task is a difficult one because the environment of the Toaster Tutor is not much like a real environment. In fact, the simulation might be more harmonious with the real world if the environment in which the toaster was presented were a workshop with tools that could be manipulated.

You may have heard of something called an aircraft simulator. To train pilots, the companies that build aircraft often construct simulators to train pilots in operating the aircraft prior to actually piloting a real aircraft. This is important when you consider that an aircraft costs billions of dollars and flying it may involve the safety of the passengers. Mistakes can be safely made in the simulator without damaging the aircraft (or people, for that matter). These simulators, which have been used for quite some time, are an example of a virtual environment.

One of the key aspects of a virtual environment is that the environment reduces the amount of effort required to suspend your disbelief. In the case of the aircraft simulator, except for the fact that a pilot will know it is a simulator, the cockpit of the simulator will exactly resemble the cockpit of the aircraft the simulator represents. To achieve the desired level of training, the suspension of disbelief is vital for the pilots to believe they are facing an actual flight situation.

Advances in computer graphics (most notably three-dimensional computer graphics), interaction devices, and processor power have brought virtual environments closer to home. Imagine a different kind of Toaster Tutor than the one that I described. In this version you put on a special headset containing stereoscopic viewers that render a three-dimensional view to your eyes and lifelike sound to your ears. You also put on two gloves, which are tethered to the computer. By monitoring the movement of your hands in the gloves, the computer can react to gestures and movements of your hands. In the headset you are presented with a customer walking into your shop and asking you to repair their toaster. They describe the problem and leave the shop. The interaction seems real, as it is rendered in three dimensions with all the advances in animating human movement and speech. You cannot help but believe the customer was a real one.

You now take the toaster (that's right take) that was brought to you by the customer and walk back into your workshop. The computer to which your headset is attached can monitor your movements and change the scene as you move, thus making it appear to you that you changed your environment. You place the toaster on your workbench. In front of you is a series of tools you can use to work on the toaster. There are also books and manuals you can examine in order to repair the toaster.

This situation describes one type of virtual reality in which the reality is presented through special hardware that is worn. One complaint about this kind of virtual reality is that the headset and the gloves are awkward. One is reminded, for example, that one is wearing a headset. This takes away from a complete suspension of disbelief.

Another kind of virtual reality is a virtual environment. A virtual environment differs from virtual reality because no special hardware is worn. The simulators described earlier are virtual environments because the environment supplies all of the necessary hardware.

Quite a few virtual environments are available for the personal computer today. The simulation-based games are the best examples of these. Although the environment they supply exists solely on the computer display, many are particularly engaging. The Toaster Tutor, although limited, is a primitive kind of virtual environment.

Perhaps the most important aspect of a virtual reality is how realistic it will be. For example, the virtual environment may supply many of the objects and mechanisms a real world environment might provide, but the problem of harmony with reality becomes even more complex when people are introduced into the virtual reality. Not only is it difficult to physically render the people, an even more difficult problem is to have them act like people—and this is where artificial intelligence comes into play.

The marriage of virtual environments with artificial intelligence begins to tap the potential by creating simulations actually behaving like their real world counterparts. For example, if you want to create an intelligent multimedia system for training salespeople, then it would make sense in this system to incorporate humans as clients in the system. For a salesperson to gain some experience with the different kinds of clients, one could envision a simulation of human personalities—an easy personality, a skeptical personality, a difficult personality. Personality types could be mixed so that different situations bring up different personality types. The virtual reality system handles rendering (animating) the people, and the artificial intelligence component of the system defines how a personality will behave.

This marriage of virtual environment to artificial intelligence opens the possibility for a richer class of system with an entirely different kind of interface. We could envision, for example, being able to ask a virtual reality guide how to accomplish a particular task. The guide would lead us through the process. A recent movie included such a guide (called an "angel" in the movie) assisting a user of the system to access data contained in the system.

The Internet

To predict or even consider the profound effects the Internet may have on traditional computing is at best scratching the surface of possibility and at worst science fiction. From the time I began writing this book, almost two years ago to now, the development and evolution of the Internet has been astounding to say the least. To consider not only the rate at which the Internet is growing but also the rate at which information is being made available on the Internet boggles the mind. Artificial intelligence has found a home on the Internet in the form of agent technology. Internet agents are programs that can travel across the Internet and perform specialized tasks. The most common type of Internet agents are those that will search the Internet for specific information. Right now we can think of the Internet as a large heterogeneous repository of information. For the most part, most of this information is static, but technology is already available to create active information in the form of applications. The ability to create and distribute applications across the Internet creates a whole new arena for intelligent multimedia applications. This final section of Chapter 9 explores some of the possibilities for the Internet and intelligent multimedia.

Masses of Information

If you have accessed the Internet then you know there is a huge and growing amount of information residing there. It is easy to get lost while traversing nodes. To some extent, the search engines now available on the Internet can assist with this problem. They can be given a text string and look out on the Internet for information matching the string. Presently this searching process makes little use of any algorithmic forms of intelligence. Work is underway to develop a significantly more intelligent system for selecting and assembling media from a heterogeneous system like the Internet. This kind of system goes by the name Intelligent Multimedia Presentation System.

The media that presently reside on the Internet consists of many forms. The predominant media is text, with static images coming a close second. In addition to these forms of media there is also sound and motion (video and animation). The Internet is by its very nature a multimedia system.

An intelligent multimedia presentation system is an ambitious project described in a document on the World Wide Web, "Intelligent Multimedia Presentation Systems: A Proposal of Reference Model." (Ruggieri et al. 1996). The idea behind such a system is this: The system consists of a series of experts who can manipulate and understand various types of media. In addition it has the ability to communicate with users to ascertain their needs for media-based systems. The expert's role in the system is to analyze the requirements specified by a user and to translate these into sets of media and application requirements that can be readily understood by the system. Within the set of experts is a design expert the role of which is to handle various aspects of the design of the presentation system and the development of the application. There is also a content expert that understands how to access and obtain various kinds of media. In some ways, you can think of the authoring tools described in Chapter 2 as a primitive ancestor of an intelligent multimedia presentation system. Whereas the authoring tool represents the means by which a presentation is created, an intelligent multimedia presentation system would conceptually use such a tool to create a multimedia application by translating user requirements and by obtaining the necessary media.

External servers and clients are part of the design proposed by Ruggieri et al. In the context of the Internet one could view the external servers as being the Internet, in which the intelligent multimedia presentation systems have access to thousands of servers. The system and its experts retrieve information from the Internet to assemble presentations as required by a user. One idea for the use of a system such as this is as an automated means to construct course materials from materials existing on the Internet. A user would outline a course, indicate the components required, and set the intelligent multimedia presentation system in motion. The system would essentially create the book for the course using materials found on the Internet. The system would indicate where it was necessary for a human to "fill in."

What makes the idea of something like an intelligent multimedia presentation system possible on the Internet is a relatively new technology that allows applications to be distributed across the Internet. Internet applications have provided for the capability of interactivity through a complex interface called the CGI or the Common Gateway Interface. This portal allows a programmer to have an Internet page and attach code to the page. The problem with this way of accomplishing application development has been that there were no standards (except for the CGI) about how this would be accomplished. Now there is a standard arising, based on the Java architecture developed by Sun Microsystems.

Java allows truly distributed applications on the Internet. Built into browsers for the Internet are interpreters that can process the Java language. Java actually consists of three components: the Java language, the Java interpreter, and the Java virtual machine. Because viewers for World Wide Web applications are presently implemented on most types of computers in use today, applications developed for the Internet are immediately portable. Applications can run across any platform on which an Internet viewer will run. This means that if I write an application for the PC version of the viewer, the same application will run on the Macintosh version of the viewer. Distribution of the application is automatic because it comes with the Internet.

In terms of intelligent tutors and other classes of intelligent multimedia applications, this presents a profound set of opportunities. Because Internet viewers can display many kinds of media over a wide area, something like the Toaster Tutor could be readily deployed over the Internet as a training application. This means that with just a desktop computer that was Internet enabled we would have the capability to access and view a tutoring program like the Toaster Tutor. One could envision a training library consisting of programs like these for reference or to be used in the field by service personnel.

One more element of the Internet is worth mentioning because it relates to the discussion of virtual environments in the previous section. With the advent of high-quality three-dimensional computer graphics, it was natural to expect that three-dimensional graphics and animations would rapidly become part of the Internet and the documents available on it. The original language for specifying Internet documents is called HTML or the HyperText Markup Language. This language, an offshoot of SGML, another language for creating annotated documents, is how a document is specified for presentation on the Internet. An offshoot of HTML is VRML, the Virtual Reality Markup Language. The purpose of VRML is to specify virtual reality environments delivered by the Internet. Thus, just as there is the potential for delivering applications like the Toaster Tutor over the Internet, such environments can be made significantly richer by incorporating VRML into their implementation.

To summarize, the Internet will provide two significant opportunities for intelligent multimedia. The first opportunity is as source of information that can be used in an intelligent multimedia application. An intelligent multimedia presentation system would automate the process of constructing applications from information residing on the Internet.

The second significant opportunity is in the ability to distribute highly interactive applications like the Toaster Tutor by way of the Internet. Portability is no longer an issue because it is guaranteed by the standardization of the viewer used to access the Internet.

Suggested Reading

AI Expert.
Although no longer published, it is an excellent source for articles about artificial neural networks and genetic programming. Some issues that contain articles of interest are listed here.

About neural networks:

June 1990, "Data Representation in Neural Networks." by James A. Anderson

October 1991, "Towers of Hanoi: Neural-Net Solution." by John Cardoso

June 1994, "Building Neural Networks with Object-Oriented Programming." by Ira Vondrák

About genetic programming and algorithms:

March 1993, "Genetic Algorithms and the Towers of Hanoi." by Sergio Morgarita

December 1993, "Genetic Algorithms: Reaching the Outer Limits." a series of articles.

February 1995, "Genetic Programming and Mimicking DNA Crossover." A series of articles.

Koza, John R., *Genetic Programming: On the Programming of Computers by Means of Natural Selection,* Cambridge, MA: MIT Press, 1993.

An excellent reference about genetic programming and related algorithms.

Masters, Tim, *Practical Neural Network Recipes in C++*, New York: John Wiley & Sons, Inc., 1993.

A good source of information about neural networks.

Ruggieri et al., "Intelligent Multimedia Presentation Systems."

This can be found on the World Wide Web. A PostScript version of this paper can be retrieved by accessing the following URL:

http://kazan.cnuce.cnr.it/IECAI/IMP-WS-call-for-papers.html

APPENDIX

CD-ROM Information

The CD-ROM included with this book contains software for many of the examples described in this book. The CD-ROM is organized in two main directories.

CHAPTERS

WINVIDEO

The CHAPTERS directory contains the following subdirectories:

2

4

5

7

8

Each of these subdirectories corresponds to a chapter. For example, subdirectory 2 contains sample programs described in Chapter 2. A chapter subdirectory may have one or more subdirectories depending on the number of examples described in a chapter. The complete directory structure descending from the CHAPTERS directory is shown in Figure A.1.

Each subdirectory containing a sample program will contain a self-contained installation package. To install any example, find the

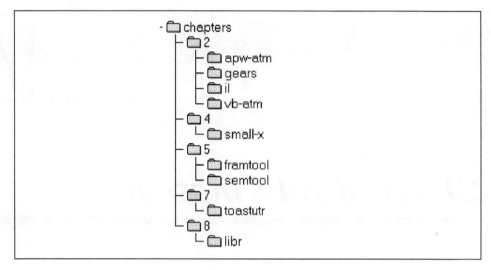

Figure A.1 Chapters directory structure.

setup.exe program and run it. Doing so will install the sample program contained in the particular subdirectory. Two of the examples are DOS-based programs. Even though they are DOS-based, Windows-based installation programs are provided.

Each subdirectory also contains a **readme.txt** file that describes the contents of the directory in which it resides. As a part of the installation process, the **readme.txt** file will be displayed.

System Requirements

To run any of the sample programs provided, your system must meet the following requirements:

80486 with 66 MHz processor (absolute minimum; Pentium preferred)

16 MB of RAM

200 MB of free hard disk storage (if you are going to install all of the sample applications)

640 × 480, 256-color SVGA display adapter

Windows 3.11 only

The WINVIDEO Subdirectory

The second subdirectory on the CD-ROM contains the installation utility for Video for Windows. In order to use the Toaster Tutor sample application (Chapter 7) you will have to install Video for Windows if you do not already have it installed. The **readme.txt** file in the WINVIDEO subdirectory describes this procedure.

Implementation Platform

Source code is provided with each of the Windows-based applications included with this CD-ROM All applications were developed with Microsoft Visual Basic Version 3.0. In addition several VBX plug-ins for Visual Basic were used. These are provided in runtime-only form, and specific documentation for them is not provided.

User Assistance and Information

The software accompanying this book is being provided as is without warranty or support of any kind. Should you require basic installation assistance, or if your media is defective, please call our product support number at (212) 850-6194 weekdays between 9 am and 4 pm Eastern Standard Time. Or, we can be reached via e-mail at: wprtusw@jwiley.com.

To place additional orders or to request information about other Wiley products, please call (800) 879-4539.

Index

A

actions, IL, 38, 49
    DEC, 57
    DISPLAY, 49–51
    DISPLAY LIST, 50–51
    ENABLECURSORMAP, 54
    INC, 57
    RESETCURSORMAP, 54
    RETURN, 40, 43
    SET, 57
    SETCURSOR, 53–54
    SET MENU, 56
    TEST, 58
    TEXT, 51–53
    VARIABLE, 57
American Standard Code for Information Interchange (ASCII), 2
AND, 51
animation, 17
    cel animation, 14
    creation programs, 17
    icon, create animation, 65
    icon, insert animation, 66
    sequence of images, 14
    and timers, 116
ANNs (artificial neural networks), 455–465, 467
any-machine simulation, 99–110
    interactivity, 106–110
    purpose of machine, 100
    what it consists of, 100
append function, 168–169
applications. *See* intelligent applications; interactive applications

artificial intelligence, 1–2, 4–5, 16
    beginning of, 153
    definition of, 6
    expert systems, 16, 18–19, 190–203
    genetic programming, 465–470, 477–478
    knowledge representation, 16, 19–22
    neural nets, 454–465, 477
    programming languages, 23
    rule-based systems, 18–19
    tasks explored by, 6
    tools for, 22–24
artificial neural networks (ANNs), 455–465, 467
ASCII (American Standard Code for Information Interchange), 2
assembler language, 99
assertFrame, 254–255
ATM simulation, Authorware, 67–96
    code for processing transaction, 79
    deposit interaction, 79
    deposit-to account, 81
    drag interaction, 88–90
    end the program, 96
    envelope sequence, 85
    flow diagram, 70–71
    start simulation again, 96
    what simulation does, 67
ATM simulation, Visual Basic, 111–130
    amount of programming, 111–112
    animated envelope, 118
    ATM amount, 117
    ATM card, 116–117
    ATM machine, 116
    background form, 113

ATM simulation, Visual Basic (*Continued*)
   button, 113–116
      selecting options, 118
      Start button, 116
   control, 115, 116
      code, 115
      events, 115
      properties, 115
   design time display, 116
   display of the ATM, 116
   icons, 116, 117
   implementation, 118–129
   LOAD event, 116
   messages, 116–117
   opening form, 113, 114
   polling, 116
   timers, 116
ATN (augmented transition network), 413–422, 425, 450, 451
attached-to, 7, 214
attribute-of relationship, 212
augmented transition network. *See* ATN
Authorware Professional for Windows, 35, 62–67. *See also* ATM simulation, Authorware
   cost, 112
   decision symbol, 65
   debugging, 66
   delays, 65
   and DLLs, 98–99
   erasing graphic elements, 65
   history of, 64
   icons, 63, 65–66, 67
      create animation, 65
      debugging, 66
      decision symbol, 65
      encapsulate code, 66
      erase, 65
      insert animation, 66
      insert delays, 65
      insert question, 65
      insert sound, 66
      insert text/graphics (display), 65, 67
      insert video, 66
      test results, 65–66
   intelligent reasoning component, 97–98
   questions, importance of, 64, 65
   sample display, 63
   semantics of, 66–67
   test results of interaction, 65–66
   to insert media, 66
   tool bar, 62, 63, 64–65
authoring tools. *See* multimedia authoring tools

automatic illustrator, 431–439
   elements of, 432–434

B

backtracking, 176, 177, 179, 182
BASIC. *See* Visual Basic
biological knowledge, 207
Books. *See* Suggested reading
border, menu definition, 55, 56
branching, 39–43
   GOTO vs CALL, 39–40
   returning, 40
   sample code, 40, 43
buzzer model, 292–302

C

CAI (computer-assisted instruction), 344
CALL, 40, 43
car function, 158, 159, 168
C language, 58–60
   factorial function, 182
   to recognize events in IL, 99
C++, data structures, 251
CBI (computer-based instruction), 344
CBT (computer-based training), 344
CD-ROM information, 479–481
cdr function, 158–159, 168
cel animation, 14
chaining, 57
characteristics-of relationship, 212
characters, 2, 12–13
class, 249–254
   instance vs class, 212
clickable area, 134–135
closed box, 33–34
code, 2
   icon to encapsulate, 66
   and labels, 216–217
   and paradigms, 99
   and Visual Basic, 111–112
Colmerauer, Alain, 170–171
colors
   menu, 55, 56
   profile of an image, 150
   text, 51
computer-assisted instruction (CAI), 344
computer-based instruction (CBI), 344
computer-based training (CBT), 344
cond function, 163–164, 165, 167
conditional expressions, 18
conflict resolution, 194
connected-to relationship, 211
cons function, 168–169

content, 9, 11
content indexing, 149
controls relationship, 7–9, 214
cost
    Authorware, 112
    hard disk drives, 3
counters, 57
    DEC, 57
    INC, 57
cursor, 53–55
    cursor map, 54
    CURSORMAP, 54
    default cursor, 54
    ENABLECURSORMAP, 54
    to reset, 53–54
    RESETCURSORMAP, 54
    SETCURSOR, 53–54
    standard cursors, 53, 54
CURSORMAP, 54
cutting and pasting, 15

D

database, 133–137. *See also* Frame Tool; multimedia database
    history of, 134
    modern databases, 134
    multimedia requirements, 141
    punched cards, 134
    relational database, 141
    rows, 141
    tables, 141
    traditional vs multimedia, 133, 151–152
    World Wide Web database, 134–137
data records, 19
data structure representation, 21–22
debugging icon, 66
DEC, 57
decision symbol, 65
decision making processes, 18
decrement, 57
definitions, 5–6
DEFINE MENU, 55–56
defun function, 159
delays, inserting, 65
development walls, 34
diagrammatic images, 14
digital knowledge, 207
digitizing, 2–3
display
    graphics, 49–51
    text, 51–53
DISPLAY, 36, 40–42, 49–51
  with variable, 50

DISPLAY LIST, 50–51
    display clause, 50–51
DLLs (dynamic link libraries), 98–99
DNA, 465
domain of instruction, 345
doorways, 33–34, 58–60
    passing information, 60–62
draggable, 48
dragging
    and Authorware, 88–90
    IL draggable, 48
    and Visual Basic, 112
drawing programs, 17
dynamic link libraries (DLLs), 98–99

E

edges, 209–210, 216, 218, 219
    creating, 221, 235–236
    deleting, 227
    drawing, 231–234
    edge record, 228, 229–230
    Edge menu, 223, 226–227
    icons, 223–224
        delete edge tool, 223
        edge creation tool, 223, 224
        edge label tool, 223
    label with program code, 216–217
elements
    diagrammatic, 14
    graphic, 14
ENABLECURSORMAP, 54
enabling technology, 3
encapsulate code, 66
encoding a picture, 2–3
END MENU, 55
ENDTEST, 58
erase, icon for, 65
eraseFrame, 258
eval function, 157, 161–163, 164–165
event definitions, 38
event-driven paradigm, 36, 63, 99
events, and IL, 38–39
    define events, 44
    event-driven paradigm, 36
    IL buttons, 46–47
    keyboard, 39, 45, 46
    MENU, 48
    mouse event, 38, 39, 44
        MOUSEDOWN, 44
        MOUSEUP, 44
    test, 47–48
    timer event, 39
    types of, 38–39

events, and IL (*Continued*)
    variable event, 39
events, and time lines, 99–106. *See also* score
expert systems, 5, 16, 18–19, 25, 190–194, 403
    conflict resolution, 194
    interpreter, 18
    pattern matching, 191
    rules, 191–194
  Small-X language, 194–203
expert system shells, 24, 25, 204
external applications, and doorways, 58–62

F

facets, 248–249
    default facet, 252
    value facet, 249
fields
    assigning, 141
    data record, 19
    of parameter structure, 61
fonts, 51
foreign language tutor, 439–448, 450
forms, in Visual Basic, 111
    ATM machine, 116
    background form, 113
    to create new forms, 111
    LOAD event, 116
    opening form, 113–115
FORTRAN, 156
frameRemovePart, 258–259
frames, 24, 248–254, 285. *See also* Frame Tool
    a-kind-of another frame, 259
    access, 256–258, 259
    class frames, 249, 253–254
    connecting, 251
    creating, 254–255,
    erase frame, 258
    facet, 248–249
        default facet, 252
        value facet, 249
    functions, 254–259
        assertFrame, 254–255
        eraseFrame, 258
        frameRemovePart, 258–259
        frameSlots, 259
        getFrame, 256
        getFrameAKOOnly, 257–258
        getFrameDefaultOnly, 258
        getFrameImmediate, 257
        isAKO, 259
        putFrame, 255
    generic, 249

inheritance, 250–251
instance frame, 249, 253–254
prototype frames, 249
remove part of a frame, 258–259
slots, 248–249, 253
    AKO slot, 251, 254
    default facet, 252
    facets, 248–249
    value facet, 249
using frames, 254
values, 252
write information into, 255
frameSlots, 259
Frame Tool, 260–261, 283–284, 285
    access frames, 264–268
    close database, 269
    copy frame, 278–279
    create database, 261–262
    delete frame element, 277
    enter frames, 264–268
    navigate database, 268–269
    open database, 262–264
    outputting database, 280–283
    save frame element, 276
    show frame hierarchy, 269–272
    show frame relationships, 272–276
future of intelligent multimedia, 453–454
    genetic programming, 465–470
    Internet, 473–477
    neural nets, 454–465
    suggested reading, 477–478
    virtual reality, 470–473

G

genetic programming, 465–470, 477–478
getFrame, 256
getFrameAKOOnly, 257–258
getFrameDefaultOnly, 258
getFrameImmediate, 257
glue, 15
GOTO vs CALL, 39–43
graphics
    DISPLAY, 49–50
    display clause, 50–51
    DISPLAY LIST, 50–51
    erasing, 65
    graphic element, 14
    inserting, icon for, 65
    with predefined effect, 51
graphs, 209–210
    edges, 209–210, 216, 218, 219
        creating, 221, 235–236

Delete, 227
drawing, 231–234
Edge menu, 223, 226–227
edge record, 228, 229–230
icons, 223–224
label with program code, 216–217
labels, 209, 210
   edge label tool, 223
   Modify Label, 224–225
   node label tool, 223
   and program code, 216–217
nodes, 209–210, 212, 213, 216–219
   creating, 221
   drawing edges, 231–234
   example, 234–235
   findnodeBoundingPoint, 230
   icons, 223
   manipulating, 230–231
   Node menu, 223, 224–226
   record definition, 228–229
grid, 101
GUI devices, 34

H

Habla, 439–448
hot areas, 134–135
   clicking on, 135
HTML (Hypertext Markup Language), 134, 476
Hypertext Markup Language. *See* HTML

I

IL (Interaction Language), 35–38. *See also* script
   actions, 49
   buttons, 36–37, 46–47
      button definition, 46–47
      displaying, 40, 41
      NOSTAY button, 47
      ON button event, 47
      sample code, 40–43
      and scrollable regions, 52–53
      STAY button, 47
   CALL, 40, 43
   chaining, 57
   characteristics of, 36–38
   cursor, 53–54
   CURSORMAP, 54
   DEC, 57
   DEFINE MENU, 55–56
   disadvantage of, 62
   DISPLAY, 40–42, 44, 49–51
   DISPLAY LIST, 50–51
   display graphics, 40, 41
   display text, 42–43
   doorways, 58–62
   draggables, 48
   ENABLECURSORMAP, 54
   END MENU, 55
   ENDTEST, 58
   GOTO vs CALL, 39–43
   graphics file format, 49
   history of, 35–36
   INC, 57
   interpreter, 38, 58
   menus, 55–56
   MOUSEDOWN, 44
   MOUSEUP, 44
   ON, 38, 40–41, 44–49
   parameter structure, 60–62
   programs in IL, 38
   RESETCURSORMAP, 54
   RETURN, 40, 43
   scrolling, 52–53
   SET, 57
   SETCURSOR, 53–54
   SETEFFECT, 51
   SET MENU, 56
   statements, list of, 37
   summary, 130–131
   TEST, 58
   test events, 47–48
   TEXT, 40, 41, 42–43, 51–53
   TIMEOUT, 49
   types of events, 38–39
   VARIABLE, 57
   variables, 57–58
images, 13–14. *See also* graphics
   diagrammatic, 14
   retrieval, 150–151
   sequence of, 14
INC, 57
increment, 57
inference, 213, 215
inheritance, 250–251
   and Smalltalk, 23
instance frame, 249
instance-of relationship, 211, 212
instructional model, 359, 365, 366, 381–390
integers
   increase value (INC), 57
   ival field, 61
   reduce value (DEC), 57
intelligent applications, tools for, 153–154. *See also* expert systems; LISP; Prolog
   suggested reading, 205–206

intelligent applications, tools for (*Continued*)
    summary, 203–204
    symbolic applications, 203
Intelligent Multimedia Presentation System, 474
intelligent multimedia systems, 4–5, 6–11, 25–27
    future, 453–454
    general structure for, 26
intelligent tutor, 26, 400–401. *See also* foreign language tutor; PROUST; toaster tutor
    domain of instruction, 345
    suggested reading, 402
    what it is, 344–345
Interaction Language. *See* IL
interactive applications. *See* Authorware Professional for Windows; IL
interactive report, 137
interactivity, 34
    and scores, 106–110
interface, 5, 26
Internet, 473–477
interpreters, 156
is-a relationship, 211
isAKO, 259
ITS (intelligent tutoring system). *See* intelligent tutor

J

Java, 475–476

K

keyboard event, 38, 39
    defining, 46
    examples, 46
kind-of relationship, 211
knowledge
    as data, 19, 21
    and data structure, 21–22
    knowledge engineering, 184
    as media, 137–140, 152
    retrieval, 140
knowledge representation, 16, 19–22, 207–208. *See also* logic representations; semantic networks
    and multimedia database, 138–140
    structures, 19
    suggested reading, 285–286
    summary, 284–285
    symbolic representations, 208
    tools, 25
Koza, John R., 466

L

labels, 209, 210
edge label tool, 223
Modify Label, 224–225
node label tool, 223
and program code, 216–217
languages, 25. *See also* natural language
let function, 167
Lingo, 106, 108
link, 134
    hot areas, 134–135
LISP (List Processing Language), 23, 24, 25, 155–157, 204
    atom predicate, 165
    basic elements, 157
    basic functions, 158–169
        append, 168–169
        car, 158, 159, 168
        cdr, 158–159, 168
        cond, 163–164, 165, 167
        cons, 168–169
        defun, 159
        eval, 157, 161–163, 164–165
        let, 167
        lispEval, 166
        loop, 167
        mapcar, 166
        null, 167
        quote, 161, 162
        return, 167
        setf, 168
    conditional statement, 163–164
    creator of, 6
    define new functions, 159
    equal predicate, 164–165
    and frame database, 280–281
    lists, 156–159
    NIL, 164, 165, 167
    procedural, 170
    recursion, 165–166
    s-expression, 158
    self-modifying, 156
    symbols, 204
List Processing Language. *See* LISP
loader, 145, 146, 148
logic, 204. *See also* Prolog
logic representations, 236–244, 284. *See also* frames
    classes, 249–254
    facts, 237–243
    inheritance, 250–251
    negation symbol, 238
    proof engine, 238
    queries, 238
        and rules, 240–241, 243
        and variables, 239

INDEX

resolution theorem prover, 238
rules, 240–244
statement, proving, 238
tener semantic network, 236–237
using, 244–248
variables, adding, 239

M

machine intelligence, 6, 153
Macromedia Director, 15, 101–110, 131
    adding scripts, 107
    Lingo, 106, 108
made-of relationship, 211–212
Mager, Robert, 440, 441, 444
Making Instruction Work, 440, 441
mapcar function, 166
McCarthy, John, 6, 156, 204
memory
    and chaining scripts, 57
    requirements, 3
    short-term, 18, 192, 193, 194–195
MENU event, 48
menus, 55–56
    DEFINE MENU, 48, 55–56
    Edge menu, 223, 226
    Edit menu, 227–228
        Copy, 227–228
        Cut, 227–228
        Paste, 227–228
    END MENU, 55
    File menu, 222
        About, 222, 223
        Exit, 222, 223
        Open, 222
        New, 222
        Save, 222–223
        Save As, 222, 223
    MENU event, 48
    Node menu, 223, 224–226
        Contents, 224
        Delete, 224, 225
        Modify, 224
        Modify Label, 225
        Modify Node, 225
        New, 224
    to redefine, 56
    SET MENU, 56
    Toaster Tutor main menu, 347
Minsky, Marvin, 6, 248
models, 287–291, 339–340
    buzzer model, 292–302
    examples, 302
        metamodel, 310–311

        PROUST, 302–307
        VCR programming, 307–310
    qualitative models, 291–292
    quantitative, 291–292
    suggested reading, 340–341
    testing, 298–302, 330–339
    toaster model, 311–339
    toaster tutor models, 364–366
        domain or mechanism, 365, 366
        instructional, 359, 365, 366, 381–390
        student, 359, 365–380
        testing the models, 391–400
mouse
    clickable area, 134–135
    cursor, 53
    events, 38, 39
        MOUSEDOWN, 44
        MOUSEUP, 44
        and ON, 44, 46
    findNodeBoundingPoint, 230
    manipulating nodes, 230–231
    sample code, 40
    what is a mouse event, 39
MOUSEDOWN, 44
MOUSEUP, 44
multimedia, 3
    advances in, 470–477
    applications, 12–16
        glue, 15
        images, 13–14
        sound, 13
        text, 12–13
        tools, 16, 17
        video, 14–15
    artificial intelligence, 4–5
    definition of, 6
    navigator, 7
multimedia authoring programs, 17
multimedia authoring tools, 33–34. *See also*
        Authorware Professional for Windows;
        IL; Macromedia Director; Visual Basic
    creating your own, 34–35
    definition of, 33
    interactivity, 34
    language-based vs graphic interface-based, 35
    need for doorways, 33–34
    overview, 130–131
    requirements, 33–34
    Visual Basic, 110–111
multimedia database, 6–8, 26–27, 133–140
    architecture, 140–151
    artificial intelligence, 6
    content, 9, 11

multimedia database (*Continued*)
  controls relationship, 7–9
  creating, 151
  data/media source, 143
  data/media type, 143
  external files, 141
  fields, 141
  functionality for, 136
  knowledge retrieval, 140
  loaders, 145, 146, 148
  operations, 145, 148
  records, 141–144
  report generator, 137
  retrieving by characteristic, 150–151
  retrieving by content, 148–150
  SEARCH operation, 148–150
  semantic relationships, 7
  suggested reading, 152
  summary, 151–152
  viewers, 145–146
multimedia manipulation programs, 17

N

name field, parameter structure, 61
natural language, 403–404, 448–451
  ATN, 413–422, 425, 450, 451
  automatic illustrator, 431–439
  foreign language tutor, 439–448, 450
  and multimedia, 405
  pedagogy, 440–444
  processing, 405–429
  and Prolog, 170–171
  propositions, 430–431, 450
  rewrite or production rules, 406
  suggested reading, 451
negation symbol, 238
Netscape's Navigator World Wide Web browser, 4
neural nets, 454–465
  suggested reading, 477
nodes, 209–210, 212, 213, 216–217, 218, 219
  creating, 221
  drawing edges, 231–234
  example, 234–235
  findNodeBoundingPoint, 230
  icons, 223
    delete node tool, 223
    node creation icon, 223
    node label tool, 223
  manipulating, 230–231
  Node menu, 223, 224–226
    Contents, 224
    Delete, 224, 225
    Modify, 224
    Modify Label, 224–225
    Modify Node, 224–225
    New, 224
  record definition, 228–229
nodes, and ANN, 456, 461
NOSTAY button, 47
null function, 167

O

ON statement, 38, 44–49
  CALL branch, 40
  GOTO branch, 39–40
  keyboard events, 46
  IL buttons, 46–47
  left mouse button, 44
  mouse events, 44
  syntax of, 45
OR, 51–52

P

pages, 134
paradigms, 99–110. *See also* time lines
  Authorware Professional, 63
  event-driven paradigm, 36, 63, 99
  language based, 131
  visual, 131
  Visual Basic, 111
parameter structure, 60–62
  definition of, 60–61
  name field, 61
  type field, 61
  vtype field, 61
part-of relationship, 211
parts, of a script, 38, 39
PASCAL, 302–307
passing information. *See also* doorways
  parameter structure, 60–61
pattern matching, 150–151, 191, 194
personal computer, 3
  and video, 14–15
photographs, digitizing, 2–3
physical image, 150
pixels, 150
point, defining, 46
polling timer, 118
Porphyry, philosopher, 209
PostScript file, 135
Principles of Semantic Networks, 209
problem-solving, assessing, 372–376
programming languages, 23. *See also* LISP; Prolog; Smalltalk

programs, 17. *See also* script
Prolog, 23, 25, 170–177, 204. *See also* logic representations
   backtracking, 176, 177, 179, 182
   bindings, 179, 181
   facts, 177–180, 182
   frame database, 280, 281–282
   proof procedure, 171–176
   queries, 178–179, 181–182
   rules, 180–183
   symbols, 177
   toaster simulation, 183–189
   a tutorial, 177–183
   unification, 176
   variables, 178–179, 181
proof engine, 238
proof procedure, 171–176
   backtracking, 176, 177, 179, 182
   unification, 176
PROUST, 302–307
putFrame, 255

Q

queries, 238
   and rules, 240–241, 243
   and variables, 239
question structure, 64
question, icon for, 65
quote function, 161, 162

R

real values, rval field, 61
records, 141–145
   and frames, 248
   in multimedia database, 137, 141–143
   in traditional database, 137
rectangles
   and cursor map, 54
   defining, 44, 46
relationships, 7
repetitive actions, 379–380
reports
   interactive, 137
   report generator, 137, 139
representation, 1–2. *See also* knowledge representation
representational symbols, 19
RESETCURSORMAP, 54
resolution theorem prover, 238
results, testing, 65–66
retrieving media
   by characteristic, 150–151
   by content, 148–150
RETURN, 40, 43
Roussel, Philippe, 170–171
rows, 141
rule-based systems, 18–19
   basic form of a rule, 18
   conditional expression, 18

S

scanning images, 14
scanning rules, 18
score, 101–110
   adding scripts, 107–109
   cast members, 108, 109
   columns, 102
   erasing, 104
   frame, 107, 108, 109
   horizontal lines, 101–102
   insert events, 102
   interactivity, 106–110
   Macromedia Director, 101, 104, 107
   show orientations, 102–103
   sound effects, 102, 104
   sprites, 107, 108, 109
screen coordinates, 51
script, 12, 38
   actions, 38
   branching, 39–40
   chaining, 57
   event definitions, 38
   examples, 40–43
   execution, 59
   parts, 38, 39
   passing information to, 60–62
   processing a script, 58–60
   returning, 40
   running, 59–60
   sections, 38
   summary, 130
   translation, 58–60
   variables, 57–58
scrollable text region, 52–53
sections, of a script, 38
semantic debugger, 303
semantic networks, 209–213, 284. *See also* semantic network tool
   class, 212
   creating, 217–218, 219
   edges, 209–210, 216, 218, 219
      creating, 221
   graphs, 209–210
   importance of consistency, 213

semantic networks (*Continued*)
   inference, 213, 215, 216
   instance, 212
   labels, 209, 216
   nodes, 209–210, 212, 213, 216–217, 218, 219
      creating, 221
   one-way relationship, 210
   relationships, 210–213
   representing, 218–219
   toaster simulation, 213–217
   traversing the network, 215–216
   Tree of Porphyry, 209–212
   using, 213–217
semantic network tool, 219, 221–236
   building the tool, 228–230
   edges
      creating, 235–236
      drawing, 231–234
      Edge menu, 223, 226–227
      edge record, 228, 229–230
      icons, 223
   Edit menu, 227–228
      Copy, 227–228
      Cut, 227–228
      Paste, 227–228
   File menu, 222
      About, 222, 223
      Exit, 222, 223
      Open, 222
      New, 222
      Save, 222–223
      Save AS, 222, 223
   icons, 223–224
      delete edge tool, 223
      delete node tool, 223
      edge creation tool, 223, 224
      edge label tool, 223
      node creation icon, 223
      node label tool, 223
   nodes
      adding, 234–235
      creating, 221, 224
      icons, 223
      manipulating, 230–231
      record definition, 228–229
      Node menu, 223, 224–226
   requirements for, 221–228
   tener semantic network, 234–236
   using, 234–236
semantic relationships, 7
   attached-to, 7, 214
   controls, 7–8, 214
semantics of visual language, 66–67

sequential analysis, 374–376
SET, 57
SETCURSOR, 53–54
SETEFFECT, 51
setf, 168
SET MENU, 56
short-term memory, 18, 192, 193
   and Small-X, 194–195
short-term memory elements (STMEs), 195
simulations
   any-machine simulation, 99–110
   ATM, Authorware Professional, 67–96
   ATM, Visual Basic, 111–130
   simulating the simulation, 391–400
   toaster, 183–189, 213–217
slots, 248–249, 253
   AKO slot, 251, 254
   default facet, 252
   facets, 248–249
   frameSlots, 259
   value facet, 249
Small-X, 194–203, 204
   IN-MEMORY test, 195–196
   rules for toaster, 195–203
Smalltalk, 23, 25
   data structures, 251
   and inheritance, 23
software, 479–480
   source code, 481
   system requirements, 480
   Video for Windows, 481
sound, 13, 66
Sowa, John, 209
Spanish tutor. *See Habla*
sprites, 107, 108, 109
STAY button, 47
STMEs (short-term memory elements), 195
story board, 12
strings, 57
   sval field, 61
student model, 359, 365–380
subtype-of relationship, 211
suggested reading
   artificial intelligence, 205
   expert systems, 206
   genetic programming, 477–478
   intelligent tutors, 402
   LISP, 205
   knowledge representation, 285–286
   models, 340–341
   multimedia database, 152
   natural language, 451
   neural networks, 477

Prolog, 205
symbolic applications, 203
symbolic expressions, 156–157
symbolic representations, 208

T

tables, 141
TEST, 58
test event, 47–48
    draggable, 48
Text, 2, 12–13
    colors, 51
    displaying, 51–53
        AND, 51–52
        OR, 51–52
        SET, 51
    fonts, 51
    inserting, icon for, 65
    reading from a file, 52
    screen coordinates, 51
    scrollable region, 52–53
    store in variable, 52
TEXT, 42–43, 51–53
thinking machines, 154–155
time-based event, 48–49
time lines, 99–106
TIMEOUT, 49
timer event, 39
time sharing, 6, 156
title, menu definition, 55
toaster model, 311–339
toaster simulation
    Prolog, 183–189
    semantic network, 213–217
toaster tutor, 343–345
    access components, 348–349
    basic idea of, 346
    buttons
        Advice, 362
        Continue, 360
        Do Action, 363
        Exit, 360
        Fix a Broken Toaster, 360–361
        Index, 364
        Make Toast, 356, 361
        No, 363
        Repair, 361
        Simulation, 363, 364
        Toaster Operational Reference Library, 360
        Toaster Technical Reference, 362
        Troubleshooting Guide, 362, 364
        video catalog, 364
        Yes, 363

    domain of instruction, 345–346
    how it works, 359–364
    intelligent tutor, 344–345
    models, 364–366
        domain or mechanism, 365, 366
        instructional, 359, 365, 366, 381–390
        student, 359, 365–380
        testing the models, 391–400
    main menu, 347
    notebook icon, 356–357
    opening screen, 347
    repair process, 352, 356
    repetitive actions, 379–380
    simulation interface, 350
    story board, 346–359
    technical reference, 348, 362, 363–364
    troubleshooting guide, 350–352, 362–363, 364
        assess use of, 378–379
    video catalog, 364
toolbar, Authorware Professional, 62, 63, 64–65
tools, 16, 153–154. *See also* expert systems; LISP; Prolog
    artificial intelligence, 22–24
    intelligent systems implementation, 25
    multimedia tools, 17
    for semantic networks, 219, 221–236
Towers of Hanoi puzzle, 457–459, 460, 468
transferring information. *See* doorways
traversing, 215
Tree of Porphyry, 209–212
troubleshooting guide, 362–363
    assess use of, 378–379
Turing, Alan, 154–155
Turing Machine, 154–155
tutor. *See* intelligent tutor
type field, parameter structure, 61

U

understanding, 367–372
unification, 176
uniform data representation, 23
union, 61

V

value facet, 249
VARIABLE, 57
variable event, 39
variables, 57–58
    assigning a value, 57
    counters, 57
    DEC, 57
    DISPLAY, 50
    INC, 57

variables (Continued)
    and logic representations, 239
    passing information, 60–62
    SET, 57
    and short-term memory, 18
    store text in, 52
    test value of, 47–48, 58
    what is a variable event, 39
VCR programming, 307–310
video, 14–15
    insert icon for, 66
Video for Windows, 481
viewers, 145–146
virtual environment, 30–31, 471, 472–473
virtual reality, 470–473
visual application. See Authorware Professional for Windows
Visual Basic, 110–111, 131. See also ATM simulation, Visual Basic
    and frame database, 280
    as a multimedia authoring tool, 110–130

forms, 111, 113
why use it, 112–113
visual programming. See also Authorware Professional for Windows
    semantics of, 66–67
Von Neumann, John, 153
VRML (Virtual Reality Markup Language), 476
vtype field, parameter structure, 61

W

wooga machine, 244–248
word processing programs, 17
World Wide Web database. See WWW database
WWW (World Wide Web) database, 134–137
    hot areas, 134–135
    links, 134
    pages, 134
    searching, 135

X

Xerox Dolphins, 170

CUSTOMER NOTE:

IF THIS BOOK IS ACCOMPANIED BY SOFTWARE, PLEASE READ THE FOLLOWING BEFORE OPENING THE PACKAGE.

This software contains files to help you utilize the models described in the accompanying book. By opening the package, you are agreeing to be bound by the following agreement:

This software product is protected by copyright and all rights are reserved by the author, John Wiley & Sons, Inc., or their licensors. You are licensed to use this software on a single computer. Copying the software to another medium or format for use on a single computer does not violate the U.S. Copyright Law. Copying the software for any other purpose is a violation of the U.S. Copyright Law.

This software product is sold as is without warranty of any kind, either express or implied, including but not limited to the implied warranty of merchantability and fitness for a particular purpose. Neither Wiley nor its dealers or distributors assumes any liability for any alleged or actual damages arising from the use of or the inability to use this software. (Some states do not allow the exclusion of implied warranties, so the exclusion may not apply to you.)